## GOVERNMENT VERSUS MARKETS

This book is the first comprehensive treatment available in the literature of the economic role of the state in a historical and world perspective. It addresses the fundamental question of what governments should do, or have attempted to do, in economic activities in past and recent periods. It also speculates on what they are likely or may be forced to do in future years. Although other recent titles in economics deal with normative theories, public choice theories, welfare state analysis, social protection, and the like, no other book has the same breadth or depth specifically on the state's viable economic role. The author's knowledge of several languages has allowed him to draw from different and often inaccessible previous publications. The investigation assembles a large set of statistical information that should prove useful to scholars and policy makers in the perennial discussion of government's optimal economic roles. It will become an essential reference work on the analytical borders between the market and the state and on what a reasonable "exit strategy" from the current fiscal crises should be.

An economist of international renown, Vito Tanzi served for 20 years as director of the Fiscal Affairs Department of the International Monetary Fund in Washington, D.C., with which he was affiliated for nearly three decades. He also taught at George Washington University and American University. Dr. Tanzi is the author of 14 books, including *Public Spending in the 20th Century: A Global Perspective* (Cambridge University Press, 2000, with Ludger Schuknecht) and *Inflation and the Personal Income Tax* (Cambridge University Press, 1980), and edited 11 other titles with contributions. A former undersecretary for economics and finance of the Italian government, he was president of the International Institute of Public Finance (IIPF) from 1990 to 1994 and is the IIPF's Honorary President. Dr. Tanzi is known for the Tanzi effect, or Olivera-Tanzi effect, which refers to the diminished real value of tax revenues in periods of high inflation owing to collection lags. He has served as a consultant to the World Bank, the United Nations, the European Commission, the European Central Bank, the Organization of American States, the Inter-American Development Bank, and the Stanford Research Institute. Dr. Tanzi received his doctorate in economics from Harvard University in 1967. He holds five honorary degrees.

# Government versus Markets

## The Changing Economic Role of the State

### VITO TANZI

**CAMBRIDGE**
UNIVERSITY PRESS

CAMBRIDGE UNIVERSITY PRESS
Cambridge, New York, Melbourne, Madrid, Cape Town,
Singapore, São Paulo, Delhi, Mexico City

Cambridge University Press
32 Avenue of the Americas, New York, NY 10013-2473, USA

www.cambridge.org
Information on this title: www.cambridge.org/9781107096530

First published 2011
Reprinted 2012

Printed in the United States of America

*A catalog record for this publication is available from the British Library.*

*Library of Congress Cataloging in Publication data*

Tanzi, Vito.
Government versus markets : the changing economic role of the state / Vito Tanzi.
p. cm.
Includes bibliographical references and index.
ISBN 978-1-107-09653-0 (hardback)
1. Trade regulation.   2. Economic policy.   I. Title.
HD3612.T35   2011
338.9–dc22          2011002621

ISBN 978-1-107-09653-0 Hardback

*To my late father*

# Contents

*Preface*                                                                    *page* ix

### PART ONE:  THE ECONOMIC ROLE OF THE STATE

1. General Introduction and Main Issues                                            3

### PART TWO:  HISTORICAL REVIEW

2. The Role of the State in the Pre–World War II Period                           39
3. Forces That Changed the Role of the State                                      72
4. Growth of Public Spending and Taxation in the 20th Century                     92
5. The Role of the State in Social Protection: Historical Landmarks              107
6. Globalization and Public Spending                                             129

### PART THREE:  THEORETICAL AND ANALYTICAL ISSUES

7. Theories of Public-Sector Behavior: Taxonomy of Government
   Types                                                                         151
8. Voluntary Exchange and Public Choice Theories                                 169
9. The Nordic European Economic Theory of Fiscal Policy                          193
10. Policy Tools and Government Roles                                            205

### PART FOUR:  THE OUTCOME OF STATE INTERVENTION

11. Evaluating the Impact of Public Spending on Socioeconomic
    Indicators                                                                   229
12. Social Protection in the Modern World: Some Quantitative
    Aspects                                                                      251

13. The Role of the State and Economic Performance in the
Nordic Countries                                                         267

PART FIVE:   ON THE ECONOMIC ROLE OF THE
STATE IN THE FUTURE

14. The Economic Role of the State in the Future: Concluding
Reflections                                                              305

*Notes*                                                                      335

*Index*                                                                      361

# Preface

There is no more fundamental question in economics than what role the state or the government should play in a country's economy. How wide and deep should such a role be in a market economy? What should the state do? How much should be left to the market and to the free economic decisions of individuals or groups of citizens? How should the state perform its role? What instruments should it use? The French poet Paul Valéry once wrote that "if the state is strong, it will crush us; if it is weak, we shall perish." Philosophers from Plato through Hobbes, Locke, Hume, Rousseau, and others, have addressed the question, focusing mainly on the political role. As in many other human activities, the secret is in finding the right balance. As noted by President Barack Obama at his inauguration, the aim is to find a government that works well.

Who decides what is the right balance? Few question that the state must play a significant role in an organized, modern society, or that organized societies need a government. The more significant question is what such a government should do and how it should do it. As with many things in life, the problem is to find the optimal dose of intervention, between one extreme, set by "centrally planned economies," where those who claim to represent the state make all the economically relevant decisions on behalf of the citizens, and the other extreme, set by the "laissez-faire ideology," where the role of the state is confined to a few basic or essential functions. To determine the right balance between these two polar conceptions ought to be the goal of economists and of intelligent and wise policy makers.

The state uses many tools or policy instruments to carry out its functions. It uses assets that are owned or have been inherited by the state, may have been bought from the market, or may even have been expropriated from their legitimate owners. It taxes individuals and enterprises on their incomes, their transactions, and their wealth. It subsidizes others. It borrows and lends money. It regulates the actions of individuals and enterprises. It prints money and uses the revenue that it receives from "seigniorage." It authorizes or forbids some activities. It certifies the qualifications of individuals who perform particular functions, such as physicians, pilots, and lawyers. Although some of the functions performed by the state are seen as necessary and useful, others may be questionable and may seem unnecessary or even harmful to some citizens. Some functions may be seen as too restrictive of individual freedom and could be delegated to the market that, if it is working well, might be able to deliver the services at lower costs.

The search for an optimal economic role of the state is an important and difficult one. It cannot be assumed that the current role is necessarily optimal. That role may have been promoted by events that required state interventions no longer considered necessary or even by mistakes. And it cannot be assumed that the role of the state in the past would be optimal today because the economy and the society may have changed, requiring different interventions. In some sense, the role of the state should continually be adapting to new developments. It must be seen as an evolutionary role that adjusts to the changing ecology of the market and, at the same time, influences that ecology. However, it should change according to certain rules or principles.

In textbooks and in articles in professional economic journals, it is often argued that the guiding principle that should justify state intervention in the economy should be "market failure." When markets fail, or are expected to fail, the state must intervene. This principle guided governmental intervention for much of the past century and especially for the past six decades. This principle may have contributed to the large growth in public spending because new, presumed, market failures were being found all the time. However, while market failure is obviously a useful principle, it fails in some fundamental aspects. First, it ignores the impact of current state intervention on the future development of private markets. Second, it tends to see market failure as a static and not a dynamic outcome of ongoing changes, including those promoted by the government itself. Third, it defines market failure in a purely technical manner, whereas for many citizens market failure may have a wider meaning. Finally, and related to the first point, the market failure approach fails to realize that, once the government intervenes in the economy to replace the market, it often creates its own monopoly in the sector or in the activity in which it has intervened. This often prevents, or at least makes more difficult, future developments of the private market or of civil society in that sector and in the economy. For political or bureaucratic reasons, the government has often shown a preference to *replace* the market rather than to correct its genuine shortcomings. Once the government has replaced the market – and, in doing so, has hired public employees and passed new laws – it has often been reluctant (or has not been allowed politically) to give up that new role.

The "market failure" approach does not recognize that the need for governmental intervention is not static: the private market is developing and changing all the time unless this process is prevented by the state. With the passing of time, the market becomes more sophisticated and potentially better able to satisfy many of the needs of the citizens. However, because the market often becomes more complex, it potentially requires different kinds of governmental intervention. It may create greater actual or perceived inequities that at least some citizens expect the government to correct. A free market is like an ecological system that undergoes a continuous process of evolution and adaptation. New technologies, new management techniques, growing globalization, and other developments have made today's markets potentially much more efficient and sophisticated in satisfying many of the people's needs; but they have also made the markets more complex and potentially less equitable. This means that, if governments directed their efforts more at promoting market efficiency and market equity and less at replacing the market because of its presumed "failures," governments could significantly reduce their spending and taxing roles while continuing to provide to most citizens the public services and the public goods that only state intervention can efficiently provide. However, the equity question would remain. Even the outcome of an efficient market might be seen as being inequitable by a majority of citizens. This equity question has become more important in recent decades and has often been used to justify more governmental intervention.

The reader should find this book informative and useful on a fascinating and enormous topic. Although it may not change many people's perception of what the state should do, if it encourages an honest and informed discussion it will have achieved a useful objective. This goal may be particularly important at this time when the financial and economic crises of 2008–9, and the government's reaction to them, have made future fiscal challenges more daunting than those in the past and the need for an efficient government role much more urgent and important.

The writing of a book such as this one is helped if the preparation of the author combines both relevant practical and academic experiences. At the cost of immodesty, I feel that I have had almost as much preparation as one can possibly have in this area. In different roles over a span of 27 years – as head of the Tax Policy Division (1974–81) and as director of the Fiscal Affairs Department of the International Monetary Fund (1981–2000) – I was in a privileged position for observing the behavior of many of the world's governments. During the 20 years that I spent as director of the Fiscal Affairs Department (FAD), that department had probably the greatest concentration of economists with a background in public finance and with Ph.D.s from the top universities in the world. FAD was also a frequent destination for some of the leading public economics scholars. They came to spend some months in a special program for visiting scholars. As a consequence, there was almost no problem or issue in public finance for which an expert could not be found. And there was almost no issue that had not been the object of some analysis or discussion in the department. I personally had to advise the governments of as many as a hundred different countries during the years that I spent at the IMF. This provided an ideal position for observing how governments operated in the real world and not just in the virtual world of theoreticians.

My IMF career had been preceded by my own strong academic background and by ten years of teaching graduate public finance. It was followed, in 2001–3, by an experience as undersecretary for economy and finance in the Italian government, a position that allowed me to experience the operations of a government from the inside. During those years, I wrote many papers and books and participated in numerous conferences that had to do with fiscal policy and, more generally, with the economic role of the state. Because of this almost unique background, narrow and purely technical issues that often drive a large part of the academic writing in this area have been deemphasized in this book. However, important theoretical issues that have real-life relevance have been discussed. Some available books that cover these theoretical issues well are now available.

Over some five decades, hundreds of individuals have influenced my thinking on economic and especially public finance questions, starting with those who first introduced me to the field of public economics. I will not attempt to list all or even many of these individuals, but I must mention a few. Because of the tyranny of time, some of them are no longer with us, including Gerhard Colm, who directed my master's thesis (on Nicholas Kaldor's expenditure tax); Otto Eckstein, who directed my Ph.D. thesis (on the relation between the personal income tax and economic growth); and Richard Musgrave, who was the second reader of my Ph.D. thesis and who influenced me in many other ways over many years. By coincidence, all three were refugees from bad governments, having left Germany in the 1930s.

In 1973–74, just before joining the IMF, I spent a sabbatical year in Italy, some of the time at the University of Rome. Part of the year was spent reading and collecting the works of Italian public finance economists who over the previous 100 years had contributed extensively to the development of public finance and had written much on the economic role of the state. In particular, I benefited from discussions with professors Sergio Steve, Cesare Cosciani, and Giannino Parravicini and with some of their assistants who became prominent economists in later years. At that time, these professors were important and influential scholars. That was a productive and especially pleasant year. It introduced me to the rich and diverse area that is the Italian *scienza delle finanze*, with its particular view of the work and the role of the government. That year had a permanent impact on my thinking which, until that time, had reflected much more the Anglo-Saxon perspective on various issues that was in vogue at the time. The Bank of Italy had partly financed that sabbatical year with a generous research grant. I am glad to convey to it a much-delayed thanks.

In more recent years, I have worked with Ludger Schuknecht, now at the European Central Bank, on some articles and on a book on public spending that have influenced parts of the present book. I also wrote several papers with another former colleague, Howell Zee. Both of these collaborations were highly productive. Finally, I conclude by thanking the librarians of the Joint Bank-Fund Library for invaluable help and Mrs. Jesusa Hilario, who patiently typed several drafts of this book. A special thanks goes to my wife, Maria, who made sure that distractions were kept to a minimum during the long period of writing. She took upon herself, with humor and kindness, the full and heavy responsibility of running the house.

PART ONE

# THE ECONOMIC ROLE OF THE STATE

The government exists not for turning life on earth into a paradise but for preventing it from turning into a complete hell.

Nikolai A. Berdyaev (1874–1948)

L'humanité ne vit pas pour avoir un gouvernement, mais elle crée un gouvernment à fin de pouvoir vivre.

Eduard von Hartmann (1842–1906)

ONE

# General Introduction and Main Issues

## 1.1. Introduction

Perhaps there is no more fundamental question in economics than the economic role that the state – or, less precisely, the government – ought to play in a democratic country with a market economy. This question recently became more urgent in view of the economic and financial crises that, just like earlier crises, stimulated many calls for more governmental intervention. This intervention was justified mostly by so-called Keynesian principles – that is, by the need to provide a boost to the weak economies. However, there were also calls for more, or better, government regulation, especially of financial markets. When governmental intervention comes through higher spending and higher taxes, as it often does, it can change for future years the economic role of the state and the status of a country's public finances.

Some observers have argued that, at least in some countries, and especially in the United States, there had been too little state intervention, especially in recent years. What is obvious from observations of historical developments and from available statistical evidence for many countries is that the economic role of the state is not fixed either in time, for the same countries, or in place, across different countries. Furthermore, at any one time or place, there is little agreement among economists and among observers in general on what that role ought to be. Therefore, the optimal role of the state continues to be a permanent and major topic of discussion in practically all countries rich and poor.

As they generally do, economists have advanced theories about what that role should be. So-called normative theories, theories developed especially during the past century and mainly in the United Kingdom and the United States, start from the assumption that there are *natural* "market failures" in

3

a market economy that need to be corrected. They ought to be corrected by the government to enhance the economic well-being of the citizens. (See, in particular, the writings by Pigou, 1924; Musgrave, 1959; and Bator, 1960.) If markets worked "perfectly," there would be no need for an *economic* role for the state, even though the state would still exist to play important political and social functions for which it would need some financial resources.[1] However, it would be a more passive and more limited role.

The normative theories assume that the state's intervention to correct for market failures is inherently benevolent and that the state is capable of correcting these failures administratively. The policy makers who act on behalf of the state are the faithful, wise, and capable agents of the electors. They have Solomon's wisdom, the knowledge accumulated by Google, and the honesty of saints. As such, they can be given monopoly powers over the needed *policies*. These *policy makers* have no personal or group interests to promote, and they pursue only the general public interest, if we assume, of course, that such an interest can be defined. At the same time, the *bureaucrats* who run the institutions that implement the policies act like competent "Weberian" bureaucrats, following faithfully and efficiently the instructions that they receive from the policy makers. No principal-agent problems develop at either the political or the administrative level (Tanzi, 2000).

Theories based on the assumption of market failure are, for the most part, tied with the economic function of the state that belongs to the general category of *allocation of resources*. An uneven income distribution in a well-working market might be a "political failure," even if it is not a "market failure" in the traditional sense. These theories stress the existence of "public goods," "semipublic goods," "natural monopolies," "externalities," and other factors (including, more recently, asymmetric information) that make private markets "fail" in their allocation function. These failures are seen as illnesses of the economy, and the government is viewed as the honest and knowledgeable doctor who can recognize the illnesses and prescribe, in the proper dosage, the correct medication capable of curing them. Consequently, the theories call for the intervention of the government to correct the failures.

Some of these market failures, such as the existence of pure public goods or of "natural monopolies," may be considered natural and unavoidable. That is, they are exogenous to the action of the state. This seems to be the normal assumption of the normative theories. Some, however, are potentially avoidable in real-life situations and could be eliminated or reduced if the state played a more forceful and efficient role *in its regulatory function*, for example, by eliminating monopolistic practices (for nonnatural monopolies) and other abuses in the market. These practices, especially in the United States, had attracted strong governmental action in the past. Recent developments in the financial and real markets, however, have highlighted the potential importance that an efficient regulatory and surveillance function by the state might have in some areas and the problems that may develop when the state does not perform, or does not perform well, this function.[2] For example, the growth of some financial institutions, to the point where they become "too big to fail," is a sign of government and not market failure. The government should and could have prevented these institutions from reaching that size with proper regulation.

After World War II, so-called Keynesian economics became popular and added another important theoretical reason for governmental intervention: *countercyclical, or stabilization, policy;* or, in a more extreme version, *fine-tuning.* This policy was justified on grounds of a special kind of market failure, the failure of the market to generate a level of aggregate demand capable of maintaining stable economic growth with reasonably full employment. Until Keynes's time, it had been assumed that a market economy with flexible prices and reasonable interest rates would always generate an adequate demand. If it did not, then prices and wages were not flexible enough, or interest rates were not at the required level. Keynes challenged this view and attributed the Great Depression to lack of adequate aggregate demand. He argued that the government should play a role in promoting levels of investment and saving that would be adequate for maintaining full employment in the economy. What "full employment" meant was a controversial issue, and the empirical measure of it changed somewhat over the years. Stabilization policy became popular especially in the 1950s and 1960s and in the first half of the 1970s. For various reasons, it lost a good deal of its popularity, especially among many academic economists, in the following two decades but came back in full fashion during the 2008–9 crisis.[3]

Economics has been more ambiguous about the precise role that the government should play in reducing income inequality, in dealing with poverty, and, more broadly, in protecting citizens against risks with economic consequences. Strictly speaking, these are different roles, although they are often confused as one. As we shall see later, these roles have become confused in the policies of many countries. There is no reason, at least in theory, why government could not improve the income distribution, for example, with negative income taxes or with other instruments, and then let the citizens deal directly through the market with their economic risks. Or, alternatively, it could let the income distribution be whatever the market generated but deal selectively with some of the more serious economic risks of particular individuals who are unable to deal directly with them.

No widely accepted theories are related to these aspects. *Some* economists, philosophers, and policy makers have advocated a government role in income redistribution (e.g., Hochman and Rogers, 1969; Rawls, 1971; and Sen, 1979; and the discussion of the welfare state of Nordic countries in Chapter 13). Over recent decades, many actions of governments have been justified on grounds of improving the distribution of income or of protecting citizens against particular risks with economic consequences. These two grounds have at times been seen as separate but more often as one objective. In the real world, governmental action has been much less related to clear market failures of an allocation kind than to vaguely defined redistributive objectives.

In an influential book, Richard Musgrave (1959) gave an important but not precise role to what he called the "redistribution branch" of the budget, a virtual branch that, together with the allocation and stabilization branches, presumably covered all the fundamental economic functions of the state. He recognized that decisions on redistribution "cannot be made by a market process" and "that a political process . . . is needed" (Musgrave, 1959, p. 19). Of course, this opens the possibility, recognized by many economists and political scientists, that the political process might not function in line with the public interests but might encourage rent-seeking activities, thus leading to unintended and less desirable results; or that it could damage the working of the market economy by having negative effects on the incentives of individuals. In earlier times, the "political process" – or, better, the operation of the existing state with its power of coercion – had often distorted markets and redistributed income from the population at large to the dominating oligarchies. In a more modern setting, with democratic institutions, as the French "laissez-faire" economist Bastiat (1864) warned, the danger is that the state becomes the great fiction by which everyone tries to make a better living at the cost of everyone else, or that the masses will promote policies that exploit the few. There has also been concern that the push for equality is likely to limit individual liberty.

## 1.2. The Role of the State in the 20th Century

If governments had based their economic policies strictly on the *theoretical* justifications advanced by economists, the role of the state – at least the one played through the traditional instruments of taxing and public spending – would have remained much smaller than it became in many countries in the later part of the 20th century. Clearly other forces must have been at work. Of course, economists do not make, and cannot be blamed for, the political decisions that determine economic policies. At best, they influence them through the impact that they have on the decisions made by policy makers, who often do not have an economic background or have a background that they acquired from "dead economists," as Keynes famously stated. Policy makers are inevitably influenced by the views of their advisers and, perhaps more, by the requests of those who elect them or finance their campaigns, helping them to stay in power with votes and financial resources. These requests reflect the *personal* or *class* interests of the voters and may in turn be influenced by the latter's economic literacy.[4] In some countries, citizens tend to see the government as the solution to many of their own problems, even problems over which governments have little influence. In others, they understand the limitations or even come to believe, as President Ronald Reagan did, that the government is often the problem.

The role of the state in the economy changed enormously from the beginning to the end of the 20th century. It is reasonable to expect that it will continue to change significantly over the course of the 21st century. The key question is how it will change. Will it continue the trend that characterized much of the past century, toward continuously growing public spending and higher taxes? Or will the direction change toward less spending and lower taxes? Will the government continue to rely mostly on the budgetary instruments of taxing and spending to promote its objectives? Or will it rely more on other instruments of economic policy, including regulations and the assumption of contingent liabilities? How will globalization influence the role of *national* governments? No crystal ball exists that can provide us with answers to these questions. The best that can be done is to speculate. In this book, we shall do that, knowing that there will be disagreement over some of the views and the arguments presented and that some of the conclusions will likely prove wrong. Especially in the last chapter, we focus on the role of the state in the future.

In order to forecast the future, it is often worthwhile to study the past for potentially useful lessons. As a famous Titian painting in the National Gallery in London, the *Allegory of Prudence*, states, "To the past the present should turn so as not to put the future at risk." However, one must be careful not to assume that past trends will necessarily continue into the future. This assumption can lead to big mistakes. There is a tendency on the part of many to take the *recent* spending role of the state as normal and even to expect, as theorized more than a century ago by the influential German economist

Adolph Wagner, that that role will inevitably keep growing in the future (a pattern that came to be referred to as Wagner's Law).

The 20th century started with a level of public spending (and of taxes) that, by today's standards, seems almost incredibly small, when measured as a share of national income. It ended the century with one in which the state was playing an enormous role, especially in "welfare states," countries that continued to claim or to be market economies.[5] It is not obvious that the role played at the end of the 20th century was more appropriate, or more natural, than the one played at the beginning, even though this is likely to be the prevalent belief. The financial and economic crisis of 2008–9 indicated that, in spite of the enormous expansion of the state's role, some basic government functions were not being performed, or were being performed badly.

Public spending as a share of gross domestic product (GDP), or of national income, grew in many industrial countries, from around 10 percent of GDP, in the 1870s, to around 40 percent of GDP in recent years, or to higher levels in several European countries (Table 1.1). A large part of this growth came in the decades after World War II, and especially after 1960. Between 1960 and the mid-1990s, the share of public spending (and of taxes) into GDP grew at record rates. By the end of the 20th century, many people were getting a large share or all of their total disposable incomes from the government.

The growth of public spending during the 20th century was caused mainly by direct responsibilities that governments assumed in many countries (especially in the second half of the century) in the provision of public pensions, public or publicly financed health services, public and compulsory education, public housing, assistance to large families, and subsidies to public and private enterprises, as well as assistance to the unemployed, the very old, the very young, the handicapped, and so on. It should be noted that most of these new responsibilities were related to particular categories of citizens and not just to those who were poor. Public spending for these activities had been almost nonexistent at the beginning of the 20th century (Table 1.2). In many countries, the state replaced existing markets or private civic activities, claiming that, by so doing, it was promoting the public interest. Citizens, who came to depend on the services provided by these public programs and on the government jobs, came to consider the government's new role as normal and essential. That role created its own strong constituencies. As George Bernard Shaw would put it, "A government that takes from Peter to give to Paul can always count on the support of [Paul]."

Table 1.1. *Growth of general government expenditures, 1870–2007 (percent of GDP)*

| Country | Late 19th century about 1870[a] | Pre-WWI 1913 | Post-WWI 1920 | Pre-WWII 1937 | Post-WWII | | | | | |
|---|---|---|---|---|---|---|---|---|---|---|
| | | | | | 1960 | 1980 | 1990 | 1996 | 2002 | 2007 |
| *General government for all years* | | | | | | | | | | |
| Australia | 18.3 | 16.5 | 19.3 | 14.8 | 21.2 | 34.1 | 34.9 | 35.9 | 35.6 | 34.9 |
| Austria | 10.5 | 17.0 | 14.7[b] | 20.6 | 35.7 | 48.1 | 38.6 | 51.6 | 51.3 | 48.0 |
| Canada | – | – | 16.7 | 25.0 | 28.6 | 38.8 | 46.0 | 44.7 | 41.4 | 39.3 |
| France[c] | 12.6 | 17.0 | 27.6 | 29.0 | 34.6 | 46.1 | 49.8 | 55.0 | 53.6 | 52.6 |
| Germany | 10.0 | 14.8 | 25.0 | 34.1 | 32.4 | 47.9 | 45.1 | 49.1 | 48.5 | 43.9 |
| Italy | 13.7 | 17.1 | 30.1 | 31.1 | 30.1 | 42.1 | 53.4 | 52.7 | 48.0 | 48.5 |
| Ireland[d] | – | – | 18.8 | 25.5 | 28.0 | 48.9 | 41.2 | 42.0 | 33.5 | 36.4 |
| Japan | 8.8 | 8.3 | 14.8 | 25.4 | 17.5 | 32.0 | 31.3 | 35.9 | 39.8 | 36.0 |
| New Zealand[b] | – | – | 24.6 | 25.3 | 26.9 | 38.1 | 41.3 | 34.7 | 41.6 | 39.9 |
| Norway | 5.9 | 9.3 | 16.0 | 11.8 | 29.9 | 43.8 | 54.9 | 49.2 | 47.5 | 40.9 |
| Sweden | 5.7[b] | 10.4 | 10.9 | 16.5 | 31.0 | 60.1 | 59.1 | 64.2 | 58.3 | 52.6 |
| Switzerland | 16.5 | 14.0 | 17.0 | 24.1 | 17.2 | 32.8 | 33.5 | 39.4 | 34.3 | 35.4 |
| United Kingdom | 9.4 | 12.7 | 26.2 | 30.0 | 32.2 | 43.0 | 39.9 | 43.0 | 41.1 | 44.6 |
| United States | 7.3 | 7.5 | 12.1 | 19.7 | 27.0 | 31.4 | 32.8 | 32.4 | 34.1 | 36.6 |
| Average | 10.8 | 13.1 | 19.6 | 23.8 | 28.0 | 41.9 | 43.0 | 45.0 | 43.5 | 42.0 |
| *Central government for 1870–1937, general government thereafter* | | | | | | | | | | |
| Belgium | – | 13.8 | 22.1 | 21.8 | 30.3 | 57.8 | 54.3 | 52.9 | 50.5 | 48.8 |
| Netherlands | 9.1 | 9.0 | 13.5 | 19.0 | 33.7 | 55.8 | 54.1 | 49.3 | 47.5 | 45.9 |
| Spain | – | 11.0 | 8.3 | 13.2 | 18.8 | 32.2 | 42.0 | 43.7 | 39.9 | 38.7 |
| Average | 9.1 | 11.3 | 14.6 | 18.0 | 27.6 | 48.6 | 50.1 | 48.6 | 46.0 | 44.5 |
| Total average | 10.7 | 12.7 | 18.7 | 22.8 | 27.9 | 43.1 | 44.8 | 45.6 | 43.9 | 42.4 |

[a] Or closest year available for all columns. Pre–World War II data are sometimes on the basis of GNP or NNP instead of GDP.

[b] Central government data for this year, New Zealand: 1960–70, and 1994–95 = 1996.

[c] 1996 and 2002 data: calculations are based on the Maastricht definition, and are smaller than those published by the INSEE, the national statistical agency.

[d] 1995 instead of 1996, because of break in data calculation.

*Source:* Tanzi and Schuknecht, 2000. Updated by author from OECD data.

Table 1.2. *Social transfers as a percentage of GDP at current prices in selected OECD countries, 1880 to 1995*

| Country | 1880[a] | 1890[a] | 1900[a] | 1910[a] | 1920[a] | 1930[a] | 1960[b] | 1970[b] | 1980[b] | 1990[c] | 1995[c] |
|---|---|---|---|---|---|---|---|---|---|---|---|
| Australia | 0 | 0 | 0 | 1.12 | 1.66 | 2.11 | 7.39 | 7.37 | 12.79 | 10.90 | 14.84 |
| Austria | 0 | 0 | 0 | 0 | 0 | 1.20 | 15.88 | 18.90 | 23.27 | 23.43 | 21.39 |
| Belgium | 0.17 | 0.22 | 0.26 | 0.43 | 0.52 | 0.56 | 13.14 | 19.26 | 30.38 | 22.45 | 27.13 |
| Canada | 0 | 0 | 0 | 0 | 0.06 | 0.31 | 9.12 | 11.80 | 14.96 | 12.90 | 18.09 |
| Denmark | 0.96 | 1.11 | 1.41 | 1.75 | 2.71 | 3.11 | 12.26 | 19.13 | 27.45 | 26.44 | 30.86 |
| Finland | 0.66 | 0.76 | 0.78 | 0.90 | 0.85 | 2.97 | 8.81 | 13.56 | 19.19 | 18.32 | 31.65 |
| France | 0.46 | 0.54 | 0.57 | 0.81 | 0.64 | 1.05 | 13.42 | 16.68 | 22.55 | 22.95 | 26.93 |
| Germany | 0.50 | 0.53 | 0.59 | n.a. | n.a. | 4.82 | 18.10 | 19.53 | 25.66 | 20.42 | 24.92 |
| Greece | 0 | 0 | 0 | 0 | 0 | 0.07 | 10.44 | 9.03 | 11.06 | 8.67 | 14.43 |
| Ireland | | | | | | 3.74 | 8.70 | 11.89 | 19.19 | 16.20 | 18.30 |
| Italy | 0 | 0 | 0 | 0 | 0 | 0.08 | 13.10 | 16.94 | 23.24 | 17.10 | 23.71 |
| Japan | 0.05 | 0.11 | 0.17 | 0.18 | 0.18 | 0.21 | 4.05 | 5.72 | 11.94 | 10.48 | 12.24 |
| Netherlands | 0.29 | 0.30 | 0.39 | 0.39 | 0.99 | 1.03 | 11.70 | 22.45 | 28.34 | 26.94 | 25.70 |
| New Zealand | 0.17 | 0.39 | 1.09 | 1.35 | 1.84 | 2.43 | 10.37 | 9.22 | 15.22 | 16.22 | 18.64 |
| Norway | 1.07 | 0.95 | 1.24 | 1.18 | 1.09 | 2.39 | 7.85 | 16.13 | 20.99 | 18.50 | 27.50 |
| Sweden | 0.72 | 0.85 | 0.85 | 1.03 | 1.14 | 2.59 | 10.83 | 16.76 | 25.94 | 12.97 | 19.01 |
| Switzerland | n.a. | n.a. | n.a. | n.a. | n.a. | 1.17 | 4.92 | 8.49 | 14.33 | n.a. | 18.87 |
| United Kingdom | 0.86 | 0.83 | 0.55 | 1.38 | 1.39 | 2.24 | 10.21 | 13.20 | 16.42 | 11.43 | 13.67 |
| United States | 0.29 | 0.45 | 0.17 | 0.56 | 0.70 | 0.56 | 7.26 | 10.38 | 15.03 | 21.36 | 22.52 |

[a] Welfare, unemployment, pensions, health, and housing subsidies. It does not include education.
[b] OECD old series.
[c] OECD new series.

*Sources:* Lindert, 2002, p. 186; OECD, 1985.

A form of fiscal illusion, combined with lack of good information or with propaganda from official or other sources, including unions of public employees, helped create the belief that this expanded government role was efficient, beneficial, and welfare promoting and that *most* citizens would be worse off without it. Most citizens were able to see the benefits that accompanied the public spending but not always the costs – the high taxes that they and others paid for financing the programs that provided the benefits or the high public debts and the various inefficiencies that often accompanied the public programs.[6] Especially when the governments provided free or almost-free services, as was often the case, the citizens tended to see the services as bargains. Behavioral economics has shown how difficult it is for people to resist the allure of things offered for free, even when these "free" things involve real but not easily recognized costs (Ariely, 2008, chap. 3). As Ariely puts it, at times "the most expensive services are free services." The "zero price effect" is very powerful and it is especially powerful in government programs. It contributes to increasing the demand well above where it would be in a non-zero-cost alternative.

In promoting this expanded role, the governments needed much larger financial resources than in the past. Thus, the tax rates and the tax levels went sharply up (Table 1.3).

The needed public resources were obtained mainly, but not only, from taxes. Higher public debts generally accompanied the higher tax levels. The tax systems were reformed by the introduction of new, high-yielding taxes – especially global and progressive income taxes, value-added taxes, and social security taxes – and occasionally by a more intensive exploitation of older taxes. The increasing share of wages and salaries in national income that was taking place during much of the 20th century (until recent years when this trend came to an end and reversed itself) made the increase in tax revenue easier. The left-leaning intellectual winds that had prevailed for several decades in many countries provided the needed ideological support for this expanded government role.

The new spending programs had the declared or implied objective of reducing economic risks faced by the majority of the citizens rather than correcting for market failures and explicitly redistributing income. Examples of risks that could reduce the real income of citizens or prevent its growth were illiteracy, limited education or training, debilitating illnesses, old age, invalidity, unemployment, and responsibility for a large number of children or other dependents. Also, gender and ethnic risks were added in some countries, leading to particular economic policies at times called "affirmative action." The expanded government role aimed at reducing

Table 1.3. *Total tax revenue as percentage of GDP, 1965–2008*

| Country | 1965 | 1975 | 1985 | 1990 | 1995 | 2000 | 2005 | 2007 | 2008 |
|---|---|---|---|---|---|---|---|---|---|
| Canada | 25.7 | 32.0 | 32.5 | 35.9 | 35.6 | 35.6 | 33.4 | 33.3 | 32.2 |
| Mexico | n.a. | n.a. | 17.0 | 17.3 | 15.2 | 16.9 | 19.1 | 18.0 | 21.1 |
| United States | 24.7 | 25.6 | 25.6 | 27.3 | 27.9 | 29.9 | 27.3 | 28.3 | 26.9 |
| Australia | 21.0 | 25.8 | 28.3 | 28.5 | 28.8 | 31.1 | 30.8 | 30.8 | n.a. |
| Japan | 18.2 | 20.9 | 27.4 | 29.1 | 26.8 | 27.0 | 27.4 | 28.3 | n.a. |
| Korea | n.a. | 15.1 | 16.4 | 18.9 | 19.4 | 23.6 | 25.5 | 26.5 | 26.6 |
| New Zealand | 24.0 | 28.5 | 31.1 | 37.4 | 36.6 | 33.6 | 37.5 | 35.7 | 34.5 |
| Austria | 33.9 | 36.7 | 40.9 | 39.6 | 41.2 | 42.6 | 42.1 | 42.3 | 42.9 |
| Belgium | 33.1 | 39.5 | 44.4 | 42.0 | 43.6 | 44.9 | 44.8 | 44.9 | 44.3 |
| Czech Republic | n.a. | n.a. | n.a. | n.a. | 37.5 | 35.3 | 37.5 | 37.4 | 36.6 |
| Denmark | 30.0 | 38.4 | 46.1 | 46.5 | 48.8 | 49.4 | 50.7 | 48.7 | 48.3 |
| Finland | 30.4 | 36.5 | 39.7 | 43.5 | 45.7 | 47.2 | 43.9 | 43.0 | 42.8 |
| France | 34.1 | 35.4 | 42.8 | 42.0 | 42.9 | 44.4 | 43.9 | 43.5 | 43.1 |
| Germany | 31.6 | 34.3 | 36.1 | 34.8 | 37.2 | 37.2 | 34.8 | 36.2 | 36.4 |
| Greece | 17.8 | 19.4 | 25.5 | 26.2 | 28.9 | 34.1 | 31.3 | 32.0 | 31.3 |
| Hungary | n.a. | n.a. | n.a. | n.a. | 41.3 | 38.0 | 37.2 | 39.5 | 40.1 |
| Iceland | 26.2 | 30.0 | 28.2 | 30.9 | 31.2 | 37.2 | 40.7 | 40.9 | 36.0 |
| Ireland | 24.9 | 28.7 | 34.6 | 33.1 | 32.5 | 31.7 | 30.6 | 30.8 | 28.3 |
| Italy | 25.5 | 25.4 | 33.6 | 37.8 | 40.1 | 42.3 | 40.9 | 43.5 | 43.2 |
| Luxembourg | 27.7 | 32.8 | 39.5 | 35.7 | 37.1 | 39.1 | 37.8 | 36.5 | 38.3 |
| Netherlands | 32.8 | 40.7 | 42.4 | 42.9 | 41.5 | 39.7 | 38.8 | 37.5 | n.a. |
| Norway | 29.6 | 39.2 | 42.6 | 41.0 | 40.9 | 42.6 | 43.5 | 43.6 | 42.1 |
| Poland | n.a. | n.a. | n.a. | n.a. | 36.2 | 32.8 | 33.0 | 34.9 | n.a. |
| Portugal | 15.9 | 19.7 | 25.2 | 27.7 | 31.7 | 34.1 | 34.7 | 36.4 | 36.5 |
| Slovak Republic | n.a. | n.a. | n.a. | n.a. | n.a. | 33.8 | 31.8 | 29.4 | 29.3 |
| Spain | 14.7 | 18.4 | 27.6 | 32.5 | 32.1 | 34.2 | 35.8 | 37.2 | 33.0 |
| Sweden | 35.0 | 41.2 | 47.3 | 52.2 | 47.5 | 51.8 | 49.5 | 48.3 | 47.1 |
| Switzerland | 17.5 | 23.9 | 25.5 | 25.8 | 27.7 | 30.0 | 29.2 | 28.9 | 29.4 |
| Turkey | 10.6 | 11.9 | 11.5 | 14.9 | 16.8 | 24.2 | 24.3 | 23.7 | 23.5 |
| United Kingdom | 30.4 | 35.2 | 37.6 | 36.1 | 34.0 | 36.4 | 35.8 | 36.1 | 35.7 |
| OECD total | 24.2 | 29.4 | 32.7 | 33.8 | 34.8 | 36.0 | 35.7 | 35.8 | n.a. |

*Source:* OECD, *Revenue Statistics, 1965–2008/Statistiques Des Recettes Publiques, 1965–2008* (2009).

these risks for most citizens below the levels they would have been without the intervention of the governments. New programs were enacted to achieve these reductions in risks. It often happened that the new programs started modestly and narrowly, benefiting initially a small group of individuals. With the passage of time, they tended to become progressively more generous and more embracing. This process has characterized many programs and must be considered a fundamental reason for public spending growth. It could almost be considered a fundamental law of public spending. The criteria that made individuals qualify for these programs were progressively relaxed, making the programs more costly. This clearly happened with disability pensions in many countries but also with the New Deal program of aid to dependent children in the United States, until it was reformed in the 1990s.

## 1.3. Assumptions behind the Growth of the Economic Role of the State

Two fundamental assumptions must have accompanied or justified the growing intervention of the state, although they were generally not spelled out or acknowledged. First, and perhaps more important, was the view that *citizens are myopic*. Left to their own, they would not, individually or collectively, take the actions needed to protect themselves and their families against economic risks. They would not save for their old age; they would not send their children to private schools at their expense; and they would not insure themselves against (or accumulate assets to pay for) occasional illnesses, unemployment, and other eventualities.[7] Second, even if they had wanted to do so, various private associations (including charitable and religious ones) would not have been capable of satisfying the citizens' needs at the desirable level. The government was expected to do better. These two assumptions justified a paternalistic and much-expanded role for the state.

In the phenomenal increase in public spending that took place in industrial countries from the first to the second half of the 20th century, the government became a huge insurance company and intermediary for the citizens. In this de facto insurance company, the citizens as a group paid fees in the form of high taxes; in turn, they were compensated with free or highly subsidized public services. As a Swedish minister of health and social affairs put it, "The basic principle of our model is that everyone contributes via taxation and everyone gets something back." However, the connection between the taxes paid (the tax prices) and the services received (the benefits) was not fully understood by many citizens, thus creating, in some of them, the belief that they were receiving "free" or "zero-cost" public services.[8] The connection, of course, related to the *whole* citizenry and not to *specific* citizens. For specific citizens, the connection between taxes paid and benefits received was and is often not close. Furthermore, it is not a random one. In this forced social contract they were required to be part of, some individuals gained or lost much more than others. For example, citizens who because of their good habits were more healthy or who had chosen to have fewer children ended up subsidizing those who were less healthy and those who had many children. Those who went to publicly financed universities were financed by the (often poorer) families of those who did not. Thus, the redistribution was not only vertical, from the top down, but also, and significantly, horizontal.[9] The presumed risk reduction for some came at a high cost for others. This horizontal redistribution was more tolerated in some countries than in others. It was often less equitable than the vertical redistribution.

Some citizens learned to game and manipulate the system to their advantage by evading taxes; staying idle while receiving benefits; going underground in their economic activities, thus avoiding taxes and regulations while even claiming unemployment compensation; faking illnesses, so that they could get paid sick leave in their public employment; faking or exaggerating disability; doing little work in their government jobs; and generally shifting a greater cost of financing the state toward honest and hard-working individuals and toward those who, because of their economic situations (such as dependent workers in large private firms), were less able to abuse the system. Phenomena such as underground economic activities, tax evasion, corruption, the taking of abusive leaves, and shirking on the job grew over the years and reached worrisome levels in several countries and especially in some of those with high taxes and high public spending.[10] This problem of horizontal inequity was already known to Plato, 2,500 years ago, when he wrote that "in their relations with the state, if there are direct taxes or contributions to be paid, the just man contributes more from an equal estate and the other less, and when there is a distribution the one gains much and the other nothing" (Plato, p. 593). It was also recognized by J. S. Mill, as well as by other writers of the past (Mill, p. 739). These horizontal inequities can transform the most equitable programs on paper into the most inequitable ones in practice.

At the same time, politicians learned that they could get votes by providing government jobs for those who voted for them or by allocating public spending to particular groups, realizing that the benefits would go to the members of the groups while the costs would be shared by all, or most, citizens. Public employment and public spending grew more than necessary, while *productive* public spending was often reduced.[11] These problems of equity and efficiency in recent years started to challenge the legitimacy of the implicit social contracts between the citizens and the state, social contracts that are supposed to be at the base of modern states. Problems of vertical and horizontal equity became more pronounced and attracted the attention of both economists and policy makers.

In high-spending and high-taxing countries, most individuals, as consumers, lost some of their ability or their freedom to make their own individual, preferred choices. Because of the high taxes they paid, they lost large parts of their private, disposable income and of their economic freedom in the use of their (before-tax) earnings.[12] If they had been free to make their own choices, many individuals would not have subscribed to the social contract that prevailed in their countries. The governments themselves lost the freedom to pursue policies that they might have preferred, because large proportions of the budget for a given year became predetermined by past programs, which were difficult to reform. This predetermination of public spending is a worrisome development of recent decades. A large and increasing number of citizens (e.g., pensioners, public employees, invalids, unemployed, people receiving welfare payments, those working in subsidized enterprises) had become dependent for their incomes, or for large parts of their incomes, on public programs and would oppose the elimination of these programs. This made it difficult for a new government to change policies enacted by previous governments. In most countries, government employees acquired legally enforced tenure on their jobs so that they could not be fired, even when their performance was poor, or when they were no longer needed. Budgets could be changed only at the margin, and the margin was often very small. In these circumstances, reform often came to mean increased spending. This, often, led to fiscal deficits and high public debts in normal times. Past policies created a kind of "path dependency" and a one-way street for governments that led toward higher spending and higher taxes.

Because of high taxes, the difference between the before-tax earnings and the (after-tax) disposable cash incomes became large, especially for dependent workers. In 2008, for example, workers without children who had *average* gross wages lost about half of their wages because of taxes in Austria, Belgium, France, Germany, Hungary, Italy, and a few other European countries (Table 1.4). Those who had wages above the average lost even more. The taxes paid on the *marginal* incomes were higher. It is difficult to argue that these high taxes do not affect incentives, even though there may be disagreement on the magnitude of the effects. These taxes were paid for the public services and for the public pensions and other cash subsidies that the citizens obtained, or expected to obtain, from the state. As mentioned earlier, the taxes paid are essentially a collective premium for *expected* collective public goods and services and for social protection.

The programs had significant redistributive effects, both vertically *and* horizontally.[13] Especially in some countries, those at the lower end of the

Table 1.4. *Taxes on the average production worker*

| Country | 2000 | 2003 | 2006 | 2008 |
|---|---|---|---|---|
| Australia | 30.6 | 28.0 | 28.3 | 26.9 |
| Austria | 47.3 | 47.4 | 48.3 | 48.8 |
| Belgium | 57.1 | 55.7 | 55.5 | 56.0 |
| Canada | 33.2 | 32.0 | 31.9 | 31.3 |
| Czech Republic | 42.7 | 43.2 | 42.9 | 43.4 |
| Denmark | 44.3 | 42.6 | 41.3 | 41.2 |
| Finland | 47.8 | 45.0 | 44.0 | 43.5 |
| France | 49.6 | 49.8 | 50.1 | 49.3 |
| Germany | 54.0 | 54.2 | 53.3 | 52.0 |
| Greece | 38.5 | 37.9 | 41.9 | 42.4 |
| Hungary | 54.6 | 50.8 | 52.0 | 54.1 |
| Iceland | 26.2 | 29.3 | 29.5 | 28.3 |
| Ireland | 28.9 | 24.2 | 23.0 | 22.9 |
| Italy | 46.9 | 45.7 | 45.9 | 46.5 |
| Japan | 24.8 | 27.4 | 28.8 | 29.5 |
| Korea | 16.3 | 16.3 | 18.1 | 20.3 |
| Luxembourg | 37.5 | 33.5 | 35.3 | 35.9 |
| Mexico | 12.6 | 16.8 | 15.0 | 15.1 |
| Netherlands | 39.7 | 37.1 | 44.6 | 45.0 |
| New Zealand | 19.4 | 19.7 | 21.1 | 21.2 |
| Norway | 38.6 | 38.1 | 37.4 | 37.7 |
| Poland | 43.1 | 43.1 | 43.7 | 39.7 |
| Portugal | 37.3 | 36.8 | 37.4 | 37.6 |
| Slovak Republic | 41.7 | 42.9 | 38.5 | 38.9 |
| Spain | 38.6 | 38.5 | 39.1 | 37.8 |
| Sweden | 50.1 | 48.2 | 47.8 | 44.6 |
| Switzerland | 30.0 | 29.7 | 29.5 | 29.5 |
| Turkey[a] | 40.4 | 42.2 | 42.7 | 39.7 |
| United Kingdom | 32.6 | 33.8 | 34.0 | 32.8 |
| United States | 30.4 | 29.9 | 29.9 | 30.1 |
| Unweighted average | | | | |
| OECD | 37.8 | 37.3 | 37.7 | 37.4 |
| EU-15 | 43.4 | 42.0 | 42.8 | 42.4 |
| EU-19 | 43.8 | 42.6 | 43.1 | 42.8 |

[a] Wages figures are based on the old definition of average worker.
*Source*: OECD, 2009.

income distribution, as a group, generally gained more in benefits than they contributed in taxes. However, at similar income levels, individuals who were, or claimed to be, more often ill, or were more idle, or had more children, or evaded more taxes, benefited more than those who did not. The more abuses there are, the greater the horizontal inequity of the system is. By and large, the public protection system contributed to a better (measured) distribution of disposable income and to lower Gini coefficients. This result has been considered to be one of the important and desirable outcomes of the large government role.

While reducing risks for many citizens and improving the countries' income distributions, this intermediation on the part of the state was inevitably costly in terms of individual liberty, efficiency in the allocation of resources, and economic growth. A pertinent question then is, What would have happened if the state had *not* stepped in with this increased spending and taxing role during the past century? As is well known, these "with and without" questions are always difficult to answer, both in economics and in other fields. Nonetheless, they are often important ones.

Ignoring the cost in terms of reduced individual economic freedom, a cost that could be high for some individuals and that received a lot of attention in the past, and that could vary from country to country, depending on the spirit of solidarity that exists,[14] the high tax rates needed to finance the expensive public-sector activities must have had a negative impact on the economic incentives of some or many citizens in their economic decisions. There is a large literature that has identified, and at times quantified, the welfare or efficiency costs of high tax rates, at least on some categories of workers. A more limited literature has done the same for spending programs. Some influential economists have gone so far as to attribute differences in the rates of growth over recent decades between the United States and European countries to differences in tax rates. However, disagreements remain on the significance of the empirical results.

The higher these welfare costs are, the less attractive the large spending role of the government appears to be *over the long run*. This would be even more so when governments are not efficient in the use of the money received – and, of course, some governments are more efficient in that use than others – and when tax revenue is collected with taxes that create more distortions.[15] If taxes had not increased, the economies of the high-tax countries probably would have grown at a faster pace, and over the long run their citizens would have had higher per capita incomes with which to buy more easily the desired social protection directly from the market, if they had chosen to do so. It can even be argued that the protection that some individuals receive from government programs may be less than what they themselves would have bought if the governments had not intervened with their programs.

For reasons identified especially by the "public choice" literature, as developed by economists James Buchanan, Gordon Tullock, William Niskanen,

Mancur Olson, and several others, government programs tend to be less efficient than the private sector's programs, because those who make the decisions (the policy makers) are pressured or have an incentive to promote their or their groups' interests.[16] Also those who administer the programs have less incentive to reduce their costs and to be efficient. There is no invisible hand that makes this self-promotion optimal. Government programs are not subjected to the discipline imposed by competition; and the individuals who operate the programs have less incentive to economize on costs. Also, when the cost of a service is zero, or is very low, there may be a demand for it on the part of individuals who do not value the service much and would not have bought it if the price they themselves paid had been explicit and higher.

Recent literature has stressed the significance of bureaucratic and political corruption that also increases the cost of public programs (e.g., Rose-Ackerman, 1999, and Tanzi, 1998). When programs become public, they often become monopolies and tools for pursuing objectives that favor the policy makers or the bureaucrats in charge. These objectives result in excessive public employment, low productivity in the delivery of services, high public-sector wages (at times pushed by unionized public employees), and creation of rents that may be in the form of bribes for some groups. In the case of public education, the public service may be used to promote objectives (e.g., patriotism, racial or gender integration) that, regardless of their intrinsic merit, are not necessarily connected with the activity of preparing individuals for the job market.[17]

Some recent studies have estimated the inefficiency that has characterized high public spending in some countries. These studies have shown that the objectives that are pursued by these programs are often obtained at too high a financial cost (see Chapter 11). One must add to these costs the macroeconomic costs generated by fiscal deficits and high public debts that often accompany high public expenditures.

It is an open question whether *many* citizens are myopic or, if they are, whether they are more myopic than the policy makers who make the spending decisions on their behalf.[18]

For example, the accumulation of large public debts in several countries and, especially, of large unfunded future liabilities in public pension systems and in some health systems can be considered as clear examples of policy makers' or governments' myopia.[19] These liabilities raise questions about the sustainability of current public programs and, implicitly, about the ability of these programs to be able to cover the *future* risks for the citizens *at the promised level*. For example, the *Relazione Annuale* of the Bank of Italy

(May 31, 2008) estimated that the unfunded liability for public pensions in Italy was about 100 percent of current GDP, or broadly equal to the Italian official public debt.[20] Thus, it is unlikely that future retirees will receive the pensions at the level and at the conditions that have been promised to them by the Italian government. For some other countries, including the United States, the estimated unfunded liabilities for pensions and especially for health programs are larger, and the current crisis has increased them. On August 5, 2010, the Social Security Board of Trustees of the United States reported that the program costs by 2015 will permanently exceed tax revenue; by 2037 the combined Trust Funds, accumulated over the years since the creation of the Social Security System, will be exhausted. In some countries, these programs have become public examples of Ponzi schemes. Payments to future beneficiaries are to be covered by the future contributions of new members. However, this pay-as-you-go equivalence disappears when demographic changes become fiscally unfriendly, as they have become in many countries.

In conclusion, the myopia of *some* citizens must be compared with the myopia of policy makers. At some future time, the potential beneficiaries of public programs will be disappointed.[21] While *some citizens* can be assumed to be myopic, for public pensions and health systems it is *the whole public system* that may be considered to be myopic. It is not obvious which myopia would have more serious consequences for the future welfare of the citizens.

## 1.4. Is a Different Economic Role of the State Possible?

For much of recorded history (until the 20th century), the world did not have governments that taxed their citizens at high rates and spent the money to finance public programs (for pensions, health, education, social assistance, etc.) on behalf of the citizens. Still the world was able to get along, and many countries grew to be more or less comfortable even though some individual citizens may have encountered difficulties because of the absence of government programs. Some social protection was provided through means other than government programs. As Kenneth Arrow observed four decades ago, "It is a mistake to limit collective action to state action." He added that "norms of social behavior, including ethical and moral codes . . . [can be] reactions by society to compensate for market failure" (Arrow, 1970, p. 79). Thus, when there are social needs, most societies tend to deal with them, sometimes more successfully than at other times. Existing "social norms" that made people behave according to shared notions of fairness helped in the past to compensate for presumed "market failure." Citizens made provisions against economic risks by giving more scope to family links, by having larger families, by saving some of their incomes at a time when saving was still seen as an important virtue, and by developing spontaneous community support networks.[22] Individuals remained economically active as long as they were able to work (rather than retiring at an officially imposed age). They had the support of extended families, social groups, and religious institutions. They participated in numerous private associations (e.g., confraternities, mutual assistance societies, credit unions). They bought services from private providers (e.g., private schools, private doctors and hospitals). The fact that at that time countries were much poorer than they are today, and thus personal incomes were much lower, meant that the assistance that individuals received from others was not generous by today's rich countries' standards. For example, see Cipolla (1969) for the poor conditions of schools in the past. If public-sector programs had existed at that time, the services provided by the state would not have been generous, as they are not generous today in poor, developing countries.

A large literature, mainly by historians and sociologists, has shown that, before governments started intervening on a large scale, with their public programs, the citizens of several countries had spontaneously developed significant private programs that, taking again into account the low income levels of the time, did a reasonable job in providing some of the basic assistance in several areas that the individuals and their families needed. For example, on his visit to the United States in the 1830s, Alexis de Tocqueville "noted with special interest the prominent place of voluntary associations in American society.... Churches, community groups, fraternal associations, and civil organizations ... did for themselves through these voluntary efforts what people in other societies expected governments and elites to do to them" (Wuthnow, 1991, p. 3). Wuthnow adds that "others have paid heed to Tocqueville's warning that needs unmet by *voluntary* efforts provide excuse for government to intervene, and with intervention comes control, and with control comes totalitarianism" (ibid., emphasis added).

The same point as the one made by Tocqueville has been made for Sweden, where, before the intervention of the state, "trade unions and other types of workers' associations formed mutual assistance associations with voluntary membership" (see Rexed, 2000, p. 9; for similar arguments, for other countries, see Alston and Ferrie, 1999; Beito, 2000; Beito, Gordon, and Tabarrok, 2002; Ritter, 1996; and Zamagni, 2000).[23]

When the public programs came into existence, these private programs were progressively crowded out. In some cases, they were *pushed out* by explicit legislation. Where the government intervened less, they continued to play a more significant role. For example, contributions to charities, hospitals, private schools, and other nongovernmental civic organizations remain important today in the United States, where the government role has been more limited, compared with most European countries. These private contributions, directly or indirectly, help reduce significantly the differences in *total* social assistance between the United States and the European countries.[24] (See Chapter 12 for statistical information.) According to Arrow's or Ariely's terminology, when the welfare state was introduced, existing "social norms" were progressively replaced by "market norms." People felt that because the state had assumed the responsibility of providing social protection, they were no longer required or expected to assist others. They no longer had a feeling of guilt in not assisting others, as they would have had before. It is also possible that, in some cases, the state intervention reduced the trust that people had in each other. In some way, part of the social capital that had existed was destroyed. Ariely also argues that citizens are more efficient in these social activities when they are prompted by social norms than by government programs.[25]

Let us consider now a simple thought experiment. Let us assume that it were possible to abolish the government programs of social assistance that now require high tax levels to be financed. In this experiment we must ignore transitional problems that, in reality, can be very important. Ignoring these problems makes the experiment seem a bit unrealistic, especially on political grounds. For example, individuals who are already retired expect and deserve to continue receiving the government pensions to which they had contributed during the working phase of their life. Those not yet retired, who have already contributed over many years to their future public pensions, expect the government to live up to its promise when they retire. Those who hold government jobs, with tenure on their jobs, expect to continue to receive their government salaries, and so on. Thus, our thought experiment must be interpreted to include a substantial transition period, a period that could extend well over one generation during which the connection of many people to government programs would be progressively reduced.

The abolition of the government programs, by reducing public spending, would significantly and progressively reduce the need for high taxes. This tax reduction would translate into corresponding significant increases in the present and future disposable (after-tax) incomes of most citizens. These higher incomes would make it possible for many among them, using the extra money in their pockets, to buy from the (domestic or possibly foreign) market some of the services (some of the protection against economic risks) that they had been buying indirectly from the government with the higher taxes that they had paid. It would be absurd to assume that the market would not be able to provide most of these services. However, it must be recognized that *some* citizens may be too poor or too handicapped to be able to buy, with their own means, the services that they were previously getting for free from the state; and some citizens who may be considered high risks may face expensive private options. These considerations shift the focus to a minority of citizens and to what could be done about them.

In the new situation, governments would face a fundamental choice: first, to wash their hands and let the citizens, in the future, do whatever they wished to do with their *extra*, disposal income (this would be a return to the situation that existed many years ago, before the public programs were created and when governments had not yet assumed any social responsibility);[26] or, second, to impose some constraints on the use of that extra income in order to attempt to continue promoting through other means the objectives that the governments had been pursuing in recent decades with their public spending programs. Regardless of the choice they made, vis-à-vis the citizens, governments would have to assume greater *regulatory* responsibilities vis-à-vis the market, to ensure that private providers of services follow socially desirable rules and that the market operated as efficiently and as transparently as it can be made to operate. In other words, the withdrawal from some spending responsibility on the part of the government would require greater responsibility in making the market work more efficiently and more transparently.

In the first alternative, the government could either assume that the citizens, for the most part, are responsible and rational (rather than myopic and irresponsible); or simply assume that, regardless of their behavior, the citizens must bear responsibility for their own actions, whatever those actions might be. In this alternative, the complete freedom of the citizens (to be responsible or irresponsible) would be respected. The only rule here is a kind of "golden rule" that states that I will not bother you if you do not bother me and I am solely responsible for my actions. This is the kind of world that very conservative economists and philosophers, and some citizens, especially in the United States, would favor. The philosopher Robert Nozick, author of *Anarchy, State and Utopia* (1974), is probably the most prominent exponent of this "minimalist state" alternative. As a reviewer of Nozick's influential book put it, "Nozick holds that each person is a separate individual with inviolable right to live as he chooses, provided only that he respects the similar right of other individuals. These rights include the rights to be free from interference...they do not include the right to any uncontracted assistance from others" (Lacey, 2001, pp. 20–21).

Critics of Nozick's position find his position rather extreme.[27] One problem with it is that, willy-nilly, when individuals live especially in an urban community, total individual freedom can generate significant negative externalities for other people who live in the same community. The greater the density of the population is, the greater are likely to be, *ceteris paribus*, potential negative externalities. This is obvious for externalities associated with contagious illnesses and extreme poverty. Thus, the role of the state in promoting or even forcing good hygiene or in forcing vaccination against infectious diseases is an old and generally accepted one. (Also see Walvin, 1988, for the consequences of the growing population density in the urban setting of London during the Victorian age that led to an increased government role.) My welfare may be reduced by others' poor hygiene and by the existence of sick people or very poor people on the sidewalks of the street where I live.[28] Of course, it could be argued that I would have the freedom to move and that my property rights do not guarantee freedom from these problems. As R. H. Coase, winner of the Nobel Prize in Economic Sciences in 1991, might put it, Does my property right include the right to be free of poor people on the street where I live?[29]

The second and less extreme alternative would be for the government to choose a paternalistic approach and encourage, or even require, that the citizens buy directly from the private market, but with their own incomes (or, in specific "deserving" cases, with cash transfers that the poorest among them might receive from the government or from civic associations), some of the protection against particular economic risks that they had been getting previously for free or at highly subsidized costs from the government against the payment of higher taxes. In this case the government would not change the *objectives* of its intervention, but it would change the *instruments* used to achieve those objectives.[30] This approach would be consistent with some of the results of experiments from behavioral economics that have concluded that some individuals tend to make irrational choices when they are completely free to choose (e.g., Ariely, 2008; Thaler and Sunstein, 2008; and Della Vigna, 2009). Many individuals may not mind being subjected to some friendly guidance, or nudge, in a kind of "libertarian paternalism," or even being subjected to some compulsion from the government, if they realize that, without that guidance or compulsion, they might choose poorly. They can thus be made to behave more rationally by being encouraged, or forced, to change their behavior. Some observers may see this as a reduction of the freedom of individuals, arguing that total freedom should include the right to be irrational.

This second alternative is not as new as it may appear and as some proponents of it have made it up to be. A paternalistic role has already been played by many governments when they have required individuals to get insurance for their cars and get the cars inspected, have fire alarms in their homes or offices, wear seat belts (or helmets) and not use cellular phones while driving, quit smoking in public places and pay more for cigarettes, get vaccination against some illnesses, live in buildings that are verified to be structurally sound, attend school until a given age, place their trash in specific containers, and so on. The government could require individuals to buy some *basic* medical insurance, to acquire some minimum pension rights (or to accumulate savings for old age through individual retirement accounts), to send children to (private) schools or provide in-house schooling, and so on.[31] These are examples of paternalism on the part of governments for activities that do not necessarily require public spending. All of these requirements have, to some extent, been imposed by the governments of some countries, including that of the United States or of some American states.

A paternalistic approach, as a substitute *for programs that previously required public spending,* exists in some limited form in several countries. Following the (1981) example set by Chile, or, perhaps, the program introduced much earlier through TIAA-CREF in American universities, several countries have introduced requirements for workers to allocate a given percentage of their earnings to personal accounts that are invested in regulated private funds and that are expected to grow in value over the long run, thus providing the workers with some financial resources when they retire.[32] These programs are based on "defined contributions" rather than "defined benefits." The law establishes the contributions required from the workers.[33] The benefits are not guaranteed in specific amounts.

The assumption that the level of future government pension *benefits* can be defined many years in advance is based on illusion. The benefits that the workers will receive from private pensions, when they retire, will depend on their contributions and on the rate of return on the money contributed to the accounts over the period. Some countries require their residents to buy private health insurances or to put money into special "health accounts" (Singapore) to be used first, in case of illnesses, before public money becomes available.[34] In many countries (United States, several Latin American countries, India), private schools have been or have become a common feature, and many families send their children to these schools, even though free public education is available. These private schools presumably provide better and more easily marketable education. Special educational accounts have also been created in some countries, including the United States.

There is little doubt that, should governments give up their quasi-monopoly power over some of these sectors (pensions, health, education), especially in today's world, private-sector alternatives would quickly appear, as they appeared when governments gave up their monopolies over airlines, telephones, and other areas. Some of these alternatives might be available abroad at lower costs. Educational and health services have become increasingly traded. Some alternatives would provide better benefits and would cost less than others. For example, India is becoming a major exporter for high-quality health services. The United Kingdom has been a major exporter of educational services. In past decades and in many countries, these alternatives were not available because governments often prohibited them; furthermore, the governments provided "free" (i.e., tax-financed) alternatives, thus sharply reducing individuals' incentive to rely on the private sector for services for which they would have to pay directly the full cost. If parents sent their children to private schools when the government continued to provide free public schools, they would still have to pay the taxes that supported public education. School vouchers that allow some children to go to private school without direct payments are now available in some countries, especially in Chile. In earlier years, markets were more closed and less sophisticated than they are, or can be, today.[35] Thus, some currently available options were not available.

Technological and policy developments have contributed over the years to make many markets *potentially* more efficient and wider than before. However, some governmental actions continue to restrain them. In a globalizing economic environment, governments would have to play a different and more effective role than in the past in regulating private markets (to prevent cartels, monopolies, and other abuses) and in forcing much greater transparency on the part of those who provide services. The regulation of some of these services must extend somehow to the global markets. The private-sector option does not imply that governments can wash their own hands and, by an act of faith, rely on invisible hands to make the system work. Rather, it implies a different government role and the use of alternative policy instruments.

Governments must provide more, better, and easier-to-absorb information to citizens, to allow them to make good choices. This important regulatory and informational role for governments has attracted limited attention in the past. Past discussions of the economic role of the state have put too much emphasis on the public replacing the private when there are market failures and not enough on correcting the market.

In this new world, the government will have to provide to the truly "deserving poor" (those who are objectively unable to work) the financial means (i.e., earmarked money) to allow them to buy from the market some of the essential, basic services that they have been getting free, or almost free, from the state. Some forms of vouchers could accomplish this objective. The government's role would thus move from providing expensive *universal* services, available to every citizen rich and poor, toward providing *targeted* and perhaps earmarked cash assistance. Universal assistance is more costly fiscally, but it is easier administratively and, especially, politically.[36] Targeted assistance is more difficult, both administratively and politically, because it requires identification of the specific groups of individuals to be assisted and decisions as to the level of income or disability at which an individual would acquire the right to public assistance.[37] Means testing is never easy because of difficulties in getting reliable information on individuals and families, especially in a mobile society, when significant tax evasion is common. In these situations the incomes declared by taxpayers are not necessarily a good criterion for identification of needs.[38] In the distant past, when there were no income taxes, and there was much less mobility, parish priests or members of mutual assistance societies had much better information on the economic situation of each family within their area (Beito et al., 2002, and Solomon, 1972).

### 1.5. Public Spending and the "Paradox of Redistribution"

Some experts would oppose the policy change proposed in the preceding section by relying on the conclusion of what has been called the "paradox of redistribution." The paradox of redistribution argues in support of high levels of public spending to achieve the objective of income redistribution. It suggests that when the incomes generated by the private market are unevenly distributed, as they generally are, a large public-sector intervention (through high public spending) can significantly reduce the income inequality, even when the public programs are universal (i.e., not targeted to the poor) and even when higher-income classes get larger shares of the total public spending (Korpi and Palme, 1998). A large part of the redistributive effect does not come from the tax side but from the spending side. The significant redistributive effect would exist even if proportional taxes were used, as long as the level of public spending is high.

Table 1.5. *Redistribution in OECD countries: Effects of taxes and public transfers*

| Country | Year | Gini coefficients | | Fiscal redistribution | Share of redistribution contributed by | | Public spending As % of GDP |
|---|---|---|---|---|---|---|---|
| | | Private income | Disposable income | | Taxes | Transfers | |
| Australia | 2003 | 0.460 | 0.312 | 0.140 | 31.8 | 68.2 | 34.0 |
| Belgium | 1997 | 0.481 | 0.250 | 0.231 | 32.0 | 68.0 | 51.2 |
| Canada | 2000 | 0.429 | 0.315 | 0.114 | 35.1 | 64.9 | 40.6 |
| Denmark | 2004 | 0.419 | 0.228 | 0.191 | 22.0 | 78.0 | 54.4 |
| Finland | 2004 | 0.463 | 0.252 | 0.211 | 21.8 | 78.2 | 50.1 |
| France | 1994 | 0.485 | 0.288 | 0.197 | 9.1 | 90.9 | 54.2 |
| Germany | 2000 | 0.473 | 0.275 | 0.198 | 25.3 | 74.7 | 45.1 |
| Netherlands | 1999 | 0.372 | 0.231 | 0.141 | 31.2 | 68.8 | 46.0 |
| Norway | 2000 | 0.403 | 0.251 | 0.152 | 25.7 | 74.3 | 39.3 |
| Sweden | 2000 | 0.447 | 0.252 | 0.195 | 19.0 | 81.0 | 55.6 |
| Switzerland | 2002 | 0.392 | 0.274 | 0.118 | 1.7 | 98.3 | 35.0 |
| United Kingdom | 1999 | 0.498 | 0.343 | 0.155 | 20.0 | 80.0 | 39.5 |
| United States | 2004 | 0.481 | 0.372 | 0.109 | 40.4 | 59.6 | 36.0 |
| Mean | | 0.446 | 0.280 | 0.166 | 24.2 | 75.8 | 44.7 |

*Source*: The data on public spending (last column) are from the European Union and the IMF. The other are from the Luxembourg Income Study, kindly made available by David Jesuit.

Table 1.5 seems to support the conclusion of the paradox of redistribution for 13 highly developed countries for which data are available. The table shows that the Gini coefficients generated by *private* incomes, before any fiscal redistribution takes place, are relatively high. They range from a lower level of 0.372 for the Netherlands to a higher level of 0.498 for the United Kingdom. The average Gini coefficient for the whole group is 0.446. However, when high private incomes are reduced by taxes, and low private incomes are increased by public transfers, the Gini coefficients, for the (after-tax and after-transfers) *disposable incomes*, are much reduced, to an average of 0.280. The Gini coefficients for *disposable* income now range between a low of 0.228 in Denmark and 0.231 in the Netherlands and a high of 0.372 in the United States.

Table 1.5 shows also that, on average, three-fourths of the redistribution – 75.7 percent – comes from public spending and only one-fourth – 25.3 – comes from the leveling effect of taxes. Only in a few Anglo-Saxon countries (the United States, Canada, and Australia) are taxes of some importance. In the United States, the absence of value-added taxes and the fact that many families have incomes that are too low to be subjected to income taxes make the tax system a more significant redistributive instrument than elsewhere.

Figure 1.1 provides a scatter diagram of total public spending as a share of GDP and of the fiscal redistribution generated by public spending and by taxes for the 13 countries shown in Table 1.5. The chart provides strong visual evidence of the impact of high public spending on the income redistribution. The higher the share of public spending into GDP is, the higher the fiscal redistribution is seen to be. The coefficient of correlation between these two variables is a high 0.82.

There is one more argument made against targeted income redistribution policies – essentially a political argument. It is often argued that high-spending, universal programs achieve more redistribution than targeted programs because the latter would not get the political support from the middle classes that they need and, thus, would not be introduced. It is concluded that, with their high levels of public spending and universal programs, the high-spending countries, and especially the welfare states, have reduced inequality more than some of the Anglo-Saxon countries because the latter have relied on targeted and not on universal programs (see also Chapter 12). This argument is based on the assumption that the middle classes suffer from a kind of "fiscal illusion." They see the advantages to them from the public spending but not the taxes that they would have to pay.

If reducing income inequality were the only or the most important objective of the economic activity of the state, and if money spent on the poor were actually received *as cash income by the poor*, as assumed by the paradox of redistribution, then the superiority of the universal programs in providing better Gini coefficients and presumably better welfare for society would be clear. However, there are at least two problems with this argument.

First, in a competitive and globalizing world, reduction in income inequality, although important, cannot be the sole or the main objective of economic policy. If that were the case, the policies pursued by the planned economies in the past, and by Cuba and North Korea today, would be praised and imitated. They delivered, or deliver, good Gini coefficients but little economic growth over the long run.[39] Because of this outcome, centrally planned economies came and mostly went.

Second, we must recognize the possibility that some (or even much) of the money that is presumably spent on the poorer income groups, for which the benefits from all that money are attributed, may be siphoned off toward those who deliver the services (e.g., schoolteachers, public administrators, nurses, doctors) through high public salaries and other channels, including

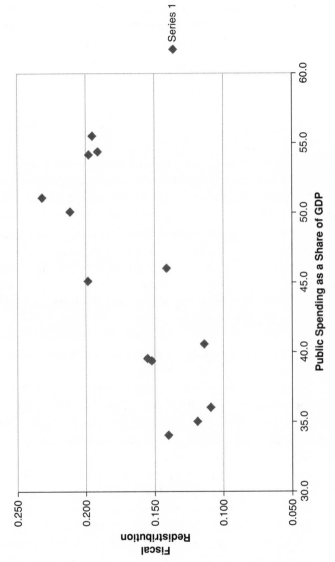

Figure 1.1 Selected countries: Public spending and fiscal redistribution.

inefficiency. Public spending may, at times, help little the intended beneficiaries but much the individuals who deliver the public services.[40] However,
it will still be attributed as a benefit to those it was intended to help. Those
who provide or deliver the public services generally do not come from the
lowest percentiles in the income distributions but mostly from the middle
classes (Tanzi, 1974, 2008; Alesina, 1998). This is an application of what
is sometimes referred to as "Director's Law." Aaron Director, a professor
at the University of Chicago, had proposed in the early 1960s a "law of
public expenditures" that stated that public expenditures, regardless of the
declared intentions, are made mainly to benefit the middle classes, while
they are financed mainly with the taxes imposed on the poor and on the rich
(Stigler, 1970). Director was probably right on the benefit side but perhaps
less so on the financing side, especially for recent years when the level of
taxation rose significantly in industrial countries and the working middle
class bore a large share of it, especially when value-added taxes and high payroll taxes were used. In these countries, "Director's Law" could be applied
to "tax expenditures" that are often more important to the middle classes
because some features of them (such as vanishing or limited deductions)
reduce their value for high-income individuals.

The "paradox of redistribution" simply assumes that the money spent on
providing services to some groups is equivalent to the real benefits received
by those groups. This assumption is often not warranted as a lot of evidence
indicates. This aspect has been largely ignored by the relevant literature.
Public spending is often accompanied by inefficiency, and this inefficiency
may come in the form of rents for those who deliver or administer the
services (see Chapter 11). Of course, how much rent goes to the providers
of public services varies among countries.

Finally, globalization and other developments are making it progressively
more difficult and more costly for countries to maintain the current high
average tax levels. Various forms of "fiscal termites" have been weakening
the tax systems of many countries (Tanzi, 2001). This means that universal
public programs are becoming more difficult to finance, without macroeconomic implications, than in past decades, when these termites were much
less active or did not exist. Over future years, fiscal termites will force
countries to adopt a different role for the state than in the recent past – a
role with less public spending and lower taxes and with more use of other
instruments of policy. Globalization and vouchers could make it easier for
countries to use targeted cash transfers that would allow citizens in low-
income groups to buy some of the services and the protection that they need

against particular risks more cheaply outside their own countries (Tanzi, 2005c). For example, health tourism has been growing in importance, allowing citizens of rich countries to buy expensive health services, at bargain prices and of acceptable quality, from poorer countries, such as India. Some educational services could also be bought, and in fact are being bought, from other countries. Some countries, as, for example, the United Kingdom, have become major exporters of educational services. In time, even the care of the very old (or of people in jail) could be bought from abroad, at adequate quality and at much lower costs.[41] There is also no valid reason why the savings to be used in old age could not be invested internationally rather than in home countries, in relatively low-risk and well-monitored investments.[42]

In all these developments, the government must play a far more vigilant and effective supervisory and regulatory role than in the past. This is a fundamental role in a market economy, one that the state has *not* played well or has not played at all in past years. There is some literature, especially associated with economists at the University of Chicago, that has questioned the role of the state in regulations.[43] Less public spending may require more and better rules and more efficient institutions necessary to enforce the rules. As the late Jean Monnet, the French policy maker who played a large role in the creation of the European Union, has been reported to have said: "Nothing is possible without men. Nothing is sustainable without institutions." The key question is whether governments would be able to create the right institutions to do so fairly and efficiently. On this question, good arguments can be advanced on both sides. If the answer to that question is positive, a new role of the state would definitely be possible and even desirable. That new role would require less public spending, less taxation, but more efficient government monitoring and guidance and more global coordination.

## 1.6. Concluding Remarks

The following chapters elaborate on some of these themes. Part II, the historical part, describes the growth of public spending during the past century and the factors that contributed to it. Part III, the more theoretical or analytical part, outlines some theories related to the role of the state in different settings and discusses policy tools that have become more important in recent years. Part IV focuses on results, in terms of significant socioeconomic indicators, that can be attributed to the growth of public spending in recent decades. The focus remains on advanced OECD countries with some occasional excursions to other countries. A concluding chapter focuses on issues that will influence the future economic role of the state. It discusses issues that have not attracted the attention that they merit. It also discusses possible changes, away from public spending, that might characterize future developments. It is argued that the use of policy tools other than spending and taxing, especially regulations, will become more important. Thus, it would be, in some sense, a return to the role of the state that existed before the 19th century. However, it would be a modern version of that role, accompanied by considerably higher public spending and taxes than at that time, and with regulations aimed at assisting the citizens and not at providing opportunities for rents to some privileged individuals. Whether the anticipated new role will be possible and will be more efficient than the recent one, only time will tell. Whether market economies may survive might depend on whether the state will be capable of exercising that role.

## References

Alesina, Alberto. 1998. "The Political Economy of Macroeconomic Stabilization and Income Inequality: Myths and Reality," in *Income Distribution and High-Quality Growth*, edited by Vito Tanzi and Ke-Young Chu (Cambridge, Mass.: MIT Press).

Alonso, Antonio, Ludger Schuknecht, and Vito Tanzi. 2005. "Public Sector Efficiency: An International Comparison." *Public Choice* 123: 321–47.

Alston, Lee J., and Joseph P. Ferrie. 1999. *Southern Paternalism and the American Welfare State: Economics, Politics, and Institutions in the South, 1865–1965* (Cambridge: Cambridge University Press).

Andreoni, James. 2006. "Philanthropy," in *Handbook of Giving, Altruism, and Reciprocity*, vol. 2, edited by Serge-Christophe Kolm and Jean, Mercier Ythier (Amsterdam: Elsevier, North-Holland), pp. 1201–65.

Angelopoulos, Konstantinos, Apostolis Philippopoulos, and Efthymios Tsionas. 2008. "Does Public Sector Efficiency Matter? Revisiting the Relation between Fiscal Size and Economic Growth in a World Sample." *Public Choice* 137, nos. 1–2 (October): 245–78.

Ariely, Dan. 2008. *Predictably Irrational: The Hidden Forces That Shape Our Decisions* (New York: Harpers and Collins).

Arrow, Kenneth J. 1970. "The Organization of Economic Activity: Issues Pertinent to the Choice of Market versus Nonmarket Allocation," in *Public Expenditure and Policy Analysis*, edited by Robert H. Haveman and Julius Margolis (Skokie, Illinois:) (Rand McNally College Publishing).

Atkinson, A. B. 2004. "Social Europe and the Contribution of Public Economics." *Rivista di Diritto Finanziario e Scienza delle Finanze*, Anno LXII, Fase. 4.

Auerback, A. J., J. Gokhale, and L. Kotlikoff. 1991. "Generational Accounts; A Meaningful Alternative to Deficit Accounting," in *Tax Policy and the Economy*, edited by David Bradford (Cambridge, Mass.: MIT Press).

Auerback, A. J., Laurence J. Kotlikoff, and Willi Leibritz. 1998. "Generational Accounting around the World." IMES (Institute of Monetary and Economic Studies, Bank of Japan), *Discussion Paper* No. 98-E-2.

Banca d'Italia. 2008. *Relazione Annuale* (Rome, May 31).

Bastiat, F. 1864. *Oeuvres Completes.* 7 vols. (Paris: Guillaumin).

Bator, Francis M. 1960. *The Question of Government Spending: Public Needs and Private Wants* (New York: Harper and Brothers).

Beito, David. 2000. *From Mutual Aid to the Welfare State: Fraternal Societies and Social Services, 1890–1967* (Chapel Hill: University of North Carolina Press).

Beito, David, Peter Gordon, and Alexander Tabarrok, eds. 2002. *The Voluntary City* (Ann Arbor: University of Michigan Press – Independent Institute).

Callan, Tim, and John Walsh. 2006. "Assessing the Impact of Tax/Transfer Policy Changes on Poverty: Methodological Issues and Some European Evidence." *Euromod Working Paper* No. EM1/06.

Cipolla, Carlo M. 1969. *Literacy and Development in the West* (Harmondsworth: Penguin Books).

Coase, Ronald. 1937. "The Nature of the Firm." *Economica* 4: 386–405.

——— 1960. "The Problem of Social Cost." *Journal of Law and Economics* 3 (October): 1–44.

Della Vigna, Stefano. 2009. "Psychology and Economics: Evidence from the Field." *Journal of Economic Literature* 47, no. 2 (June): 315–72.

de Molinari, Gustave. 1849. *Les Soirées de la Rue Saint-Lazare: Entretiens sur les Lois Economique et Défense de la Propriété.* Translated as *Le Serate di Rue Saint-Lazare* (Macerata: Liberi Libri, 2009).

De Viti de Marco, Antonio. 1936. *First Principles of Public Finance* (London: Jonathan Cape). Previously published in Italian.

Down, Anthony. 1957. *An Economic Theory of Democracy* (New York: Harper).

European Commission. 2008. *Public Finances in EMU* (Brussels).

European Foundation for the Improvement of Living and Working Conditions. 2008. *Second European Quality of Life: First Findings* (Dublin).

Gustafsson, Bjorn. 2008. "The Swedish Model in the Era of Integration and Globalization," in *Institutions for Social Well-Being: Alternatives for Europe,* edited by Lilia Costabile (London: Palgrave Macmillan), pp. 171–97.

Haveman, Robert. 1994. "Should Generational Account Replace Public Budgets and Deficits?" *Journal of Economic Perspective* 1: 55–111.

Hochman, H. M., and J. D. Rodgers. 1969. "Pareto Optimal Redistribution." *American Economic Review* 59: 542–57.

Korpi, Walter, and Joakim Palme. 1998. "The Strategy of Equality and the Paradox of Redistribution." *American Sociological Review* 63, no. 5: 661–87.

Lacey, A. R. 2001. *Robert Nozick* (Princeton: Princeton University Press).

Lindert, Peter H. 2002. "What Drives Social Spending? 1780 to 2020," in *When Markets Fail: Social Policy and Economic Reform,* edited by Ethan B. Kapstein and Branko Milanovic (New York: Russell Sage Foundation, 2002), pp. 185–214.

McCaffery, Edward J., and Joel Slemrod, eds. 2006. *Behavioural Public Finance* (New York: Russell Sage Foundation).

Mill, John Stuart. 2004. *Principles of Political Economy* (Amherst, N.Y.: Prometheus Books).

Musgrave, Richard. 1959. *The Theory of Public Finance* (New York: McGraw-Hill).

Myrdal, Gunnar. 1954. *The Political Element in the Development of Economic Theory* (Cambridge, Mass.: Harvard University Press). Originally published in Swedish in 1929.

Nozick, Robert. 1974. *Anarchy, State and Utopia* (New York: Basic Books).

OECD. 1985. *Social Expenditure, 1960–1990* (Paris: OECD).

2009. *Taxing Wages* (Paris: OECD).

2010. *Revenue Statistics of OECD Countries* (Paris: OECD).

Pigou, Arthur. 1924. *The Economics of Welfare*. 2nd ed. (London: Macmillan).

Plato. 1961. Republic I, in *The Collected Dialogues of Plato*, edited by Edith Hamilton, Bollinger Series 71 (New York: Pantheon Books).

Rawls, John. 1971. *A Theory of Justice* (Cambridge, Mass.: Belknap Press of Harvard University Press).

1974. "Some Reasons for the Maximin Criterion." *American Economic Review* 64: 141–46.

Rexed, Knut. 2000. "Public Sector Reform: Lessons from the Nordic Countries, the Swedish Experience." Swedish Agency for Administrative Development. Mimeo (May 19).

Ritter, Gerhard A. 1996. *Storia dello Stato Sociale* (Rome: Laterza). Translated from *Der Sozialstaat Entstehung und Entwiklung im Internationalen Vergleich* (Munich: R. Oldenbourg Verlas, 1991).

Rizza, P., and P. Tommasino. 2008. "Will We Treat Future Generations Fairly? Italian Fiscal Policy through the Prism of Generational Accounting," in *Fiscal Sustainability: Analytical Developments and Emerging Policy Issues*, edited by Daniele Franco. Banca d' Italia, Workshop on Public Finance (April).

Rose-Ackerman, Susan. 1999. *Corruption and Government: Causes, Consequences and Reform* (Cambridge: Cambridge University Press).

Say, J. B. 1841. *Traité de économie politique* (Paris: Guillaumin).

Savedoff, William D., and Pablo Gottret. 2008. *Governing Mandatory Health Insurance* (Washington, D.C.: World Bank).

Sen, Amartya. 1979. "Personal Utilities and Public Judgments: Or What Is Wrong with Welfare Economics?" *Economic Journal* 89: 537–89.

Solomon, Howard M. 1972. *Public Welfare, Science and Propaganda in Seventeenth Century France* (Princeton: Princeton University Press).

Stigler, George J. 1970. "Director's Law of Public Income Redistribution. "*Journal of Law and Economics* 13 (April): 1–10.

1989. *The Economic Role of the State* (Cambridge, Mass.: Basil Blackwell).

1975. *The Citizen and the State: Essays on Regulation* (Chicago: University of Chicago Press).

Tanzi, Vito. 1974. "Redistributing Income through the Budget in Latin America." Banca Nazionale del Lavoro, *Quarterly Review*, no. 108: 65–87.

1998. "Corruption around the World." *IMF Staff Papers* 45, no. 4 (December): 559–94.

2000. "Rationalizing the Government Budget," in *Economic Policy Reform: The Second Stage*, edited by Anne Krueger (Chicago: University of Chicago Press), pp. 435–52.

2001. "Globalization, Technological Developments and the Work of Fiscal Termites." *Brooklyn Journal of International Law* 26, no. 4: 1261–84.

2005a. "Social Protection in a Globalizing World." *Rivista di Politica Economica*, Anno XCV, Serie III (March–April): 3–23.

2005b. "The Economic Role of the State in the 21st Century." *Cato Journal* 25, no. 3 (Fall): 617–38.

2005c. "The Role of Government and Public Spending in a Changing World." *Rivista di Diritto Finanziario e Scienza delle Finanze*, Anno LXIV, Fasc. 3: 321–39.

2007. "Fiscal Policy and Fiscal Rules in the European Union," in *Europe after Enlargement*, edited by Anders Aslund and Marek Dabrowski (Cambridge: Cambridge University Press), pp. 50–64.

2008. "The Role of the State and Public Finance in the Next Generation." *OECD Journal on Budgeting* 8, no. 2: 1–27.

2010. "Complexity in Taxation: Origin and Consequences." Mimeo (November).

Tanzi, Vito, and L. Schuknecht. 2000. *Public Spending in the 20th Century: A Global Perspective* (Cambridge: Cambridge University Press).

Thaler, Richard H., and Cass R. Sunstein. 2008. *Nudge: Improving Decisions about Health, Wealth, and Happiness* (New Haven: Yale University Press).

Tooley, J. 1996. *Education without the State* (London: Institute of Economic Affairs).

U.S. Government. 1962. *Economic Report of the President* (Washington, D.C.: GPO).

Walvin, James. 1988. *Victorian Values* (Athens: University of Georgia Press).

West, E. G. 1970. "Resource Allocation and Growth in Early-Nineteenth Century British Education." *Economic History Review* 23: 68–95.

World Bank. 2008. *Governing Mandatory Health Insurance*. Edited by William D. Savedoff and Pablo Gottret (Washington, D.C.).

Wuthnow, Robert. 1991. "The Voluntary Sector: Legacy of the Past, Hope for the Future?," in *Between States and Markets: The Voluntary Sector in Comparative Perspective*, edited by Robert Wuthnow (Princeton: Princeton University Press).

Zamagni, Vera, ed. 2000. *Povertá e Innovazione Istituzionale in Italia: Dal Medioevo ad Oggi* (Bologna: Il Mulino).

# PART TWO

# HISTORICAL REVIEW

I do not know which makes a man more conservative – to know nothing but the present, or nothing but the past.
    Keynes, *The End of Laissez-Faire*, p. 16

# TWO

# The Role of the State in the Pre–World War II Period

## 2.1. Introduction to the Historical Review

The following five chapters in Part II present a historical review of the changing economic role of the state. Much of the review deals with the 19th and 20th centuries. The review discusses various factors and refers to some economists who contributed to changes in the perception of what responsibilities states have in the economy and to actual changes in the economic activities of governments over the two centuries. As a background to that review, it should be recalled how attitudes toward poverty, income distribution, and the opportunities faced by individuals changed over long periods of time. While recognizing some exceptions and some differences among countries, we can distinguish three general periods.

In the first period, which extended from the Middle Ages to the first half of the 19th century, the social and economic status of a person depended largely or almost exclusively on birth. Family and family connections were by far the most important factors. Poverty (or a low-class status) was seen as a natural condition of part of humanity. Sergio Ricossa ([1986] 2006) quotes the words of Giordano da Rivalto (o da Pisa), a monk who was a famous theologian and preacher at the beginning of the 13th century: "If all were king, who would work the land? God has ordained that there must be rich and poor so that the rich are served by the poor, and the poor are helped by the rich" (my translation). Ricossa adds that Giordano's position was the view of the church, which took a great interest in helping the poor through a network of charitable institutions that were financed by the rich. The view of the existence of a natural order was not limited to the 13th century and to Italy. Sir Llewellyn Woodward (1962), in his book on the *Age of Reform, 1815–1870*, reported that, for the first half of the 19th century in England, the attitude toward poverty was similar. Alexis de Tocqueville, in his 1835 essay "Memoire sur le pauperisme," shared the same view. In his 2009 book on *The Future of Liberalism*, Alan Wolfe has confirmed Woodward's view about the 19th century attitude toward inequality. As he put it, "Realism demanded that we accept the world as it was, and the world that then existed was inegalitarian to the core" (p. 65). R. K. Webb concurred:

Even more important in explaining the country's failure [in the early part of the 19th century] to help the poor by legislation were pervasive attitudes among the upper and middle classes towards the question of... social welfare. To some, effective regulations seemed impossible in a rapidly changing economy; to others, no human intervention could alter a divinely ordained social order in which the poor were an inevitable and necessary part. Still others – a small minority – were convinced of the futility of intervention by the political economists' doctrines of laissez-faire. (Webb, 1980, p. 158)

On February 1834 the English Parliament voted a law to help the poor, and soon a sixth of the population of England would be getting some assistance for being poor (Tocqueville, [1835] 1998, p. 39). In the second half of the 19th century, attitudes toward poverty started to change, in part because of political developments in many countries and in part because, as a consequence of the Industrial Revolution, some individuals of humble origins were becoming rich, thus creating a new "bourgeoisie" with increasing financial and political power. In this period, growing pressures were directed toward passing legislation directed at promoting more *equality of opportunities* among individuals – for example, voting rights, the rights of workers, the rights of women, and the rights of children. This period extended, in some form, until World War I or until about the Great Depression. Thus, from the natural acceptance of poverty or of birth-related class status, societies started moving toward concern for the creation of opportunities. This would allow at least *some* individuals to escape poverty and the class they were born into. (See also on this change chapter 3 of Wolfe's book.)

A theme that runs through much of the literature of the 19th century concerns the likelihood that higher political participation by the citizens and general elections in which an increasing share of the population could vote would generate demands for assistance and for redistribution of income and wealth by the masses. More and more categories of individuals, and not just the poorest, would press for governmental assistance to promote equality of conditions. These pressures would bring higher spending, higher taxes, and eventually more centralization of political power, putting the liberty of individuals, *qua* individuals, in danger of the tyranny of the majority. The greater the push for equality was, the greater would be the limitations on the liberty of the individuals. And, while equality was considered a mere fact, liberty was considered an important value. This theme was expressed forcefully in Tocqueville's [1835] 1998 essay mentioned earlier. That theme would remain popular to the present day in conservative political circles. A countertheme was that poverty promotes significant negative externalities for society because of the crimes and the moral degradation that it is supposed to cause. Because of this, the poor need to be assisted and reformed through the use of government programs. This theme has remained popular with the Left.

Starting with the Great Depression, the concern started to shift again, from equality of opportunity toward the *equality of outcomes*. It was no longer sufficient to help the poor to cope and survive; the new, ambitious, abstract goal became that of promoting equality of outcomes. In an egalitarian society, differences in living standards, and especially in access to "basic goods," became more and more unattractive and bothersome to the sensitivity of many. Ignoring the socialist experiments in various countries that pushed the goal of equality to an extreme and tended to suppress individual liberty, the welfare states became the most explicit attempts by governments in market economies to promote the goal of equality, or at least the goal of lifting the standards of living of all citizens, within a free society, above some minimum level that was not the minimum biological level of the past.

Perhaps it should be added that this change would inevitably bring much controversy because, quite apart from the implications for liberty mentioned earlier, to some people equality seemed an unnatural goal. In their view, it conflicted with the laws of nature and biology. Human beings are social animals. They like to live in groups so that their *individual* freedom is always, to some extent, limited and conditioned by the dynamic and the circumstances of the group to which they belong. However, the institution of hierarchy has, with rare exceptions, always been present. It starts from within the family, in which the husband almost always had more power than the wife, the parents more than the children, the male children more than the female children, the firstborn more than the others, and so on. Larger groups have historically reflected similar hierarchies, which in some societies became the traditional castes that continue to exist in some countries today. The long period of the Middle Ages reflected these hierarchies, which determined how the gains from collective actions were distributed within the groups. Thus, in some "natural" or "biological" or "historical" sense, egalitarianism, regardless of its moral virtue and some rare exceptions, might seem to some to go against this age-old natural order. Therefore, the search for and the goal of the equality of outcomes were and still are strongly resisted by many, who equate it with a challenge to individual liberty. It remains a highly controversial goal in market economies. (See also Burke, 2000; and Wolfe, 2009.)

To the extent that the goal of equality inevitably requires some restrictions on the liberty of some individuals, it has been contested on political grounds by Robert Nozick and conservative commentators who assign greater weight to individual freedom than to equality of outcomes and believe that the latter constrains the former.

## 2.2. The Polar Roles of the State

The economic role that the state, or less precisely the government, plays, or is expected to play, in a modern country depends on several factors. Among these, the most important are the extent to which the individuals who make up the population of a country feel that they are integral parts of a community; the political system that selects the policy makers and establishes the rules within which they operate; the views of the policy makers and the political pressures and constraints to which they are subjected; and the choices that previous policy makers or governments made in past years that have often established a path for successive governments from which it is not easy to depart. These choices are inevitably affected by the prevailing intellectual winds. On some of these issues in recent years, economists and political scientists have made significant contributions, especially related to the second factor listed. The work of the school of public choice is relevant because it has put the emphasis on the rules (such as constitutional rules) that constrain or should constrain government behavior. Over the long run, however, even constitutional rules may become endogenous to the system because they can be, and often are, changed.

The contributions of these economists and political scientists have typically assumed a market economy with democratic political systems and have focused on organizational or institutional issues within these governments. Thus, to some extent they have suffered from what the late Lord Robbins described as "provincialism in time." Although we briefly review that literature in later chapters, here we identify two diametrically opposed roles that set a lower limit (a floor) and an upper limit (a ceiling) to the economic role that governments can play. In doing this, we shall have to pay a visit to what Schumpeter (1954) called the "lumber room" of old ideas. Later, we show that, in most countries, the economic role of the state falls somewhere between two polar cases.

In the first of these polar roles, the responsibilities of the government or the state are limited because the citizens themselves, with the help of a presumably well-functioning market, and with the use of their own efforts and incomes, are expected to take care of most of their needs, both personal and social. In these societies, the individuals are free to organize themselves in civil groups to pursue communities' or social objectives. In this case, the state is left with a limited role, one aimed mainly at correcting *significant* market failures, at producing essential public goods, or, occasionally, at complementing market outcomes. The government may also intervene in situations, such as major disasters, when *all else fails* (Moss, 2002). During disasters, most people expect the government to step in and play a leading role, unless foreign governments do that, as happened in the Haitian or, to a lesser extent, the Pakistani disasters of 2010. This is broadly the role that economists generally associate with an economic system that goes under the name of "laissez-faire." This system prevailed in some form mostly in the 19th century and in the conception of so-called classical economists.

The alternative role, and its polar opposite, is one in which most economic decisions are made largely by political representatives of the people or of the working class, who presumably act for the state. Some or most of these "representatives" may be self-appointed, so that the term representative does not necessarily refer to elected officials. In this system, the state takes upon itself the responsibility for the economic welfare of the citizens and for making most economic decisions. It appropriates (most of) the means of production; it prohibits (most) private property; and it leaves little scope for market forces that, in this system, almost cease to exist, because they are not allowed to operate. Most economic decisions are "commanded" by the state and are coordinated through a central planning process. S. C. Strumilin, Russia's party economist during Stalin's time, is reported to have said that "our task is not to study economics but to change it. We are bound by no law." This system leaves little economic freedom to individuals and has no use for their economic incentives, which it discourages and tries to stamp out. The individuals become property of the state, which can use them as it considers appropriate. Their *personal* preferences, *qua* individuals, carry no weight. The policy makers are the sole interpreters of the needs of society (or of the "working class"). This system is normally referred to as a "centrally planned system" or as a "command economy." (For a scholarly account of the "command economy," see Kornai, 1992.)

These two polar cases have been traditionally identified with the names of two famous economists, Adam Smith and Karl Marx, although many other economists were involved in developing them and there are questions about the extent of responsibility that these two economists carry for the use that was made of some of their ideas. These two economists wrote two of the most influential economics books ever written. Adam Smith, who considered himself mainly as a moral philosopher rather than an economist, wrote *The Wealth of Nations* (1776), a book that is believed to have set the stage for the economic system called "laissez-faire" and that influenced the economic development of today's advanced countries. In 1759 Smith had published another important book, *The Theory of Moral Sentiments*, which had a more philosophical bent and which some historians consider the more important of Smith's work (see, e.g., Herman, 2001; and Himmelfarb, 2004). As we show later, the attribution of "laissez-faire" to Smith may not be entirely appropriate.

Karl Marx, who was "a philosopher, a historian, an economist, a linguist, a literary critic, and a revolutionist," wrote *Das Capital* (1867; first English edition, 1886), a book that helped set the stage for a centrally planned, or command, economy. A recent biographer of Marx notes that "within one hundred years of his death [in 1883] half of the world's population was ruled by governments that professed Marxism to be their guiding faith. Marx's ideas have transformed the study of economics.... Not since Jesus Christ has an obscure power inspired such global devotion – or been so calamitously misinterpreted" (see Wheen, 1999, p. 1). Marx's funeral, on March 17, 1883, had been attended by only 11 mourners.[1] (For a list of socialist countries in 1987, see Kornai, 1992, pp. 6–7.)

Both *The Wealth of Nations* and *Das Capital* – directly or, more often, through interpretations by followers – had enormous influence on policy makers and policy making in different parts of the world, and at different times. Historically, the influence of Marx was much more direct and obvious, and more easy to identify, than that of Smith. Policy makers have often appealed to one or the other of these books, often without having read them, in guiding or in justifying their policies. It must be recognized that Adam Smith and Karl Marx, and the systems they helped create, defined *polar* cases. In today's world, the economic role of the state in most countries reflects a space or a position that is distant from these two poles: most economic systems are now neither laissez-faire nor command economies. The state's responsibilities are now generally far greater than theorized by Smith and his followers, but they are less overwhelming than they were under command economies. In a few countries the role of the state is today closer to Marx's; in many it is closer to Smith's. So-called welfare states, which came into full existence especially in the 1960s and 1970s, assign an economic role to the state that is much wider than that attributed to Adam Smith. However, they leave a lot of scope to market forces and individual activities that guarantee private property, although they limit the returns to it with high taxes and regulations such as zoning laws. Also, the few remaining centrally planned economies have acquired significant market features. Political competition from market economies and globalization have forced them to do so. In general, it can be concluded that the economic role of the state is perhaps at this time closer to Smith's view than to Marx's. However, two or three decades ago there were many more countries than now in Marx's camp, and for a while there was fear that that camp might win the competition of ideas.

Central planning had its first real-life application in Russia, after the Bolshevik Revolution of 1917. (See, inter alia, Rostow, 1953; and Kornai, 1992.) After World War II, it was exported to many countries that, politically or ideologically, fell under the influence of Russia and of the communist ideology. These included China and several other Asian countries, Eastern Europe, and some countries from Africa and Latin America. Other countries, such as India, were influenced by the concept of central planning, although they did not become command economies. For about 70 years, from 1920 to 1990, the Marxist ideology became a real challenge, both intellectually and practically, to the economic thinking associated with the name of Adam Smith or with classical or neoclassical economics. It also attracted the interest of many economists, including some major ones, in Western countries.[2] The collapse of the Soviet Union and the fall of communism, around 1990, initiated a process of transition of many countries from central planning, or command economies, toward market economies, thus raising the economic significance of Adam Smith and reducing that of Karl Marx (Stiglitz, 1994; and Tanzi, 1993 and 2010). Over the next couple decades, the kind of liberal economics that had originated with Adam Smith, in a modern version and reinterpretation, reacquired prominence in many parts of the world. During this period, and especially in the 1990s, calls to give a greater scope to the market became stronger than they had been for some time. These calls often asked for a reduced role of the state. Of course, it was a modern version that still contemplated a much larger government spending role than had been visualized by Adam Smith and by classical economists.

The economic crisis that affected many countries starting in 2008 led again to criticism against "laissez-faire" or market economics and to calls for an expanded role of the state, as had happened during the Great Depression. Some of these calls were connected with the Keynesian view, back in fashion, that the world economies needed a major fiscal stimulus to aggregate demand to pull the countries out of the crisis. Some calls, however, were directed at increasing, on a sustained basis, the economic role of the state in various sectors, including financial markets, health, education, infrastructure, research, energy, and assistance to failing enterprises such as banks. Industrial policy was back in fashion. It is too early to predict what the long-run effect of these calls on public spending and on the economic role of the state will be.

Historically, economists think of laissez-faire economics as the kind of economic system that existed in many, but not all, now-advanced countries, for the century that ended before World War I or, perhaps, before the Great Depression. In some countries there was limited laissez-faire because governments were active in controlling trade and in promoting various industrial sectors even when their public spending was low. Still, this period was the closest, real-life experiment with the economics attributed to Adam Smith and with the economic role of the state theorized or recommended by him and by his European and American followers, who contributed to what came to be called classical economics. As we discuss later, Adam Smith himself may have had less to do with "laissez-faire" than commonly believed. In any case, around 1880–90 laissez-faire policies started losing some of their attraction and governments became more interventionist.

The Russian experiment of 1920–90, as well as that of other countries under Soviet influence in the decades after World War II, was the closest, real-life experiment with Marxist economics. The laissez-faire and the Marxist experiments never overlapped historically in their pure versions, except perhaps to some extent in the decade of the 1920s. The Marxist experiment coexisted for the most part with "mixed economies" and not with "laissez-faire" economies.

In laissez-faire economies, the direct *economic* role of the state was narrow and limited to a few basic functions.[3] In the centrally planned economies, it was invasive and overwhelming: the state owned most properties and assets; it determined the employment and the wages of workers and the saving and investment of the country; it decided what would be produced and the prices at which the output would be sold. It was responsible for most investments, normally carried out by state-owned enterprises, as well as for imports and exports. In these economies the public sector accounted for close to 100 percent of the countries' total production. As a consequence, it was impossible to distinguish public from private finance, because almost all was public. Decisions by policy makers, endorsed by the communist parties, almost totally replaced the dynamics of the market. These decisions determined the actions of the state-owned enterprises. Economic decisions by individual citizens did not count, and their economic incentives were suppressed because they might conflict with social goals, such as an egalitarian society. People with strong, personal economic incentives were seen as being antisocial, because their incentives would lead to the inequality of incomes (Tanzi, 2010). The state promoted its social spending mostly through huge state-owned enterprises. These were responsible for providing employment, health care, pensions, and other benefits to the workers. There was no formal unemployment because the state enterprises were required to absorb all the available labor even when they did not need it.[4]

Centrally planned economies did not fare well in the long run. Central planning proved unsustainable because the system was excessively rigid and inefficient, especially for complex, modern economies. It was easy to plan for an economy when it produced mostly a few agricultural products and a few other standard items, such as Mao shirts, but much more difficult to plan for an economy with thousands of diversified products and services. Mathematically trained economists attempted to develop sophisticated systems, including input-output analysis, to cope with the increasing complexity of the economy. But, in the end, the system became too complex and failed.

At the beginning of the communist experiment, the Austrian economist Mises (1922) had forecast that the experiment would fail because rational economic calculations would be difficult or impossible to make under "socialism." Another famous Austrian economist, in 1944, provided a more complete explanation of why this would be so. Simply the information contained in thousands of prices, freely established by the market, that makes it possible for strangers to cooperate and produce what individuals want would be missing in a centrally planned economy (Hayek 1944). Hayek added, more controversially in the view of some, including Paul Samuelson, that the need to control economic activity would inevitably lead to political tyranny. Thus, it would be impossible to have a command economy with a truly democratic political process.

As countries' economies became more complex, the lack of incentives and of the information contained in freely established prices in a market economy would become progressively more damaging, and the need for planners to control people's behavior would become heavier. As Boettke put it, "It is not the size of government that matters, but the scope, and Hayek argues that unintended and undesirable consequences emerge when government's scope expands beyond its administrative capacity" (2005, pp. 1046–47). The conclusion that large public sectors lead to repression and perhaps tyranny was controversial. While Keynes declared himself in agreement with virtually the whole content of Hayek's 1944 book, others, including George Orwell and Paul Samuelson, were highly critical of its conclusions. Schuessler (2010), however, has reported that "Hayek didn't oppose all forms of government intervention." She quoted him to the effect that "the preservation of competition" is not "incompatible with an extensive system of social services." Hayek's views may not have been uniformly popular in the years following the publication of his book, when larger public sectors were becoming favored by economists; in fact, in my recollection, Hayek's work was never assigned or even discussed at Harvard during the years when I was studying for my doctorate in economics at that university, in the early 1960s.

Once the revolutionary and almost religious enthusiasm that had accompanied the coming into power of communist parties evaporated, apathy, corruption, inefficiency, and the problems identified by Mises and Hayek set in. A few countries are still trying today to maintain that system, such as North Korea and Cuba, although Cuba has introduced some market features in its economy. Neither of these countries is a paragon of economic efficiency. However, their policy makers might argue that efficiency is not the main goal of their economies. Provision of basic necessities to everyone and equality in outcomes are. Other countries, including China and Vietnam, continue to be controlled by so-called communist parties, but these countries have de facto abandoned communist economic principles. They have become, effectively, if not officially or totally, mixed economies dominated by totalitarian regimes, with some elements of economic planning. For the time being, their totalitarian regimes are not hurting their economic performance. They may even facilitate the creation of badly needed infrastructure by removing political obstacles that are common to democratic regimes. In time, as they become more developed, they will require more democratic political institutions and more clearly identifiable rule of law.

## 2.3. Adam Smith and the Economic Role of the State

The economic role that the state plays in a market economy is of course not the same in all countries, and it does not remain constant over time. Over the past centuries it changed dramatically and generally became much more important from the beginning to the end of the 20th century. The starting point for analyzing that role remains *The Wealth of Nations*, which was published in the same year as the American Declaration of Independence but was many years in the writing. Smith's book was written in part as a reaction against "mercantilism" or, in his terminology, "the mercantile system." Smith described the overwhelming and negative interference in economic activities by the governments of his day and especially by his own government, mainly through their regulatory or authorizing power and through impediments on trade. In these societies, many activities had to be authorized by governments that could create monopolies that benefited particular favored individuals or groups and forbade others from carrying out some activities. Smith was particularly upset with the treatment of, and the constraints imposed on, the American colonies and India. In the "mercantile system," market forces played a reduced role, even though private property was allowed and markets existed where goods and services were bought and sold.

It is generally believed that Smith's book set the stage for the "laissez-faire" period, during which the state reduced governmental discretion and attempted to leave more freedom to market forces (and not just in foreign trade) and to the economic actions of individuals.[5] Smith's ideas contributed to this change. The laissez-faire period lasted, in a reduced form after around 1880, until the late 1920s when strong reactions against some of its presumed shortcomings were set in motion by various political, economic, and intellectual developments. Up to that time it had been challenged mainly by socialist writers, by some economists of the German school, and by occasional mainstream thinkers. Although governmental intervention had increased, starting around the 1880s, and public spending had started to grow before that time, the role that Adam Smith played in laissez-faire policies deserves some attention.

It has been common, especially in recent years, for economists and financial operators to consider Adam Smith as the main promoter of laissez-faire economics, the discoverer of the "invisible hand," and generally the godfather of "free-market capitalism." Furthermore, most economists base their negative feelings about "mercantilism," or about what Smith referred to as the "mercantile system" (i.e., about a developmental economic role of the state), on views attributed to Smith. Some of these views may perpetuate what might well be considered historical inaccuracies. Because of the important role that Adam Smith has played in the development of economics and, more important for this book, in the definition of the economic role of the state, it may be worthwhile to present here what in my view is a more faithful interpretation of Smith's views.

It has been reported that "Adam Smith . . . is one author who is more quoted than read" and also that "there is at least one Adam Smith interpretation for every European nation" (Reinert and Reinert, p. 14). German scholars discussed for a long time what they defined as "Das Adam Smith Problem" (ibid.; and Himmelfarb, 2004, p. 53). Herman (2001, pp. 215–20) has referred to the "myths" about Smith's theories. Buchan (2006, p. 2) has pointed out that Adam Smith, the supposed godfather of laissez-faire capitalism, never used the expression laissez-faire, which had been in use in France before Smith's time. Furthermore "the phrase 'invisible hand' occurs [only] three times in the million-odd words of Adam Smith's that have come down to us and not on one of these occasions does it have anything to do with free-market capitalism." Generally, historians read Smith's books, whereas most contemporary economists base their knowledge of him on limited, secondhand accounts.[6] Part of the problem is that some of Smith's views evolved from his first book, *The Theory of Moral Sentiments*, published in 1759, to his second book, *An Inquiry into the Nature and Causes of the Wealth of Nations*, published in 1776. Both books were several years in the making, and, when published, were considered very important, especially by philosophers. (The first chair in economics in the world, located at the university of Naples and occupied by Antonio Genovese, was not established until 1754.) Over the years, some of Smith's views were adjusted and reinterpreted by "classical economists" to bring them closer to their own preferences. Thus, Smith came to be seen as the originator of the kind of laissez-faire economics that was in part developed later. A broadly similar destiny would characterize Keynes's work and, perhaps, Marx's.

Adam Smith was born in 1723, well before the beginning of the Industrial Revolution, a revolution that would dramatically change the world that had existed up to his time. His father was a customs inspector, an activity that probably influenced Smith's own thinking. In order to understand the impact that *The Wealth of Nations* would have on British society, it is perhaps important to mention that, at that time, "to inherit wealth and to live on rents were more noble than to work and to produce" (Ricossa, 2006, p. 19, my translation). While Smith wrote one of the most influential books in economics of all times, he considered himself primarily a "moral philosopher" and held the chair of moral philosophy at the University of Glasgow in Scotland. His basic philosophy is best understood in relation to that of his friend David Hume, who had become famous for having written *The Treatise of Human Nature*, which was considered a masterpiece. Hume believed that human beings are driven essentially by "passion" and by "self-interest" and by little else. There was thus little left for socially inspired behavior. As a consequence, all societies need some stable center of authority, an anchor, a government, capable of keeping individuals in line by punishing transgressors and redirecting destructive passions. For Hume, liberty is needed to preserve individuals *qua* individuals, while authority is needed to preserve society *qua* society. As he put it, "there is a perpetual...struggle...between Authority and liberty, and neither of them can ever absolutely prevail in the contest" (quoted in Herman, 2001, p. 203).

By contrast, Smith had a more positive or more optimistic view of human nature. He believed that human beings have a natural sense of identification with other human beings, a kind of "fellow feeling" that makes them participate in the happiness and suffering of others. Human beings are also conditioned by what other human beings think of them. This "fellow feeling" and this sense of identification with other human beings are enhanced by cultural progress. Cultural progress is in turn promoted by commerce, an activity that increases contacts among human beings, increases wealth, and requires the establishment of shared rules. Commerce thus acquires a commanding importance in Smith's world.

In a world in which commerce had been looked down upon, Smith's idea was revolutionary; surely, it was not an activity in which nobles should engage in.[7] Furthermore, in the popular conception, the idea of exchange traditionally had been associated with that of being cheated.[8]

Another important element in Smith's new world, another building block, was the idea that commerce is promoted by "the division of labor" – that is, by specialization, which in turn increases the productivity of workers and promotes economic and cultural progress. Smith used the famous example of the pin factory to make the latter point. The more specialization there is, the greater is the productivity of workers, and greater is the need for exchange and commerce. Smith seems to have gotten the idea of the importance of specialization and the example of the pin factory from the fifth volume of the French *Encyclopedie*, which had an article called "Epingle" (pin; see Himmelfarb, 2004, p. 17).

This is where the government enters Smith's world. The government can impede the development of commerce though mercantilist policies and thus slow down cultural progress by putting obstacles to it. He believed that this is what the British government had been doing especially in the trade of England with America and India. His criticism of the "mercantile system" reflected his views of these policies. These policies were not consistent with the development of commerce. On the other hand, he believed that the government could facilitate and encourage commerce by creating administrative and physical institutions and by providing social services that promote and facilitate rather than impede trade and other exchanges.

Smith provided a detailed list of government duties, which became famous and a great influence on later writing and thinking. The list reflects Smith's view of the ways in which governments can protect and promote commercial exchanges, thus leading to a better society. The list must be seen as a considerable *expansion* and *redirection* of the economic role of the state in his time rather than a restriction in that role. It should be recalled that Smith was writing *before* the Industrial Revolution at a time when the view that people had of government actions was dismal. Thus, it may be a mistake to consider Smith's list as restrictive and implying a minimalist role of the state, even though it may appear so from the perspective of our time. It must also not be seen as being identical with what later laissez-faire economists, many of whom were French and were opposing the growing government role in France at that time, wanted the state to do.

Writing in 1897, Augusto Graziani, an influential Italian author of a major public finance textbook, would say that the "doctrine of Smith had been vulgarized by J. B. Say" (1897, p. 34). Say wanted the state to be out of the way, whereas Smith wanted to give the state a limited, well-defined, useful, and productive role. But there obviously was considerable overlap between Smith's and the classical economists' views. Say was the French economist who enunciated the famous "Say's law," which states that the supply creates its own demand. By implication, the government should not interfere in the productive activities of the market.

Smith's economic role of the state was linked with the economic function that we now call *allocation of resources*. He did not believe in, or perhaps did not imagine, a government role related to what could be called "social justice," or, in today's terminology, redistribution. He believed that the increase in productivity that would come with more specialization and more commerce would make everyone wealthier in an absolute sense, including the working classes, which would benefit from higher wages and from some trickle down. He favored high wages because they made workers "more active, diligent, and expeditious." He was aware that the system he was advocating (later called "capitalism") could well lead to more inequality of wealth. Thus, in the debate of our days, on whether governments should promote growth or equity, he would come out on the side of growth because growth would increase the *absolute* incomes of the workers. However, he had no problem with the state's assistance to the very poor, those who could not take care of themselves, an assistance that, in England, had been provided since 1601. He even supported proportional taxation and taxes on luxury products, rather than on necessities, "to contribute...to the relief of the poor." His concern again was not the income distribution but the absolute income of the working class. In any case he had no illusion that the governments that existed at his time could or would engage in the redistribution of income from the top down. Given the kind of government that existed in those days, historical experience had taught the population (and Smith) that the outcome of a policy of redistribution would be the reverse.

Interestingly, Smith worried about the impact that specialization could have on the psychology of workers, as Karl Marx would a century later. He felt that spending 12 to 14 hours a day on narrow tasks, in confined areas, as was common at that time and would become even more common as the Industrial Revolution progressed, would lead to the narrowing of workers' interest and to some alienation from the society around them. This would reduce the general interest, the *bene commune*, a concept that had first appeared in Florence in the 13th century and that referred to the welfare of the whole community. This concern led him to advocate a state-enforced and partly state-financed system of education aimed at teaching young children to read, write, and learn the basics of arithmetic. The parents of the children would be required to pay some small fee to cover part of the cost of the schools. It would take a century before the principle of free, compulsory public education would be introduced in Britain, by the Foster Act of 1870.

Finally, it should be stressed that "Smith was no fanatical dogmatist . . . he made exceptions to the doctrine of laissez-faire which many of his later disciples forgot" (Webb, 1980, p. 93). He had no illusion that laissez-faire policies and the "invisible hand" would *always* contribute to "public welfare." While he had a lot of confidence in the working of a free market and in the positive contribution that commerce would bring to a good society, he had less trust in the businessmen and the merchants who operated in it. He wrote about "the bad effects of high profits," about the fact that merchants were always asking for protection, and about their "mean capacity" and their "monopolizing spirit." He concluded that the worst of all governments would be one made up of a company of merchants (see Buchan, 2006, pp. 109ff.; Himmelfarb, 2004, pp. 55ff.; Herman, 2001, pp. 218–20; and Smith himself, 1776, various places). Therefore, the *Wealth of Nations* cannot be considered "an apologia for big business and the merchant class" (Herman, 2001, p. 218). And there was definitely no glorification of "greed" in Smith's thinking.

One is left with the clear impression that, given the chance, Smith would be in favor of monitoring the activities of the merchants to prevent abuses. However, he had no illusion that the kind of government that existed in his time would ever be able to do it fairly and objectively, as the mercantilist experience had taught him. Whether a more modern government would be able to exercise this role effectively is left unanswered. In conclusion, it may not be correct to assume that Smith would be against regulations imposed by a good government, as is normally assumed. In a clear example of faulty logic, many have assumed that because Smith was against the regulations associated with mercantilism, he must have been against any kind of regulation. This is the same as assuming that doctors would be against all medicines because they are against some that are harmful.

Before going to Smith's famous description of the economic role of the state, there is another issue that merits some mention. It is a highly controversial one that has attracted much attention by economists for centuries. Especially economists interested in economic development have paid much attention to it in recent decades. However, economists specializing in public finance have largely ignored this issue, assuming, wrongly in the view of the author of this book, that it falls outside public finance or public economics. This is a potential *developmental role of the state*. The question is whether, as it has normally been assumed by most modern economists in developed countries, the state should let the market play its role in the growth of the economy of a country and should not intervene except perhaps by financing basic research, promoting good education, and assisting in the development of some essential infrastructure.

It should be recalled that the promotion of economic growth is not listed among the fundamental roles of the state, in Musgrave's 1959 influential book and in most textbooks in public finance. Smith's criticism of the "mercantile system" essentially follows this orthodox approach,[9] an approach that was strongly endorsed by J. S. Mill (1848, pp. 836–43) and reinforced two centuries after Smith by the work of Hayek and others. Hayek (1988) wrote about the "fatal conceit" of policy makers making decisions that only the market should make. On the other hand, there is the reality that most politicians have a hard time resisting the temptation to pursue various forms of industrial policies (including those associated with protection); Keynesian fiscal policies, at times justified as promoting growth; and tax policies that provide tax incentives presumably to accelerate development in some sectors. In all these cases the declared objective of policy makers is faster growth or development. Often these policies fail, *but not always*. Thus, among the positive (if not the normative) goals of governments one should add the pursuit of economic growth.

This is not the place to defend or criticize these policies but simply to point out that Smith's views on this issue were not and have not always been shared by all economists. The "right" development role of the state, one that *at some stage of development* supports in various ways industries that face increasing returns, can allow some countries to grow faster and become more developed. *The Origins of Development Economics*, a book edited by Jomo and Reinert (2005), provides an interesting discussion of this issue. It points out that Venice and the Netherlands, in the 15th and 16th centuries, had been successful users of development policies and had grown to become the richest lands on earth (in spite of lack of natural resources); so had England in the 15th and 16th centuries and the United States in the 19th century. One could add the more recent experiences of Korea, China, Taiwan, Singapore, and other countries. It is difficult to believe that these countries would have developed as fast as they did if the government had remained neutral. Of course, this does not mean that the continuation of these policies would be worthwhile. Also, it does not mean that these policies are always or even often successful, as the Latin American experience with import substitution in the 1960s and 1970s and that of many African countries indicate.

Early Italian economists are reported by Jomo and Reinert to have made important contributions to this area. Among them Antonio Serra deserves special attention. In 1613 he published *Breve Trattato delle Cause che Possono far Abbondare l'Oro e l'Argento dove non sono Miniere* (A Short Treatise on the Causes That Can Bring Gold and Silver Where There Are No Mines), a book that Schumpeter (1954), in his *History of Economic Analysis,* considered as the first scientific book in economics. Serra had shown that promoting activities with increasing rather than diminishing returns can lead to growth. "Catching up" for countries that start from behind – as, for example, South Korea – may require particular interventions that governments may be successful in providing. The fact that governments often fail in their attempts to promote faster economic growth is not an argument against the validity of this conclusion, although it can be against an enthusiastic endorsement of it.

Between the 16th and the 18th centuries, development policies (or mercantile policies) contributed to "state building" and vice versa in some countries (Jomo and Reinert, 2005). It should be repeated, however, that development policies are often unsuccessful and unnecessary. It is easy to show that these policies often fail. But that is also true of many other policies. It all depends on the context and on the government's ability to pursue the right ones and not let these policies become good excuses for rent-seeking activities as they often do (Ekelund and Tollison, 1981). Thus, the context in which policies are used and the precise role that the state plays are important.

In conclusion, it can be argued that among the government goals of allocation of resources, distribution of income, and stabilization, the goal of economic development or growth must be explicitly recognized as a separate one, even though promoting this goal can lead to frequent government failures.

In book 5 of *The Wealth of Nations*, the part that deals with the "Revenue of the Sovereign or the Commonwealth," Adam Smith outlined his views on what role the state should play in the economy. The question of what role should the state or the government be expected to play in an economy based on private ownership and with private markets was addressed at length by Smith. He stressed that the government should defend the economic choices of individuals and called attention to the "inevitable failures" that occur when governments attempt to direct industries or the employment of individuals in specific directions, as they had done during the "mercantile system" and earlier periods. Thus, he would be skeptical about the merits of "industrial policy" or of the "import substitution policies" that became popular in recent decades. He stressed that "no human wisdom or knowledge could ever be sufficient" in avoiding "delusions" when the government assumes this role. This position was strongly reaffirmed by Hayek (1988) in recent decades.

As mentioned earlier, Smith was concerned about the creation of "monopoly powers" in the economy, and, in making a point often forgotten or ignored, he commented on the propensity of private individuals to establish monopolies or cartels whenever they could. If there is this propensity, and if it creates abuses and potential difficulties, only the government could, at least in theory, take action to prevent the monopolies and the cartels from coming into existence or from operating. This implies an important (theoretical) regulatory role for the state. Perhaps for this reason, there have been various attempts to prove, or to argue, that monopolies cannot exist unless the government creates them; or, if they do exist, that they are not damaging. Smith would have been skeptical about "market fundamentalism," the ideology that became predominant in recent decades and that aimed at removing most government regulation of economic activities, believing in the self-regulating power of the market. Smith's view implies an important, potentially positive role for the government: that of preventing the establishment of private monopolies and of other abuses by unscrupulous individuals. This role can in principle also be exercised through the courts, which can punish abuses, as argued by some economists, but this route can be too expensive for many of those who suffer the abuses. It must be stressed that Smith would not favor economic regulations of markets, except for those aimed at controlling activities that generate significant negative externalities or at restricting the creation of private monopolies and limiting abuses. Today, Smith might favor reasonable environmental, health, or security-related regulations, as well as some regulations imposed on banks or on the financial market for the protection of those who invest their savings in them. He would certainly be bothered by the excess profits and the excess bonuses in the financial industry.

The basic, implicit, but rarely acknowledged position of Adam Smith – that when certain conditions do not hold, government ought to intervene – was challenged two centuries later by a group of Chicago school economists that included Frank Knight, Milton Friedman, Aaron Director, Ronald Coase, and George Stigler. They challenged Smith's view and those of Alfred Marshall and Arthur Pigou, who had built on some of Smith's original intuition.[10] The Chicago school questioned almost any governmental intervention and probably helped create the intellectual foundation for what came to be called "market fundamentalism" (see Van Overtveldt, 2007; and Ebenstein, 2007). The main conclusion of the Chicago school was that when the government intervenes, either with public spending or with its regulatory power, it normally fails, and government failure can cause more damage than the failure that its intervention was intended to correct. Only a detailed empirical analysis of government programs can determine whether this conclusion is correct, as George Stigler (1968) stressed during his career.

As for a specific, *positive* role of the state, a role often associated with public spending, Smith stressed two aspects: first, the need to provide services that are essential for an organized society, especially one based on commerce, but are not likely to be provided, or to be provided in needed quantity, by private markets. In this he was principally concerned about administrative services (such as registration of births, deaths, marriages, and properties), the protection of property rights and some contracts, the provision of justice, and the protection of citizens from internal or external dangers. In some sense he was anticipating the concept of public good that would be defined more precisely much later by various economists. He also identified the need for the state to build large public works (roads, harbors, canals) and to provide some essential services that, because of their high costs or their nature, would not be provided by private individuals.[11] He stressed that the provision of these services should be as efficient as possible and that fees should be charged for them whenever possible. He would not favor any kind of featherbedding or the use of public enterprises to create jobs.

Among the activities that justified government spending, he identified defense, because it protects the whole society against foreign dangers; because no private person would have an interest in paying for it; and because no private provider would be able to charge the citizens for this protection. He favored the public provision of justice, including personal protection, for similar reasons.[12] Once again, this government role was important for the development of commerce. Infrastructures could be provided by the state but, as much as possible, should be paid for, by those using them, through tolls, fees, or other means. Thus, he seems to be in favor of privately financed infrastructures, whenever possible. In 19th-century England, privately owned and run infrastructures were common. Using information gathered by an English commission, de Molinari argued in 1849 that in England these private infrastructures were much better maintained than those in France, where they tended to be publicly financed and operated. For education, Smith seemed to make a distinction between elementary, or basic, education, which provided literacy and some knowledge of arithmetic, and could be (partly) publicly financed or subsidized, and higher education, which should normally be paid fully by those who benefited from it.

The view that higher education should be paid by the students and not by the state was shared by economists during the 19th century, including, for example, by F. S. Nitti, who wrote a popular Italian public finance book, *La Scienza delle Finanze* (first published in 1903) that was translated into many languages. Nitti, a prolific writer who became a minister and prime minister in the Italian government, endorsed most of Smith's views on the economic role of the state in his book, indicating that these views were still influential around 1900. Carlo Cipolla, a prominent economic historian, has shown that, while in Italy the obligation for children between 6 and 12 years to attend elementary schools already existed in the 19th century, only 1 or 2 percent of public budgets was allocated to educational spending (Cipolla, 1996, pp. 96–97), and there was no enforcement of the rule that children should attend school.

Smith's and his followers' views on the role of the state were based on their own observations. Their views came in part as a reaction against the widespread state interference in the economic activities of individuals, which had characterized the mercantilistic period, or the "mercantile system," when many activities needed the authorization of government. Smith's views on the positive economic role of the state *stressed the allocation of resources* necessary for the protection of individuals from other individuals and from foreign powers (defense and police protection), for the protection of property, and for the enforcement of contracts (justice). These expenses were necessary to allow commerce to develop without interferences, and commerce was considered important. He also stressed the importance of making the market operate efficiently by preventing monopolies, cartels, and other private abuses and through the elimination of regulations that restricted legitimate economic transactions and activities. He did not have illusions about the role of governments in his time and noted that "civil government . . . is in reality instituted for the defense of the rich against the poor" (see Smith, 1776, p. 715).[13] Classical economists endorsed this view, thus justifying a very restricted role for government in income redistribution.

In Smith's writing there was no mention of a government *role in redistributing income and in stabilizing the economy.* He would not have trusted the governments of his time in those roles. These roles would be introduced, mainly in the 20th century, when the nature of governments changed and the popular perception of what the government could and should do also changed. This was a reflection of the fact that the political power of those who might be helped by a redistributive role also increased. Smith recognized that in exceptional circumstances (mainly wars) the government might be justified in going into debt, as England would a few decades later during the Napoleonic Wars. However, he was highly critical of public debt (see book 5, chapter 3), as had been other economists in his time and before his time. (See Hume, 1955; see also Mill, 2004, pp. 796–802.) The view that government budgets should be kept in equilibrium, not necessarily every year but in the medium run, went back all the way to Cicero, the Roman statesman, and was widely accepted until the "Keynesian revolution."[14]

Smith recognized the need *to assist the very poor,* a role that had been undertaken by the community and not by the state, before Elizabeth I's reign in England, and by the church in Scotland (Trevelyan, 1942, pp. 433–34; also Ritter, 1991; Solomon, 1972, for the protection of the poor in 17th-century France; and Zamagni, 2000, for similar policies in Italy). As Solomon put it, "The principle was long established that each parish was responsible for its poor" (p. 22). The same point has been made for Sweden in relation to villages and towns. According to Knut Rexed, "One of the heritages from the early clan societies [in Nordic countries] was a strong emphasis on taking care of and protecting other members of the same local society. Each village and town was collectively responsible for its poor, its sick, its disabled and its orphaned" (2000, p. 8). Smith and many in his time did not see this as income redistribution but as a way of removing potential problems created by poverty. Poverty was seen as a creator of negative externalities and had to be dealt with.[15] It must be repeated that Smith's view of the role of the state, in spite of its limitations, was far more liberal (i.e., far more pro-state) than that of many classical economists of the 19th century.

Especially in the first half of the 19th century, it would have been impossible to have a high level of public spending because the tax level was very low; those who controlled the actions of the government would not have allowed the imposition of higher taxes on themselves (the aristocrats, who owned most of the productive assets, controlled the government); and the capacity to administer programs and the expertise necessary to do so were not available. The growth of public spending would have to wait until political power shifted to the people, through broader representation; it became possible to increase the tax level; and the public administration acquired more capacity to administer (see Woodward, 1962, book 4, pp. 444–72).

## 2.4. The Level of Public Spending in the 19th Century

A question that immediately comes to mind when reading *The Wealth of Nations* is, What level of public spending would be required in a world guided largely by Adam Smith's principles? That is a world in which the state would limit its action to defense, internal security, administration, basic education, care of the very poor, and some infrastructure projects. According to information available from many countries now considered advanced, for which data are available, public spending, as a share of national income, rose from around 10 percent of GDP in 1870 to around 13 percent before World War I.[16] This was a period of intense globalization, one in which economic policy was perhaps closest to Adam Smith's principles (see Table 1.1). That period was not the "Stone Age." It was also very different from the world that had existed more than a century earlier, at the time when Adam Smith wrote *The Wealth of Nations*. On the contrary, it was a period of intense modernization, benefiting from a century of the Industrial Revolution and important scientific discoveries and technological advances. It was the period when electricity was introduced in many countries; the Galleria, dedicated to Vittorio Emanuele II, that became a model for indoor, modern shopping centers, was built in Milan; railroads were built in many countries, allowing an increasing number of people to cover greater distances in less time; much of modern Paris, including the famous Metro and the Eiffel Tower, were built; the Suez and later the Panama canals were opened; French impressionism became popular; and cars and airplanes were being introduced. Thus, we are talking about public spending *in relatively modern and fast-developing economies*. Furthermore, the data on public spending at that time had been inflated by the servicing of large public debts incurred in earlier wars or in preparation for future wars.

In his monumental work on public finance in the 19th century, after complaining about waste in government expenditure and the multiplication of special accounts in the government finances, which makes this work sound very modern, Paul Leroy-Beaulieu (1888) mentions that public spending had been contained until around 1840 but then it had started growing fast, because of the advent of parliamentary regimes and democratic movements (see especially pp. VI and 9). The level of public spending shown for the later part of the century – 10 or 13 percent of GDP – already reflected the growth of public spending after 1840. In another book, published in Italy in 1897, Augusto Graziani, an Italian economist, wrote that "the increase in public spending is a phenomenon so widespread and characteristics of modern states that it cannot be attributed to accidental or pathological causes" (1897, p. 171, my translation). Thus, the level of public spending as a share of national income at the end of the 19th century, in spite of its low value compared with today's levels, was already seen as the result of a process that was leading to higher public-sector involvement in the economy and to unproductive spending.

In another monumental treatise on public finance (a thousand pages long) published in 1903, F. S. Nitti lists the causes that had led to the growth of public spending in the 19th century: the continuous increase in military spending; large public works, connected with the introduction of new technologies, such as electricity, steam engines, railroads, telegraphs; increase in public debts; and various forms of "social prevention" activities assumed by the state. In this he argues that the action of the state is necessary to "prevent" negative development. He mentioned in this context specifically hygiene and sanitary measures and argues that only the state can take these measures. This is the same point made by Walvin (1988). The fact that this was also a period of intense urbanization made these measures particularly important. Finally, he mentions the increasing participation of the popular classes in public life.[17] (See Nitti, 1903, pp. 113–16 of the 1972 edition.)

The level of public spending before World War I must be compared with levels that in several European countries by the late 20th century approached or, in a few countries, exceeded 50 percent of GDP (Table 1.1). These new levels reflect a hugely expanded conception of what the state should do.

In spite of the concerns on the part of economists living in that period about the growth of public spending, the period between 1870 and 1913 is generally considered as one in which laissez-faire policies generally prevailed. The spending role of the state in the economy was still limited, and tax levels were also low. At that time, however, there was a lot of social action aimed at introducing social legislation related to voting rights, the rights of women, workers' rights, children's rights, and so on. This can be interpreted as the period when governments became interested in creating more equal opportunities for citizens through social legislation. But, in spite of the modest absolute increase in public spending and the growing role played by governments in changing and in enforcing some important social legislation by creating more effective bureaucracies, the *direct* economic role of the state remained modest and mostly laissez-faire. It was not far from Smith's conception.

The spirit of the time can perhaps best be captured by mentioning the views about the level of taxation expressed by the earlier-mentioned important French economist, Paul Leroy-Beaulieu. This author had extensive knowledge of fiscal developments worldwide and his two-volume 1888 treatise on public finance contains detailed statistical information on the public finances of many countries. Leroy-Beaulieu felt that he could determine empirically a desirable lower and a maximum level of the ratio of taxes into national income, what we now call the tax burden. He considered total tax levels of 5–6 percent of national income as "very moderate." He added that this should be the normal tax level in a country with little public debt and modest military spending, though he recognized that public debt and wars raise that level. This was close to the level that prevailed in the United States at that time. Taxes between 6 and 12 percent could still be considered "normal." Taxes above 12–13 percent of national income became "exorbitant" and damaging to economic growth. Leroy-Beaulieu added that these high tax burdens might exist in some countries, "but certainly the progress of the national wealth would be slowed down: the liberty of the industry and that of the citizens would in this case be threatened and limited by the vexation and the controls ('inquisitions') that necessarily follow the tax complication and the tax increase" (1888, pp. 127–28, my translation). He anticipated by a century a lot of the recent literature on the potential negative impact of high taxation on economic growth and on the liberty of individuals. For the sake of the historical record, we might also cite Benjamin Franklin's view of high taxation. In his famous 1758 booklet, *The Way to Wealth*, he stated, "It would be thought a hard government that should tax its people one tenth of their time, to be employed in its service." Thus, for Franklin, a tax burden of 10 percent was seen as excessive.

Before the outbreak of World War I, economic thinking in the United States still reflected similar views. At that time, public spending in the United States had been lagging behind that of other industrial countries (see Table 1.1). In 1913, when the U.S. Congress was debating the introduction of an income tax that, in the proposed legislation, would be applied with a 1 percent basic or minimum rate and with a marginal (top) tax rate of 6 percent (on the part of incomes exceeding a half million U.S. dollars, at 1913 prices), a professor of public finance at Harvard University stated at congressional hearings that these rates were "clearly excessive." When the U.S. federal income tax was finally enacted in that same year, at still a 1 percent basic rate but with a 7 (and not 6) percent marginal tax rate (still applied on the part of income over a half million dollars), the chairman of the Ways and Means Committee in the U.S. Congress declared, in his intervention, that the tax "would produce more money than the mind of man would ever conceive to spend" (see Tanzi, 1988, p. 99). The proposal to introduce the federal income tax had led to an epic political fight between proponents and opponents of the tax. Its introduction required an amendment to the U.S. Constitution. Also in 1913, Sweden introduced a very basic, universalistic social insurance program, and some basic social legislation started to be introduced in several European countries. These social legislations led Tony Atkinson (2008, p. 22), an expert on welfare states, to believe that before 1918 the welfare state was already in place. However, if it was a welfare state, it was one that could be financed with very low levels of taxation and did not generate much public welfare.

The statistical evidence available indicates that before World War I the tax burdens of major countries (and the level of public spending) were on average around 13 percent of national income. In this period, Colbert's famous statement – that the art of taxation consists of "plucking the goose to obtain the largest amount of feathers with the minimum amount of hissing" – was clearly a guiding principle. There was then still little tolerance by the populations for high taxes.[18] The main taxes used before World War I were foreign trade taxes; property taxes based on cadastral values (i.e., on values determined administratively and based on physical characteristics of properties) or on characteristics such as the number of windows and the width of the houses; presumptive taxes on various business activities or professions; excise taxes on items such as tobacco, salt, ironware, wine, and playing cards; and, occasionally, taxes on transfer of property and local poll taxes. Marriages and funerals also occasionally attracted some taxes.

A natural question is, How could taxes have been so low at that time? Didn't governments need more revenue to carry out their essential functions? The answer to this question is partly found in the roles that both the *demand* for tax revenue, on the part of governments, and the *supply* of tax revenue available to them played. Let us focus first on factors that shaped the *demand* for tax revenue. In general, as we already saw, governments concentrated on the truly *fundamental* role of the state, a role close to the one outlined by Adam Smith. Such a role did not need a lot of money, and, even today it would not require much money if governments chose to  pursue

Table 2.1. *Social transfers, as a percentage of GDP, at current prices in selected countries, 1880 to 1930*

| Country | 1880 | 1890 | 1900 | 1910 | 1920 | 1930 |
|---|---|---|---|---|---|---|
| Australia | 0 | 0 | 0 | 1.12 | 1.66 | 2.11 |
| Austria | 0 | 0 | 0 | 0 | 0 | 1.20 |
| Belgium | 0.17 | 0.22 | 0.26 | 0.43 | 0.52 | 0.56 |
| Canada | 0 | 0 | 0 | 0 | 0.06 | 0.31 |
| Denmark | 0.96 | 1.11 | 1.41 | 1.75 | 2.71 | 3.11 |
| Finland | 0.66 | 0.76 | 0.78 | 0.90 | 0.85 | 2.97 |
| France | 0.46 | 0.54 | 0.57 | 0.81 | 0.64 | 1.05 |
| Germany | 0.50 | 0.53 | 0.59 | | | 4.82 |
| Greece | 0 | 0 | 0 | 0 | 0 | 0.07 |
| Ireland | | | | | | 3.74 |
| Italy | 0 | 0 | 0 | 0 | 0 | 0.08 |
| Japan | 0.05 | 0.11 | 0.17 | 0.18 | 0.18 | 0.21 |
| Netherlands | 0.29 | 0.30 | 0.39 | 0.39 | 0.99 | 1.03 |
| New Zealand | 0.17 | 0.39 | 1.09 | 1.35 | 1.84 | 2.43 |
| Norway | 1.07 | 0.95 | 1.24 | 1.18 | 1.09 | 2.39 |
| Sweden | 0.72 | 0.85 | 0.85 | 1.03 | 1.14 | 2.59 |
| Switzerland | | | | | | 1.17 |
| United Kingdom | 0.86 | 0.83 | 1.0 | 1.38 | 1.39 | 2.24 |
| United States | 0.29 | 0.45 | 0.55 | 0.56 | 0.70 | 0.56 |

*Notes:* Transfers include welfare, unemployment, pensions, health, and housing subsidies. Please note that it excludes spending for public education. 0 = known to be zero; blank = not yet a sovereign state or known to be positive, but number is not available.
*Source:* Adapted from Lindert, 2002.

it. There were almost no government *cash* transfers; most spending was direct. The spending was limited to the financing of large infrastructures and of some enterprises that provided services especially within municipalities, some essential administrative institutions, the defense of the country, the protection of individuals and property, the limited financing of basic education, the payment of salaries and some pensions to public employees, and a few other similar activities such as asylums for the insane and the very old and the very young that did not have any family.

The government's role did not include public spending for the stabilization of the economy, for the redistribution of income between different categories of individuals, or for redistribution across generations. However, it did include, as mentioned earlier, limited resources for assisting the very poor. There were almost no "social transfers" – that is, government expenditures (in cash or in kind) aimed at protecting citizens against particular risks, such as illnesses, old age, unemployment, invalidity, and so on. Such transfers did not exist or were very small (Table 2.1). These social transfers started acquiring some importance in the 1930s partly because of the Great Depression and partly because of changing attitudes about what the role of the state in the economy should be. There were few transfers to *private* enterprises or, for that matter, to the rest of the world. In the period before World War I, the main need for significantly *higher* public revenue had come from occasional wars and from servicing the public debt that resulted from the wars.

A factor that progressively, and especially in the 20th century, would lead to demands for higher public spending, and thus to higher taxes, was *universal suffrage*. As reported earlier, in the 19th century this factor had already attracted the attention of several economists and political scientists. Another factor would be urbanization that was accompanied by growing needs for some social services and for a larger government role. Walvin (1988) provides an interesting account of the role of urbanization in the Victorian era and its impact on the government role.

In his book on *Public Choice Analysis in Historical Perspective* (1992), Alan Peacock, a major public finance economist in recent decades, wrote that "one of the great political debates of the 19th century concerned the consequences of introducing a universal franchise" (p. 42). The debate concerned two related aspects, although it was mainly focused on the first of them. The first was the "relation between the extension of the franchise and the securing of the operation of free market principles." The second was the impact that universal franchise would have on taxation, public spending, and the role of the public sector. The fear, on the part of economists, was that universal franchise would cause the majority of voting citizens who did not have any property to lose respect for property rights. Economists considered these rights as one of the pillars of a market economy. (This debate is reported in detail in chapter 2 of Hutchison, 1981.)

The debate had attracted the interest of Tocqueville (1835) and of James Mill (1819), the father of John Stuart Mill. The fear that universal franchise would destroy the market economy was especially strong in Europe and even more so in England, where property was much more concentrated. Tocqueville (p. 150) had felt that this would be less of a problem in the United States where most citizens owned some property, often in the form of land. Mill's fear led him to propose that the franchise be limited, in England, to males over 40 years of age. Perhaps it should be mentioned that in the 19th century *wealth ownership* was far more important than *income*. It was more visible, more tangible, and more permanent than income. With the passing of time, and with economic developments that brought widely owned public enterprises and wealth held in the form of stocks and other financial instruments, wealth became less visible and less tangible, and the attention shifted to income. Also, with the passing of time income from labor grew in importance as a consequence of the growth of human capital.

The impact of universal franchise on taxation and public spending has attracted less attention than it deserves. The activity of the public sector was pulled away from the provision of public goods and the establishment of basic institutions toward the redistribution of income and the protection against economic risks. It can also be added that, when women were given the right to vote, public spending became more beneficial to women, as it was in the welfare states.

In the United Kingdom, the percentage of household heads with voting rights rose from 4.2 in 1867 to 74.2 in 1911 and to higher levels later (Lindert, 2002, p. 191). The same was happening in other countries. As Lindert put it, "There was so little social spending of any kind before the twentieth century primarily because political voice was so restricted" (p. 190). Lindert emphasizes the importance of the *demand* side for public services, which in some sense is different from explanations of the growth of public spending that stress other considerations, such as the "Baumol hypothesis," that argue that economic growth raises the cost of providing government services because of the lower productivity gains in the production of those services, compared to the productivity growth in the private sector (Baumol, 1967).

The Italian economist, De Viti de Marco, one of the major contributors to the Italian *scienza delle finanze*, which was influential a century ago, had also worried that universal suffrage in societies with uneven income distributions would lead the poorer citizens to demand public services that would benefit them while shifting the tax burden on the richer few. The masses would support with their votes public programs that would benefit them and vote for taxes that would be paid by the rich (De Viti de Marco, 1936). The latest Italian edition of this book, *I Primi Principi dell'Economia Finanziaria*, had been published in 1928, with earlier editions having appeared in the later part of the previous century. A mathematical version of De Viti de Marco's view was provided by Hagertrom (1938). Hagertrom, like De Viti de Marco and others, predicted that democracy would lead to radical egalitarianism and consequently to higher public spending. In more recent decades, this preoccupation led some exponents of the public choice school of economics (a school that developed mostly but not exclusively in the United States in the 1960s and 1970s), such as James Buchanan, Francesco Forte, and others, to advocate constitutional limits to taxation, as exist in the Swiss Constitution (Forte, 1985). In Buchanan's view, these limits are needed to constrain populist pressures on governments that could damage economic activities and limit individual freedom (Brennan and Buchanan, 1980).[19]

The public choice school, and especially James Buchanan, acknowledged the influence of the *scienza delle finanze*. Buchanan recently listed De Viti de Marco's book among the 10 books "that had exerted the greatest influence on [his] work and [his] ideas generally" (Buchanan, 2003, p. 283). That school had never lost sight of the political pressures on the policy makers that influence political decisions and the outcome of economic policy.[20] It rejected the view of "government solely as a policy mechanism" (Peacock, 1992, p. 7). The "limits to taxation" are part of a broader movement, which became popular in recent years, to impose *fiscal rules* to public spending, to taxation, to public debt, and to fiscal deficit. The Netherlands was the first country to impose limits to public spending, while Switzerland had imposed limits to taxation in its constitution.[21] The European Monetary Union imposed limits on fiscal deficit and public debts, leaving to the member countries the choice of the levels of taxation and spending. In a spreading movement, other countries have imposed, in more recent years, other kinds of limits on fiscal variables (Kopits, 2007). It should be realized that, to some extent, this is a return to the fundamental rule of Cicero: the need to keep budgets in balance *over the medium and long run*.

*Supply* considerations and factors that shaped the *supply* of public revenue are also significant historically. In the pre–World War I environment, if the demand for public spending had been much higher, it might not have led to significantly higher tax revenue because of the difficulties that existed at that time in raising tax levels. The difficulties were several: first, the middle class was still small, and the taxation of the larger poorer classes would have provided little revenue, while the taxation of the rich would have been politically difficult because they still significantly controlled the political decisions. Second, the structure of the economy imposed limitations on tax collection. For example, the share of formal wages and salaries in national income was low; large establishments, capable of withholding taxes at source (on incomes paid by them, or on their sales) were still few; the share of agriculture in the economy was high; and informal activities predominated. These characteristics would have made it difficult, though perhaps not impossible, to raise significantly higher tax levels (Tanzi, 1994). Additionally, the "technology of taxation" was still rudimentary. The major revenue producers of later years (the global income tax, social security contributions, and the value-added tax) were still unknown or not widely used. Social security contributions were not collected because there were still no fully developed social security or pension systems. In spite of these limitations, several countries were able to double their tax burden during World War I, but to levels that were still much lower than today's.

Just before or during the outbreak of World War I, several countries introduced *national* income taxes. These countries included, inter alia, the United States, France, and Germany. Britain already had income taxes levied at very low rates, but it increased their importance in this period.[22] In Germany, Saxony had had an income tax. In Britain, the income tax had been introduced more than a century earlier, during the wars against Napoleon. It had been abolished in 1816. Apparently it had been so despised that the act that abolished it specified that the records of the tax payments be destroyed. The tax was reintroduced in 1841 (Webb, 1980, p. 158).

For the countries that entered World War I, the conflict provided a political opportunity, a "cover," for politicians who wanted to raise the level of taxation permanently. Several governments took advantage of this opportunity. Still, the opposition to taxes was so great at that time that only small shares of the war expenses were covered by taxes. The shares were 16.7 percent in Germany and 26.2 percent in Britain. They were lower in France, Italy, and Russia. France even delayed the collection of income taxes until 1916. Excess profit taxes were more easily introduced, to limit the war profits that some enterprises would make because of the war. (See Stevenson, 2007, pp. 180–81; and Ferguson, 2007, pp. 318–19.)

The war was financed to a large part through borrowing and the printing of money. The latter led, in several of the countries, to hyperinflation that destroyed the wealth of the middle classes and helped wipe out the debt accumulated by the governments during the war.[23] So, indirectly, through the inflation tax, taxpayers paid for the costs of the war. The total financial cost of the war has been estimated at U.S. $82.4 billion, at 1913 prices. This was a huge sum for the time. Because of the war costs, by 1917 public spending had risen to 76 percent of net national product in Germany, 70 percent in Britain, and more than 100 percent in France. During the war, "the soldiers' families were allocated separation allowances, and the disabled, widows and orphans needed assistance, as did thousands of refugees" (Stevenson, 2007, p. 179). Some of the expenses continued after the war so that taxes remained above the low level they had reached before the war. A "ratchet effect" occurred. It helped raise the level of public spending in future years. That ratchet effect would be higher after World War II when governments were also expected to play a larger role in the economy and when resistance to high taxes had weakened (Peacock and Wiseman, 1961).

# References

Atkinson, Tony. 2008. "European Union's Social Policy in Globalization Context," in *Institutions for Social Well-Being: Alternatives for Europe*, edited by Lilia Costabile (Houndmills: Palgrave Macmillan), pp. 15–32.

Baumol, William J. 1967. "Macroeconomics of Unbalanced Growth: The Anatomy of Urban Crisis," *American Economic Review* 57: 415–26.

Boettke, Peter. 2005. "On Reading Hayek: Choices, Consequences and the Road to Serfdom." *European Journal of Political Economy* 21 (December): 1042–53.

Brennan, G., and J. M. Buchanan. 1980. *The Power to Tax: Analytical Foundations of a Fiscal Constitution* (Cambridge: Cambridge University Press).

Buchan, James. 2006. *The Authentic Adam Smith: His Life and Ideas* (New York: W. W. Norton).

Buchanan, James. 2003. "Endnote," in *The Theory of Public Finance in Italy from the Origins to the 1940s*, edited by D. Fausto and V. De Bonis (Pisa-Rome: Istituti Editoriali e Poligrafici Internazionali).

Burke, A. L. 2000. "The Price of Everything: On Human Values and Global Markets" (July). http://www.nnn.se/n-model/price/price.htm.

Cipolla, Carlo. 1996. *Storia Facile dell'Economia Italiana dal Medioevo a Oggi* (Milan: Oscar Mondadori).

Clarke, Peter. 2009. *The Rise, Fall and Return of the 20th Century's Most Influential Economist* (New York: Bloomsbury Press).

de Molinari, Gustave. 1849. *Les Soirées de la Rue Saint-Lazare: Entretiens sur les Lois Economique et Défense de la Propriété.* Translated as *Le Serate di Rue Saint-Lazare* (Macerata: Liberi Libri, 2009).

De Viti de Marco, Antonio. 1936. *First Principles of Public Finance* (London: Jonathan Cape). Translated from *I Primi Principi dell'Economia Finanziaria* (Rome: San-paolesi, 1928).

Dunoyer, Charles. 1825. *L'Industrie et la Morale Considérées dans leurs Rapports avec la Liberté* (Paris: A. Sautelet).

Ebenstein, Lanny. 2007. *Milton Friedman* (New York: Palgrave Macmillan).

Ekelund, Robert B., and Robert D. Tollison. 1981. *Mercantilism as a Rent-Seeking Society: Economic Regulations in Historical Perspective* (College Station: Texas A&M University Press).

Fausto, Domenicantonio. 2003. "An Outline of the Main Italian Contributions to the Theory of Public Finance." *Il Pensiero Economico Italiano*, anno undicesimo 1: 11–41.

Fausto, D., and V. De Bonis. 2003. *The Theory of Public Finance in Italy from the Origins to the 1940s* (Pisa-Rome: Istituti Editoriali e Poligrafici Internazionali).

Ferguson, Niall. 2007. *The Pity of War* (New York: Basic Books).

Forte, Francesco. 1985. "Control of Public Spending Growth and Majority Rule," in *Public Expenditure and Government Growth*, edited by Francesco Forte and Alan Peacock (Oxford: Basil Blackwell), pp. 132–42.

Franklin, Benjamin. 1758. *The Way to Wealth* (Bedford: Applewood Books, 1986).

Frey, Bruno. 1985. "Are There Natural Limits to the Growth of Government?," in *Public Expenditure and Government Growth*, edited by Francesco Forte and Alan Peacock (Oxford: Basil Blackwell), pp. 101–18.

Graziani, Augusto. 1897. *Istituzioni di Scienza delle Finanze* (Turin: Fratelli Bocca Editori).

Hagerstrom, K. G. 1938. "A Mathematical Note on Democracy." *Econometrica* 6: 381–83.

Hayek, F. A. 1944. *The Road to Serfdom* (Chicago: University of Chicago Press).

   1988. *The Fatal Conceit: The Errors of Socialism*, edited by W. W. Bartley III (Chicago: University of Chicago Press).

Herman, Arthur. 2001. *How the Scott Invented the Modern World* (New York: Random House).

Himmelfarb, Gertrude. 2004. *The Road to Modernity* (New York: Vintage Books).

Hume, David. 1955. *Writings on Economics*, edited and introduced by E. Rotuein (London: Thomas Nelson and Sons).

   [1739]. *A Treatise of Human Nature.*

Hutchison, Terence W. 1981. *The Political and Philosophy of Economics: Marxians, Keynesians and Austrians* (Oxford: Basil Blackwell).

Jomo, K. S., and Erik S. Reinert. 2005. *The Origins of Development Economics* (London: Tulika Books).

Kopits, George. editor 2004. *Rules Based Fiscal Policy in Emerging Markets* (London: Palgrave Macmillan).

   2007. "Fiscal Responsibility Framework: International Experience and Implications for Hungary." *MNB Occasional Paper* 62.

Kornai, Janos. 1992. *The Socialist System: The Political Economy of Communism* (Princeton: Princeton University Press).

Labriola, Arturo. 1943. *L'Attualitá di Marx* (Naples: Alberto Morano Editore).

Leroy-Beaulieu, Paul. 1888. *Traité de la Science des Finances*, 2 vols., 4th ed. (Paris: Guillaumin).

Lindert, Peter H. 2002. "What Drives Social Spending? 1770 to 2020," in *When Market Fails: Social Policy and Economic Reform*, edited by Ethan B. Kapstein and Branko Milanovic (New York: Russell Sage Foundation), pp. 185–214.

MacCulloch, Diarmaid. 2003. *The Reformation: A History* (New York: Viking).

Marx, Karl. 1867. *Das Capital.* Translated as *Capital: A New Abridgement.* World's Classics (Oxford: Oxford University Press, 1995).

McLean, I. 2006. *Adam Smith: Radical and Egalitarian? An Interpretation for the 21st Century* (Edinburgh: Edinburgh University Press).

Mises, L. 1922. *Socialism* (Indianapolis: Liberty, 1981).

Moss, David A. 2002. *When All Else Fails* (Cambridge, Mass.: Harvard University Press).

Mill, James. 1819. *An Essay on Government*, with an Introduction of Ernst Barker (Cambridge: Cambridge University Press, 1937).

Mill, John Stuart. [1848] 2004. *Principles of Political Economy* (Amherst, NY: Prometheus Books).

Muller, Jerry Z. 1993. *Adam Smith in His Time and Ours* (New York: The Free Press).

Musgrave, Richard. 1959. *The Theory of Public Finance* (New York: McGraw-Hill).

Nitti, Francesco Saverio. 1903. *La Scienza delle Finanze* (Bari: Editori Laterza, 1972).

Peacock, Alan. 1992. *Public Choice Analysis in Historical Perspective*, Raffaele Mattioli Lectures (Cambridge: Cambridge University Press).

Peacock, Alan, and Jack Wiseman. 1961. *The Growth of Public Expenditure in the United Kingdom* (Princeton: Princeton University Press).

Rexed, Knut. 2000. "Public Sector Reform: Lessons from the Nordic Region: The Swedish Experience," Swedish Agency for Administrative Development. Mimeo (May 19).

Ricossa, Sergio. [1986] 2006. *La fine dell'economia: Saggio sulla perfezione* (Catensac, Italy: Rubettino Editore).

Robbins, Lionel. 1952. *The Theory of Economic Policy in English Classical Political Economy* (London: Macmillan).

Rostow, W. W. 1953. *The Dynamics of Soviet Society* (New York: W. W. Norton).

Schuessler, Jennifer. 2010. "Hayek: The Back Story." *New York Times Book Review* (July 11), p. 27.

Schumpeter, Joseph. 1954. *History of Economic Analysis* (New York: Oxford University Press).

Serra, Antonio. 1613. *Breve Trattato delle Cause che Possono far Abbondare l'Oro e l'Argento dove non sono Miniere* (Naples: Lazzaro Scorriggio).

Simons, H. C. 1934. *A Positive Program for Laissez-faire: Some Proposals for a Liberal Economic Policy*, Public Policy Pamphlet No. 15 (Chicago: Chicago University Press).

Smith, Adam. [1776] 1999. *The Wealth of Nations* (London: Penguin Books).

Solomon, Howard M. 1972. *Public Welfare, Science and Propaganda in Seventeenth Century France* (Princeton: Princeton University Press).

Stevenson, David. 2007. *Cataclysm: The First World War as Political Tragedy* (New York: Basic Books).

Stigler, George. 1968. "The Government of the Economy," in *A Dialogue of the Proper Role of the State*, by G. J. Stigler and P. A. Samuelson (Chicago: University of Chicago Business School), pp. 3–20.

Stiglitz, Joseph E. 1994. *Whither Socialism?* (Cambridge, Mass.: MIT Press).

Tanzi, Vito. 1988. "Trends in Tax Policy as Revealed by Recent Development and Research." *International Bureau of Fiscal Documentation Bulletin* 42, no. 3 (March).

1994. "Taxation and Economic Structure." *Public Choice Studies*, no. 24: 35–45.

ed. 2003. *Transition to Market* (Washington, D.C.: IMF).

2010. *Russian Bears and Somali Sharks: Transitions and Other Passages* (New York: Jorge Pinto Books).

Tocqueville, Alexis de. [1835 and 1840] 1965. *Democracy in America* (Oxford: Oxford University Press).

1835. "Mémoire sur le paupérisme," in Tocqueville, *Democrazia e poverta'* (Rome: Ideazione Editrice, 1998).

Trevelyan, G. M. 1942. *English Social History* (London: Longmans, Green).

Van Overtveldt, Johan. 2007. *The Chicago School* (Chicago: Agate).

Walvin, James. 1988. *Victorian Values* (Athens: University of Georgia Press).

Webb, R. K. 1980. *Modern England*. 2nd ed. (HarperCollins).

Weber, Max. 1947. *The Theory of Social and Economic Organization* (London: Free Press of Glencoe).

Weinburg, M. 1978. "The Social Analysis of Three Early 19th Century French Liberals." *Journal of Libertarian Studies* 2, no. 1: 45–63.

Wheen, Francis. 1999. *Karl Marx* (London: Fourth Estate).

Winch, Donald. 1978. *Adam Smith's Politics* (Cambridge University Press).

Wolfe, Alan. 2009. *The Future of Liberalism* (New York: Alfred A. Knopf).

Woodward, Llewellyn. 1962. *The Age of Reform, 1815–1870*, 2nd ed. (Oxford: Clarendon Press).

Zamagni, Vera, ed. 2000. *Povertá e Innovazioni Istituzionali in Italia* (Bologna: Il Mulino).

# THREE

# Forces That Changed the Role of the State

## 3.1. The Impact of the Industrial Revolution and Reactions to It

Between 1776, when Adam Smith published *The Wealth of Nations*, and the period around World War I, several important developments took place in the now industrialized countries. These developments changed dramatically the world that had existed until Smith's time. They contributed to putting pressure on the limited role of the state and on the level of public spending, conceptualized by Adam Smith, which had prevailed during the laissez-faire period, especially until sometime around 1880. They also stimulated various nongovernmental responses to these developments. Smith had written his book at the very beginning of the Industrial Revolution, when the world was not much different from that at the time of the Roman Empire, and before that "revolution" would start changing the economic and social relations that had existed. "[The] industrial revolution was the most revolutionary of all revolutions" because it changed radically the world that had existed before (Ricossa 2006, p. 63, my translation). At the time Smith wrote *The Wealth of Nations*, most people lived in rural areas and did not vote, and governments mostly represented the rights of the ruling class against the masses.

The Industrial Revolution, together with the political movements that accompanied it, in part as the outcome of the French and perhaps the American revolutions and of new political thinking, would in time transform the character of the economies and of the economic and social relations in the advanced countries. These economies would be progressively transformed from being largely agricultural and rural to increasingly industrial and urban. Increasing commerce within and between countries would play a major role in this transformation. With the passing of time, this change would lead some economists to argue that the role of the state, as advocated by Adam Smith and especially as it was practiced during the laissez-faire period, was too limited and too restrictive. It was no longer right for a modern industrial society. The ongoing changes would help set in motion forces that in time would lead to higher public spending and tax levels. Furthermore, with the Industrial Revolution came a new class of often-enriched manufacturers and businessmen who, because of their often-humble background and newly acquired wealth, had less respect for the traditions and the relationships that had existed earlier. Inherited beliefs started to be challenged by self-made, practical men.

In much writing on the economic role of the state by those who describe the laissez-faire period, there seems to be a view that laissez-faire, especially in much of the 19th century, was mainly a philosophical or ideological choice. However, at that time, and until the late part of the 19th century, "public opinion, even the opinion of the poor, did not expect government to cure poverty." There was then a prevalent belief, shared by J. S. Mill and Nassan Senior in England, "that the state never did things well." Senior pointed out that "it is as difficult to elevate the poor as it is easy to depress the rich. In human affairs . . . it is much easier to do harm than good" (see Woodward, 1962, p. 446). Senior believed that "the state might provide parks, open spaces, museums, and picture galleries" that were very scarce in the fast-urbanizing world of that time but not much else beside Smith's traditional functions (p. 446). No one believed that the state could engage in public expenditure on a large scale for purposes of social betterment (p. 17). Woodward (p. 16) adds this:

A great deal of the talk about laissez-faire must be discounted, or at least put into its proper context. In many cases the arguments concealed an admission that a problem was insoluble . . . the policy of *laissez-faire* was not the result of a new and optimistic belief in the progress of society through private enterprise. It was rather an acknowledgement that the fund of skill and experience at the service of society was limited.

A similar attitude was echoed by Keynes (1926, p. 12) when he wrote that "the ineptitude of public administrators strongly prejudiced the practical man in favor of 'laissez-faire.' . . . Almost everything which the State did in the eighteenth century in excess of its minimum functions was, or seemed, injurious or unsuccessful."

However, "although the older generation of economists and writers on public matters . . . were suspicious of state interference, they recognized the limits of private action, and the need for equality of opportunity, if competition were to be fair between individuals" (Woodward, 1962, p. 445).

The intellectual reaction against the laissez-faire attitude would initially come from Germany, a country in which the ongoing process of industrialization (which was bringing smokestacks and other unattractive features to the countryside, starkly depicted by German paintings of that period) was not universally seen as bringing benefits to society and was even demonized by some. It was no coincidence that it was in Berlin that the first world conference for the protection of workers took place in 1890. Karl Marx and other German socialist writers had formulated, especially in the second half of the 19th century, their critical theories against private property and capitalism. They saw industrialization as a process that would bring the creation of large monopolies, economic crises, the exploitation of workers, the progressive impoverishment of the masses, and in time the eventual collapse of capitalism. Marx contemplated the possibility of drastically reorganizing economic and social relations, by getting rid of markets and, eventually, nations. However, even ignoring Marx and other socialist writers, who, in England, were dismissed as "low radicals," some mainstream economists started calling for a larger role of the state in the economy (Trevelyan, 1942, and, more recently, Musgrave, 1998).

An influential German economist, Adolf Wagner, for example, was sharply critical of what he called "the false doctrine" of Adam Smith, which in his view made the activity of the state seem inherently unproductive. Probably Smith would disagree with him because he would see the state's activity as promoting commerce and thus civilization. Wagner's writing referred to a more profound and beneficial concept of the state that had existed in German thinking and had its roots in German philosophy.[1] This is the "communal state" described by Musgrave (1998), a state that is connected with and is an expression of the community. It is distinct from the one that is related strictly to the activities of individuals. For Wagner, the state "does not have just a function of protection" *of individuals* and "should not be considered as an arbitrary creation" and "as a necessary evil, but as the very necessary condition and, at the same time, the supreme form, of social life." That state is linked to the survival of the community, *as a community*, with its distinctive features, history, traditions, social values, and unwritten rules, and not just to the service of the individual. Social life could not exist without some social organization. When societies become more advanced, that organization becomes the state. He rejected the theory of the state based exclusively on the individual, a theory inherent in Smith's and Hume's thinking, which dominated and has continued to dominate Anglo-Saxon thinking. At the same time, Wagner rejected the socialist view, which was then gaining currency, a view that tended to ignore the individual or to suppress the individual under the weight of the community's will. He argued that "the state should not be seen as solely the guarantor of [individual] rights but as the promoter of civilization and welfare." Wagner referred to the optimistic view of the working of the market "in the school of Smith" and found various shortcomings in that market and in the competitive system. In this he seemed to ignore the concerns that Smith himself had expressed about the market. Wagner's views would have attracted a large following at the present time, when the market economy has come under strong attacks and many have regretted the disappearance of community spirit. Wagner referred significantly to the *role of the state in the distribution of national income*, a role that he thought should be important and that in fact became more important over time and especially in the 20th century.

Because of their historical importance, it may be worthwhile to cite directly from Wagner's conclusions (translated by the author of this book from the Italian edition of Wagner's book, 1891, p. 14): "The system of [public] spending, of taxation, and of [public] debt must be organized in a way to reduce some social and economic shortcomings that derive from it." Wagner was, thus, aware of the potential welfare and macroeconomic costs of these policies. He went on to note that "even inconveniences that do not derive from the functions of the state . . . should be removed with an opportune social policy. From this follows the need for increase in the financial resources of the state to allow it to exercise new and diverse functions." Wagner favored higher taxes and a larger share of public spending in national income in order to promote *social objectives* – that is, the objectives of the community. His views contrasted sharply with those expressed in France around the same time by Leroy-Beaulieu, as reported earlier. He went on to argue that taxation must contribute to a redistribution of national income.

Wagner's writing was influential and helped change some of the laissez-faire views that still prevailed in Europe in the later part of the 19th century. Around 1900 he was a much-cited economist, often cited more than Smith. He saw the state in a kind of biological or evolutionary role, a role that would change and grow with the passing of time, to better adjust to the changing economic and social environment. This growth would be tied with and be directed toward the promotion of social objectives. It is difficult to decide whether Wagner's views on the long-run growth of the public sector were normative (what should be) or positive (what will be). "Wagner's law" of the growth of the public sector has often been interpreted as an almost mechanical, positive law. It probably was not.

In England, even though socialist ideas were not popular, by the end of the 19th century, reactions against laissez-faire had also acquired some momentum, in part promoted by the writings of John Stuart Mill, who died in 1873, and other writers. Mill's views on the role of the state are described in book 5 of his *Principles of Political Economy*. They are still worth reading. He made an important distinction between the "necessary" and the "optional" functions of government. Mill embraced the philosophy of utilitarianism, according to which happiness is the result of the actions of individuals. It should be noted that the focus was on happiness and not on the income level. Actions should be judged by the impact that they have on happiness. Like Wagner, he advocated a better distribution of wealth (not income) through the use of direct (but not progressive) taxation and especially of inheritance and gift taxes, which could be progressive, by reducing the possibility that the children of the rich would automatically continue to be rich, thereby making the equality of opportunities more difficult to achieve. He supported universal suffrage and the promotion of social legislation *enforced by an effective public bureaucracy*. These policies did not necessarily involve more public spending. They were aimed at changing social relations in society rather than necessarily at promoting a greater spending role by the state (Mill, 1859).

In Italy, Pope Leo XIII reacted to the growing popularity of socialism and to the ongoing intellectual debate with an encyclical, the *Rerum Novarum* of May 15, 1891, which listed, among the duties of governments, the defense of private property, the protection of workers in their work against those who exploited them, a just wage, and a campaign to educate workers to save.[2] Thus, the *desired* role of the state was changing more rapidly than assessed by the increase in public spending, which was also changing but more slowly. The pope did not explicitly support a large government role through higher public spending, though he hinted at some government role in social protection.

Wagner's writings became popular with those who represented the Italian national government at that time. They accepted the inevitability of the growth of public spending, to deal with the growing complexity of the economy. It has been claimed that Cavour, the first Italian prime minister after the Italian unification, had even anticipated it and that, once a formal statement of that "law" became available, it was widely accepted by students and practitioners of public finance in both Italy and in other countries. The growing intervention by the state in economic affairs was opposed by those who had a more liberalist view of the economy, such as the two leading Italian economists at the time, Vilfredo Pareto and Maffeo Pantaleoni, and, at the political level, by Silvio Spaventa, a major political figure (De Cecco and Pedone, 1995, p. 257).

In an important paper written in 2004, Tony Atkinson pointed out that the Industrial Revolution had brought with it three important developments that would in time have implications for the economic role of the state: the concepts of unemployment, retirement, and business cycles. These developments probably influenced Wagner's thinking in the late 19th century. In this period, "Germany [had] become a great industrial state; the new methods of modern machinery and large capital [had] created forms of employment unknown before; huge urban agglomerations [had] been called into existence; [and] the 'domestic' industries [were] being destroyed" (Atkinson, 2004, pp. vii–viii). The destruction of these "domestic" industries had made the skills of many individuals, especially artisans, obsolete. The latter had seen their work replaced by machines and their incomes fall.

In the new world being created by the Industrial Revolution, a growing number of individuals were forced to leave their homes and families in the rural areas where they were born and move to the "urban agglomerations" to be close to the factories where they now worked. This process of internal migration was similar to that now taking place in China. At that time, however, daily mobility was still limited to the distance that people could cover on foot, so workers had to live close to the places where the factories were located.[3] People could suddenly find themselves without a job and without an income in an urban environment in which they no longer could rely on the support and the safety net that had been provided by the extended family and by the community in the rural settings where they had lived. The modern concept of unemployment was the consequence of a society in which increasing numbers of people were employed as workers on informal, time-limited contracts (often daily or even hourly contracts) by manufacturing enterprises. These contracts favored the enterprises and not the workers. The workers could be dismissed at any time without much thought or compensation and had to work at very low wages. The introduction of machines sometimes reduced their wages, and in some cases the workers reacted by breaking the machines (Thomis, 1970). This condition of the workers had inspired not only the pope's encyclical of 1891 but also the Berlin Conference on Industrial Legislation of 1890, which "marked the beginning of international cooperation for the protection of labor" (Ashley, 1904, p. ix).

With the passing of time, workers gained increasing protection and the right to unionize, among other rights. This progress did not always come peacefully. Before the Industrial Revolution, people either had been self-employed, mainly in agricultural or artisanal activities, or had been attached on a permanent basis, often in a position of dependence or even servitude, to powerful families. These individuals could and did experience poverty, even extreme poverty, but not unemployment in the modern sense. In some sense the families for whom they worked had some permanent obligations toward them. The obligations extended to the families or the dependents of the workers.[4] At that time, average life expectancy was low, about 45 years. This reduced the economic problems associated with old age. Most people remained active until they died, and their death was often fairly sudden, being caused by infectious diseases or accidents. Chronic, old-age diseases were rare because relatively few people reached old age.

Similarly, the modern notion of *retirement* can be interpreted as a permanent form of unemployment, after a certain age, for the retired individuals. Retirement did not exist in the past, and it still does not exist today in many traditional societies. In developing countries, it is limited to the share of the population that is fortunate enough to have had regular jobs in the official economy during their working life. Because these people are entitled to a pension, they can *retire*. Most of the poorer people, who remain in the informal sector, do not have access to a pension and often cannot officially retire.[5] The idea that, regardless of the physical or mental condition of a person, the person must "retire" at a given date is something new and radical.

Retirement requires the existence of public or private pensions or sufficient savings accumulated during the working age, when there is not an extended family to support the retiree. Pensions are supposed to allow the retired individuals to sustain themselves and their dependents after retirement. In a modern society with job tenure, and with salaries that, regardless of productivity, increase or remain constant in many jobs, when the age of the individuals rises, employers may find it advantageous to have an age limit at which they can force the older and presumably less productive workers to leave their employment. These older individuals become a progressively poorer bargain for the employers. When they retire, and in the absence of a family safety net, the workers need to fall back either on a pension or on accumulated savings.[6]

When retirement rules were first introduced in many countries more than a century ago, most workers worked in *manual* jobs. Some of these jobs were very hard and demanded physical strength and endurance. At that time, a major social issue was the reduction in the number of working hours that often extended to 12 or more hours a day. Therefore, it made sense to set retirement at a given and not too advanced age. However, in today's world, because of the change in the composition of the output produced and the greater use of machines, few jobs require physical strength and endurance – perhaps no more than a small percentage of all jobs. Working hours have been much reduced compared to work patterns in the past as a result of important changes in social legislation. The eight-hour workday was a major social victory.[7] Furthermore, because people tend to live much longer now than in the past, the illness-free and healthy portion of their life has increased substantially and, in many countries, continues to increase with time.[8] Thus, policies that require workers to retire at a certain, and still relatively young, age seem less justifiable. These policies are now slowly being reformed.

An efficiency-based argument for setting retirement at a relatively young age is that technological developments are more easily assimilated by young people, especially during their school years, so that the productivity of more senior workers tends to lag, especially in societies with fast technological advances in which experience becomes less important than technical ability. If technological developments are learned and assimilated mostly in schools, and companies do not wish to spend money training workers (who may leave their companies, taking their new acquired skills with them), then the older workers become, the more detached they may become from current technological developments.[9]

Unemployment, retirement, and business cycles – developments that increase the probability of becoming unemployed in certain periods and that were becoming more common and attracting the attention especially of socialist writers during the 19th century – created different potential justifications for more governmental intervention, although not necessarily for more public spending. This is the argument advanced by Atkinson. When the workers moved to the cities, many cut themselves off from the potential support that came from their extended families and from mutual assistance associations, cooperatives, and other civil institutions that often were active locally. These institutions had become important by the time that the *Rerum Novarum* was issued.

In the *Rerum Novarum*, Pope Leo XIII expressed concern about the ongoing disappearance of "corporations of arts and trades," the medieval "guilds" that had been common and had provided some coordinated social assistance for members engaged in similar activities. The pope felt that the disappearance of these "corporations" reflected an abandonment of the Christian spirit. He worried that workers might be left without defense against the "greed" of employers and against "savage competition," which did not reflect the Christian spirit of compassion and cooperation that had characterized the societies of the past. He was particularly worried by usury and speculation.

## 3.2. Private Responses to the Industrial Revolution

Cooperation among human beings was common long before public institutions for social well-being were established by governments. Spontaneous
cooperation must have been born at least since men needed to cooperate
to keep alive the flames they had started or to hunt successfully. It has been
reported that a cooperative already existed in 44 B.C. among the workers
who unloaded ships in the port of Ostia, near Rome. Cooperatives existed
in the *collegia* of the Romans and the *agapi* of the first Christians, who
stressed unconditional love for fellow men. They were common in the Middle Ages. (See Rizzi, 2003, for the following description.) The cooperative
movement was stimulated by the Industrial Revolution and, before the state
started intervening, contributed to the protection against some risks and
gave workers some protection against unscrupulous employers. The movement prospered especially in England, France, Germany, and parts of Italy
and spread to other countries. In Germany, the cooperative movement grew
rapidly. The number of cooperative societies rose from 38 in 1864 to 568 in
1900. The number of members grew from 7,700 in 1864 to 522,000 in 1900.
In Saxony, 75 percent of workers belonged to these cooperatives (Ashley,
1904, pp. 118–19).

In England, Robert Owen, who was "among the first English thinkers to
realize that the evils of industrialism were not incurable and that the new
machinery might be used to abolish poverty" (Woodward, 1962, p. 130),
started a movement in the early part of the 19th century for the common
management of canteens (cafeterias), schools, laundries, and other needed
facilities. It was specifically a response to the Industrial Revolution. In
Rochdale, a little town of the Lancashire, near Manchester, that had become
the capital of the cotton industry, the Rochdale Society of Equitable Pioneers
was created by 28 weavers in 1844. It was the first modern cooperative and
had the goal of providing its members with products of basic necessity at
reasonable prices. The founders of this cooperative are remembered as "the
equitable pioneers." The cooperative aimed at making a small profit that
was distributed among the members, in proportion to their purchases, at the
end of each year. The "principles of Rochdale" – one vote for each member
and no discrimination of any kind – continue to influence the cooperatives
of today.

The Rochdale Society expanded into many shops, some enterprises, a
hospital, a public library, reading rooms, and even a savings bank. The
society organized some schools to educate those in the poorest social classes.

By 1891 it had a million members. By 1863 there were more than 400 cooperatives in England and the movement had spread to Scotland.

The cooperative movement in France took a more socialist trend. It was promoted by Pierre Joseph Proudhom and Louis Blanc, who were influenced by "utopistic socialism," some of it of Catholic inspiration (Nitti, 1971). *Ateliers nationaux* were public enterprises created, after the 1848 revolution, to guarantee work to low-class workers. These enterprises were sustained by the state. In France, both consumption and production cooperatives became common, and some began providing credit. The theorist of the "cooperative republic" was Charles Gide, whose goal was to ban profit from economic activities. Thus, it was a clearly socialist movement.

In Germany, the cooperative movement spread to credit institutions. The main driver of this movement was Herman Schulze-Delitzsch. These credit cooperatives were primarily engaged in providing "minicredit." They started by providing cheap credit to shoemakers and carpenters, because at that time there were enough shoemakers and carpenters to make the project viable. By 1850 Schultze-Delitzsch had created the first cooperative bank in the world. Credit to some members was provided using the deposits of other members. Obtaining credit required not collateral but the endorsement of a kind of commission made up of some members that attested to the honesty of the borrowing member. By 1859 the General Federation of Cooperatives was created.

In 1840 Friedrich Wilhelm Raiffeisen created in Germany the first Catholic rural bank. So-called Raiffeisen Banks soon spread in the rural areas of German-speaking territories. Their objective was to allow agricultural workers to obtain credit at reasonable interest rates to buy cattle, seeds, and some equipment for their farms. In 1849 Raiffeisen created a kind of minicredit initiative through the "association for the assistance of agricultural workers without means." This initiative required better-to-do citizens to provide minicredits to the poorest citizens. Thus, minicredit is not as recent an invention as many believe.

In 1852 Raiffeisen moved to Heddesdorf and focused his effort on low-income workers. In 1861 he created the first "cooperative credit system of Raiffeisen." This cooperative depended exclusively on mutual assistance. Its dependence on Christian ethics made it different from "popular banks." By 1888 there were 445 such cooperatives, and the concept soon spread to other countries. By the second half of the 19th century, there were three cooperative systems in existence: the English one that focused on cooperation *in consumption*; the French one that focused on cooperation *in production*;

and the German one that focused on cooperation *in the provision of credit*. The German system spread to Italy, where Catholic rural credit cooperatives became common. The Cassa di Gambarore, near Venice, was the first such cooperative in Italy, created on February 26, 1890.

These innovations were in addition to the more highly developed systems of social protections that were sponsored by religious groups, confraternities, mutual assistance societies, and similar groups.

In recent years globalization may have added further reasons for public assistance and, according to some economists, for more public spending (Rodrik, 1998; and Williamson, 1997). Marx had worried about the impact of globalization as early as in 1848.[10] Whether this additional push for government intervention should best be exercised through higher public spending or through other policy instruments, such as regulations that forced individuals to buy directly from the market protection against the risks of being unemployed or the risks of old age or invalidity, is not important at this point. In either case the role of the state, interpreted broadly, would have become larger, although the increase in the level of public spending would depend on how that role was exercised.[11]

In conclusion, major structural changes in the economy that took place over the past two centuries created new pressures on governments to widen their intervention or on society to develop new institutions to deal with them. Governments responded to these pressures through new legislation that at times required higher public spending. As the widespread suspicions about the bad role that the state had played in the past (when state powers had been used to favor the interests of the aristocrats) started receding, citizens became more willing to give greater powers to the government. They also started to demand better services. However, the response by governments was often delayed. As a consequence, the spending levels that had prevailed until the early part of the 20th century might be seen as too low even by individuals who would broadly share Adam Smith's views on the economic role of the state.[12] The question remains as to how much higher they needed to become.

### 3.3. Changes in Intellectual Winds

In addition to the *structural* changes in the economies that created government responsibilities not anticipated by Adam Smith, there were developments of a more *intellectual* or *political* nature that pushed governments toward more public spending. At the purely intellectual level, there were influential writers such as Adolf Wagner and, later, John Maynard Keynes, who advocated larger responsibilities for the government. As mentioned earlier, Wagner predicted, or advocated, that public spending would (or should) grow in line with economic development, because the more modern and advanced economies became, the more government services (and public spending) they would need.[13] Public spending was seen by Wagner as a kind of needed input for the expansion of the economy. Other German economists and social scientists endorsed Wagner's views. They saw the state as an organic entity and an expression of the community that exists almost independently from the individual citizens (and from the policy makers) living at a particular time. As the waters of a river, individual citizens come and go, but the community and the state (the river) remain. Acceptance of a difficult-to-change constitution or a monarchy implies such continuity to a large extent.

Wagner had advocated that the government should aim at redistributing income and wealth, from the better to do to those with lower incomes, a position partly endorsed by John Stuart Mill.[14] In this role, the state would intentionally collect more tax revenue from richer people and finance public services that would benefit those with *lower* incomes, and not necessarily the poor. This was a different role from the one that had been pursued by many communities and civil and religious institutions since the Middle Ages. These communities and institutions had allocated resources for the care of orphans, the handicapped, the very old without families, and the very poor – that is, for people who were not able to care for themselves and did not have family members to do so. The reason for this past redistribution was basic need and not lower income. Wagner's view set the stage for the "redistribution branch" in Musgrave's famous trilogy of the categories that justified governmental intervention: namely, allocation of resources, redistribution of income, and stabilization of the economy.[15] Because of his "radical" views, Wagner was attacked by perhaps the leading American public finance economist of the time, Edwin R. Seligman, the professor of public finance at Columbia University, for proposing what Seligman called pejoratively "fiscal policy."[16] This was reportedly the first use of this expression in the English language. With the Keynesian revolution, "fiscal policy" changed meaning and, for many economists, especially in the United States, it became a synonym of stabilization policy, rather than of redistribution policy (Eckstein, 1964, p. 101).

In a small, fascinating, and little-known book, based on two lectures delivered in 1924 at the University of Oxford and in 1926 at the University of Berlin – *The End of Laissez-Faire* (1926) – John Maynard Keynes called for an expanded intervention by the state in the economy. He specifically identified two areas in which the state needed to intervene. Interestingly, neither of them would necessarily require more public spending at a time when public spending in industrial countries had increased as a share of GDP but still averaged less than 20 percent of GDP. The greater government intervention was needed because, in Keynes's view, for various reasons some needs of citizens were not being satisfied by the private sector.

The first need for state intervention comes when "the ideal size for the unit of control and organization lies somewhere between the individual and the modern state"; Keynes suggested that "semi-autonomous bodies" within the state could be recognized and would be required to promote "solely the public good." He mentioned, as examples of such bodies, "the Universities, the Bank of England, the Port of London Authority, even perhaps the Railway Companies." However, he went on to state that when Joint Stock Institutions "have reached a certain age and size, to approximate to the status of public corporations... [they tend] to socialize themselves." This happens when "the owners of the capital, i.e., the shareholders, are almost dissociated from the management." Keynes specifically mentioned "a big railway, or big public utility enterprise, but also a big bank or a big insurance company." The recognition of the "semi-autonomous body" status would be particularly appropriate "if their great size or semi-monopolistic position renders them conspicuous in the public eye and vulnerable to public attack." He concluded that "semi-autonomous" corporations should be preferred to "organs of the Central Government for which Ministers of State are directly responsible" (pp. 41–45)

The second need is that of "separating services which are *technically social* from those which are *technically individual.*" "The important thing for Government," Keynes specifies, "is not to do things which individuals are doing already, and to do them a little better or a little worse; but to do things which at present are not done at all." Thus, he implied that some things were not being done. After recognizing that "particular individuals... are able to take advantage of uncertainty and ignorance" and that "big business is often a lottery" that generates "great inequality of wealth," "unemployment of labour," and "the impairment of efficiency and production," he concludes that "the cure lies outside the operations of individuals" who may even benefit from the disease. The cure must be sought "in the deliberate control of the currency and of credit by a central institutions" and "in the collection and dissemination on a great scale of data relating to the business situation, including the full publicity, by law if necessary, of all business facts which it is useful to know" (pp. 46–48). Thus, Keynes is assigning to the state the function of regulation of big business and the requirement of full disclosure on the part of the latter. These views seem highly topical in the aftermath of the 2008–9 economic crisis.

As to two other examples of this second need for state intervention, Keynes mentions the coordination on the part of the government of savings and investment decisions and the need for "a considered national policy about what size of Population . . . is most expedient for the country to have," paying attention not just to the size but also "to the innate quality" "of its future members" (p. 49).

In the middle of the Great Depression, Keynes wrote and published his seminal book – perhaps the third-most important book in economics ever written (together with Adam Smith's and Karl Marx's), in terms of its impact on policy – *The General Theory of Employment, Interest, and Money* (1936). That book created a completely new role for the government, the role of trying to stabilize the economy at a full-employment level. This new role for the state had not existed before, although the use of public works in times of crisis had occasionally been proposed and used. Although this new role did not have a *direct* impact on the level of public spending, it would have a large *indirect* impact.

In the years after the publication of *The General Theory*, an increasing number of economists came to believe that a higher level of public spending by itself would make an economy more recession proof. They embraced and advocated the new stabilization role proposed by Keynes, that the governments should compensate, with its fiscal action, for lack of private demand in the economy, a condition that many considered likely, because of a presumed natural tendency to underconsume or underinvest by individuals. Because it was always politically easier to increase spending or reduce taxes than to do the opposite, the Keynesian role inevitably promoted a policy asymmetry that would inevitably lead to higher public spending over the long run.[17] However, in spite of current perceptions, Keynes did not have a *direct* involvement in promoting large increases in spending. He may have been the least Keynesian among the Keynesians.

## 3.4. Impact of Political Developments

Government economic policies are, of course, not influenced only, or perhaps even mainly, by the thinking of economists but, more significantly, by political developments. Some of these developments were the challenges that came from new economic experiments or economic models being followed by Soviet Russia and to a lesser extent by the fascist regimes in Germany, Italy, and some other countries. Both socialist and, to a lesser extent, fascist ideologies created pressures for a larger role of the state in the economy. Socialists or communists ideologies pushed for an overwhelming economic role for the state in both the allocation of national resources and the distribution of national income. These experiments, and especially the one going on in Russia in the decades after the 1917 Bolshevik Revolution, attracted a large following among Western intellectuals, especially but not only in European countries. Various intellectuals saw virtues in that experiment but tended to ignore defects.[18] They in turn pressured the governments of democratic and market-oriented countries, including those of the United States, the United Kingdom, France, Canada, and Australia to increase public spending.

The governments of these countries were put on the defensive and often responded by creating new social programs or by expanding existing ones, giving rise to a "mixed economy," a concept that became particularly popular in the 1950s and 1960s. The Great Depression, an event that was seen by many as a massive failure of market economies, gave a further impetus to these policies. In the United States, the "New Deal," which included the introduction of "social security" for the whole working population and the regulation of the financial markets, aimed at correcting the presumed failures in the market economy and at increasing the role of the state in sustaining and redistributing incomes. The move toward "mixed economies" or even, in some countries, toward mature "welfare states" was set in motion. Over the next two generations, these changes would bring a dramatic expansion in public spending in many countries.

The economic role of the state in a market economy that had prevailed until the Great Depression would change dramatically between the 1920s, a decade that can be seen as representing the end of laissez-faire as pursued by countries, and the 1940s or 1950s, which can be seen as the beginning of an era of mixed economies and welfare states. Some would argue that the end of laissez-faire had come much earlier, perhaps as early as 1890. The change in public spending between the 1920s and the 1950s was gradual in most countries but less so in the United States, where the share of total public expenditure in GNP rose sharply from 9.9 in 1929 to 28.4 in 1958.[19] It would then accelerate in many countries over the next two decades but much less in the United States, where a conservative Republican administration would slow down that growth in the decade of the 1950s and resistance to tax increases made higher public spending more difficult in later years. This acceleration would require new policies and new legislation.

In 1959 Richard Musgrave systematized the new thinking in his influential book, *The Theory of Public Finance* (1959). It identified the three separate goals for governmental action mentioned earlier.[20] Once again, it is a bit puzzling that Musgrave did not include growth or development among the specific government goals, because the pursuit of growth is often claimed to justify many (often not very good) government policies. At about the same time that Musgrave was finishing his book, economists from Northern European countries were developing a "Theory of Fiscal Policy" that would guide the fast-increasing public spending, connected with the introduction of welfare states, then taking place in those countries. Both Musgrave and the Northern European economists were attempting to integrate the theory of economic policy with fiscal policy. However, while Musgrave's book was more related to the *goals* of governmental action, the "Theory of Fiscal Policy" was more focused on the *relationships* between *instruments* of policy and governmental *goals*, in the hope that econometric models, which were becoming popular at that time, would link both quantitatively and efficiently the policy instruments to the policy goals, whatever these were.

In *The Rise and Decline of the State*, Van Creveld wrote that "the [actual] move toward the welfare state started during the [second world] war" (1999, p. 354). According to him, Churchill and Roosevelt wanted to compensate the workers of their countries for the effort and sacrifices they had made during the war. In the "Atlantic Charter" of 1941 these policy makers referred to "freedom from want" as an objective to be promoted by their governments after the war. They believed that if only a part of the war production could be appropriated by the state and used to deal with poverty and unemployment, much could be achieved in securing "freedom from want."[21]

In 1942 the Beveridge Report, published in England, suggested a way to introduce major social reforms after the war. Van Creveld cites the prime minister of Australia, who declared during World War II that "government should be the agency whereby masses should be lifted up" (1999, p. 355). This surely was a long way from laissez-faire and reflected optimism about what governments could do and how well they could do it. Other writers, including Tony Atkinson, would see other and much earlier origins for the welfare state.

The expansion of the government role required two important steps: increasing taxes and creating specific programs that would use the additional revenue. The Beveridge Report provided a potential road map toward the latter. The programs would need additional public employees to administer them and would benefit particular groups. Thus, they would create growing constituencies that would have an interest in supporting the expanded role of the state (Peacock 1979, especially pp. 105–17). Van Creveld concludes that "after 1945 the confluence of... different modes of thought caused state intervention in the economy to explode" (1999, p. 357). The creation of new programs would require new thinking and, in democratic countries, new legislation. In spite of the growing popularity of state intervention, there was still strong opposition to it from traditional and conservative groups, which continued to influence policy.[22] Years would pass before the ideological change would result in significantly higher public spending and in higher levels of taxation in most countries. Different countries would respond at different speeds to the pressures for higher spending. The lowest speed, over the long run, would be that of the United States.

Only one of the three goals mentioned by Musgrave – allocation – can be considered an *essential* governmental function. No organized society can exist without this goal being satisfied to some extent by a government and without the institutions needed to satisfy that goal.[23] Thus, this function would set a *minimum* role of the state and a minimum level of public spending. The other two goals are new and to some extent optional. Countries, or political jurisdictions, have existed for thousands of years without these two goals being pursued by governments, or even being recognized as valid goals. As mentioned earlier, redistribution, where it was pursued in the past, was generally in the wrong direction, from the population at large toward those who controlled the government apparatus. However, in the past half century, views changed dramatically and one got the impression that each of the two new goals overwhelmed in importance everything else. Consequently, there may have been some crowding out of the allocation function, especially by the redistributive function. An argument can be made that governments, in recent years, have been doing less than they should in allocation and more than they should in stabilization and redistribution. In some countries, criminals are set free because of lack of jails. In others, infrastructures are in a deplorable state. In others, environmental problems have become extreme. In some others, judicial processes take much too long because there are not enough judges.

Under various claims, including that of reducing economic risks, income redistribution became a justification and the explanation for the large increase in public spending that took place in many countries after World War II. Much of the increase in public spending in the past half century can be connected in some ways with attempts at redistributing income across different groups, and not necessarily from the top to the bottom of income classes. To some extent, the objective progressively changed from redistributing income across income groups toward protecting (most or all) citizens against particular risks with economic consequences. This shift changed some government programs from selective to universal, making them very expensive. A larger level of public spending was also believed to contribute to economic stabilization, at a time when the Great Depression was still in many people's mind.[24] Countries with higher levels of public spending were thought to be less exposed to and thus more protected against recessions.

We shall have to wait to see whether the crisis of 2008–9 affected countries with high levels of public spending less than those with low levels.[25] Over the years, a lack of symmetry in stabilization policies has contributed to increasing the shares of public spending in gross domestic product. Increases in spending, enacted during slowdown or recessionary periods, were not neutralized by reductions in spending during periods of recovery. Thus, the pursuit of active stabilization policies contributed over the years to increases in the level of public spending. Once again, it will be interesting to observe whether the share of public spending in GDP, which was increased during the current crisis, will soon revert to the level that had existed in the years before the crisis.

## 3.5. Main Conclusions

Until the later part of the 19th century, it would not have been feasible to have had a larger economic role of the state, in terms of public spending, for several reasons: it would have been difficult to raise high tax levels, because those who could have paid the taxes (those with higher ability to pay) were the same individuals who controlled the government decisions; because of bad historical experiences, people resisted giving more power to the state, fearing the interference of the state in their lives; and even if the government could have accessed more revenue, it would not have had the capacity to administer this revenue because of the lack of expertise at a time when experts could not be imported from abroad as they did not exist and the quality of the bureaucracy was low.

The expansion in public spending came when people were given more power and became less concerned about giving more power to the government; changes in the economies created more taxable capacity; and government bureaucracies acquired more capacity to administer additional resources and monitor programs.

Multiple factors contributed to the change in the role of the state. Among these, particular importance must be assigned to the extension of the franchise and the progressive introduction of universal suffrage; the impact of the Industrial Revolution on individuals and families; structural changes caused by the Industrial Revolution on the economy, including urbanization; changing views on the role that the state should play on economic questions; the impact of major economists, especially Adam Smith, Karl Marx, and John Maynard Keynes; and the competition that came from the Russian experiment.

The growing intervention by the state crowded out alternative, spontaneous ways of coping with the forces unleashed by these factors. However, the state was not a passive policy instrument. It was often an active player that promoted the interests of those who controlled it or benefited from its policies.

## References

Angelopoulos, Angelos. 1950. "Les Principes Directeurs d'une Nouvelle Politique Financiere," in *Archivio Finanziario: Raccolta Internazionale di Scritti di Cultura Finanziaria*, vol. 1 (Padova: CEDAM), pp. 11–19.

Ashley, W. J. 1904. *The Progress of the German Working Classes in the Last Quarter of a Century* (London: Longmans, Green).

Atkinson A. B. 2004. "The Future of Social Protection in a Unifying Europe," revised version of the First Kela Lecture delivered in Helsinki (November 3).

De Cecco, Marcello, and Antonio Pedone. 1995. "Le istituzioni dell' economia," in *Storia dello Stato Italiano: dall' Unita' a Oggi*, edited by Raffaele Romanelli (Rome: Donzelli Editore), pp. 253–300.

de Jouvenel, Bertrand. 1952. *The Ethics of Redistribution* (Cambridge: Cambridge University Press).

Ebenstein, Alan. 2001. *Friedrick Hayek: A Biography* (London: Palgrave).

Eckstein, Otto. 1964. *Public Finance*, 2nd ed. (Englewood Cliffs, N.J.: Prentice-Hall).

Friedman, Milton. 1962. *Capitalism and Freedom* (Chicago: University of Chicago Press).

Galbraith, J. K. 1958. *The Affluent Society* (Boston: Houghton Mifflin).

Hegel, George W. F. 1956. *The Philosophy of History* (New York: Dover Publications).

Heller, Walter W. 1967. *New Dimensions of Political Economy* (New York: W. W. Norton).

Keynes, John Maynard. 1926. *The End of Laissez-Faire* (London: Hogarth Press).

    1936. *The General Theory of Employment, Interest, and Money* (San Diego: Harcourt Brace Jovanovich).

*Le Encicliche Sociali: Dalla "Rerum Novarum" alla Centesimus Annus.* 2003. (Milan: Paoline Editoriale Libri).

Marx, Karl. 1995. *Capital: A New Abridgement* (Oxford: Oxford University Press).

Mill, John Stuart. 1859. *On Liberty* (repr., Harmondsworth: Penguin Books, 1974).

    2004. *Principles of Political Economy* (Amberst, New York: Prometheus Books).

Musgrave, Richard. 1959. *The Theory of Public Finance* (New York: McGraw-Hill).

    1998. "The Role of the State in the Fiscal Theory," in *Public Finance in a Changing World*, edited by Peter Birch Sorensen (London: Macmillan), pp. 35–50.

Nitti, Francesco Saverio, 1971, *It Sociolismo Caltolico* (Bari Editori Laterza).

Peacock, Alan. 1979. *The Economic Analysis of Government and Related Themes* (Oxford: Robertson).

Ricossa, Sergio. 2006. *La Fine dell' Economia: Saggio sulla Perfezione* (1986; Catanzaro: Rubettino Editore).

Rizzi, Franco. 2003. *Banca di Credito Cooperativo di Carate Brianza, Un Secolo di Storia Caratese* (Carate Brianza: BCC Credito Cooperativo).

Rodrik, Dani. 1998. "Why Do More Open Economies Have Bigger Government?" *Journal of Political Economy* 106, no. 5 (October): 997–1032.

Seligman, Edwin. 1909. *Progressive Taxation in Theory and Practice. 2nd ed.* (Princeton: American Economic Association).

Smith, Adam. 1776. *The Wealth of Nations* (Harmondsworth: Penguin Books, 1999).

Stein, Herbert. 1984. *Presidential Economics: The Making of Economic Policy from Roosevelt to Reagan and Beyond* (New York: Simon and Schuster).

Thomis, Malcolm I. 1970. *The Luddites: Machine-Breaking in Regency England* (New York: Schocken).

Trevelyan, G. M. 1942. *English Social History* (London: Longmans, Green).

Van Creveld, Martin. 1999. *The Rise and Decline of the State* (Cambridge: Cambridge University Press).

Viner, Jacob. 1937. "Mr. Keynes on the Causes of Unemployment." *Quarterly Journal of Economics* 48, 1 (November) 39–76.

Wagner, Adolf. 1891. *Sviluppo della Scienza delle Finanze Collezione Diretta da Emanuele Morselli* (Padova: CEDAM, 1960). German editions, 1883 and 1890.

Wheen, Francis. 1999. *Karl Marx* (London: Fourth Estate).

Williamson, Jeffrey G. 1997. "Globalization and Inequality, Past and Present." *World Bank Research Observer* 12, no. 2 (August): 117–35.

Woodward, Llewellyn. 1962. *The Age of Reform, 1815–1870* (Oxford: Clarendon Press).

# FOUR

# Growth of Public Spending and Taxation in the 20th Century

## 4.1. From World War I to the 1960s

In the now rich countries of the Western world, the levels of taxation and of public spending generally increased after World War II, though until 1960 the increase was relatively slow.[1] During World War II, there had been large tax increases in several countries to finance the war. Except for the war years, the tax to GDP ratios remained below or around 30 percent of GDP in most industrial countries until the early 1960s. It increased sharply after 1960. The important exception in the tax increase was the United States. For several countries, 1960 can be considered the tipping point for the coming of mature "welfare states," or for "mixed economies."

There had been significant increases in the levels of taxation during World War I (to finance part of the huge spending for the war), followed by slow growth until World War II when, as had happened in the First World War, but in larger amounts, taxes were increased to finance the new war.[2] Tax levels for general governments were only 11 percent of GNP in 1925–29 in the United States; 20 percent in France in 1924–25; and less than 10 percent until 1930 and still below 20 percent up to 1950 in Sweden. They were about 25 percent of GNP in 1924–25 and around 30 percent of GNP in the early 1960s in the United Kingdom. In the United States, they were around 28 percent of GNP in the 1960s, a large increase from the levels in the 1920s. From the end of World War II until about 1960, there were relatively modest changes; tax levels remained low compared with the shares of GDP that they would reach in many other countries in later years. The fall in military spending after World War II accommodated some of the increase in civilian spending in some countries, including the United States.

In the United States, federal *outlays* that do not include those of state and local governments rose from 3.4 percent of GDP in 1930 to 10.7 percent of

GDP in 1934. This increase is much larger than is generally assumed to have taken place in recent writing about that period. For the rest of the decade of the 1930s, the outlays generally fell from the peak. In 1940 the share of federal outlays into GDP was 9.8 percent. After 1940 they increased rapidly to finance the war and reached a record of 43.6 percent of GDP in both 1943 and 1944. After the war they fell rapidly to 11.6 percent of GDP in 1948, not far from the 1934 level. After 1948 the share of federal outlays in GDP started rising again and reached a level of 20.4 percent of GDP in 1953, before the change to the Republican Eisenhower administration. There would not be any significant increase in federal outlays, above the 1953 level, until 2009, for which year the estimated outlay would jump to 28.1 percent of GDP, because of the economic crisis and the government response to it. Federal *receipt* (that excludes state and local government data) reached a maximum of 20.9 percent of GDP in the middle of World War II, in 1944. That percentage would be equaled only in the year 2000 before falling again, significantly, during the Bush years, after 2000. The 2009 estimate of 15.1 percent of GDP was lower than in any year since 1951 (see the U.S. Office of Management and Budget, 2009, table 1.2, pp. 24–25).

The reasons for the increases in tax levels, that started around 1960, in many countries were several:

1. Popular views about the desirable government role in the economy had changed, and economists were responding and contributing to this change with their writing and with new theoretical concepts that highlighted market failures and promoted the need for the state to correct for those failures through public spending.

2. By the second half of the century, in most countries, universal (or almost universal) suffrage had given voice to a large part of the populations, giving substance to De Viti de Marco's and other economists' worry that universal suffrage would lead the (poorer) majority of the populations to demand policies that would benefit them, presumably at the cost of those with higher incomes, rather than at the cost of their future incomes. At this time, few entertained the possibility that these policies might, in fact, not benefit the poor and the middle class because of their possible effects on the supply side of the economy. Supply side economics would appear only a couple decades later.

3. The impact of two world wars had allowed governments to raise tax rates during the wars. Thus, the administrative mechanism for doing so had been put in place, and many taxpayers had experienced the payment of higher taxes. After the wars, these mechanisms and tax

increases had been maintained in some countries, partly to service the large public debts acquired during the wars, partly to help the veterans of the wars and their families, and partly to introduce new programs.[3] (See especially Peacock and Wiseman, 1961, for the effect of wars on public spending.)

4. Changes in the structure of the economies were facilitating tax collection. Two of these changes were the growing shares of wages and salaries in national income that were especially important for income taxes and social security contributions; and the growing importance of large firms capable of withholding taxes at the source. There is also some evidence that until the 1960s the "administrative costs" of tax collection had declined because of the growing use of mass taxes collected at source. The methods of tax collection had shifted some of the collection cost to the taxpayer. A third change was significant technological or administrative breakthroughs in taxation, such as "global" income taxes, applied with highly progressive rates on the *total* taxable income of citizens; and, in the 1960s and later, the introduction of value-added taxes in several countries. It also helped that in this period the countries' economies were still relatively closed, so that tax competition that would characterize the later period of globalization was still not a problem. Countries could increase tax rates and tax revenue more easily than they would be able to do in later years when the economies became more open and capital and highly skilled labor became more mobile. (See Tanzi, 1995.)

In conclusion, the increase in tax levels can be explained by *demands* for higher public spending, coming from a part of the population that had acquired more political power, and by a higher *supply* of tax revenue due to technological and administrative developments in taxation and to structural changes in the economies.

## 4.2. From the 1960s to the 1990s

The decades of the 1960s to 1990s were the ones when major changes occurred in the public finances of many countries and when the activities of governments in the economy grew the most (see also OECD, 1985). In some sense, the pressures that had been building up since the 1930s started having political and practical effects. By the end of the century, tax revenue, as a percentage of GDP for European countries, rose by an average of about 15 percentage points (and much more for some of these countries).[4] See

Table 4.1. *Total tax revenue, 1960–2007 (percentages of GDP)*

| Country | 1960 | 1980 | Highest level reached (year in parentheses) | 2000 | 2008 |
|---|---|---|---|---|---|
| Canada | 23.8 | 31.0 | 36.7 (1998) | 35.6 | 32.3 |
| United States | 26.5 | 26.4 | 29.5 (2000) | 29.5 | 26.1 |
| Australia | 22.4 | 26.7 | 31.1 (2000) | 31.1 | 27.1 |
| Japan | 18.2[a] | 25.3 | 29.9 (1989) | 27.0 | 28.1 |
| New Zealand | 27.3 | 30.6 | 38.0 (1989) | 33.6 | 32.7 |
| Austria | 30.6 | 40.0 | 44.6 (2001) | 42.6 | 42.7 |
| Belgium | 26.5 | 41.3 | 45.2 (1998) | 44.9 | 44.2 |
| Denmark | 25.2 | 43.0 | 50.1 (1999) | 49.4 | 48.2 |
| Finland | 27.7 | 35.7 | 47.2 (2000) | 47.2 | 43.1 |
| France | 34.1[a] | 40.1 | 45.1 (1999) | 44.4 | 43.2 |
| Germany | 31.3 | 36.4 | 37.2 (1995) | 37.2 | 37.0 |
| Greece | 17.8[a] | 21.6 | 35.9 (1996) | 34.1 | 32.8 |
| Ireland | 20.5 | 31.0 | 36.8 (1988) | 31.7 | 28.8 |
| Italy | 24.4 | 29.7 | 43.2 (1997) | 42.3 | 43.3 |
| Luxembourg | 27.7[a] | 35.7 | 39.9 (1983) | 39.1 | 35.5 |
| Netherlands | 30.1 | 42.9 | 45.5 (1987) | 39.7 | 39.1 |
| Norway | 31.2 | 42.4 | 44.5 (1986) | 42.6 | 42.6 |
| Portugal | 16.1 | 22.9 | 36.6 (2007) | 34.1 | 35.2 |
| Spain | 14.1 | 22.6 | 37.2 (2007) | 34.2 | 33.3 |
| Sweden | 27.1 | 46.4 | 52.2 (1990) | 51.8 | 46.3 |
| Switzerland | 19.0 | 24.7 | 30.0 (2000) | 30.0 | 29.1 |
| United Kingdom | 28.5 | 35.1 | 39.0 (1982) | 37.1 | 35.7 |
| Average | 25.0 | 33.3 | 39.8 | 37.9 | 34.7 |

[a] 1965.

*Source:* Arranged from unpublished OECD data.

Table 4.1, for the changes in tax levels, and Table 1.1, for the changes in public spending. The additional revenue came from a variety of sources. In the first two decades after World War II, the main contributor was the (personal) income tax. This tax was an ideal instrument for the time and came to be seen by many policy makers and tax experts as a "dream tax." For example, during World War II, 90 percent of American taxpayers considered the income tax as a "fair tax," according to survey data published by the American Enterprise Institute (2005). The marginal tax rates for income taxes became very high and generally stayed high for several decades after World War II, until globalization and tax competition forced them down.

Until the 1970s several countries (including the United States and the United Kingdom) had marginal tax rates for the income tax that at times exceeded 90 percent. These high rates even inspired a Beatles' song, *The Taxman*. Its lyrics went, "I shall tell you how it will be, one for you, nineteen for me, 'cause I am the taxman." The song was composed in 1966 when the top marginal tax rate in the United Kingdom was 96 percent! In the United States the marginal tax rate had been lowered, from 91 percent in 1963 to 70 percent for the 1965–66 period, by the Kennedy administration, partly to stimulate the slow-growing economy as an early application of Keynesian thinking that by that time had become very popular.[5] These rates do not include the taxes imposed by many local governments (states and counties) in the United States. In the United States the 70 percent rate for the federal income tax remained in effect until Reagan's presidency, when it was sharply reduced first to 50 percent and then again to 28 percent for a few years by the 1986 tax reform. It was raised again in the early 1990s but was still a long distance from the previous level.

The personal income tax, applied with its highly progressive rates, was seen by economists and policy makers to have many virtues. Because it was "income elastic," it automatically provided a growing share of revenue over the years when nominal income increased, either because of real growth or because of inflation (Tanzi, 1980). This gave governments the politically attractive option of claiming to reduce taxes, when they did not need the revenue increases. It could be argued that tax payments were based on the "ability to pay" of taxpayers, because the tax rates were progressive. At least in its legal version, the tax could be made as progressive as policy makers desired, to reflect their concern for equity. It was an ideal instrument for social engineering, particularly important in a world that was seen to be full of "merit goods," that is, of goods the consumption of which deserved to be subsidized by the government through the tax system: one of these goods was housing, which, in the United States, was favored with a particularly generous tax expenditure (the deductibility, from taxable income, of nominal interest paid on mortgage).[6] This "tax expenditure" became an important subsidy to housing, especially in the 1970s, when inflation became relatively high, thus affecting nominal interest rates while the deduction of interest payments from the taxable income was unlimited. At a time when there was still worry about underconsumption, and when the higher income classes were assumed to save too much, the personal income tax was believed to help maintain aggregate demand by reducing aggregate private savings while the government spent the revenue collected. It could be fitted (or tailor-made) for the specific circumstances of individuals or families, thus facilitating financial engineering and social policy. Finally, the personal exemption could be made high enough to leave out of the tax net individuals and families with low taxable incomes.

With the manipulation of income taxes, tax administrations could be made to administer social policies indirectly through "tax expenditures," which complemented, and at times replaced, explicit public expenditures. It was an option that the United States' political system would prefer. It is a well-known fact that tax expenditures can substitute for direct public spending (see, e.g., Van den Ende, Haberham, and den Boogert, 2004). At least 10 OECD countries, including 6 of the G-7 countries, now publish "tax expenditure budgets" that estimate the revenue losses to the governments (and the benefit to taxpayers) caused by these tax expenditures. These revenue losses, or tax expenditures, subsidize some favored categories of private spending and play a role similar to that which could be played by public spending. Thus, tax administrations became similar, in some of their functions, to social ministries.

In the decades after World War II, the personal income tax was seen to have two other virtues considered important: it had countercyclical power, at a time when business cycles were a major preoccupation of policy makers; and it was considered an efficient tax because at that time most economists dismissed its potential negative effects on work effort and incentives.[7] Few academic articles dealt quantitatively with these potential disincentives before the decade of the 1980s, when new econometric studies started to raise concerns about the potential disincentives (see Tanzi, 1988). Furthermore, though it may now seem strange, books on income taxation, written in those years, did not even mention "tax evasion" or "the underground or shadow economy" as potential problems associated with income taxes – for example, Musgrave (1959), Pechman (1971), and Goode (1964).

By the 1960s there was strong political and intellectual pressure on most governments to increase public spending significantly and to find new revenue sources to finance it (Tanzi, 2004b). The political climate had been changed by the increasing popularity of the "Keynesian revolution" and by calls advocating a mixed economy. Economists and politicians became convinced that governments could improve people's lives through public programs and higher public spending. Public spending became popular and politically attractive to politicians, who could win elections by proposing new government programs.[8] By 1965, tax revenue as a share of GDP had grown to 26 percent for the whole group of OECD countries. Several European countries – France, Germany, the United Kingdom, Austria, Belgium, Finland, the Netherlands, and Sweden – by this time had tax levels that exceeded 30 percent of GDP. In 1965 the highest tax burden was found in Sweden (35 percent of GDP), followed by France (34.1 percent), Austria (33.9 percent), and the Netherlands (32.8 percent). In Sweden, between 1950 and 1965, the share of taxes into GDP had risen by more than 15 percentage points. It would increase by at least another 15 percent of GDP in the following two decades, thereby completely changing the fiscal and social landscape of Sweden within a little more than a generation. Similar increases took place in Finland and Denmark. (See Chapter 12, below, for more details.) These three countries, with Norway and Iceland, formed the nucleus of the type of mature welfare states associated with Nordic countries.

In several European countries, the period between 1960 and the middle 1990s witnessed the fastest increase in public spending and in tax levels of their history and, in several countries, the establishment of mature and universal welfare states. In spite of the very fast increase in tax levels, the growth in spending often exceeded the growth in taxes, thus leading to fiscal deficits and to increases in public debts that caused macroeconomic difficulties in later years in some of the countries. For example, for the 12 original countries of the European Monetary Union, the share of public debt in GDP rose from 31 percent in 1977 to 75.4 percent in 1996 (Tanzi, 2004a). However, at that time Keynesian economics had reduced the fear that fiscal deficits had induced in earlier periods. The Ciceronian world had been replaced by the Keynesian world.

In the period after 1965, the increase in tax revenue came from three main sources:

1. Between 1965 and 1985, the introduction of value-added taxes in many European countries contributed about 4 percent of GDP in *additional* revenue. The VAT replaced existing turnover taxes in these countries, so that its *total* revenue was greater than the *additional* revenue that it contributed. The United States did not introduce a VAT. Because of this, it could not finance much higher public spending levels.[9] Perhaps, this, more than any other factor, explains the lack of growth of total taxation in the United States between 1960 and 2007 (Table 4.1). Of all the countries in the table, the United States is the only one in which the share of total taxes into GDP increased the least over almost a half century. Between 1960 and 2008 its share of total government receipts into GDP increased from 25.2 percent to 28.1 percent. Furthermore, all the increase was at the state and local government level.[10] In 2007 the United States shared with Japan and Switzerland the lowest levels of taxation among OECD countries shown in the table.

2. The growth in social security "contributions" would generate, on average, about 6 percent of GDP in additional revenue in that period. The growth of these taxes came from the higher tax rates on the share of wages subject to tax, and, to a lesser extent, from the rise in the shares of wages and salaries in national income taking place at that time in several countries. In this period, these revenues often exceeded the payments that pension systems had to make because of the high number of workers and the low number of retirees. Therefore, these systems accumulated assets and helped finance other public spending. As often happened with other spending programs, pension systems also became progressively more generous over the years.[11] Demographic developments have been changing this feature, setting the stage for large problems in pension systems in future years in many countries, when the ratio of retirees to employed workers will rise significantly and the share of wages in national income will fall.[12]

3. An impact on income tax revenue came automatically from increases in *real* incomes and in *prices*. The increases in nominal incomes pushed taxpayers into higher marginal tax rates, thus automatically raising revenue (Tanzi, 1980). This automatic increase in tax revenue was called a "fiscal drag" because it was supposed to slow down (to be a drag on) the economy, unless the extra revenue was spent. If it was spent, it contributed to aggregate demand, according to Haavelmo's "balanced budget multiplier." The "fiscal drag" became important especially during the inflationary years of the 1960s and 1970s when it provided several governments with substantial additional revenue without the need to change legislation. This revenue was generally spent rather than returned to the taxpayers. Income taxes (on both individuals and enterprises) contributed about 5 percent of GDP in *additional* revenues in 1965–85. The "fiscal drag" would in time attract attention and would generate demands for the indexation of tax brackets *for inflation* to remove its effect on revenue. Some countries introduced indexation of income brackets for inflation[13] (Tanzi, 1980). However, there was no indexation for the effect on revenue from real growth or from distortions of capital income bases (e.g., interest rates, capital gains, profits) for inflation.

On average, these three tax sources raised the share of taxes into GDP, for the European countries, by about 15 percentage points over the 1965–85 period. This additional revenue helped finance the fast-rising social spending taking place. As mentioned, in the United States there was no value-added tax, and the increase in social security taxes was much more contained.[14] The United States was spending more on defense than the European countries. As a consequence, social spending increased much less than in the European countries, in spite of President Johnson's "War on Poverty." After the breakup of the Soviet Union, in the early 1990s, the fall in defense spending in the United States (the "peace dividend") accommodated rising social spending without major tax increases and with relatively little increase in *total* public spending.[15]

By the end of the century, two countries, Sweden and Denmark, had tax burdens that exceeded 50 percent of GDP (Table 4.1). According to OECD data, Sweden's reached a record of 52.2 percent of GDP in 1990. These were probably the highest tax burdens ever recorded in the history of the world.[16] Six other countries had tax burdens that exceeded 45 percent of GDP, compared with 30 percent in the United States. The U.S. level would even fall during the George W. Bush administration, as a consequence of tax cuts.[17]

An interesting feature that has not attracted much attention is that there was much less growth in government *real* expenditure – that is, in the public expenditure associated more (though not exclusively) with the direct *allocation* role of the government. These expenditures (for public employees and for the purchase of goods and services including defense and the building of infrastructure) absorb real resources directly and are thus distinguished from cash transfers to individuals and enterprises. In some countries, and especially in Nordic European countries, significant income redistribution or universal protection against some risks is pursued through the direct provision of public services, provided mostly free, or at highly subsidized prices, to relevant categories of citizens. In these countries, *real* public expenditure (or final consumption expenditure) rose more than in other countries. This particular type of spending grew, on average, by about 6 percent of GDP in a century for the countries for which information is available. Compare Table 1.1 with Table 4.2.

Table 4.2 provides data on final consumption expenditure for general government for 18 selected countries. The data are shown as percentages of GDP. The table shows that this expenditure remained on average around 20 percent of GDP over the 1995–2008 period. However, there was considerable difference across countries. In 1995 the five countries with the lowest ratios were Japan, the United States, Luxembourg, Greece, and Ireland. They had an average expenditure of 15.7 percent of GDP. The five countries with the highest ratios were Sweden, Denmark, the Netherlands, France, and Finland, with an average expenditure of 24.4 percent of GDP. Thus, the difference

Table 4.2. *Final consumption expenditure of general government in selected countries (percentages of GDP)*

| Country | 1995 | 2000 | 2005 | 2008 |
|---|---|---|---|---|
| Belgium | 21.4 | 21.3 | 22.7 | 23.2 |
| Spain | 18.1 | 17.2 | 18.0 | 19.4 |
| Germany | 19.6 | 19.0 | 18.7 | 18.1 |
| Italy | 18.0 | 18.4 | 20.3 | 20.2 |
| France | 23.7 | 22.9 | 23.7 | 23.2 |
| Portugal | 17.6 | 19.3 | 21.4 | 20.8 |
| Netherlands | 23.8 | 22.0 | 23.7 | 25.5 |
| Austria | 20.4 | 19.1 | 18.5 | 18.8 |
| Ireland | 16.3 | 13.6 | 15.1 | 17.7 |
| Finland | 22.8 | 20.3 | 22.3 | 22.3 |
| Luxembourg | 15.9 | 15.1 | 16.5 | 15.2 |
| Greece | 16.0 | 17.8 | 17.0 | 16.9 |
| Denmark | 25.2 | 25.1 | 26.0 | 26.7 |
| Sweden | 26.6 | 26.0 | 26.4 | 26.4 |
| Great Britain | 19.3 | 18.5 | 21.3 | 21.6 |
| United States | 15.4 | 14.3 | 15.7 | 16.7 |
| Japan | 14.7 | 16.9 | 18.1 | 18.5 |
| Canada | 21.3 | 18.6 | 18.9 | 19.6 |
| Australia | n.a. | n.a | n.a | n.a |
| Average | 19.8 | 19.2 | 20.3 | 20.6 |

*Source:* European Commission (AMECO). Unpublished data based on Eurostat definitions introduced in year 1995.

between the two groups was 8.7 percent of GDP. The latter countries are generally considered welfare states. In 2008 the five countries with the lowest percentages were Luxembourg, the United States, Greece, Germany, and Ireland, with an average of 16.9 percent of GDP. Japan had been replaced by Germany. The group with the highest percentages was made up of Denmark, Sweden, the Netherlands, Belgium, and France. Finland had been replaced by Belgium. The average for the group was 25 percent of GDP. The difference between the two groups had been reduced marginally, from 8.7 in 1995 to 8.1 percent of GDP.

Table 4.3 provides information on *cash* transfers for the same countries as in Table 4.2. The table excludes transfers in kind. Cash transfers averaged around 15 percent of GDP, but once again there were significant differences among countries. In 1995 the five countries with the highest cash transfers were Finland, Sweden, Austria, Denmark, and France with an average of 19.8 percent of GDP. The five countries with the lowest shares were Japan, Portugal, Ireland, the United States, and Canada, with an average of 11.1

Table 4.3. *General government cash transfers in selected countries (percentages of GDP)*

| Country | 1995 | 2000 | 2005 | 2008 |
|---|---|---|---|---|
| Belgium | 16.3 | 15.2 | 15.8 | 15.9 |
| Spain | 13.6 | 12.0 | 11.6 | 12.4 |
| Germany | 17.6 | 18.4 | 19.2 | 16.9 |
| Italy | 16.3 | 16.4 | 17.0 | 17.7 |
| France | 17.9 | 17.1 | 17.7 | 17.5 |
| Portugal | 11.2 | 11.7 | 14.9 | 15.6 |
| Netherlands | 15.2 | 11.3 | 10.9 | 10.4 |
| Austria | 19.7 | 18.9 | 18.8 | 18.1 |
| Ireland | 11.7 | 7.8 | 9.5 | 12.3 |
| Finland | 21.9 | 16.2 | 16.6 | 15.4 |
| Luxembourg | 14.3 | 13.1 | 14.4 | 13.4 |
| Greece | 13.5 | 14.8 | 16.3 | 19.1 |
| Denmark | 19.5 | 16.2 | 16.3 | 14.9 |
| Sweden | 20.1 | 17.1 | 17.0 | 15.1 |
| Great Britain | 15.0 | 12.6 | 12.9 | 13.1 |
| United States | 11.8 | 10.6 | 11.9 | 12.9 |
| Japan | 8.4 | 10.1 | 11.3 | 12.1 |
| Canada | 12.2 | 10.3 | 9.9 | 9.9[a] |
| Australia | n.a. | n.a | n.a | n.a. |
| Average | 15.3 | 13.9 | 14.6 | 14.6 |

[a] 2007.

*Source:* European Commission (AMECO) unpublished data.

percent of GDP. The difference between the two groups was 8.7 percent of GDP. Broadly the same countries appear in the two groups as in Table 4.2. In 2008 the first, high-spending group comprised Greece, Austria, Italy, France, and Germany with an average of 17.9 percent of GDP. The low-spending group was made up of Canada, the Netherlands, Japan, Ireland, and Spain with an average of 11.4 percent of GDP. The difference between the two groups was reduced to 6.5 percent of GDP. This table shows some major changes over the period. Portugal, Greece, and Japan sharply increased their cash transfers, while the Netherlands, Finland, Denmark, Sweden, and Canada significantly reduced their cash transfers.[18] It should be noted that the first group includes countries that are now facing major fiscal difficulties, while the second group includes countries with much better fiscal accounts.

From the early part until the end of the 20th century, defense spending fell as a share of GDP, while public investment changed little. Therefore,

Table 4.4. *Total general government spending, 1995–2009 (percentage of GDP)*

| Country | 1995 | 2000 | 2005 | 2008 | 2009 |
|---|---|---|---|---|---|
| Australia | 36.7 | 34.4 | 36.2 | 34.1 | n.a. |
| Austria | 56.2 | 51.4 | 50.0 | 48.9 | 52.3 |
| Belgium | 52.3 | 49.1 | 52.1 | 50.0 | 53.6 |
| Canada | 47.3 | 39.9 | 38.0 | 39.6 | 43.8 |
| Denmark | 59.3 | 53.5 | 52.6 | 51.9 | 55.9 |
| Finland | 61.5 | 48.3 | 50.1 | 48.9 | 54.3 |
| France | 54.4 | 51.6 | 53.3 | 52.7 | 55.2 |
| Germany | 48.3 | 74.6 | 46.8 | 43.7 | 47.9 |
| Greece | 45.7 | 46.6 | 43.7 | 48.3 | 50.0 |
| Iceland | 53.4 | 36.4 | 45.7 | 43.2 | n.a. |
| Ireland | 41.2 | 45.6 | 33.7 | 42.0 | 46.9 |
| Italy | 52.5 | 47.3 | 48.1 | 48.8 | 51.6 |
| Japan | 36.7[a] | 39.0 | 38.4 | 37.2 | 40.5 |
| Korea | 20.8 | 29.3 | 31.6 | 28.7 | n.a. |
| Luxembourg | 39.7 | 37.6 | 41.5 | 37.7 | 43.3 |
| Netherlands | 51.5 | 44.8 | 44.8 | 45.9 | 49.5 |
| New Zealand | 41.9 | 41.3 | 40.8 | 39.7 | n.a. |
| Norway | 51.5 | 58.2 | 55.6 | 39.9 | n.a. |
| Portugal | 43.4 | 43.4 | 47.7 | 45.9 | 51.6 |
| Spain | 44.4 | 39.2 | 38.4 | 41.1 | 45.2 |
| Sweden | 65.2 | 55.6 | 55.0 | 53.1 | 55.9 |
| Switzerland | 34.6 | 36.3 | 35.0 | 33.7 | n.a. |
| United Kingdom | 43.9 | 39.1 | 44.1 | 47.3 | 51.2 |
| United States | 37.1 | 3.9 | 36.3 | 38.8 | 42.2 |
| Average | 46.6 | 43.8 | 44.1 | 43.4 | n.a. |

[a]1996.

*Source:* National Accounts of OECD Countries, OECD Paris, 2008; and European Commission, unpublished data.

*the largest growth came in expenditure on subsidies and transfers,* which were mainly, though not exclusively, made *in cash,* as shown in Table 4.3 for the more recent period. This expenditure increased from about 1 percent of GDP, in the early part of the 20th century, to about 25 percent of GDP, by the end of the century. This was an extraordinary increase. Perhaps better than any other indicator, it reflects the change in the economic role of the state during the 20th century. In 2008, the latest year for which *final* data are available, total general government expenditure as a share of GDP for OECD countries ranged from a minimum of 28.7 percent in Korea (and 34.1 percent in Australia) to a maximum of 53.1 percent in Sweden, 52.7 percent in France, and 51.9 percent in Denmark. These figures would rise

Table 4.5. *Change in total tax revenue, 1960 to 2007 (percentages of GDP)*

| Country | Differences | |
| --- | --- | --- |
| | 2008–1960 | Reductions from highest level to 2008 |
| Canada | 8.5 | 4.4 |
| United States | − 0.4 | 3.4 |
| Australia | 4.7 | 4.0 |
| Japan | 9.8 | 1.8 |
| New Zealand | 6.4 | 4.3 |
| Austria | 12.1 | 1.9 |
| Belgium | 17.7 | 1.0 |
| Denmark | 23.0 | 1.9 |
| Finland | 15.4 | 4.1 |
| France | 9.1 | 1.9 |
| Germany | 5.7 | 0.2 |
| Greece | 15.0[a] | 3.1 |
| Ireland | 8.3 | 8.0 |
| Italy | 18.9 | +0.1 |
| Luxembourg | 7.8[a] | 4.4 |
| Netherlands | 9.0 | 6.4 |
| Norway | 11.2 | 1.9 |
| Portugal | 19.1 | 1.4 |
| Spain | 19.2 | 3.9 |
| Sweden | 19.2 | 5.9 |
| Switzerland | 10.1 | 0.9 |
| United Kingdom | 7.2 | 3.3 |
| Average | 11.7 | 3.1 |

[a] 1965–2008.

*Source:* Arranged by author from OECD data.

significantly in many countries in 2009 because of the economic crisis that reduced GDP and led governments to sharply increase spending (Table 4.4). It should be noted that between 1995 and 2008 there were significant reductions in the average level of government spending, especially in Austria, Canada, Denmark, Finland, Germany, the Netherlands, Norway, and Sweden. Thus, all the big spenders from the North of Europe reduced their level of public spending. All these countries faced the 2008–9 financial crisis without major financing difficulties.

Table 4.5 provides a quick view of the growth of tax levels in OECD countries between 1960 and 2008. The leaders in this growth were two countries that created the most mature form of welfare state (Denmark and Sweden) and two countries that started the period with exceptionally low levels of taxation and that have been catching up at a very fast pace (Spain and Portugal). The table shows also the extent to which the United States has been an outlier. Surprisingly, after the United States and Australia, Germany is the other country in which the level of taxation grew the least over the almost half century.

Table 4.5 shows also that practically all the countries reached the highest level of taxation some time *before* 2008. During the first decade of the 21st century, and until the crisis, many tried to reduce the tax burden from the highest level reached. The largest reductions were in Ireland, the Netherlands, Sweden, Canada, Luxemberg, New Zealand and Finland, with reductions of between 8 to 4 percent of GDP. In a later chapter, we discuss the consequences of these reductions that were, in some countries, accompanied by even larger reductions in the level of public spending.

## References

American Enterprise Institute. 2005. *Taxpayers Surveys* (Washington, D.C.).

Franco, Daniele. 1993. *L'Espansione della Spesa Pubblica in Italia* (Bologna: Il Mulino).

Goode, Richard. 1964. *The Individual Income Tax* (Washington, D.C.: Brookings Institution).

Heller, Walter W. 1966. *New Dimensions of Political Economy* (New York: W. W. Norton).

Musgrave, Richard. 1959. *The Theory of Public Finance* (New York: McGraw-Hill).

OECD. 1985. *Social Expenditure, 1960–1990: Problems of Growth and Control* (Paris: OECD).

Peacock, Alan, and Jack Wiseman. 1961. *The Growth of Public Expenditure in the United Kingdom* (Princeton: Princeton University Press).

Pechman, Joseph A. 1971. *Federal Tax Policy* (New York: W. W. Norton).

Samuelson, Paul. 1947. *Foundations of Economic Analysis* (Cambridge, Mass.: Harvard University Press).

Stein, Herbert. 1984. *Presidential Economics: The Making of Economic Policy from Roosevelt to Regan and Beyond* (New York: Simon and Schuster).

Tanzi, Vito. 1980. *Inflation and the Personal Income Tax* (Cambridge: Cambridge University Press).

1988. "Trends in Tax Policy as Revealed by Recent Developments and Research." *International Bureau of Fiscal Documentation Bulletin* 42, no. 3 (March) 97–103.

1995. *Taxation in an Integrating World* (Washington, D.C.: Brookings Institution).

2004a. "The Stability and Growth Pact: Its Role and Future." *Cato Journal* 24, no. 1–2: 57–69.

2004b. *A Lower Tax Future? The Economic Role of the State in the 21st Century* (London: Politeia).

2010. *The Charm of Latin America: Economic and Cultural Impressions* (Bloomington: iUniverse).

Tanzi, Vito, and Ludger Schuknecht. 2000. *Public Spending in the 20th Century* (Cambridge: Cambridge University Press).

Toder, Eric. 2000. "Tax Cuts or Spending: Does It Make a Difference?" *National Tax Journal* 53, part 1(September): 361–71.

U. S. Office of Management and Budget. 2009. *Historical Tables*, Budget of the U.S. Government, Fiscal Year 2010 (Washington, D.C.: GPO).

Van den Ende, Leo, Amir Haberham, and Kees den Boogert. 2004. "Tax Expenditure in the Netherlands," in *Tax Expenditure-Shedding Light on Government Spending through the Tax System*, edited by Hana Polackova Brixi, Christian M. A. Valenduc, and Zhicheng Li Swift (Washington, D.C.: World Bank), pp. 131–54.

# FIVE

# The Role of the State in Social Protection

## Historical Landmarks

### 5.1. Introduction

In previous chapters we discussed the growth of public spending and of taxes that took place over the past century, in the so-called advanced countries. We also outlined some of the factors that contributed to that growth. The public spending and the taxes that financed the new social activities started to be justified not on grounds of assisting the very poor, as in the past, but on grounds that the social spending provided protection to increasing shares and growing categories of the population against risks that had economic consequences for the citizens. The governments' programs, financed by the public spending, were generally assumed to make it easier for citizens to cope with the economic risks of modern living. It was thus argued that they increased the welfare of the citizens.

This risk-focused justification was different from the one used in the past to support assistance to the very poor, as for example with various programs of assistance in France, Italy, and other European countries, or with the English Poor Law of 1601. In Islamic countries the "Zakat," one of the five Pillars of Islam, had been for a long time a "social tax" that provided resources to assist the elderly, the widows, the orphans, and the disabled, all individuals that could not take care of themselves, in those countries (Crone, 2005).

The new social programs that started to be introduced were not guided by compassion, or by the assumption that extreme poverty generated negative externalities as earlier, but by the new and radical belief that citizens are *entitled* to some social assistance from the state. Thus, the principle of obligation by society vis-à-vis some of its members who might not qualify as very poor or deserving poor came into center stage. Particular categories of citizens were identified for assistance. As time passed, the public spending was progressively directed toward larger shares of the population, and in some cases it came to cover the whole population, or at least the whole population of workers. Thus, conceptually, it was fundamentally different from the earlier, limited safety nets. In many cases, the formal protection provided by the modern public programs had a pro-worker rather than pro-poor bias. It was specifically focused on workers and their families and was promoted by labor unions, at a time when labor unions had acquired strong political powers. Workers had found it easier to organize and acquire "voice" in ways that the poor had not.

Protection against risks with economic consequences cannot and does not necessarily come only from government programs. It could come from spontaneous actions of individuals, especially when they act rationally, have a sense of community, and live in a free society with a relatively well-working market economy; or in one in which the extended family or other social but nongovernmental networks are free and willing to operate. These spontaneous actions are more likely to take place when the government encourages them and/or provides some logistic assistance. However, when the government intervened, it was often to restrain these private actions and to compete with the private programs. In previous chapters, it was mentioned that the protection that became available from government programs during the past century was not always *a net addition* to the existing private protection. It would be a mistake to assume that the government always stepped in to fill a clear or complete vacuum. In reality, in many cases it replaced, with formal government programs, the informal network of assistance that had existed before its intervention and that had been provided by various private and religious sources.

Before governments started to intervene on a large scale, individuals and members of their immediate families had received assistance when in need and to varying degrees, from various sources.

1. Members of their extended families assisted those in need. We tend to forget that the size and concept of family has tended to shrink with economic development. There is a negative relation between size of family, as perceived by its members, and the level of economic development. The higher level of the latter has reduced the number of those who can help, or are expected to help, family members in need. There has been a big change in social norms in this area.[1] In some countries of Asia, there are still legal obligations on family members to assist other members in need.

2. Friends, neighbors, and other members of the community where the individuals lived volunteered assistance. Because mobility was limited

in earlier times, especially in rural communities, individuals tended to have more social relations and more "social capital." They were more disposed to help one another.

3. Churches and other religious affiliations were active in social work and in providing assistance to the poor, especially in some countries. Before the Reformation in the 16th century, the Catholic Church had been active in all the European countries. The astonishing number of monasteries, convents, and parishes that had existed indicates the important role that religion and religious orders had played in these charitable and educational activities. As one writer put it, "In the course of the centuries an immense number of foundations had been made for religious, charitable, and educational [activities], and had been provided with rich material resources. Churches, monasteries, hospitals, and schools had often great incomes and extensive possessions" (Kirsch, 1911, 39). Until the 16th century, the church had had available more than half of all the land of the then Catholic countries of Europe. Parishes and monastic orders had played a major role in this social work all over Europe. This kind of assistance was often provided when the need for assistance became apparent and not, ex ante, in anticipation of future needs.[2] The church lost many of these possessions either after the Reformation, when they were confiscated by the Protestant governments, or, later, after anticlerical governments came into power in non-Reformation countries, such as France and Italy, in the 18th and the 19th centuries. It is an open question whether the governments were more capable in using these assets as efficiently as the church had done for the objective of assisting the poor. In any case, the appropriation by the states of these church properties also transferred to the state and to other organizations the need and the responsibility to take over some of these pro-poor activities and the need to create alternative systems of assistance, as happened in England with the Poor Laws of 1601.

4. In the 19th century, that need was partly filled by an increasing number of confraternities, cooperatives, mutual assistance societies, credit unions, and the provision of informal credit provided by those in the communities that supplied goods and services. In a society where individuals knew one another and where there was trust, such credit was common. However, usury became a problem at times.

In spite of obvious shortcomings, this kind of social protection had played a significant function in several countries. Community organizations especially became important during the second half of the 19th century. In evaluating the effectiveness of this informal social protection, it is necessary to repeat that at that time the countries were still very poor and their per capita income was very low by today's standards. Average incomes were lower than they are in China today.[3] Therefore, if government programs had existed, the quality of the services offered would have been very basic, as it still is today in developing countries.

The Industrial Revolution contributed to the changes in some of the existing social arrangements. Furthermore, the intellectual winds that had been set in motion by the Enlightenment and by the French Revolution started to promote the notion that different arrangements, based on basic "human rights" of individuals against society, rather than compassion toward the poor, might be desirable and possible. Socialism, which wanted to promote equality of *outcomes* and not just of *opportunities*, became popular with many workers who had become progressively better organized and more vocal. The success of this movement might have endangered the concept of property rights, which was particularly dear to economists and of course to those who owned the properties. Existing informal "safety nets," often based on the compassion and the charity of others rather than on the rights of the individuals themselves began to look inadequate. The antireligious bias of the French Revolution had created animosity against religiously based social assistance, at least in some countries on the European continent. Greater mobility reduced trust and community spirit and created difficulties with community- or family-based social assistance, which tended to be local. Pressures were created on both private enterprises and governments to begin to play larger roles. Both were pushed to create more formal arrangements, based on individual rights and not on the charity of institutions, to replace the informal ones that had existed. In some countries, it was the enterprises that responded more quickly, thus eventually helping to create an enterprise-supported or "hidden welfare state" (Howard, 1997). In others, it was the state that entered the field of social protection in a massive way.

Two different kinds of welfare states would eventually come into existence. One would be more prevalent in Europe. The other would be more prevalent in the United States and in some Anglo-Saxon countries. The European version would itself have several models. In the middle of the 19th century, after the riots of 1848, the intellectual debate, a debate that would go on for decades, on whether poverty could be better fought through state intervention or by relying on laissez-faire policies became intense. It has continued to our present days.

On January 26, 1850, Louis Adolphe Thiers, the slightly center left, republican French historian and major political figure in 19th-century

France – he was several times minister and in 1870 became president of France – speaking to the French Legislative Assembly, presented in the name of a Committee for Public Assistance some conclusions on how to deal with economic and poverty problems. The conclusions are worth reporting: the state should have ready, at any one time, a portfolio of worthwhile public work projects to be executed during periods of crisis; it should facilitate emigration; it should improve hygienic conditions in areas where workers lived; and it should promote the creation of mutual assistance societies (Prins, 1888). These recommendations reflected the prevailing views of the time, at least in France.

After the widespread turmoil of 1848 in France and in Europe, the debate on whether poverty could be fought with state intervention or with "laissez-faire" became sharper. Many economists continued to be concerned that state intervention would sap the energy of the workers and would reduce their propensity to save, while creating exaggerated expectations of what the state could do for them. With the passing of time, the governments of some countries would start to create universal and publicly financed programs of social assistance. In others, the intervention of the state would remain more limited. In this and later chapters, we discuss different organizational models that were followed in later years by different groups of countries. We shall focus more specifically on the welfare states created by the Nordic countries of Europe that are seen as the most ambitious intervention by governments in the social area. These are complex issues. The alternative models of assistance followed by countries have too many details to be described adequately in a book such as this one. Therefore, the aim here is to provide broad rather than detailed pictures.

Before moving to the description of the main historical legislations on social protection, it may be useful to outline, in the most schematic fashion possible, the options that were available to the countries when the governments started to intervene.

The first option could have been to build on and encourage the informal network of safety nets that already existed in many countries, as recommended by Minister Thiers to the French Legislative Assembly. As we saw earlier, some informal safety nets already existed through mutual assistance societies and other arrangements. Others were being created throughout the 19th century and early 20th century. Also as Pope Leo XIII had said, a greater effort could have been made to encourage workers to increase their savings, perhaps by improving the institutions that could accept and safely invest their savings.[4] In some countries, including Italy, the government lent its bureaucratic support to this objective by creating postal savings systems that allowed workers, in every urban center where a "post office" was located, to save in a simple, costless, and relatively safe way. It is, of course, difficult to assess what would have happened if governments had *not* entered, or had not entered massively, the area of state-provided social protection. Would the various private arrangements that already existed develop more, thus making public intervention less necessary? We shall never know. The governments could have encouraged the relevant social, private activities in various ways, as recommended by Minister Thiers. For example, they could have done so by not taxing these activities or by subsidizing them to some extent, or encouraging them in other ways, perhaps with some bureaucratic or administrative assistance.

The second option would have been to focus the attention on "workers" and to encourage employers to divert some of the wages they paid to workers toward channels that would protect the workers or even provide some relevant training to some of them. These channels could have been the setting aside of some savings for rainy days and for old age or of funds to be used for illnesses and training. In this option, the role of the state would have shifted largely to *regulating* and *monitoring* the actions of the workers and the enterprises. This would, however, have favored workers who worked for large enterprises in the formal economy. The self-employed and those who were in the informal sector and many in the agricultural sector would have remained dependent on the informal networks. This, in fact, happened in some industrial countries, including Italy, and in several developing countries.

The third option would have been that of requiring all citizens to acquire with their own means some basic minimum insurance against particular risks, such as old age, early death, and illnesses. This option would have needed to be accompanied by subsidies to the poorer individuals or by programs of assistance to the "deserving poor," those who did not have any income to buy the minimum insurance because of physical or mental handicaps and did not have family members to assist them; or those who had incomes that were too low to be able to buy these insurances. In this option the government would need to perform three functions: regulate the insurance activities, assist financially the "deserving poor," and promote a better-working market economy. Workers would receive salaries not reduced by high taxes or by forced "contributions." Therefore, they would be more financially capable, given the average income level of the country, to buy directly the needed protection from the market. To some extent this is the model that Chile has been developing and following in the past three decades, with considerable success especially for pensions. Some European countries have been following a similar model for health. An increasing number of countries have in recent years followed this alternative, with respect to pensions.

The fourth option would be one in which the government took upon itself the financial responsibility of providing to *all the citizens* some basic degree of social protection. This option would push up significantly both public spending and the level of taxation necessary to finance the spending, because the expenditure would have to be financed through general taxation unless there were cross-category transfers, say, from workers to nonworkers. This has largely been the option chosen by mature welfare states, although some modifications have been introduced in recent years.

Of course, another option could have been for governments to do absolutely nothing and to let private and voluntary arrangements develop without any guidance or assistance. Those who favor a minimalist role of the state would favor this option. Some would argue that this option would maximize individual liberty and personal incentives. It would keep taxes and public intervention at a minimum and would not force anyone to do anything that he or she would not wish to do voluntarily. No individual would be forced to pay taxes that would be used to assist others. This option does not imply that the result would be a community without any protection for individuals and families in need. The informal networks would remain active, or be revived, and voluntary participation could even be stimulated by the lack of governmental intervention. As Adam Smith already recognized, and as statistics on charitable contributions and other evidence indicate, most individuals have a basic sense of charity or sympathy for others.[5] For example, many contribute spontaneously to requests for assistance in cases of major disasters and voluntarily to charities. The government could still retain an important and fundamental role: that of making the market economy as efficient as possible, thus eliminating rents and creating a flexible labor market that would assist those searching for jobs and able to work. For this it would require an effective and efficient use of regulations aimed at eliminating abuses and arbitrary distortions and not at creating rents for some groups.

In the real world, today, we do not find any of these options in its purest form. In most countries, we find combinations of these options. However, there are some identifiable patterns in the way countries have created arrangements and institutions for social protection. In the rest of this chapter, we report briefly on *major* social legislation introduced by some countries over the past century or so, legislation that has had a major impact on formal programs of social assistance worldwide. Of course, in addition to these major social landmarks there were many other smaller and lesser-known legislative initiatives. It should be added that none of these options would be necessarily best for every country or for every society. Each country has its own history and its own peculiarities and characteristics. Therefore, an option that may be good for one country may not be good for another. Countries should select the option that works best for them. When they copy the options of other countries, the result may at times be disappointing.

## 5.2. The 1880s' Bismarck Legislation in Germany

Social protection (or social insurance) broadly defined, implying a significant government role, is generally considered a European "invention." Its origin has at times been traced to the "Workmen's Compensation for Norwegian Miners," a program enacted in 1842. However, in 1786 in the Republic of Venice, a fund had already been created to assist sailors who had become disabled (Geremia, 1961, pp. 619–20). In 1847 and 1853 "poor relief laws" were enacted in Sweden. In spite of these early examples, the birth of modern social protection is often traced to the legislation introduced by Otto von Bismarck in the decade of the 1880s, when he was chancellor of the German Empire. During that decade he promoted several laws aimed at providing safety nets for German workers. These laws had a great impact on social legislation in Europe and elsewhere. A short description of these laws may highlight their importance for the modern world.

Bismarck was not a leftist but a shrewd, political pragmatist. With the social legislation that he promoted, he wanted to achieve several political objectives. Among these were, first, to reduce the attraction that the radical and socialist ideas of Marx, Engels, and others were having on German workers. These radical ideas were attracting a lot of attention at that time and an increased following among German and other workers. By promoting the pro-worker social legislation, Bismarck hoped to divert the workers away from these socialist ideas. At that time, workers were becoming a powerful, political force that could no longer be ignored. A second objective may have been to reduce the influence of Catholics, especially in the South of Germany (and especially in Bavaria), an influence linked in part to the network of their charitable or social activities, which continued to exist in those areas. A third objective may have been that of increasing loyalty toward Germany, especially on the part of workers from non-German minorities.

Whatever the motives, Bismarck promoted and enacted three important and pioneering laws: the Health (or Sickness) Insurance Bill of 1883;

the Accident Insurance Bill of 1884; and the Old Age and Infirmity (or Disability) Bill of 1889. These laws aimed at protecting workers against the economic effects of sickness, accidents, and old age, at a time when no country had public or publicly supported programs to assist workers against these risks.[6] The Health Insurance Bill provided health care in case of sickness for about two-thirds of the German workers. In case of sickness they received both medical care and small cash allowances. The cost of the insurance was divided between the employers, who were required to pay one-third, and the workers, who were required to pay two-thirds of the total. The provision of the health care was administered by local health offices. Thus, the government's involvement was not financial but largely bureaucratic or regulatory (Fay, 1950).

The Accident Insurance Bill of 1884 for workmen provided insurance for accidents that occurred at the place of work. For this protection the employers were responsible for the full cost. Thus again, there was no direct *public* money involved. The Old Age and Infirmity (or Disability) Bill of 1889 extended coverage beyond the industrial workers and included other workers. About 13 out of 16 "wage earning workpeople" (about 81 percent) had a right to a small pension if they became permanently disabled or if they reached the age of 70. At a time when life expectancy at birth was about 45 years, few lived long enough to benefit from the small pension.[7] However, the important point is that *the pension became a right of the worker and was no longer an act of charity*. The cost of the pension system (which was estimated to amount to about 2 percent of wages) was divided among the employers (two-fifths), the government that contributed 50 marks to each pension, and the workers who contributed the rest. Thus, for pensions there was for the first time a government direct financial obligation. Often "patriarchal" businesses paid the worker's part. In a sign that political trading is not a recent invention, Bismarck won the industrialists' agreement to this program by agreeing to the imposition of some import tariffs that they wanted. By this time, laissez-faire was being challenged in several countries. In Italy, for example, the challenge had started in the decade of the 1880s (Are, 1974).[8]

A few important conclusions follow from the description of Bismarck's legislation. First, the assumption of the responsibility on the part of the state for pensions to workers, combined with the imposition of tariffs on imports, can be seen as attacks against the laissez-faire view that in Germany and other European countries had reached the greatest degree of support around 1875 but had started to decline by the 1880s. Second was the progressive expansion of workers' rights that took place after the initial introduction of the Bismarck-sponsored legislation. With the passing of time, more and more individuals came to be covered by this legislation, making it progressively more universal in its coverage[9] (see also Flora, Kraus, and Pfennig, 1983 and 1987). Third, although Bismarck's legislation was innovative and important, it had a limited immediate impact on German public finances, because the state financial responsibility was limited. What Bismarck did that was of great importance was to have established the principle of state-supervised compulsory insurance. Table 1.1 shows that in 1913, or two decades after the enactment of the social legislation, and in spite of the considerable expansion in the programs over the years, the share of total public spending in Germany was still only 14.8 percent of GDP. Table 2.1 provides more support for this conclusion. Nonetheless, Bismarck's legislation had a major impact on the world and must be seen as a major and perhaps the most important landmark in social legislation.

### 5.3. Roosevelt, Johnson, Clinton, and Obama Social Legislation in the United States

Before discussing the Beveridge Report, which was to have a major impact on programs of social protection around the world after World War II, we should also describe some major developments in the United States, especially those related to the introduction of the Social Security System in the 1930s and the "War on Poverty" in the 1960s. For the sake of completeness we also briefly report on later legislation. The "Social Security System" was introduced in the United States in 1935 by Franklin Delano Roosevelt. In his message to Congress on June 8, 1934, President Roosevelt promised to undertake "the great task of furthering the security of the citizen and his family through social insurance." By 1934 more than half of the American states had already some state laws related to pensions for old age. Roosevelt's social security was, however, a *national* program. He had also wanted to establish a system of health insurance, but strong opposition to it made this goal impossible.[10] This goal would have to wait for the Obama administration to introduce the Patient Protection and Affordable Care Act of 2010.

The American Social Security System, introduced in 1935, covers several programs such as Old Age, Survivors Benefits, and Disability Insurance (OASDI) and Aid to Dependent Children (ADC). Measured in terms of the size of the total payments that it now makes to beneficiaries every year, the Social Security System is the largest government program in the whole world. The system has been amended several times since its creation. It is financed by taxes on wages up to a given income level, thus making these taxes regressive, paid in equal proportions by employees and employers. Self-employed workers pay the full amount. The system is supposed to be based on a pay-as-you-go principle. Temporary surpluses are invested in U.S. government bonds.[11] Up to now, the system has accumulated large assets but the assets will be exhausted at some future date (2037?), as expenditures become significantly higher than revenue. Program costs have started exceeding tax revenue by this time (2010). Generational accounts, which discount future streams of revenue and expenditure, indicate large deficits in this system under the assumption of unchanged legislation and under realistic assumptions for growth, interest rate, life expectancy, and other significant variables. The benefits received by pensioners are taxed. The normal retirement age is 65, an age significantly lower than the one used in Bismarck's legislation, in spite of the fact that life expectancy has increased remarkably since Bismarck's time. To be entitled to a pension, workers must now make "social security contributions" over at least a ten-year period. The system is work related. Nonworkers do not contribute to it and are excluded from its benefits. The system has some strong but not very transparent redistributive elements in it. Some beneficiaries get more than they contribute, while others less than they contribute.

When the Social Security System was first introduced in the middle of the Great Depression, the bill that was presented to Congress, reportedly written in a way that few could understand, met with a lot of initial resistance, including the constitutional question of whether the federal government had the right to force workers and enterprises to be part of this program. The program was seen as an attack on individual freedom and/or a challenge to the rights of the states. There was also some concern that workers would start paying taxes immediately while the government would start paying the first pensions only several years later. This might potentially damage the economy. The government would accumulate surpluses for a long time in this special account because contributions would exceed payments. The introduction of the Social Security System was blamed by some economists for the economic slowdown that occurred in 1937, at a time when the economy had been moving slowly out of the Depression and national income was returning to the 1929 level.

Over the years, Social Security has received praise by some and continued criticism by others. Some critics have pointed out that the implicit rate of return on the contributions that many participants make to it is much lower than the value of what the beneficiaries would have received if their contributions had been invested directly in the market. The system has also

Table 5.1. *United States: Federal government payments to individuals for social programs (percentage of GNP)*

| Year | Total | Social security | Employee retirement benefits | Medical care | Public assistance and food | Unemployment benefits | Other |
|------|-------|----------------|------------------------------|--------------|----------------------------|-----------------------|-------|
| 1940 | 1.61 | 0.12 | 0.38 | 0.10 | 0.44 | 0.47 | 0.10 |
| 1945 | 0.83 | 0.16 | 0.30 | 0.07 | 0.25 | 0.04 | 0.01 |
| 1950 | 4.53 | 0.36 | 0.67 | 0.28 | 0.52 | 0.67 | 2.02 |
| 1955 | 3.38 | 1.17 | 0.64 | 0.20 | 0.52 | 0.49 | 0.35 |
| 1960 | 4.56 | 2.24 | 0.70 | 0.20 | 0.61 | 0.52 | 0.28 |
| 1965 | 4.69 | 2.51 | 0.71 | 0.25 | 0.65 | 0.39 | 0.18 |

*Source:* Arranged from tables I and IX, on pp. 397 and 405 of Stein, 1984.

been criticized by some economists for discouraging the incentive to save for retirement on the part of workers.[12] On the other hand, its supporters have praised its redistributive features. For these and several other reasons not discussed here, the Social Security program has remained controversial, at least with some groups, to this day (see, e.g., Tanner, 2004). However, it has also continued to have many strong supporters (Diamond, 2004). Over the years, the program has been expanded to cover disability and medical expenses for beneficiaries, making it much more expensive than at the beginning. President George W. Bush attempted to introduce partial privatization in 2005 but gave up in the face of stiff opposition from the program's defenders.

The Social Security Act of 1935 included Title IV, a program of Aid to Dependent Children. It was intended to help poor mothers, who at that time were mostly widows rather than single mothers, to raise small children. Such programs had been introduced by many states, mostly between 1910 and 1920. By 1935 some 40 states had them. The Social Security Act of 1935 offered to cover a third of the cost for the states that had this program. In some way, it was an example of national governments taking over some private or, in this case, subnational activities in social assistance. Beside the Social Security Act, many of the permanent changes introduced by President Roosevelt were of a regulatory nature, and some were outside the public finance areas. Table 5.1 provides data that show the impact of Roosevelt's legislation on social spending, until President Johnson's War on Poverty in the mid-1960s.

A great expansion in social expenditure in the United States came from President Johnson, with his War on Poverty. The War on Poverty would

inflate the U.S. budget for many years to come. For a while, price inflation increased tax revenue through the "fiscal drag." Also demographically
friendly developments, such as the baby boom after World War II that
increased the number of workers in the 1960s and beyond, contributed
to social security contributions while containing payments, because few
people were retiring. This made it easier for the federal government to
finance the fast-rising social expenses. Reductions in defense spending also
contributed to the available revenue for social spending, especially after
the end of the Vietnam War. With the passing of time, the impact of the
changes, introduced by the War on Poverty on public spending, became
more pronounced.

In a message to Congress, on March 16, 1964, President Lyndon B. Johnson announced his "War on the Sources of Poverty." He affirmed that, "for
the first time in our history, it is possible to conquer poverty," even though
the programs proposed "will not eliminate all the poverty in America in a
few months or a few years." The programs were presented as "a total commitment by this President, and this Congress, and this nation, to pursue
victory over the most ancient of mankind's enemies" (see U.S. Government,
1965). The main legislative proposals were presented by President Johnson
in his State of the Union Address on January 4, 1965. The address includes
several initiatives that would broadly expand the role of the U.S. federal
government in the economy in future years. The most important among
these were the Elementary and Secondary Education Act of 1965, which
would provide federal assistance for various educational programs, and the
Social Security Act of 1965, which would introduce the government in
the health sector through Medicare, a program of assistance directed to the
recipient of social security, and through Medicaid, a program directed to
welfare recipients. These last two programs and especially the first would
become progressively more expansive with the passage of time because of the
increasing number of beneficiaries and the higher inflation rate in the health
sector. For this, intergenerational accounts provide large (discounted) current net liabilities that are a kind of hidden debt. This is a time bomb that
will worry future U.S. administrations.

The War on Poverty, or the "Great Society" legislation of the Johnson
administration, made it also possible for some individuals, who were neither
elderly nor disabled, to live, at the government's expense, without working.
This was a truly radical change in policy. The benefits that the individuals
received were of different kinds. They included general welfare payments,
food stamps, special payments for pregnant women and for young mothers,
Medicaid benefits, and housing benefits received from the states. In 1968,

4.1 percent of all American families were headed by nonworking women who were receiving welfare benefits. By 1980, this percentage had increased to 10 percent (Frum, 2000, p. 72).

Expenditure for "human resources" – which includes education, training, employment and social services, health, income security, social security, and veterans benefits and services – that between 1940 and 1960 had been under, and in some years considerably under, 5 percent of GDP, started rising in the 1960s, especially after the War on Poverty came into effect. In 1965, outlays for "human resources" were 5.3 percent of GDP. By 1970, they were 7.4 percent of GDP. By 1980, they were 11.5 percent. After reaching 12.4 percent of GDP in 1983, there was some containment for a couple of decades, promoted by a reform of the system. However, by 2010 they are estimated to have reached almost 16 percent of GDP (see U.S. Office of Management and Budget, Historical Tables, 2009). There has obviously been a large change in social expenditure in the United States over the past half century. The large change in this category has been partly masked by the large fall in defense spending over the period.[13]

Let us now return to Title IV of the Social Security Act of 1935, the title that dealt with Aid to Dependent Children. The introduction of this program had been followed by its expansion and by continuing controversy until the Clinton reform of 1996 changed it.

In 1960 the name of the program was changed from Aid to Dependent Children to Aid to Families with Dependent Children (AFDC). Thus, the focus shifted from children to families, and the scope of the program grew. It was extended to cover children with both parents, when one of them was unemployed; the age of the children covered by the program was raised to 18 years, if they were in school; children in foster homes were covered; and the share of the costs covered by the federal government was raised from one-third to one-half. This represents a classic example of what often happens to government-financed programs. They start small and tend to grow, in scope and coverage, over the years.

The AFDC program, administered by the U.S. Department of Health and Human Services, over the years faced several legal challenges, mostly aimed at expanding it and at making welfare a right of the recipients and not a privilege or an act of charity that could be denied at the discretion of those who administered the program. For a while, the administrators had managed to keep some power of discretion on who was entitled to the benefits, but this power was continually being challenged from the left and eroded.

Although the sums involved were never enormous – by the time it was drastically changed in 1996, this program was spending U.S. $24 billion per year – the program was subjected to criticisms from the right. It included the accusation that it had created dependency on welfare. As the benefits increased, as would be expected, so did the number of individuals who asked for support. Between 1936 and 1969 the number of families receiving welfare through this program rose from 162,000 to almost 2 million. Some charged that it encouraged increased births among unmarried or divorced women, thus contributing to the rise of the number of illegitimate children; that these illegitimate children contributed to the rise of crime rates and the creation of urban slums; and that it created a cycle of poverty because it caught participants in a welfare trap.[14] It was often pointed out that some families had been trapped by these programs for several generations, during which no family member had ever worked. A final claim was that the program was keeping women from marrying even when they had or lived with partners, thus leading to increasing evidence of welfare fraud.

The Aid to Dependent Children of 1935 was replaced by the Personal Responsibility and Work Opportunity Reconciliation Act in 1996 (the Clinton Welfare Reform Act). The new act kept President Clinton's promise "to end welfare as we know it." The objective of the new act was to encourage those who had been receiving welfare to look for jobs and to make welfare a second chance and not a way of life. This would break the intergenerational dependency on welfare benefits that had been developing over the years. As reported by President Clinton, in an article published in the *New York Times* on the 10th anniversary of the change (August 22, 2006), over the decade "welfare rolls . . . dropped substantially, from 12.2 million in 1996 to 4.5 million today." Of course, a strong economy helped but "sixty percent of the mothers who left welfare found work" and child poverty dropped significantly.

The ADC program provides a good example of a process that has become common in many expenditure programs and that has contributed to a kind of natural increase in public spending over time. It is a process that might point to *a fundamental law of public program development*. A new program is at times introduced to help a specific, limited group of beneficiaries, say, widowed women with small children. When the new program is introduced, it looks lean and has a limited scope and a well-defined set of beneficiaries who are easy to identify. The spending is limited. It seems to be a reasonable program directed at clearly deserving potential beneficiaries, such as poor, widowed women with small children. With the passing of time, pressures to expand the number of beneficiaries and to enlarge the scope of the program, by relaxing some of the requirements to qualify, begin to rise. Standards are slowly relaxed and the number of beneficiaries goes up, together with the expenditure for the program.

A program that may have seemed inexpensive when it was introduced becomes progressively more expensive. What is worse, the program also becomes less equitable, because the beneficiaries that are added are likely to be less deserving of assistance than the original ones but often get the same government benefits. This introduces the common problem of horizontal inequity in public assistance, discussed in Chapter One. The ADC program provides an example of this common process. An even better example is provided by disability pensions in which the concept of disability has been progressively relaxed in most countries, so that two "disabled" persons, with widely different degrees of incapacity to perform useful tasks, often end up getting identical pensions. The number of individuals getting disability pensions has grown remarkably in some countries (the Netherlands and Italy among others), making these expensive public programs. In some cases, individuals who seem to be fit for many jobs end up retiring before the time of most normal pensions and while still qualifying for other pensions, as it seems to happen among policemen in some rich American counties. This is another example of the horizontal inequities that social programs help generate. Many other examples of this process could easily be found.

The 1996 act ended welfare as an entitlement, required those who received welfare to start working after two years on the program, put a lifetime limit of five years to the total time that recipients could receive benefits financed by federal funds, restricted funds available to unmarried women under 18 years of age, and restricted any welfare payments to immigrants. The reform has been widely seen as having helped restore the work ethic and having been a success in reducing poverty among children.

On March 21, 2010, the U.S. House of Representatives passed H.R. 4872, the Patient Protection and Affordable Care Act (PPACA). President Obama signed the bill into law on March 23, 2010. The law created a mandate for most U.S. residents to acquire health insurance. They would be punished if they did not. Individuals and families could receive subsidies from the government if they could not afford the full cost of the insurance. This is an important change for the United States. However, it cannot be considered a landmark for social legislation because the United States simply joined several other countries in enacting this type of law. At the time of this writing, the full implication of this complex legislation is still being discussed, and the Republican Party has promised to abolish this legislation. How much it will cost the U.S. government over the long run is still a hotly debated and very important issue. Perhaps because of the complexity of this legislation, this reform does not seem to have attracted the popular endorsement that had been expected.

## 5.4. The Beveridge Report in the United Kingdom

The other important milestone in the history of social insurance and social protection is the Beveridge Report, which contributed significantly to the creation of the British welfare state after World War II and also influenced other countries. The report led to the expansion of the National Insurance System, a system that had been first introduced in limited form in 1911, and to the creation of the National Health Service. The report was prepared by a government committee under the chairmanship of Sir William Beveridge, an economist who had been director of the London School of Economics, and was published on December 2, 1942, when Great Britain was in the middle of World War II (Beveridge, 1942). It was broadly welcomed, and there was huge interest on the part of the British population in its published version. However, because of the war, its implementation would have to wait until 1945 when the war was over and the Labor Party won the general election.

The report highlighted three "guiding principles" or recommendations: to think in a "revolutionary" way toward social protection and not in a "patching" way; to realize that by providing "income security" social insurance would attack only "want," considered as only one of the "five giants on the road to reconstructions. . . . The others [were] Disease, Ignorance, Squalor, and Idleness" (to deal with the other four "giants" would require more than "income security"); and to promote cooperation between the actions of the state and of individuals. In offering security for service and contribution, the state "should not stifle incentive, opportunity, [and] responsibility; in establishing a national minimum, [the state] should leave room and encouragement for voluntary action by each individual to provide more than that minimum for himself and his family."

In time, the 300-page report led to the passage of the Family Allowances Act of 1945; the National Insurance (Industrial Injuries) Act of 1946; the National Health Service Act of 1946; the Pension Act of 1947; the Landlord and Tenant (Rent Control) Act of 1949; and the National Insurance Acts of 1948 and 1949. The need to provide family allowances, based on the number

Table 5.2. *Welfare spending in the United Kingdom: 1900–1995 (percentage of GDP)*

|  | 1900 | 1910 | 1921 | 1926 | 1936 | 1946 | 1956 | 1966 | 1976 | 1981 | 1995 |
|---|---|---|---|---|---|---|---|---|---|---|---|
| Education | n.a. | n.a. | 1.69 | 2.02 | 2.17 | 1.75 | 3.26 | 4.59 | 6.20 | 5.54 | 5.09 |
| Health | n.a. | n.a. | 0.41 | 1.41 | 1.69 | 1.72 | 3.11 | 3.69 | 4.91 | 5.19 | 5.74 |
| Social Security (including housing benefits) | n.a. | n.a. | 4.26 | 4.65 | 5.30 | 4.53 | 5.16 | 6.94 | 10.18 | 11.45 | 13.13 |
| Total | 2.6 | 4.16 | 6.36 | 8.08 | 9.16 | 8.00 | 11.52 | 15.22 | 21.28 | 22.18 | 23.96 |

*Source:* Glennerster, 1998, annex, table 2A.1, p. 25.

of dependent children, was stressed by the report. Thus, large families were seen to deserve more public support.

The Beveridge Report and the legislation that it produced intended to provide an expansion of the economic role of the state far beyond that suggested by the Bismarck legislation or even by the Roosevelt legislation. For the Beveridge Report, the final destination would be a mature and high-spending welfare state. It would introduce legislation that conflicted frontally with a market economy, as, for example, the Rent Control Act of 1949. Table 5.2, on the development of welfare spending in the United Kingdom between 1900 and 1995, shows a sharp increase in that spending between the mid-1940s and 1981, followed by a more modest growth afterward when a conservative government was in charge and tried (with limited success) to reduce the scope of governmental intervention in the economy.

Tables 1.1 and 1.2 give some idea of the size of the increase in public spending in the United Kingdom that was accounted for by the rise in *social* spending. It can be seen that what happened in the United Kingdom after the Beveridge Report was, quantitatively and qualitatively, significantly different from what happened in Germany after Bismarck, or in the United States after the New Deal (see also Hills, Ditch, and Glennerster, 1994, and Peacock, 1954, for more information on the United Kingdom).

## 5.5. Keynes and Social Legislation

Before bringing this chapter to a close, there is a kind of historical puzzle that should be addressed, even if briefly. Today, it is common to attribute to J. M. Keynes the merit, or the blame (depending on one's political viewpoint), for the large expansion in the role of the state in the economy of many countries that took place since the time when he published *The General*

*Theory* in 1936. Policy makers often define as "Keynesian" their policies that increase public spending. During the recent financial and economic crises (2008–9), there have been many calls to increase public spending "along Keynesian lines." Some have even attributed the birth of the welfare state to Keynes.

There is no question that Keynes called for a larger role of the state in the economy. He called for an end to "laissez-faire" in lectures in 1924 and 1926, when, some would argue, "laissez-faire" had already been abandoned in several continental European countries, such as Germany and Italy, although economists still broadly supported it, especially in the United States. Keynes believed that when organizations become too large – or, in today's parlance, "too big to fail" – it might be better to make them "semi-autonomous bodies" with the specific task of promoting public goods and with more regulatory controls on them. In today's world, post offices, subway systems, or railroads might be good examples. In his view, very large institutions and especially large enterprises tend "to socialize themselves." He saw his proposal as an alternative to socialism (at a time when socialism had become very fashionable), in which ministers would become directly responsible for the decisions of economic institutions. He saw a state role in the "dissemination on a great scale" of business data and in forcing full disclosure. In today's words, this would reduce the frequency of asymmetry in information among individuals. Many would agree with him today on the objective to force enterprises, and especially banks, to become more transparent. He clearly "distrusted markets and believed, rather, in alternative means to improve society, resting on persuasion and intellectual ingenuity" (Marcuzzo, 2010, p. 7). Thus, he was far from the economists of the Austrian school, including Mises and Hayek, who believed in the magical power of the market and downplayed its shortcomings. Most importantly, he did not believe that private markets *automatically* delivered full employment, and he saw unemployment as a major social problem. His fear was that the free working of the market would fail to automatically bring investment in line with a country's saving and, as a consequence, it would deliver the economy to socialism. Therefore, he advocated a government role, especially in promoting adequate investment and in maintaining the needed level of aggregate demand.

Thus, Keynes believed that "laissez-faire" should be complemented by significant state intervention and that classical economics should be replaced by a new kind of economics that recognized various market failures. Yet, he did not provide any clear statement that the government must promote more social spending or even a welfare state. If Keynes had something to do with higher public spending, it may have been as an indirect by-product of stabilization policy. An argument can be made that stabilization policy is often accompanied, for political reasons, by a natural asymmetry that, over the long run, leads to a larger share of public spending into GDP. The reason is that policy makers are more ready, and find it easier, to increase public spending during recessions than to cut it during booms. This asymmetry leads to progressively higher share of public spending into GDP over the long run. However, this is a by-product of stabilization policy and not an objective of Keynes's economics. Keynes thought that economic policy should be guided by well-informed and able individuals, by a kind of "intellectual aristocracy" that would not suffer from political biases and from the previously mentioned policy asymmetry. This attitude has, at times, been called the "Harvey Road mentality" (see Buchanan, Burton, and Wagner, 1978; and Rowley, 1987).

Keynes seems to have been somewhat detached from the public debate that led to the Beveridge Report and to the social legislation of 1945, except for a few epistolary exchanges with Beveridge. An explanation for this detachment that has been advanced is that between 1941 and 1945 he spent a lot of time in the United States and in Canada. This was the time when the creation of the Bretton Wood institutions (IMF and World Bank) was being studied and prepared, and he was very much engaged with this important project. However, indirect indications, such as his letter at this time to Colin Clark, then a major economist, in which he agreed with Clark's view that a tax burden of 25 percent of GDP would set an upper limit to tax revenue in a country, and his statement that in meetings on Keynesian economics in the United States in the early 1940s he felt as if he were the only "non-Keynesian" in the room, seem to confirm Skidelsky's conclusion that "Keynes was not a passionate social reformer," in spite of his revolutionary thoughts in economics (Skidelsky, 2000, p. 265; and Marcuzzo, 2010). By the way, while Keynes agreed with Clark's upper limit to the level of taxation, Paul Samuelson was highly critical of that limit (Samuelson, 1967, p. 39).

In conclusion, it may be incorrect to attribute to Keynes the blame for the growth of public spending that took place during the second half of the 20th century. For sure, he had little to do with the creation of welfare states.

### References

Are, Giuseppe. 1974. *Economia Politica nell' Italia Liberale (1890–1915)* (Bologna: Il Mulino).

Ashley, W. J. 1904. *The Progress of the German Working Classes in the Last Quarter of the Century* (London: Longmans, Green).

Barro, Robert J. 1978. "The Impact of Social Security on Private Saving: Evidence from the U.S. Time Series." American Enterprise Institute, *AEA Studies*, 199.

Beveridge, Sir William. 1942. "Social Insurance and Allied Services." Report by Sir William Beveridge Presented to Parliament by Command of His Majesty (November).

Buchanan, James M., John Burton, and Richard E. Wagner. 1978. *The Consequences of Mr. Keynes* (London: Institute of Economic Affairs).

Crone, Patricia. 2005. *Medieval Islamic Political Thought* (Edinburgh: Edinburgh University Press).

Diamond, Peter. 2004. "Social Security." *American Economic Review* 94, no. 1 (March): 1–24.

Fay, S. B. 1950. "Bismarck's Welfare State." *Current History* 18 (January): 1–7.

Feldstein, Martin. 1974. "Social Security, Induced Retirement, and Aggregate Capital Accumulation." *Journal of Political Economy* 82 (September–October).

Flora Peter, Franz Kraus, and Winfried Pfennig. 1983 and 1987. *State, Economy and Society in Western Europe, 1815–1975*, vol. 1, *1983*, vol. 2, *1987* (Chicago: St. James Press).

Frum, David. 2000. *How We Got Here: The '70s* (New York: Basic Books).

Glennerster, Howard. 1998. "New Beginnings and Old Continuities," in *The State of Welfare: The Economies of Social Spending*, edited by Howard Glennerster and John Hills, 2nd ed. (Oxford: Oxford University Press), chap. 2.

Hills, J., J. Ditch, and H. Glennerster. 1994. *Beveridge and Social Security: An International Retrospective* (Oxford: Clarendon Press).

Howard, Christopher. 1997. *The Hidden Welfare State; Tax Expenditures and Social Policy in the United States* (Princeton: Princeton University Press).

Kirsch, J. P. "The Reformation," in *The Catholic Encyclopedia* (New York: Robert Appleton Company, 1911).

Maddison, Angus. 1999. "Perspective on Global Economic Progress and Human Development." Academy of the Social Sciences/1, *Annual Symposium*.

Marcuzzo, Maria Cristina. 2010. "Whose Welfare State? Beveridge versus Keynes," in *No Wealth but Life: Welfare Economics and the Welfare State in Britain, 1880–1945*, edited by R. Backhouse and T. Nishizawa (Cambridge: Cambridge University Press).

Peacock, Alan, ed. 1954. *Income Redistribution and Social Policy: A Set of Studies* (London: Jonathan Cape).

    1993. "Keynes and the Role of the State," in *Keynes and the Role of the State*, edited by D. Crabtree and A. P. Thirlwall (London: Macmillan).

Prins, M. A. 1888. *Le pauperisme et le principe des assurances ouvrières obligatoires* (Brussels: Th. Falked).

Rowley, Charles K. 1987. "John Maynard Keynes and the Attack on Classical Political Economy," in *Deficits*, edited by James M. Buchanan, Charles K. Rowley, and Robert D. Tollison (Oxford: Basil Blackwell), pp. 115–22.

Samuelson, Paul. 1968. "The Economic Role of Private Activity," in *A Dialogue on the Proper Economic Role of the State*, by G. J. Stigler and P. A. Samuelson (Chicago: University of Chicago Business School), pp. 21–39.

Schlesinger, Arthur M., Jr. 1959. *The Coming of the New Deal* (Boston: Houghton Mifflin).

Skidelsky, Robert. 2000. *John Maynard Keynes: Fighting for Britain, 1937–1946* (London: Macmillan).

Stein, Herbert. 1984. *Presidential Economics: The Making of Economic Policy from Roosevelt to Reagan and Beyond* (New York: Simon and Schuster).

Tanner, Michael D., ed. 2004. *Social Security and Its Discontents: Perspectives on Choice* (Washington, D.C.: CATO Institute).

U.S. Government. 1965. *Papers of U.S. Presidents, Lyndon B. Johnson, 1963–1964* (Washington, D.C.: GPO), pp. 375–380.

U.S. Government, Office of Management and Budget. 2009. *Historical Tables; Budget of the U.S. Government, Fiscal Year 2010* (Washington, D.C.: GPO).

# SIX

# Globalization and Public Spending

## 6.1. Introduction

The past two decades have been characterized by a growing attention to a phenomenon that has generally gone under the name of globalization. Many articles and books have been written about this phenomenon, and violent demonstrations have occasionally been organized against international meetings of the World Trade Organization, the IMF, the G7-G8, the G20, or other institutions or organizations to protest the alleged damaging effects of globalization. Some critics of the phenomenon have been asking policy makers to put an end to it. The 2008–9 financial and economic crises, in part closely associated with the globalization of the financial market, brought about sharp falls in international trade. If that crisis had continued, it might have challenged the process of globalization in its recent forms and brought it to an end, as the Great Depression did to the previous period of globalization.

As is often the case with many words in common use, globalization has many faces and many meanings. Consequently, it is not easy to define it precisely, for it means different things to different people. For some it conveys the image of a world that has become a "global village . . . in which distance and isolation have been dramatically reduced by electronic media." This definition, provided by *Merriam Webster's Collegiate Dictionary* (10th edition), points to one aspects of the phenomenon, an aspect that, for sure, is of marginal relevance to a large proportion of the world's population that may not have witnessed yet much genuine reduction in distance and isolation. For others, globalization has made the world "flat," thus facilitating connectivity and reducing the cost of transaction between countries and among people (Friedman, 2005).

In some different ways, globalization is not really a new phenomenon, because it has been going on for centuries. For example, Columbus's trip to the Americas can be seen as a clear manifestation and promotion of globalization. Among the many changes that it brought about, Columbus's trip would in time cause a person of Japanese descent (Fujimori) to become president of a country (Peru) that had been the center of the until then unknown empire of the Incas! Magellan's trip around the world was another manifestation of globalization because it opened trade routes between the Atlantic and the Pacific. The openings of the Suez and the Panama canals were other examples. Manifestations of globalization were also the conquests of Alexander the Great, the expansion of the Roman Empire, and the conquests of Genghis Khan. During Roman times the Roman philosopher and scientist Seneca, who died in Pompeii during the eruption of the Vesuvius, was already complaining that imports from India and China were damaging the Roman economy! These events changed large areas of the world in fundamental ways and connected different regions, before the current wave of globalization.

In this chapter, we focus on economic aspects of globalization and particularly on the impact that it may have had on the economic risks, faced by the citizens of countries exposed to this phenomenon, and on the role that the government may have played through its public spending in protecting citizens against these risks – in other words, the hypothesis is that globalization changes the economic role of the state in some fundamental ways, forcing an increase in public spending.[1] We argue that the story is a complex one and that recent attempts on the part of some economists to establish clear relationships between measures of globalization (such as the openness of the economy) and measures of the government's role in social protection (such as public spending) are not convincing.

Unless one focuses on the communication revolution of the past couple decades, which clearly has brought major changes to the world, the process of economic globalization has been going on for a long time, accelerating in some periods, when new technologies or new policies helped it, and slowing down or, for some periods, even reversing itself, in periods when wars, plagues, economic crises, or policy changes created obstacles to it. Obviously, different parts of the world, and different income classes within countries, have been affected differently by these events, some more positively than others.

There is a broad consensus among economists that the period that went from the middle of the 19th century until the beginning of the First World War in 1914 was a period of intense globalization. In this period or at least in the earlier part of it, laissez-faire economics broadly coincided with and facilitated globalization, although some policy changes had started to challenge laissez-faire policies especially toward the end of that period. Technological developments (railroads, electricity, cars, telegraphs, steamships) and the economic policies of the time, which for the most part gave free reign to market forces, together with the gold standard, which in a way provided a world money standard for intercountry payments, made this a period of intense globalization. Many countries became more open than they had been previously to trade, capital movements, and even to the movements of people. Millions emigrated to new countries in this period (Solimano, 2008 and forthcoming). Indexes of openness to trade and to capital movements for *industrial countries* were, at that time, broadly similar to those registered in recent years (Baldwin and Martin, 1991). The First World War interrupted that period, but it continued after the war, until the Great Depression again sloved it down.

Much of the information available and the attention on the part of economists to globalization has come from, or been directed to, the industrial countries. Information on other countries has been limited. Some of these other countries were at the time colonies of European powers, so that their commercial relations with the rest of the world were determined by the policies of those powers. The latter often constrained the economic relations of the colonies to the motherland. Recent research has indicated that the Latin American countries, which by the 1870–1914 period were mostly independent, may not have been as "globalized" as the industrial countries. In fact, the Latin American countries had the world's highest tariffs in that period.

According to Coatsworth and Williamson (2004, p. 67), "Tariffs in Latin America were far higher than anywhere else from the 1860s to World War I, long before the Great Depression. Indeed, tariff rates in Latin America were even on the rise in the decades before 1914." However, Coatsworth and Williamson conclude that "revenue needs were... the key to these exceptionally high tariffs, and this motivation had its roots in the exceptional levels of military conflict in the region." In other words, military conflicts created strong needs for higher tax revenue, not globalization. This was the same motive that would lead to the increase in public spending and, to a lesser extent, in tax levels during World Wars I and II in industrialized countries.

Given the prevailing structure of the economies at that time, which depended mostly on agricultural production, tax revenue could be obtained mainly from foreign trade taxes. In that period, the United States also depended on foreign trade taxes for a large share of its government revenue. This conclusion is consistent with that reached by the "general theory of tax structure change," a theory that was popular four decades ago among economists interested in taxation. This theory, ignored in recent writings, had shown that foreign trade was the best "tax handle" for many developing countries. The larger the share of imports and exports of a country was, the easier it was to raise higher revenue. The reason was that it was easier to tax goods that were channeled through a few ports or frontier passes. (See Tanzi, 1973, for a description of this theory; and Musgrave, 1969, for a discussion of "tax handles.")

## 6.2. Globalization and Public Spending

As shown in earlier chapters, in the period between 1870 and 1913 governments played a limited though increasing and essential role in the economy. Public spending in general, and especially that for social protection, was small by modern standards, although it was growing (see Table 1.2). As reported earlier, at that time the share of total public spending in GDP averaged around 12–13 percent (see Tanzi and Schuknecht, 2000; Maddison, 1997; Lindert, 2003; and Table 1.1). At the same time, there were many activities undertaken by churches, civil organizations, or extended families that provided some basic protection to many individuals and families against various economic risks. To a large extent, the protective policies of the welfare states or the mixed economies that developed later crowded out many of these nonstate activities. Thus, the successive growth in public spending may have contributed less to an increase in net protection against economic risks than generally assumed. This is an area that has not been well researched by economists, which leaves the impression that government programs for social protection always filled a vacuum and represented a noncontroversial net-positive improvement in reducing economic risks (but see Beito, Gordon, and Tabarrok, 2002; Solomon, 1973; Zamagni, 2000; Ritter, 1996; and Wuthnow, 1991). As Ritter put it, "With respect to the history of social protection, comparative research has not paid enough attention to the vast assistance provided to the poor by association of mutual help" (p. 32, author's translation from the Italian edition of the book).

Events after 1913, but especially after 1929, brought an end to the globalizing trends and policies that had characterized the previous decades. These events were World War I and, especially, the Great Depression and World War II. At the same time, autarkic policies were introduced by the governments of Germany, Italy, Japan, Russia, and other countries. These policies contributed to the closing of these and other countries' economies in the 1930s. These events were not conducive to the creation of a "global village" or a "flat world." In these periods, policy makers lost their enthusiasm for openness, policies changed, and the world went through a long period when borders became relatively closed for trade and very closed for the movements of financial capital and, to some extent, for persons. After World War II, many countries, and especially developing countries, adopted policies of import substitution that attempted to force or accelerate the industrialization of their economies by restricting imports, especially for final goods and services. Raúl Prebisch became the intellectual guide for this movement, especially in Latin America. Protectionism became a popular policy.

As we saw earlier, it was exactly in this period that the role of the state in the economy, as measured by public spending, accelerated. In many countries, welfare states or "mixed economies" started coming into existence, first slowly and then at a faster pace. Public spending, as a share of GDP, more than doubled, from its low but increasing level, between 1913 and the 1950s. It grew explosively in the rest of the century. This phase lasted at least until the early 1990s when a new period of opening of markets and of globalization began. It is, thus, important to realize that the growth of public spending *had nothing, or little, to do with globalization.* On the contrary, it took place *before* the world became globalized, in the current round, and well before much of the recent discussion of globalization started. In fact, public spending and taxes showed some tendency to fall in the more recent years, at least until the 2008 financial crisis (see Table 4.5).

In the second half of the 1970s, intellectual winds started changing again, this time in the opposite direction from that of the 1950s and 1960s. Conservative, libertarian economic ideas, such as those of Milton Friedman and Friedrich Hayek, and of other exponents of the "Chicago school," which had been considered a kind of radical fringe until that time, gained attention, helped by the stagflation of the period that challenged some basic macroeconomic assumptions, such as the Phillips curve. The Keynesian ideas[2] that had dominated the two preceding decades came under scrutiny and attack and, for a while, lost some of their attractiveness, especially in academic circles (see especially Lucas, 1973 and 1976; and Prescott, 1986). Articles were published about the end of Keynesianism, and ideas based on rational expectations and/or Ricardian equivalence came to dominate academic thinking. The fact that individuals with strong conservative views, such as Margaret Thatcher and Ronald Reagan, could be elected to lead two important and influential countries was a forceful indication of this change

(Clarke, 2009). Both Friedman and Hayek were awarded the Nobel Prize in economics.

This period brought progressively more opening of countries' economies, more capital movements, and more skeptical attitudes vis-à-vis the large role that governments had assumed over previous years in the running of the countries' economies. In some ways the world witnessed a fundamental change from a "Keynesian revolution," which had focused on the demand side of the economy, to a "supply-side revolution," which put the emphasis on the impact of economic policies, including high taxes, on the supply side of economies. Both of them had been genuine revolutions because they changed in fundamental ways, at least for many economists and policy makers, the way they saw the economic role of the state and the working of the economy. The attention of many economists shifted, at least partly, from the demand to the supply side of the economy for the first time in several decades.[3]

This period culminated in what came to be called the "Washington Consensus." That "consensus" represented in some sense the affirmation (or reaffirmation) of the role of the market over the role of the state in the economy, after a long interlude. It was accompanied, at the same time, by the fall of the centrally planned economies, due to the political disintegration of the Soviet Union, and the need for the previously command economies to start on the road to transition toward becoming market economies (see Tanzi, 2010a, for an informal, impressionistic account of these changes). In the early 1990s this promarket attitude became popular and led to important policy changes that promoted market activities in an increasingly globalized context. For example, it brought large-scale privatization of state enterprises in many countries and opened to the private sector the possibility of investing in infrastructure through what came to be called "public-private partnerships"[4] (Harris, 2004). Because the privatized enterprises, especially in developing countries, were often bought by foreigners, public-private partnerships contributed also to large cross-country capital movements.

This phase of globalization in the past two decades was given its special characteristics by technological developments in the communication field and by policies that allowed the liberalization of capital movements. The "Internet network," built largely with private money, made it possible for individuals to communicate rapidly with individuals in other parts of the world where computers were available. This created a global and instantaneous "connectivity" that had not existed or was not thought possible before. The exchange and storage of huge amounts of data became cheap, rapid, and easy. The drastic fall in the price of computers over the years, and their growing computing capacity, increased their popularity and their use. They became particularly important for facilitating the movements of financial capital and the development of a global financial market, which exploded in terms of daily trading. The combination of new technology and new policies, together with better-developed payment systems capable of handling millions of transactions a day, made it possible to shift huge amounts of money around the world in seconds. The fact that the financial market became global and that it was little regulated contributed to these changes.

These developments, combined with facilitating policies, allowed for the creation of a huge and truly global financial market that linked the economies of countries and the financial operations of their banks and enterprises in a way never witnessed before. Governments and many private agents could now access the market, as providers of funds or as borrowers, at levels and with a facility that would have been impossible in earlier times. Unfortunately, as is often the case, the development of needed institutions always follows the need for them. The absence of global and efficient regulations over this global activity and of regulatory institutions contributed to the financial crisis of 2008–9. To some extent, what happened in the recent financial crisis gave some weight to Keynes's views of the market. He had defined it as "a lottery" (Keynes, 1926, p. 47). Recently some economists have referred to it as "casino capitalism" (Sinn, 2010).

International speculation was facilitated by these developments as well as by the likelihood of behavior driven by "herd instincts," "contagion," and pressure to conform and generate competitive short-run profits (Galbraith, 1990; Shiller, 2008; and Posner, 2009).[5] The conditions for more frequent and deeper financial crises were in place (Tanzi, 2007). A statement by Harold James (2001, p. 200) is worth quoting: "What made the Great Depression 'Great' was a series of contagious financial crises in the summer of 1931 and the subsequent trade response." It should be mentioned that the closing of some countries' economies in World War I because of the war had been followed, in the decade of the 1920s, by their reopening, which lasted more than a decade. Globalization before 1913 had taken place long before the communications revolution and the development of a global financial market, even though the telegraph had played a significant role in that period and significant capital movements had taken place facilitated by the gold standard. The past two decades have witnessed more frequent and deeper financial crises than earlier decades. The 2008–9 crisis was just the latest, most global, and deepest of the many recent banking crises (Reinhart and Rogoff, 2009).

These financial crises have at times led to sharp falls in the countries' gross domestic products, to large fiscal costs associated with the subsequent restructuring of the banking sectors, to (short-term) sharp increases in unemployment and in poverty in the affected countries, and to calls on the governments of some countries to provide "safety nets" for the populations. These calls became particularly strong during the financial crises that occurred in Southeast Asia in 1997–98, because the countries most affected by these crises (Korea, Thailand, and Indonesia) did not have modern, government-provided safety nets. In these countries, the existing safety nets had depended mostly on social norms, such as life employment for employees in private enterprises, and on the support of families. In these countries, some individuals who had belonged to the working middle classes found themselves in poverty almost overnight when the enterprises in which they had worked closed down. We shall have to wait to assess the full effect of the recent global financial crises. But some of its potential effects on the public finances have become evident. Many countries, including the United States and the United Kingdom, have come out of the crisis with far worse fiscal situations than they went in and with different and inflated economic roles of the state (see Tanzi, 2010b, and Chapter 14). For some countries the financial crisis has morphed into a fiscal crisis.

Social protection can be considered an economic as well as a social imperative. Thus, in today's world some "safety nets" should be in place. However, these can take various forms, as argued in the first chapter. A strong case can be made, and has been made, that globalization has implications for the role that the state should play in a country's economy. It can be and has been argued that the more globalized the countries become, the greater should be the economic and especially the protective role of the state. According to this line of reasoning, globalization *should* lead to increases in public spending and especially in *public spending for social protection.* This normative statement was changed into a positive one in the influential writing by Dani Rodrik (see especially Rodrik, 1998).

The connection between globalization and public spending cannot be limited to the role that the state should play to protect individuals from economic risks that may increase because of globalization. That connection must also be considered in terms of the role that the state is capable of playing and its implication for the economy. When the role of the state extends beyond the capacity of its policy makers and its administration, or beyond the state's capacity to finance it, the results are never good. That role might itself be affected by globalization because globalization may reduce the control that policy makers have over some policy instruments and may reduce the country's capacity to collect taxes.

Much of the increase in public expenditure in industrial countries over the past several decades was connected with spending for public pensions, assistance to the aged, public health, and programs linked to larger families, including the care and the education of children. This spending is clearly related to important economic risks associated with becoming old or ill, being illiterate, having many children, and so on. However, while real and significant, these risks, and especially those associated with old age and poor health, do not derive from globalization. Whether a country is globalized or not, its citizens will get old, and some will become ill. Globalization does not raise the probability of these risks except in the event that it makes it easier for infectious diseases to cross frontiers.

The same is to a large extent true for public spending on education. Whether a country is globalized or not, it will be better off with an educated population; and the more children there are, the higher will be the expenses for education. However, in this case globalization does not cause the birthrate to go up, although it could be argued that a globalized country will have a greater need for better-educated workers to be more competitive. To the extent that more spending for education and research helps in this direction and that it is mostly government financed, some link to globalization might exist. In conclusion, only a small part of public spending can be said to have become necessary because of higher risks created by a more open economic environment.

Details on the growth of total public spending on various categories of public spending as shares of GDP for 18 industrial countries for more than a century can be found in Tanzi and Schuknecht (2000). The categories include defense, education, public health, pensions, unemployment benefits, interest on public debt, and public investment.

## 6.3. Testing for Links between Globalization and Public Spending

In an often-cited paper, Dani Rodrik advanced the thesis that there is "a robust association between an economy's exposure to foreign trade and the size of government," measured by the ratio of public spending to GDP. For Rodrik, "the explanation is that government expenditures are used to provide social insurance against *external* risk" (Rodrik, 1998, p. 997; emphasis added). In other words, globalization raises the openness of a country's economy, and this larger exposure to foreign trade, coupled with "volatility of the terms of trade and the product concentration of exports," increases external risk and leads to "greater volatility in domestic income and consumption." This increased volatility can be reduced by a larger share of government spending in GDP. The public budget becomes the shock absorber for the higher risks of individual. Rodrik concluded that "causality should run from exposure to external risk to government spending" (p. 998). He then proceeded to provide some empirical backing to his thesis. On the basis of his empirical analysis, he concluded that "governments have expanded fastest in the most open economies" and especially "in economies that are subject to the greatest amounts of external risk" (p. 1028).

This is indeed a powerful and important hypothesis. Rodrik referred to an earlier paper, by David Cameron (1978), that had also linked tax revenue statistically to the economy's openness. However, he ignored the large literature by public finance economists, which in the decades of the 1960s and 1970s also had found a relation between openness and tax burden. These economists had argued that the causation of the relationship was different from the one assumed by Rodrik. Put simply, for these writers openness provides a convenient "tax handle" for governments that would like to increase tax revenue but are unable to do so through taxes other than those associated with trade (see, e.g., Tanzi, 1973 and 1967; Musgrave, 1969). For these writers, external risks had little to do with the level of taxation or the level of public spending. The spending role of government was larger in more open economies simply because these economies found it easier to collect more taxes. This literature focused explicitly on developing countries because it was assumed that industrial countries had more control on the level of taxation and on the use of specific tax categories.

There are some theoretical questions about the relationship between trade liberalization and individual income risk. As pointed out by Krebs, Krishna, and Maloney (2004), in the short run the reallocation of capital and labor across firms and sectors brought about by trade reform and by increasing openness can raise individual income risk. However, beyond the short run a better-integrated world economy would produce more stable prices and better macroeconomic outcomes. Their assessment is that, "theoretically, the openness-volatility relationship is ambiguous, that is, the theoretical literature does not offer strong prior on the sign or magnitude of this relationship [for the long run]." It could be added that a country that has made the initial adjustment to join this new open world as, say, Germany or Chile did, would have an easier ride in future years. Thus, a process of *trade integration* that is gradual rather than sudden could make the world economy and the economies of specific countries more stable and thus reduce, rather than increase, income risks. However, there is no certainty of this. Furthermore, this conclusion refers to globalization related to trade and *not necessarily to that related to capital movements.*

When financial markets are linked, sudden capital movements, especially if associated with portfolio investments and with speculation rather than with real investments, could increase risks by creating financial crises, even over the longer run. These sudden capital movements often originate from the domestic policies of the affected countries, but they can also be induced by contagion or by developments in major industrial countries, such as sudden, large changes in interest rates or in the credit that they make available. This happened in the United States in the early 1980s when the Federal Reserve Bank sharply and suddenly increased interest rates to fight U.S. inflation. This increase in interest rates may have contributed to the Latin American debt crisis and to that region's "lost decade." Of course, the domestic policies of the Latin American countries also played an important part. They had borrowed too much abroad, using the money to finance consumption or bad investments. Before the 2008–9 crisis, excessive credit to the housing industry in the United States and very low interest rates promoted by the Federal Reserve Bank until 2004 led to excessive investment in housing and set in motion forces that led to the global crisis.

There had been a lot of talk in recent years about reforming the "architecture" of the international financial system. Unfortunately the talk had not been followed by concrete actions (Tanzi, 2000). A reform of this architecture, which introduced *efficient* regulation of financial activities at the global level, combined with sound macroeconomic policies at the national level, which increased transparency and sharply reduced foreign borrowing (especially foreign borrowing associated with large structural fiscal deficits or misaligned exchange rates), would reduce the risks deriving from free capital movements. The greater provision of good data on the part of many countries and financial institutions would also lead to better investment decisions and reduce the probability of these crises. Unfortunately, while some limited progress was made after the 1997–98 crisis in Southeast Asia in the provision of national data, the progress was not sufficient, disequilibria continued, the architecture of the international financial system was not reformed, and data about the activities of hedge funds and other major actors in the financial market remained scarce.

Apart from these considerations, related to the impact of openness on income-related risk, it has been pointed out that there are two possible and conflicting hypotheses about the impact of globalization on public spending: one is the "efficiency hypothesis"; the other is the "compensation hypothesis" (Garrett, 1999; and Garrett and Mitchell, 1999).

The efficiency hypothesis stresses the fact that high levels of public spending, especially if directed toward welfare payments, reduces a country's ability to compete globally. The reason is that this welfare spending, which necessarily raises the level of taxation in a country, makes the country's economy less efficient. Therefore, as the global market becomes more integrated, and more open to competition, pressures are created to make the economy more efficient. These pressures may lead to the liberalization of labor markets, to the reduction of inefficient regulations and to the introduction of efficient ones, to the freeing of goods market, to the privatization of public enterprises, and even to the reduction of tax rates and public spending.

One consistent result of these trends during the recent globalization has been the widespread drop in marginal tax rates for the personal income tax and in the tax rates that apply to capital income and to the profits of enterprises. Over the past two decades, these rates have dropped sharply in practically all industrial and developing countries. These pressures to become more efficient have been recognized. For example, Harold James (2000, p. 213) wrote that "states are faced by contradictory pressures: on the one hand, to reduce tax levels, because of the enhanced mobility of factors of production; and on the other, traditional consideration requiring additional expenditures."

The efficiency hypothesis can be combined, especially for states that have high tax burdens, with a concern that globalization may have created "fiscal termites" that are progressively weakening the bases of tax systems and that will make it progressively more difficult, or more costly, for countries to maintain high tax levels. We refer to this as the "fiscal termites hypothesis." Table 4.5 shows that almost no OECD country had reached the highest level of taxes in 2008, the last year for which data were available and the last year before the financial crisis affected tax revenue. Most countries reached the highest level around 2000 and started reducing the tax level in more recent years, before the 2008–9 crisis. Because of the "fiscal termites," the role of the state must be reconsidered in order to reduce public spending, making it more efficient while possibly preserving the protection against significant risks (Tanzi, 2001 and 2002).

The compensation hypothesis, on the other hand, is essentially Rodrik's hypothesis that argues that public spending must be increased to compensate workers for the higher risks and for the costs associated with globalization and, possibly, to improve the quality of "human capital" through training and education, so that the countries' economy can remain competitive in a more integrated global economy. Thus, in some ways social spending can acquire some of the characteristics of public goods, because it can contribute to the country's competitiveness. Public spending can also help maintain political support for globalization and for promarket policies. Without this support, populism could become a strong force, leading to inefficient policies such as protection against imports and inefficient forms of industrial policy.

These are to some extent competing hypotheses. It is possible that some countries might opt for the policies implied by the first hypothesis, while other countries may try to follow the policies of the second.

## 6.4. Empirical Tests

A detailed empirical analysis of these two contradictory hypotheses is beyond the scope of this book, but a few observations are in order.

First, it is improbable that, as Rodrik maintains, "the social welfare state has been the flip side of the open economy." As we saw in earlier chapters, the intellectual winds that produced the welfare state were long in coming and became strong exactly in the years when the economies became *less* open. The Keynesian revolution and the creation of mixed economies and welfare states happened in a period when economies that had been relatively closed became even more isolated. The level of public spending grew relatively little in the 1870–1913 period, when the economies were particularly open and before they started closing temporarily and significantly because of the First World War. On the other hand, as we reported earlier, by 1926 Keynes was calling for an end to "laissez-faire" (Keynes, 1926). In the early 1950s, long before the current globalization process got under way, there were already complaints about the increase in public spending and the creation of welfare states (see de Jouvenel, 1952) and calls for the creation of what could be considered a welfare state in the relatively closed American economy (Galbraith, 1958).

Second, Rodrik's sample of OECD countries is biased by the fact that the countries where public spending grew the most in the period covered by Rodrik (mostly those of northern Europe) are all small countries that, being small, tend to be more open. These are also countries with more ethnically homogeneous populations. It has been shown in several studies that countries that are more ethnically homogeneous tend to have higher levels of public spending. (See. inter alia, Alesina, Glaeser, and Sacerdote, 2001; and Alesina and La Ferrara, 2003.)

Third, there are major problems with the data *when the sample is expanded by Rodrik beyond the OECD countries* to the "100 plus-country sample" that includes the developing countries. These problems are not random but systemic. There is no data source that gives public spending *for developing countries for the general government.* Comparable data that include subnational public spending for these countries simply do not exist systematically beyond the OECD sample. The mother of all data sources, the IMF *Government Finance Statistics,* provides data for *central* government only. Because larger countries (e.g., Brazil, Argentina, Mexico, Nigeria, India, South Africa, Russia, Indonesia, China) have often large subnational governments, the spending of which does not show in the data, and because these countries, because of their size, tend to be less open, this statistical deficiency biases the relationship between openness and public spending. Interestingly, the most closed Latin American economy – Brazil – is also by far the country with the largest level of public spending – more than 40 percent of GDP in recent years. The next most closed economy, Argentina, follows Brazil with public spending of well over 30 percent.

A study that attempted to deal with this problem by assembling from various sources more comprehensive data for public spending from 1973 to 1997 for 14 Latin American countries concluded that "*the most striking finding is the strong* negative effect of trade openings on changes in aggregate social spending" (see Kaufman and Segura-Ubiergo, 2000, p. 6, emphasis added, and 2001). This result is not surprising to anyone familiar with the Latin American situation. Trade opening leads to the fall of foreign taxes, and capital liberalization leads to the fall of taxes on incomes from capital sources. This forces countries to spend less. There is a large literature on the negative impact of trade opening on tax revenue for developing countries (see, inter alia, Ebril, Stotsky, and Gropp, 1999; Peters, 2002; and Abed, 2000). There is also evidence that taxes on incomes from financial sources have fallen in most countries.

Finally, it is worthwhile to show that, over the past two decades, when the process of globalization became particularly intense, the countries with the most open economies were the ones that *reduced* the total public spending the most.

Tables 1.1 and 4.4 provide information on what happened to public spending in some of the most open OECD countries in recent years, during the period when concerns about globalization became intense. Public spending fell significantly rather than increased. This behavior supports either the efficiency hypothesis or the fiscal termites hypothesis. More likely it reflects some combination of the two because their effect on public spending would be the same.

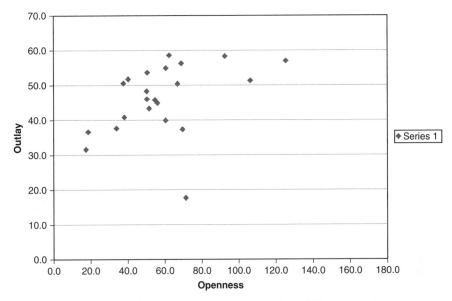

Figure 6.1. Openness versus outlay: 1987.

Another way of addressing the link between openness and public spending for industrial countries is to plot openness against public outlay, as done by Rodrik. We do this for two years, 1987 and 2002. In Figure 6.1 public outlay is on the vertical axis and openness is on the horizontal axis, both for 1987. Figure 6.2 has the same information for 2002. The period between 1987 and 2002 was one of intense globalization. Openness is defined as imports plus exports as percentages of GDP. For these countries, the spending data for *general* government are available from the OECD. The openness data are from IMF sources.

Figure 6.1, for 1987, seems to support the Rodrik hypothesis: openness and public spending are positively correlated for OECD countries. The correlation between the two variables is positive and equal to 0.41. Figure 6.2 shows the same statistics for 2002. Because the period between 1987 and 2002 was one of intense globalization, the scatter diagram for 2002 should show a closer positive relationship between the two variables than the scatter diagram for 1987. However, this is not what happened. The two variables seem to be much less correlated in 2002 than they were in 1987. In fact, the correlation coefficient falls from 0.41 for 1987 to an insignificant 0.07 for 2002.

A far better empirical test is one that correlates *changes* in public spending over the 1987–2002 period against *changes* in openness over the same period. If more openness brings about more public spending, as theorized

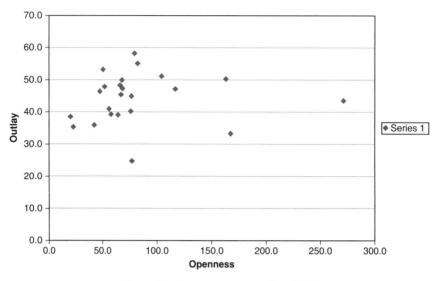

Figure 6.2. Openness versus outlay: 2002.

by Rodrik, there should be a positive relationship between these two variables. Figure 6.3 provides a scatter diagram that shows changes in openness on the horizontal axis and changes in public spending on the vertical axis. The scatter diagram shows clearly that the relationship is negative rather

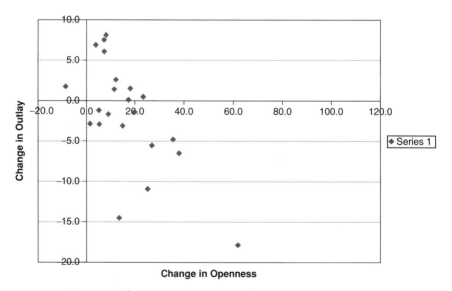

Figure 6.3. Change in openness versus change in outlay: 1987–2002.

than positive. The more open the economies of the countries became, the less their governments spent. This is confirmed by the correlation coefficient that is negative and equal to $-0.67$. This chart points to the validity of the efficiency, or the fiscal termite hypothesis, rather than the compensation hypothesis. Thus, it would seem that the compensation hypothesis can be put to rest with respect to public spending. However, as we argue in later chapters, public spending is only one of the tools available to governments to promote their roles. Rodrik may have been wrong in concluding that globalization raises public spending, but he might be right in assuming that globalization requires a different and possibly a larger role of the state. That role would use other policy instruments than public spending.

## References

Abed, George. 2000. "Trade Liberalization and Tax Reform in the Southern Mediterranean Region," in *Trade Policy Developments in the Middle East and North Africa*, edited by B. Hoekman and H. Kheir-el Din. (Washington, D.C.: World Bank), chap. 3.

Alesina, Alberto, E. Glaeser, and B. Sacerdote. 2001. "Why Doesn't the U.S. Have a European Style Welfare State?" *Brookings Paper on Economic Activity* (Fall).

Alesina, Alberto, E. Glaeser, B. Sacerdote, and Eliana La Ferrara. 2005. "Ethnic Diversity and Economic Performance." *Journal of Economic Literature* 43, no. 3: 762–800.

Baldwin, Richard, and Philipp Martin. 1991. "Two Waves of Globalization: Superficial Similarity, Fundamental Differences," in *Globalization and Labor*, edited by Horst Siebert, Institute für Weltwirtschaft, University of Kiel (Kiel: Moh Siedeck).

Beito, David, Peter Gordon, and Alexander Tabarrok, eds. 2002. *The Voluntary City* (Ann Arbor: University of Michigan Press – Independent Institute).

Cameron, David. 1978. "The Expansion of the Public Economy: A Comparative Analysis." *American Political Science Review* 72: 1243–61.

Clarke, Peter. 2009. *The Rise, Fall and Return of the 20th Century Most Influential Economist* (New York: Bloomsbury Press).

Coatsworth, John H., and Jeffrey G. Williamson. 2004. "The Roots of Latin American Protectionism," in *Integrating the Americas*, edited by Antoni Estevedoardal, Dani Rodrik, Alan M. Tayer, and Andres Velasco (Cambridge, Mass.: Harvard University Press), pp. 37–74.

de Jouvenel, I. Bertrand. 1952. *The Ethics of Redistribution* (Cambridge: Cambridge University Press).

de Molinari, Gustave. 1849. *Les Soirées de la Rue Saint-Lazare: Entretiens sur les Lois Economique et Défense de la Propriété.* Translated as *Le Serate di Rue Saint-Lazare* (Macerata: Liberi Libri, 2009).

Ebril, Liam, Janet Stotsky, and Reint Gropp. 1999. *Revenue Implications of Trade Liberalization,* Occasional Paper 180 (Washington, D.C.: IMF).

Friedman, Thomas. 2005. *The World Is Flat: A Brief History of the Twenty First Century* (New York: Picador; Farrar, Straus and Giroux).

Galbraith, John Kenneth. 1958. *The Affluent Society* (Boston: Houghton Mifflin).
  1990. *A Short History of Financial Euphoria* (New York: Penguin Books).
Garrett, Geoffrey. 1999. "Globalization and Government Spending around the World." Paper presented at the 1999 Meeting of the Political Science Association, Atlanta, September 1–5.
Garrett, Geoffrey, and Deborah Mitchell. 1999. "Globalization and the Welfare State," Yale University. Mimeo.
Gaspari, D. 1881. *Il Progresso delle Societá di Mutuo Soccorso* (Sanseverino, Marche: Corradetti).
Geremia, Giusto. 1961. "La previdenza sociale in Italia nell'ultimo secolo," in *L'Economia Italiana dal 1861 al 1961: Studi nel Primo Centenario dell'Unitá d'Italia* (Milan: Dott. A. Giuffré Editore).
Harris, Stephen. 2004. "Public Private Partnerships: Delivering Better Infrastructure Services." *Working Paper* (Washington, D.C.: IADB).
James, Harold. 2000. *The End of Globalization: Lessons from the Great Depression* (Cambridge, Mass.: Harvard University Press).
Kaufman, Robert, and Alex Segura-Ubiergo. 2000. "Globalization, Domestic Politics and Welfare Spending in Latin-America: A Time-Series Cross-Section Analysis, 1973–1997." *Working Paper*, June 2. Washington D.C.: The World Bank.
  2001. "The Political Economy of the Welfare State in Latin America." (The World Bank, Mimeo).
Keynes, John Maynard. 1926. *The End of Laissez Faire* (London: Hogarth Press).
Krebs, Tom, Pravin Krishna, and William Maloney. 2004. "Trade Policy, Income Risks, and Welfare." Mimeo.
Lucas, Robert E., Jr. 1973. "Some International Evidence on Output-Inflation Trade-Offs." *American Economic Review* (June).
  1976. "Economic Policy Evaluation: A Critique." *Carnegie-Rochester Conference Series on Public Policy* 1 (1976).
Musgrave, Richard. 1969. *Fiscal Systems* (New Haven: Yale University Press).
Peters, Amos. 2002. "The Fiscal Effects of Tariff Reduction in the Caribbean Community," InterAmerican Development Bank. Mimeo.
Posner, Richard A. 2009. *A Failure of Capitalism* (Cambridge, Mass.: Harvard University Press).
Prescott, Edward C. 1986. "Theory Ahead of Business-Cycle Measurement." *Carnegie-Rochester Conference on Public Policy* 25.
Reinhart, Carmen M., and Kenneth Rogoff. 2009. *This Time Is Different; Eight Centuries of Financial Folly* (Princeton: Princeton University Press).
Ritter, Gerhard A. 1996. *Storia dello Stato Sociale* (Rome: Editori Laterza).
Rodrik, Dani. 1998. "Why Do More Open Economies Have Bigger Government?" *Journal of Political Economy* 106, no. 5 (October): 997–1032.
Schlesinger, Jr., Arthur M. 1959. *The Coming of the New Deal* (Boston: Houghton Mifflin).
Shiller, Robert J. 2008. *The Subprime Solution* (Princeton: Princeton University Press).
Sinn, Hans-Werner. 2010. *Casino Capitalism: How the Financial Crisis Came About and What Needs to Be Done Now* (Oxford: Oxford University Press).
Solimano, Andres, ed. 2008. *The International Mobility of Talent, Types, Causes, and Development Impact* (New York: Oxford University Press).

forthcoming. *Broken Borders: The International Mobility of People and Elites in the Global Age* (Cambridge: Cambridge University Press).

Solomon, Howard M. 1973. *Public Welfare, Science and Propaganda in Seventeenth Century France* (Princeton: Princeton University Press).

Tanzi, Vito. 1967. "Determinants of Government Revenue Shares among Less Developed Countries; A Comment." *Economic Journal* 77, no. 306 (June): 403–5.

——— 1973. "The Theory of Tax Structure Change." *Rivista di Diritto Finanziario e Scienza delle Finanze.*

——— 2000. "Taxation and the Architecture of the International Economic System," in *Financial Globalization and the Emerging Economies*, edited by J. A. Ocampo, S. Zamagni, R. French-David, and C. Pietrobelli (Santiago, Chile: CEPAL and Jacques Maritain Institute), pp. 139–50.

——— 2001. "Globalization, Technological Developments and the Work of Fiscal Termites." *Brooklyn Journal of International Law* 26, no. 4 (August): 1261–85.

——— 2002. "Globalization and the Future of Social Protection." *Scottish Journal of Political Economy* 49, no. 1 (February): 116–27.

——— 2007. "Complexity and Systemic Failure," in *Transition and Beyond*, edited by Saul Estrin, G. Kolodko, and M. Uvalic (London: Palgrave), pp. 229–46.

——— 2010a. "Recent Fiscal Developments and Exit Strategies." *CES ifo Forum* 11, no. 2: 105–10.

——— 2010b. *Russian Bears and Somali Sharks: Transition and Other Passages* (New York: Jorge Pinto Books).

Tanzi, Vito, and Ludger Schuknecht. 2000. *Public Spending in the 20th Century* (Cambridge: Cambridge University Press).

Trevelyan, G. M. 1942. *English Social History* (London: Longmans, Green).

Wuthnow, Robert, ed. 1991. *Between States and Markets: The Voluntary Sector in Comparative Perspective* (Princeton: Princeton University Press).

Zamagni, Vera, ed. 2000. *Povertá e Innovazione Istituzionale in Italia: dal Medioevo ad Oggi* (Bologna: Il Mulino).

# PART THREE

# THEORETICAL AND ANALYTICAL ISSUES

The government does not solve problems, but finances them.
Ronald W. Reagan

The question we ask today is not whether our government is too big or too small, but whether it works.
Barack Obama

# SEVEN

# Theories of Public-Sector Behavior

## Taxonomy of Government Types

### 7.1. Introduction

In the previous chapters, we have provided information on the growth of public spending over more than a century in several countries and have discussed the impact that various factors, as well as important economists, may have had on that growth. We now turn out attention to the results and the consequences of high public spending and consider various theories that have been advanced by economists to help explain the behavior of governments. In this chapter, we focus on "primal types" of states and offer some classifications that may be of use in assessing ways in which governments behave. We start with Italian contributions that contain seeds for later development in fiscal theory. Except for James Buchanan, and, to a lesser extent, Richard Musgrave, Alan Peacock, and a few others, these seeds have not been fully recognized by non-Italian public finance scholars. However, especially through the work of Buchanan, they have had some limited impact on the public finance literature.

Public finance has been a major field of study, separate from economics, in Italy for perhaps longer than in most other countries. The first chair in public finance was established at the University of Pavia in 1878, and its first occupant was Giuseppe Ricca Salerno, who was the author of one of the earliest public finance textbooks (Salerno, 1880). Chairs in public finance continue to exist today in various faculties (economics, statistics, law, and political science). There were full treatises in public finance as early as the middle of the 19th century (see, e.g., Bianchini, 1855). Because of this, the Italian *scienza delle finanze* developed early, deeply, and further than in other countries, with the possible exception of Germany.[1] However, linguistic obstacles limited and continue to limit the impact of the Italian school. Still, today, there are several Italian-language journals that concentrate on public finance, and there is an association, the Societa' Italiana di Economia Pubblica (SIEP), that holds annual congresses on public economics. (In the United States, there is a tax association but not a separate one in public finance or public economics.) While the contributions of the Italian school are very extensive and diverse, what is reported here describes only some of those contributions and highlights a few aspects of particular significance to the issue of the role of the state in the economy.

## 7.2. The Theory of Fiscal Illusion

De Viti de Marco was one of the major contributors or founders of the Italian *scienza delle finanze*.[2] (Other major contributors to that tradition included Barone, Pantaleoni, Mazzola, Pareto, Fasiani, Puviani, and Einaudi.) After pointing out that public finance "studies the *productive* activities of the state, which are directed toward the satisfaction of collective wants" (De Viti de Marco, 1936, p. 34; emphasis added) and that "collective wants presuppose the existence of a community" (p. 37), he assumes that "the members of society agree in desiring that public goods shall be produced according to the law of least cost" and that "every citizen tends to maximize his consumption of public goods, at the same time attempting to pay the least possible amount" (pp. 35–36). These statements summarize much of the later literature in public finance.

De Viti de Marco makes the interesting observation that "collective wants... arise from a certain '*conflict*' *of interests* between the groups that make up the national and international social structure"; the state "intervenes in order to regulate and make possible the co-existence of the antagonistic activities of such groups" (p. 38; emphasis added). Therefore, the state acts as a referee. The collective wants that he lists – defense and internal security, enforcement of contracts and conflict resolution, activities with important negative externalities such as those with respect to hygiene, and regulation of natural monopolies – have all the characteristics of dealing with conflicts of interest between groups (or nations).[3] The assumption here seems to be that the state is more efficient in dealing with these conflicts than arrangements attempted by private citizens. One can assume that in this economist's view, the state's intervention reduces the transaction costs for the production of public goods. In some way, De Viti de Marco's position reminds one of Adam Smith's, that the role of the state is predominantly needed to reduce conflicts and make commerce easier. However, there is no reference to Adam Smith in De Viti de Marco's work.

After stressing that in public finance political elements or factors are always present and active, De Viti de Marco postulates that there are essentially two different "extreme" or "limiting" types of political constitution, the *absolute state* and the *popular state*. However, he believes that most real-life states reflect some combination of the two. He recognized that bureaucracies at times acquire dictatorial power in these states. He, thus, anticipates the principal-agent problems that would attract attention in more recent years. He also points out that, especially in the popular state, pressures by interest groups can lead to unproductive spending. The possibility that public spending becomes more unproductive is a characteristic that becomes more relevant when states are more popularly based. One reason is that "with the substitution of a system of finance based on taxation for one based on patrimonial finance, there came a rapid increase in public expenditure [when states became more popularly based]" (p. 69). Reliance on taxation made the supply of funds to governments more elastic. He also predicted a growing reliance on "fees" for public services in the future.

De Viti de Marco concluded that the income of each citizen can be considered as an index for measuring the demand for general public services so that taxes could be made proportional to income. It should be recalled that he was writing at a time when the state did not play much of a role in redistributing income so that the output publicly produced, mainly consisting of public goods, benefited everyone. The income could be considered a good, though not necessarily a perfect, index of the benefits that individuals received from the public spending.

A century and a half ago, John Stuart Mill had wondered whether "direct or indirect taxes are the most eligible." After observing "the unpopularity of direct taxation" and contrasting it "with the easy manner in which the public consent to let themselves be fleeced in the prices of commodities," Mill reached the conclusion that "an Englishman dislikes, not so much the [tax] payment, as the act of paying."[4] He called this preference for indirect taxes an "infirmity of the popular mind." His final assessment was that "if our present revenue . . . were all raised by direct taxes, an extreme dissatisfaction would certainly arise at having to pay so much."[5] Thus, the implication was that indirect taxes are necessary evils used by the government to make possible the raising of needed revenue. Or, if we look at it from a different angle, indirect taxes allow governments to raise more revenue and to spend more.[6] In Chapter 2, we saw how despised the income tax was in England in the 19th century.

While Mill's argument was related to the choice between direct and indirect taxes, Vilfredo Pareto made essentially the same point vis-à-vis the choice between taxes and public borrowing. While not contesting the Ricardian argument of the equivalence, *for a fully rational individual,* of the burden of extraordinary (i.e., once-and-for-all) taxes and public loans, Pareto observed that no taxpayer makes the Ricardian calculations. Therefore, the choice on the part of the authorities between loans and taxes is made by taking into account the taxpayers' *subjective* perception of their respective burden. Pareto's conclusion is reminiscent of Mill's: "Deficit financing is one way of inducing the citizens to accept what they would not accept with taxes. For example, if during the [first world] war the governments had tried to collect through taxes as much as they collected through loans, it is very likely that they would not have succeeded"[7] (Griziotti, 1944). As we reported in an earlier chapter, much of World War I was financed by loans and by money creation rather than by higher taxes. Thus, public debt and indirect taxes allow governments to get citizens' support for higher spending. In the decade of the 1960s and 1970s, economists rediscovered the "Ricardian equivalence" and used it to challenge Keynesian countercyclical policies based on deficit financing (Bailey, 1962; Barro, 1974).

Hugh Dalton, another Englishman who, in addition to having written one of the classic books in public finance, had the distinction of having held the office of chancellor of the exchequer, sided with the "plain man" in the conviction "that the best tax is that which is least felt, that is to say which causes the least inconvenience and conscious sacrifice to those who pay it."[8] Dalton quoted approvingly a Cambridge rule to be followed by the authorities in choosing among taxes: "The rich should pay more taxation than they think, while the poor should think they pay more than they do."[9] Thus, Dalton was recommending the use of fiscal illusion for both groups.

The basic point that these important writers were making, and one that incidentally was ignored by much of the modern public finance literature, which has been obsessed with rationality and optimal taxation, is that individuals are not computers that can assess fully and dispassionately the costs and the benefits of taxation (and of other policies). They are human beings with instincts and biases who may react in ways that are consistent not with "rational" behavior but with the ways individuals define rational behavior. Behavioral economics is finally giving some weight to this point. To some extent, the writers mentioned here anticipated intuitively some of the results recently found through experiments conducted by behavioral economists (for a recent survey of these experiments, see Della Vigna, 2009; also Smith, 2008).

While for Mill and Dalton the realization that individuals suffer from fiscal illusions did not become the keystone of a full-fledged theory of public-sector behavior, for Amilcare Puviani, an Italian writer of the turn of the 20th century, fiscal illusion was connected with a particular view of how governments operate. Puviani identified in fiscal illusion one instrument through which governments promote the growth of public spending that benefits the sectors or the groups that they represent.

Puviani made the most important systematic contribution to the theory of the *subjective* burden of taxation. In an unusual and, for a long time, forgotten book, he introduced the concept of "fiscal illusion."[10] In a very limited sense, this concept was implicit in some of the writing of Mill, Dalton, Pareto, and others. However, and this is a fundamental difference, while for the others it was mainly related to the attitude of taxpayers toward particular aspects of taxation or borrowing and thus was not in any way an interpretation or a description of the modus operandi of governments, for Puviani it became the cornerstone of his interpretation of how governments operate and implicitly of a *positive* theory of public-sector behavior. For Puviani, fiscal illusion became an instrument that policy makers can use, and often use, in the pursuit of their objectives. Furthermore, the concept was extended to cover both taxation and public expenditure. Fiscal illusion makes it possible for government to raise more revenue and to sustain a higher level of public spending. Occasionally it can also help accommodate or justify unproductive spending pushed by interest groups. Thus, it makes it easier for governments to accommodate the forces, mentioned earlier, that push for higher public spending and is an important concept in explaining the growth of public spending.

In Puviani's conception, governments do not aim at maximizing the difference between *objective* benefits, derived from public expenditure, and *objective* costs of financing that expenditure as, for example, is assumed by the modern pure theory of public expenditure (discussed in the next chapter)[11] and by all the literature that assumes that governments promote the "public interest" or a "welfare function." For Puviani, governments aim at maximizing the difference between *subjective* and often presumably objectively erroneous evaluations of the benefits of public expenditures and of their subjective costs. More importantly, this maximization process is not a static but a dynamic one: governments do not (or, at least, may not) passively accept and exploit these subjective and erroneous evaluations of costs and benefits *as they are* at any one time. On the contrary, they are actively engaged in *promoting* and/or *reinforcing* these errors through the active creation and use of "fiscal illusions." Therefore, fiscal illusions are not just random errors on the part of taxpayers but also systematic, government-induced errors. These illusions become instruments of governments and may be associated with or promoted by the increasing complexity of legislation. As legislation becomes progressively more complex, it becomes easier to generate fiscal illusions (see also Chapter 14).

Fiscal illusions are "errors . . . that the political body uses to reach its objectives" and these errors concern both "revenues" and "public expenditures."[12] These illusions can be positive or negative. The positive ones "consist in [making taxpayers] see things that do not exist,"[13] as, for example, in making them believe that a given public expenditure is actually solving a problem or making a genuine positive contribution to public welfare, when in fact it is not. The negative fiscal illusions occur when taxpayers do not see or feel the total burden of a tax actually paid or of a public debt incurred.[14] By promoting or reinforcing these illusions governments try to strengthen what Puviani calls the "contributive push," which we could simply call "taxpayers' compliance."[15] It is obvious that, when these fiscal illusions exist, the financial public-sector equilibrium, in terms of both level and structure of taxation and expenditure, will be different from the one implied by the (modern) pure theory of public expenditure.

There are various ways in which governments create and/or take advantage of fiscal illusions.[16] For example, governments will often rely on taxes that are included, or "wrapped up," to use Dalton's expression, in the prices of the products because, in this case, the taxpayer is less likely to be aware of the tax that he is paying and will thus not feel the sacrifice. This is the case with value-added taxes, as imposed in Europe, which, unlike the retail taxes imposed by U.S. state governments, are not shown separately; or with taxes that are shifted so that the actual burden falls on taxpayers other than on those meeting the legal obligation. Second, governments will not change the basic tax laws too often because taxpayers become particularly insensitive to taxes that have been levied for a long time ("old taxes are good taxes"); on the other hand, *minor amendments aimed at benefiting particular groups* of taxpayers will be frequent as they will often go unnoticed and unreported. This has been a problem in the United States where the number of pages dealing with income taxes in laws or regulations has grown astronomically over the years. This has made the tax system progressively more complex, thus increasing the cost of compliance (Tanzi, 2010). Third, governments will take advantage of shifts in public opinion that reduce the taxpayers' resistance to new or additional taxes.[17] Fourth, governments will avoid relying on just one or two taxes because, up to a certain point, the greater the number of taxes is, the lower is the taxpayers' resistance to the total tax burden. Fifth, governments will collect the tax when and in the way that is least painful to the taxpayer (e.g., with withholding at the source). Sixth, governments will rely on borrowing rather than on higher permanent taxes or even on (once-for-all) extraordinary taxes, as public borrowing will not result in an immediate, obvious burden. Seventh, governments will rely on deficit financing, financed not by borrowing from the public but from the expansion of the monetary base, as this "inflation tax" will not be seen as an obvious tax by the taxpayers. Eighth, governments will introduce taxes, clearly intended to be permanent, as temporary. Finally, governments will introduce new spending programs when the cost of these programs appears low (e.g., unemployment compensation during periods of full employment, social security programs that do not require payments for pensions until much later). The costs of these programs often become clear only much later.

When citizens are subjected to fiscal illusions, they will act in ways that may no longer be regarded as rational in an objective or optimal sense but that are rational from the point of view of the citizens, given the information that they have acquired. Therefore, fiscal illusions change the reality for the citizens so that their behavior may be consistent with their sense of reality that is distorted by the illusions. In addition, the creation of fiscal illusions can be seen as an intentional creation of informational asymmetry on the part of the government. Thus, asymmetry in information is not just a problem for the private market. "Lemons," a la Akerlof, can also exist in the public sector where it is the government that sells them.

## 7.3. Primal Types of States in the Italian Tradition

Puviani's theory can help explain to varying degrees actual, as distinguished from abstract, government behavior. In other words, it can be used to develop a *positive* theory of public-sector behavior. In order to do so, however, Puviani's theory must be combined with other Italian contributions. The Italian public finance literature, though not Puviani, identified and discussed three primal types of states:[18] the monopolistic (or predatory), the individualistic (or corporate), and the paternalistic (or tutorial). The importance and the use of public illusions are assumed to vary among these. Each of these forms of government behavior is likely to have characterized some countries at some historical point in time. It is also likely that this classification fits some current governments. It should be recalled that a classification of states in monarchies, aristocracies, and democracies goes back all the way to Aristotle and to Machiavelli. However, there is no direct matching of this classification with the one of the Italian school.

## Monopolistic State

In the monopolistic type, which is the one closest to Puviani's and Pareto's own conception of how governments operate, a ruling class, group, or party comes to control the government's apparatus of a country and uses it *to maximize the interests of the group's members*.[19] There is little genuine concern for the "public interest" interpreted as the interest of everyone. Rather, most governmental actions are ultimately aimed at favoring or even at maximizing the welfare of the subset of the population that controls or influences the government apparatus. This subset can be small and thus be removed from the majority. Or it can be a larger part of the population. The government might create government jobs for those most active in supporting the party in power; or it might promote public investments or even public education that benefits those groups or those regions that support the ruling group.[20] Of course, when the government promotes the interests of the majority of voters, it ceases to be a monopolistic state. Coercion need not necessarily be the main instrument for promoting the ruling class's interest; often, and especially in a more democratic setting, fiscal illusion is.

Fiscal illusions become important instruments used to achieve the objectives of the ruling class in the monopolistic state. These illusions are promoted and exploited by monopolistic governments to achieve their self-promoting objectives. They will induce the population to increase the acceptability of public spending, intended to benefit disproportionately the ruling class, by promoting positive fiscal illusions that exaggerate the benefits that the general public derives from the public expenditure. They will aim at increasing the acceptable level of taxation, or of borrowing by promoting negative fiscal illusions that hide the true (or objective) burden of taxation. This process results in structures and levels of taxation and public expenditure that are different from those that would be promoted by governments that behaved according to theories that are based on the premise that taxpayers' preferences, within a democratic context, are not distorted by fiscal illusions. The public expenditure will benefit disproportionately the groups that control the government. The burden of taxation will fall mainly or disproportionately on the rest of the population. The preferred taxes will be those for which fiscal illusions are easiest. The budgetary process will be such as to hide the true beneficiaries. This may be achieved by making the process and the budget document very complex. Extrabudgetary accounts, hidden expenditures, complex laws, and other such operations or options will be common.

A look around the world indicates that monopolistic governments, which were very prevalent in the past, have not disappeared, even though with the passing of time they may have come to depend less on coercion and more on fiscal illusions. The objectives sought have changed less than the instruments used. The reason is that even a monopolistic government finds it useful to promote its (selfish) objectives by relying on fiscal illusions, rather than simply on coercion or brute force, because it wants to remain in power, and this will be facilitated by some acceptability for its programs on the part of the citizenry. Thus even a monopolistic government will try to justify its actions in terms of the public interest. Populism may be one expression of such governments. Of course, a monopolistic government's ability to maximize the welfare of its members is often limited by various legal or sociopolitical constraints, including constitutions.[21] However, in the absence of fiscal illusions, the cost of remaining in power would be higher.

It may have been one of the limitations of Puviani's work to assume universality for the monopolistic type of state in the same way as it may be one of the limitations of the normative literature on public-sector behavior to (implicitly) assume universality for the individualistic state and voluntary exchange. It is easy to see some connection between Puviani's theory of fiscal illusion and some of the assumption of the school of public choice (Wagner, 2003). Wagner has pointed out that until recently the assumption of rationality on the part of economists tended to rule out fiscal illusions. However, when there is asymmetry in information, an individual may be fully rational and still be subjected to fiscal illusions. In conclusion, it can be realistically concluded that most governments rely on some fiscal illusion, but some more than others.

### Individualistic State

In the individualistic state, which is the one implicitly or explicitly assumed by much Anglo-Saxon public finance literature, not only does the individual have a voice in determining the role of the state, but the state exists only to serve him or her. It is not clear how the interests of the unborn or the spiritual interests of the dead are accounted for in this individualistic state. Musgrave notes that "the satisfaction of social wants must be based on the preferences of individual consumers or voters."[22] In other words, there are no natural *collective* wants but only those chosen by the individuals who make up the community. However, for technical reasons, there are pure public goods that make the connection with individual wants difficult. For example, defense is a pure public good, but different citizens are likely to value it differently (Tanzi, 1972b). The public interest is the summation of the welfare (measured cardinally) of all the individuals composing society at a given point in time.[23] There must not be any difference between the objectives of the taxpayers as a group, in terms of structure and level of taxation and public spending, and those of the governing body. Therefore, in this conception there should be no scope for the government's exploitation of fiscal illusions. The government not only should avoid promoting those illusions but should be actively engaged in educating the citizens so that they can avoid these "errors" with respect to revenues and expenditure. All decisions involving taxation and public spending should be based on illusion-free, educated, conscious and objective evaluations of the costs and the benefits associated with them.[24] The government will favor taxes the burden of which can be easily identified by those who pay them (broad-based individual income taxes, sales and excise taxes for which the tax is shown separately from the price of the commodity, and so on). The budgetary process will be all inclusive and transparent. Only in this way would the resulting equilibrium be consistent with a truly, objective welfare maximization. We shall see in the next chapter that this individualistic conception of the role of the state was prevalent in the public finance literature that prevailed in the United States in the 1950s and later.

### Paternalistic State

In the paternalistic or tutorial type of state, the public interest is no longer assumed to be the summation of the interest of all the individual citizens, as they themselves would see it in an illusion-free world, but it can, and usually does, transcend that summation. In this case the governing body, in the interest of the "community" or the state – which may acquire a mystical, Hegelian look – can transcend the interests of the individual citizens, as perceived by them, and pursue policies that may diverge from those of an individualistic type of state. The state may correct for the perceived myopia of particular citizens, in order to promote collective interests as it interprets the interest of the "community" or even those of individuals who act irrationally or who impose unwittingly costs on other citizens. These policies may include those to protect the environment for future generations and to ensure the continuity of the nation or of the community. In other words, the interest pursued by the governing body may diverge from the public interest that would result from the mechanical summation of the welfare as seen by all the individuals composing society at a given time, if we assume that such a summation was possible.[25] In this kind of state, income redistribution is likely to play a more important role than in the individualistic state, although this is not necessarily true.

In the pursuit of these policies, governments might correct for presumed "irrationality" of some citizens and might even be aided by the creation or the exploitation of some fiscal illusions, if these help correct for the irrationality or help promote the genuine, long-run goals of the state, as interpreted by the policy makers. However, the key difference is that this will be done not in the selfish interest of the group of individuals comprising or controlling the government, as was the case with the monopolistic state, but in the interest of "society" or the "country" or the "people" or the "community" or the "nation" or some other abstract concept, as interpreted by the well-intentioned policy makers. This concept is not limited to the mechanical summation of the interests of the individuals *who live in a country at one time.* The interests of future generations (and past generations) play a role.

In paternalistic states, even though the objectives of the governments may be fundamentally different from those in monopolistic states, so that the use of fiscal illusions could be considered as benign, the end result would still be a public sector with levels of taxation and of public spending different from those of the individualistic state. The leaders will not refrain from amending the preferences of the voters if they feel that those preferences are not consistent with the long-run interests of the community. This is the aspect that has made this concept of the state very unattractive to many public finance scholars. The fact that some dictators have claimed to act on behalf of this kind of state when they have limited the liberties of the citizens has contributed to the opposition to it. However, it ought to be recognized that the concept has some theoretical merit and can claim some distinguished pedigree.

The concept of the paternalistic state can perhaps be related to the rule by philosopher-kings, as in Plato's *Republic*, or, in a more democratic setting, to the "Harvey Road mentality" that some public choice theorists (e.g., Buchanan, Burton, and Wagner, 1978) attributed to Keynes. According to Peacock (1992, p. 10), Keynes believed that" the United Kingdom should be governed by an intellectual aristocracy ... who could persuade the public and the politicians to follow their prescriptions." Presumably, this intellectual aristocracy would promote its own interpretation of the public interests and would be insulated from political pressures and without personal biases. The MITA bureaucrats, who for many years ran Japan's economic policies when Japan was much admired, may have been an example of such an intellectual aristocracy. The policy makers of the welfare states of the Nordic countries of Europe may also reflect this type of state, at least according to some interpretations.

These primal types of government may never be found in their pure form in the real world. To varying degrees, all governments exhibit characteristics belonging to all of these types.[26] But for some countries, at some historical juncture, the monopolistic tendency may prevail; for others, the paternalistic traits may appear dominant. For this reason, one should expect to find most governments, to varying degrees, taking advantage of existing fiscal illusions and perhaps even creating or promoting some.

The *positive* theory of public-sector behavior helps explain or define the broad behavior of the public sector in a universal context; it is not limited geographically or historically. Especially in its individualistic version it does not invalidate the modern normative theory of public finance – the theory built on the fundamental contributions of Wicksell, Lindahl, Musgrave, Samuelson, and others – which not only assigns a benign role to the state but also rules out intentionally promoted fiscal illusions. There is a close relation between the normative theory and that of the individualistic state. It does, however, bring about a redimensioning of that theory by arguing that its validity and relevance are limited in time and space.

## 7.4. Primal Types According to Musgrave

In one of his last articles, published when he was almost 90 years old, Musgrave (1998) provided a classification of governments that bore some similarity with the Italian classification of primal types of economic roles of the state but was more influenced by the German and Austrian tradition in public finance and by Musgrave's own long and remarkable life and professional experience in several countries. Musgrave identified four primal types of states that covered a historical perspective beginning in the period before the 18th century and ending in modern times and a geographical perspective that spanned over many countries. The four types are the service state, the welfare state, the communal state, and the flawed state.

Musgrave's *service state* is broadly similar to the minimalist, but essential, state role that we identified earlier with Adam Smith and his classical economist followers. It is a state that corrects for (some of) the market's *allocative* shortcomings, or presumed failures, and performs essential minimal functions that cannot be delegated to the private market. Its role is connected mainly with the existence of pure public goods, large physical and institutional infrastructures, and *significant* externalities.[27] The main government tool for its intervention in the service state is exhaustive (i.e., real) public spending. Public spending must be kept at a minimum so that the tax level can be kept low. High taxes have damaging effects on incentives and on the economy, and spending above that minimum level tends to be inefficient and unproductive. In this "service state," there seem to be no role for income redistribution as an end in itself or for the stabilization of the economy. However, to the extent that extreme poverty exists and that it creates *significant* negative externalities, some spending can be allocated to deal with it. Thus, assistance to the "deserving poor" is justified, but fairness per se has no role in this spending function.

The *welfare state* is different from the service state because it admits distributional concerns, not connected with externalities associated with poverty. Fairness becomes important in guiding government policy. In the welfare state, society develops a view of what income distribution is considered fair, and the government promotes policies that aim at achieving that income distribution, even if these policies create some economic inefficiencies and may slow down the rate of growth of the economy. A major focus is no longer the existence of "poverty" but the "fairness" of the income distribution. Relative poverty replaces absolute poverty as the reason for governmental action. Gini coefficients, or other measures of income distribution, become important statistics, while in the service state only extreme poverty was important. This would imply that a country in which the market generated a good income distribution, before governmental intervention, would not need much governmental intervention.

In the *welfare state* the economic role of the government expands beyond narrow resource allocation to deal with more general market failure. More externalities attract the attention of the government. That role also includes fairness and, presumably, stabilization. According to Musgrave "the [welfare] state [still] implements the choice of individuals and their preferences" presumably as expressed through elections (1998, p. 35). He believes that the concern for fairness derives directly from individual preferences and not from those of the leaders. Individuals do not like an income distribution that is uneven and support redistribution even when they are on the losing side. The actions of individuals are expected to take into account the impact of those actions on the community. Thus, in Musgrave's interpretation, the actions by the government reflect the preferences of the citizens, and those preferences now include an aversion to high income inequality and to other consequences such as environmental degradation. This implies that the citizens of different countries, say Americans vis-à-vis Swedes, could have different preferences with respect to income redistribution, thus justifying different policies. The welfare state seems to harbor less worries than the service state about the disincentive effects of high taxes or of income redistribution policies.

Musgrave does not explain how individual preferences are amalgamated to allow policy decisions based on them or whether the preference of each citizen is given the same weight.[28] Presumably he would rely on the views of the policy makers chosen in free elections.[29] They would be the interpreters of the citizens' preferences. In any case there is no explicit economic theory that guides the redistributional function of the state. That function is the result of an undefined political process so that it becomes futile to speak of optimal outcomes.

The *communal state* seems to be related to but is not necessarily the same as the Italian paternalistic state. This type of state has also not been well received by economists, especially by those raised in the Anglo-Saxon, individualistic tradition and especially by followers of the school of public choice. These economists have always put the individual at the center of the action and well above the community. Communities are not supposed to have a mind or goals. Only individuals have goals. The goals of a community are assumed to be just the summation of the goals of the individuals who form the community at a given time. However, as Musgrave put it, in the communal state "the state is no longer a mere handmaiden to overcome externalities or to add distributional adjustments, made in line with the private preference of its members. While before the perspective was essentially individualistic, the state or community, as distinct from the private members that compose it, now has its own direct role to play" (1998, p. 42). The state acquires its own existence, an existence that is independent from that of the individuals living in the country or the community *at a given point in time*. As an Italian writer put it "the state is a living organism that has its own justification to exist and that extends its existence over time above that of the citizens who at any one time make up the community."[30] The unanswered question is, of course, who speaks for the state. The influence of George Hegel's philosophy is obvious. Communities, and especially old ones, develop traditions, history, community goals, and written and often unwritten rules of behavior that provide some guidance and a modus operandi to the government and may constrain individual behavior. These rules make up what sociologists call "social capital." In this conception, the state becomes like a river, the water of which changes all the time, but the river remains. The river is the state; the water represents the individuals.

In this community, as members of the community, individuals may have obligations and rights that extend beyond the specific rules issued by the government at a given time through its laws and regulations. There are always some norms or principles that are connected with traditions and ethical behavior and not just with formal rule of law. Thus, in some sense and to some extent, this is a principles-based more than a rule-based society. Of course, the principles may not always be desirable ones, as seen by those who are outside the community or even by some within the community. It would be difficult to understand the role of castes in India, or some other traditions in traditional societies, without understanding the existence of the community. A communal state is more likely to give more weight to the interests of the unborn and to future generations and may thus lead to what could be viewed as better decisions in some issues, such as global warming, that compare the immediate interests of the individuals living at the present time with those who will be living in future times. In a communal state, an assumption occasionally made by theoretical economists that individuals live forever becomes more acceptable.

In his article, Musgrave provides a rich historical and philosophical background for the "communal state." One gets the impression that, in his advanced age, he has come to admire and to feel nostalgic about the "communal setting of *Finanzwissenschaft* in the nineteenth-century German traditions." In this article, he reported at some length the views of Adolph Wagner and other thinkers and commented that, while "the distinction between private and public goods is straightforward [because it is based on technical characteristics], that *between communal and private wants is complex*" (1998, p. 46, emphasis added). He concluded that "the distinction between the role of individuals as private persons and as member of their community deserves serious consideration," implying that that distinction had not received such consideration. He added that "to view the world as based on private and self-interest-oriented concerns [of individuals]... leaves out a significant part of the social setting in which individuals function" (ibid.).[31]

It is easy to sympathize with Musgrave and to wonder why the notion that there are "communal wants" and "communal goods" has not received more attention on the part of public finance scholars, even though sociologists have often talked about social capital and have regretted the reduction in that capital in recent societies.[32] The existence of communal goods imposes obligation for both the state and the individuals and for the enterprises that belong to it at a given moment. These obligations often extend beyond the observance of rule of law. This becomes a society that is, at least in part, principle based in which the obligations of individuals go beyond those codified by formal laws and regulations. It is a society that is not just based on formal, legislated rules but also on ethical principles. This aspect is often stressed by the teachings of the Catholic Church and by papal encyclicals, which at times appear to favor an antimarket economy.

The occasional exploitation of these notions by authoritarian regimes should not be a sufficient reason to reject them because communal wants and goods clearly exist and play a significant role in the actions of governments. For example, it is difficult to explain why governments spend a lot of money to build expensive monuments, to protect the countries' cultural heritage,[33] to organize costly parades, to subsidize various national or even regional or communal cultural activities, to promote the activities of "national champions," and to promote "national interests" in various other ways without acknowledging the existence of communal wants and a communal conception of the state. National monuments do not seem to fit the category of private goods or public goods. They are in a category of their own and are definitely "communal goods." And there are many of them.

The *flawed state* is linked to but is not the same as the monopolistic state in the Italian tradition. It is a state where public-sector failure is common and where "fiscal illusion" is likely to be an important tool for governments. In this state, however, explicit coercion is also an important government tool. It is a state where narrowly based vested interests have replaced elites and where, according to Musgrave, "sector struggles" have replaced "class struggles." A flawed state may also be one in which principal-agent problems have become dominant, where corruption is common, and where the bureaucracy may no longer be a reliable instrument for implementing the policies planned at the top. Perhaps a difference from the monopolistic state is that the latter is more efficient in pursuing the interests of those who control the state. In the flawed state no one may be in full control of its activities. In the current jargon this would be called the failed state.

## References

Arrow, Kenneth J. 1951. *Social Choice and Individual Values* (New York: John Wiley & Sons; rev. ed., New Haven: Yale University Press, 1963).

Bailey, M. J. 1962. *National Income and the Price Level* (New York: McGraw-Hill).

Barro, Robert. 1974. "Are Government Bonds Net Wealth?" *Journal of Political Economy* 82, no. 6: 1095–1117.

Bianchini, Lodovico. 1855. *Principi della Scienza del Ben Vivere Sociale e della Economia Pubblica e degli Stati* (Naples: Dalla Stamperia Reale).

Bowsky, William M. 1969. "Direct Taxation in a Medieval Commune: The Dazio in Siena," in *Economy, Society and Government in Medieval Italy: Essays in Memory of Robert L. Reynolds*, edited by David Herliky, Robert S. Lopez, and Vsevolod Slessarev (Kent, Ohio: Kent State University Press), pp. 204–21.

Buchanan, James M. 1960. "La Scienza delle Finanze: the Italian Tradition in Fiscal Theory," in *Fiscal Theory and Political Economy, Selected Essays* (Chapel Hill: University of North Carolina Press), pp. 24–74.

1967. *Public Finance in Democratic Process* (Chapel Hill: University of North Carolina Press).

Buchanan James, David Burton and Richard Wagner. 1978. The consequences of Mr. Keynes (London: Institute for Economic Affairs).

Dalton, Hugh. 1967. *Principles of Public Finance* (New York: Augustus M. Kelley).

Della Vigna, Stefano. 2009. "Psychology and Economics: Evidence from the Field." *Journal of Economic Literature* 47, no. 2(June): 315–72.

De Viti de Marco. 1888. *Il Carattere Teorico dell'Economia Finanziaria* (Rome: Pasqualucci).

1936. *First Principles of Public Finance* (London: Jonathan Cape).

Fasiani, Mauro. 1951. *Principi di Scienza delle Finanze*, vols. 1 and 2 (Turin: G. Giappichelli).

Fausto, Domenicantonio, and Valeria De Bonis, eds. 2003. *The Theory of Public Finance in Italy from the Origins to the 1940s* (Pisa: Istituti Editoriali e Poligrafici Internazionali).

Griziotti, Benvenuto. 1944. "Fatti e Teorie delle Finanze in Vilfredo Pareto." *Rivista di Scienza delle Finanze*, 136–40.

Mosca, Gaetano. 1884. *Teoria dei Governi e Governo Parlamentare* (Turin: Loescher).

1966. *La Classe Politica*, a cura di N. Bobbio (Bari: Laterza).

1993. *Storia delle Dottrine Politiche* (Bari: Laterza, 1933).

Mill, John Stuart. 2004. *Principles of Political Economy* (Amherst, N.Y.: Prometheus Books).

Mueller, Dennis C. 1979. *Public Choice* (Cambridge: Cambridge University Press).

Musgrave, Richard A. 1959. *The Theory of Public Finance* (New York: McGraw-Hill).

1998. "The Role of the State in the Fiscal Theory", is *Public Finance in a Changing World*", edited by Peter Birch Sørensen (London: Macmillan Press LTD): 35–50.

Pareto, Vilfredo. 1951. *I Sistemi Socialisti* (1902; Turin: UTET).

1923. *Trattato di Sociologia Generale*, vol. 3, 2nd ed. (Florence: Barbera).

Parravicini, Giannino. 1970. *Scienza delle Finanze: Principi* (Milan: Dolt. A. Giuffre Editure).

Peacock, Alan. 1992. *Public Choice Analysis in Historical Perspective Raffaele Mattioli Lectures* (Cambridge: Cambridge University Press).

Putnam, Robert D. 2000. *Bowling Alone* (New York: Simon and Schuster).

Puviani, Amilcare. 1973. *Teoria dell' Illusione Finanziaria* (1903; Milan: ISEDI).

Ricca Salerno, Giuseppe. 1890. *Scienza delle Finanze*, 2nd ed. (Florence: G. Barbera Editore).

Sen, Amartya. 1999. "The Possibility of Social Choice." *American Economic Review*, 89, no. 3 (June): 349–78.

Smith, Vernon L. 2008. *Rationality in Economics* (New York: Cambridge University Press).

Tanzi, Vito. 1972a. "Taxpayer Preferences and the Future Structure of State and Local Taxation," in *Issues in Urban Public Finance*, New York Congress, edited by International Institute of Public Finance (Saarbrücken, 1973), pp. 459–66.

1972b. "Exclusion, Pure Public Goods, and Pareto Optimality." *Public Finance* 27, no. 1: 75–78.

1974. "Redistributing Income through the Budget in Latin America." Banca Nazionale del Lavoro, *Quarterly Review*, no. 108, pp. 65–87. (March).

Thomas, William. 1549 [1963]. *The History of Italy*, edited by George B. Parks (Ithaca, N.Y.: Cornell University Press for The Folger Shakespeare Library).

Wagner, R. E. 1976. "Revenue Structure, Fiscal Illusion and Budgetary Choice." *Public Choice* 25 (Spring): 45–61.

2003. "Public Choice and the Diffusion of Classic Italian Public Finance," in *The Theory of Public Finance in Italy from the Origins to the 1940s*, edited by Domenicantonio Fausto and Valeria De Bonis (Pisa-Roma: Istituti Editoriali Poligrafici Internazionali), pp. 271–82.

Weil, Henri. 1950. *Hegel et l'État* (Paris: Librairie Philosophique J. Vrin).

EIGHT

# Voluntary Exchange and Public Choice Theories

## 8.1. Introduction

Part II of this book described how the economic role of the state evolved, during the 19th and the 20th centuries, from one in which "the Mafia would [have been] a more accurate characterization of the state, [to one] concerned with the "public good...a state that is self-consciously concerned with the performance of the economy is a relatively modern phenomenon...associated with the rise of 'representative government'" (North, 1989, p. 108).[1] With the passage of time, the redistribution of income (from the top down and horizontally, depending on the distribution of economic risks and benefits) became an important objective and, together with the stabilization of the economy, was added as a relative newcomer to the legitimate goals pursued by governments.

While political discussions of the role of the state go back to Aristotle, Plato, Socrates, Machiavelli, and various philosophers during the Enlightenment in Europe and during the creation of the United States of America, in the previous chapters we discussed how a few major economists, and especially Adam Smith, Karl Marx, and John Maynard Keynes, contributed through their writings and those of their followers to the evolution in that role, over the 19th and 20th centuries, in the economies of the world. Directly or indirectly, each of these economists had an important impact on how governments saw their function and their responsibility in the economy. Smith was mostly concerned about the allocation of resources to facilitate commerce; Marx, with the redistribution of income (and especially wealth); and Keynes, with the function of stabilization. It can be added that each of these economists would probably have been surprised, and occasionally shocked, at how his ideas were interpreted, transformed, used, and often abused by his followers.

Through perhaps no fault of his, Adam Smith became "the apostle of capitalism" and "the puppet of conservatives." They pushed his ideas about the operation of markets far beyond where he probably would have liked (Buchan, 2006).[2] We have learned that China's current premier reads Adam Smith (see the "Lex Column," *Financial Times*, February 4, 2009). Amartya Sen has recently pointed out that Smith never used the term "capitalism," and he "did not take the pure market mechanism to be a free standing performance of excellence." Furthermore, he was a "defender of the role of the state in providing... education and poverty relief" and was "deeply concerned about the inequality and poverty" (Sen, 2009, pp. 27 and 28). Of course, Sen may also be pushing his interpretation of the work of Smith.

Karl Marx "would have been appalled by the crimes committed in his name" (Wheen, 1999, p. 2). As to Keynes, he was clearly a "reluctant Keynesian" whose main goal was to save capitalism from socialism during the Great Depression. As to the growth of public spending and taxation, which has often been attributed to or justified by Keynes's ideas, it may be repeated that, in a letter sent to the Australian economist, Colin Clark, Keynes agreed with Clark's thesis that a share of total taxes into national income of 25 percent was probably the maximum tolerable level before all kinds of negative consequences and inefficiencies would be set in motion. Clark's thesis had been stated in a paper published in 1945 (Clark, 1964). This tax percentage should be compared with the levels reached in the 1990s by many countries (Table 1.3).[3] Surely Keynes would have been horrified by these levels. Sen has called attention to Keynes's "relative neglect of social services" and to the fact that "he was relatively less engaged in analyzing problems of unequal distribution of wealth and of social welfare" (Sen, 2009. p. 29). And, as reported in the previous chapter, Keynes may have believed that economic policy should be formulated by a select group of intellectuals.

The late 1950s or early 1960s can be identified as the "tipping period" when the economic role of the state changed rapidly in many countries, even though that role had been changing slowly at least since the 1890s or even earlier. By the 1950s, the various political and intellectual pressures that had been building up for some time, some associated with the Industrial Revolution, converged and pushed many governments to rethink drastically, and not just superficially or rhetorically, on what the role of the state in the economy should be. In this period, the minimalist role of the state, the "service state" in Musgrave terminology, that had characterized the past, and which at some times and places may have made the state look like a Mafia, came to an end and started to be replaced, permanently, by one that expressed concern for the "public good" or the "public interest."[4]

## 8.2. The Voluntary Exchange Theory

The new role of the state would require far higher taxes and public spending than in earlier decades, except for the war years. The government would play a bigger role in allocating national resources and, especially, in distributing national income. Who should finance the higher spending? Who should benefit from the spending that would be more and more of a redistributive kind? How could this new role be played efficiently and fairly? Were there economic principles and rules that could guarantee that the results obtained from this higher spending would be beneficial or even optimal? What impact would the electorate have in determining this allocation of resources and public spending? What impact would those who made the specific decisions have? Would they simply follow the instructions of the electorate or pursue their own agenda? While in the public discussion the debate would often focus on specific programs, the debate among economists would also be centered on the economic role of the state.

In the past, some economists, including Wicksell and Lindahl from Sweden, Sax from Austria, and some scholars from the Italian school (Mazzola, Pantaleoni, De Viti de Marco), had addressed similar questions. However, given the limited scope of governmental intervention in their time and the more immediate spending needs (for wars, servicing of public debts after the wars, building of essential infrastructure in response to new technologies, and essential administrative services), these questions did not have the urgency that they would acquire in the 1950s and later years.

The period around 1950 saw the beginning of the so-called scientific phase of public finance and economics. Except for a few major economists (such as John Kenneth Galbraith and Milton Friedman) who continued to write for the general public, economists started to direct their writing more toward one another. Economic writing became more technical and, often, more mathematical. Mathematics became the chosen language of many economists who agreed with Samuelson that "mathematics is a language." According to Buchanan (1983, p. 13), "Economic theory ... had shifted to a discipline of applied mathematics."[5] Krugman (1991, p. 6) noted that "economics tends ... to follow the line of least mathematical resistance." Elaborate econometric models, based on a Keynesian framework that stressed the importance of macrovariables and on the improved national accounts statistics that had become available, were developed. Important new tools of analysis, intended to remove politics from policy decisions so that inefficiency in the use of public resources would be kept at a minimum, were created. Much writing was directed at refining tools, including budgetary tools, that could help policy makers make good decisions in spending policies.[6] In this period, the attention of mainstream public finance scholars, which in the past had concentrated on the revenue side of the budget, shifted to the spending side.

This was the period when "cost-benefit analysis," applied to public works, was developed. The basic concept went back a long time, to the work of Jules Dupuit, a French engineer, who in 1844 had discussed the measurements of the benefits and the costs of public works (Dupuit, 1952). Otto Eckstein, 1958, developed, as his doctoral thesis at Harvard, the modern version of cost-benefit analysis.[7] He became an important Harvard professor and went on to form a consulting firm that specialized in creating elaborate econometric models of the economy. The new concept of cost-benefit analysis was soon revised to accommodate unemployment, poverty, and "nonefficiency objectives" in so-called social cost-benefit analysis, thus introducing in the analysis, under "new clothes," considerations that were largely political. The belief was that unemployment and poverty tended to make social costs and social benefits, for public works, different from financial costs and benefits. A person hired when (or in an area where) there was high unemployment cost less, socially, that one hired when, or where, there was less unemployment. A dollar of benefit received by a poor person had more value than a dollar received by a rich person. Therefore, more public spending could be justified, when "social" considerations were taken into account. Cost-benefit analysis became part of new budgetary techniques (the "budget's new clothes") that included planning, programming budgeting systems (PPBS), zero-base budgeting (ZBB), and performance budgeting. These new techniques were expected to bring disciplines (and to give weight to social objectives) in the spending decisions of governments (see McKean, 1968; and Merewitz and Sosnick, 1971). However, as Peacock put it, "It is an intriguing question how the economic analysis of 'market failure' led to the supply of ideas creating its own demand" (1992, p. 7). This was an example of the application of "Say's Law" to the production of ideas. That law, named after the 19th-century French "laissez-faire" economist J. B. Say, says that the supply creates its own demand.

The economic analysis of "market failure" led to a sharply rising demand for the services of economists in the government. Or, perhaps, it was the other way around. Robert Fogel, who, in 1993, shared the Nobel Prize in economics with Douglass North, pointed out in his book *The Fourth Great Awakening and the Future of Egalitarianism* (2000) that in the United States there had been "little demand for . . . specialists in Washington until the onset of the great Depression" and that a "turning point in the government demand for economists came in 1932." "By 1938, the middle of Roosevelt's second administration, the number of economists employed by the government had risen to five thousand. Today, [as of 2000], that number stands at over twenty thousand." As Fogel points out, "Most of the new corps of specialists accepted the precepts of modernism and embraced its egalitarian ideals. They looked for guidance . . . to the journal of their discipline" (2000, p. 130).

Some questions were asked as to the nature of the government. Was it representative of the individuals living within the country at a given time or of something different? Was it to reflect in its decisions the wills of the living citizens, *qua* individuals, or transcend those wills? If it was supposed to reflect those wills, how could they be aggregated? As we have seen, some of these questions had been asked more philosophically, by European and especially by German economists, earlier. As Joseph Stiglitz would stress later – in a book on *The Economic Role of the State* published in 1989 – unlike clubs and other private associations, the state is characterized by two special features: membership is universal for the citizens born in the country and they do not choose to become members but become de facto members at birth.[8] Furthermore, the state has the exclusive or monopoly power over the use of (legitimate) force to compel citizens to do or not to do certain things; or to punish them for not complying with the laws and the rules imposed by the state. The legitimacy of the laws is not questioned except through complex legal and political procedures. The state can force citizens to pay taxes, serve in the military, fight and even die in wars, obey regulations, and so on. It can punish them financially, or even send them to jail, for not complying with rules or laws. At the same time, it provides citizens with some protection and with free, or highly subsidized, benefits and services.[9] Thus, there are clear costs and benefits of being a citizen of a country. These costs and benefits are not distributed equally, or even in proportion to income, across the population, as De Viti de Marco believed that they should be, or that they were. Because of this, coercion is necessary. To the two conditions mentioned by Stiglitz, which are also found much earlier in the works of Seligman and Fasiani, one should add another condition, stressed by Fasiani, that the state, unlike private clubs and other private associations, has a permanent existence. Individuals and private associations come and go, but the state remains. Fasiani stresses that only the state incorporates all three of these characteristics.

Even in a democratic context, there are implicit (or forced) exchanges between the state, on one side, and the citizens, on the other. These can be considered to be part of the social contract between the state and the citizens, which is never based on unanimity rule but generally on a simple majority rule that forces everyone to obey the laws of the land. Taxes paid by *all* citizens *as a group* can be assumed to be "prices" paid for *all* the public services that they receive. Superficially, this exchange makes the process appear similar to that of an individual who pays, with his own money, for goods that he buys from the private market. The difference is that each private good that is bought from the market by a private citizen is bought voluntarily; therefore, the private exchange can be assumed to be a truly voluntary one. However, the same cannot be said for public goods and services. The payments for these public goods and services do not reflect free decisions on the part of *each* individual taxpayer. For *individual* citizens, the exchanges with the government are in some sense forced. This problem becomes more significant when the taxes are high and the tax revenues are used to provide free or highly subsidized services that benefit especially particular groups of citizens and not necessarily all citizens. In this context what may appear to be true for the whole citizenry is not necessarily true for individual citizens, unless they are imbued by a high degree of altruistic spirit and/or feel that those who receive the benefits are, in a sense, part of their family or their immediate community. Even when the exchange may be assumed to be voluntary *for the whole community*, because the decision has been reached democratically through fair majority voting, it may not be a voluntary one for many individual citizens.

The idea of taxes as pseudoprices (tax prices) for the whole community had been common in the German *Finanzwissenschaft* and in some of the early writing in the Italian *scienza delle finanze*.[10] On the other hand, the Anglo-Saxon literature for a long time had tended to see government activity as largely unproductive, that is, producing little of real value that the citizens would want to pay for willingly. Thus, the less government there was, the better it would be. In the Italian tradition, the basic question had been whether the prices for the basic services offered by the government tended to be too high for reasons connected with bad taxes or with the nonoptimal use of the tax revenue because of the appropriation of some benefits by the ruling class.[11] In the Anglo-Saxon literature, the question had not been the possible exploitation on the part of the ruling class but the implicit view that public spending was inherently unproductive.

In the private sector, *each* person buys freely the goods that he or she likes and in the quantities and qualities desired, given his or her spending capacity. Given full information on both sides, each legitimate transaction can be assumed to be "welfare improving." If I buy or exchange something, it means that what I get has greater value to me (under the assumption of full and symmetric information) than the money or the goods I give in exchange. Mutatis mutandi, the same is true if I sell something. The market determines the equilibrium prices at which exchanges take place. If the market is working well, the free transactions in the private sector establish outcomes that can be considered Pareto optimal: nobody can be made better off without making someone else worse off. Resources are invested in the goods and services that people desire, and prices guide these investments. For several reasons, however, this is often not the case in the public sector.[12]

Just like private goods, public goods are costly to produce and/or provide; however, they are not sold at market prices, and people do not have the freedom to buy or not to buy them, and in the quantity or the quality that they desire. One cannot buy the amount of police protection or of national defense that he or she desires. Once produced, in whatever quantity or quality, public goods are provided free or at highly subsidized prices, and they benefit or can benefit anyone who lives in the country and accesses them. People cannot be excluded from benefiting from them, regardless of whether, as taxpayers, they have contributed or not to the financing of the goods. Thus, the problem of potential free riders is always present. Furthermore, for *pure* public goods, even if the nonpaying individuals could be excluded, which is not possible, it would be inefficient to do so because the cost of adding additional beneficiaries is zero, once the public goods have been provided. Additional consumers can be added at no extra cost, because their addition does not subtract benefits from others.

Under a system of truly *voluntary* exchange, between the state and the individual citizens, it would be convenient for individuals not to contribute to the cost of provision of the public goods, thus becoming "free riders"; or, alternatively, to understate the benefits that they get from a particular public goods in order to reduce their tax payment. For *pure* public goods, it is generally and practically impossible for the state to force citizens to "reveal their true preferences." These are nonrival goods in consumption and do not have the characteristic of excludability. Thus, inevitably, decisions on how much to produce, what to produce, and how to make citizens pay for the public spending *become political decisions. The participation of individual citizens is inevitably "forced."* There is no *voluntary* exchange in this context. The Italian *scienza delle finance* always recognized this. Furthermore, as it was argued earlier, if the government is able and has an interest in creating some fiscal illusions, even the assumption that the citizens vote for programs having full knowledge of their true value cannot be accepted. Fiscal illusion has the capacity of creating asymmetry in perception between the government and the citizens who vote.

Some literature that developed in the 1950s and that was partly built on earlier contributions from Sweden and Austria promoted the view that in democratic countries the exchange between citizens and governments could be "voluntary." The idea that, somehow, it might be possible in a democratic, representative government (as exists in many countries) to simulate, or to find a virtual equivalent of, a "voluntary exchange" between the citizenry and the state, which would democratically lead to Pareto efficiency or to optimality in the public-goods sector, attracted the attention of some of the best minds in economics before 1960, including Richard Musgrave, who had written his doctoral thesis in the late 1930s on the topic; Paul Samuelson (1954, 1955), who wrote some of the most frequently cited papers; and Kenneth Arrow (1951). These authors had followed leads suggested by Wicksell and Lindahl several decades earlier. Their goal was to develop the technical conditions for a "voluntary exchange" that would lead to an optimal allocation of resources (to a Pareto optimum), in both the private and the public sector, and to the maximization of a "social welfare function" to reach an *optimum optimorum*.[13] This would be a kind of economic nirvana. Could the "unseen hand" of the government perform a function similar to Adam Smith's "invisible hand" in the market? This question challenged some of the top economic minds in the 1950s.

One requirement was the existence of a virtual, all-knowing "philosopher king" or "social planner" who could play the role (in Plato's mold) of a "benevolent dictator." The planner would need to have perfect knowledge; to be totally objective and honest; and to be able to weigh accurately the preferences of the citizens in order to make the needed changes, as to the amount and type of taxes that each citizen would pay and the public goods to be provided. Nothing but the "public interest" would influence the "benevolent dictator's" decisions. He would have to be capable of identifying the public interest and the conditions needed to maximize it. Brilliant theoretical papers were written and discussed. However, as was the case with the scholastic or theological debate during the Middle Ages to determine how many angels could stand on the tip of a pin, brilliant theories did not translate into useful, practical applications. The theories could not solve an essentially unsolvable problem. Therefore, in spite of the accolades that the theories received from economists, they did not have an impact in the future evolution of the economic role of the state *in the real world*. That role continued to be influenced largely by political considerations conditioned by changing intellectual winds and pushed by the interests of pressure groups that were becoming progressively more powerful. Governments provided more and more goods and services that were not pure public goods and engaged in activities that were not fully justified by economic theory. Increasingly, the existence of externalities and of relative poverty created justifications for more and more public-sector intervention. Growing concerns about equity and stabilization added other justifications.

This is not the place to discuss in detail the theories or the specific reasons why those theories failed to have much of an impact on the future growth of public spending. There are several excellent books that have discussed those theories, including those by Dennis Mueller (1979 and later editions) and Cornes and Sandler (1986). A few comments may, however, be appropriate. These comments are not presented in order of their importance.

First of all, while the membership of the citizens in the state that represents a country may be universal, so that they are all supposed to be subject to the state's obligations and to vote, in the real world many citizens can try to escape from their obligations in several ways. Taxes may be evaded and are often violated on a large scale.[14] Economic activities can go underground.[15] Regulations can be ignored. Some citizens, and especially those with higher skills and incomes, may migrate to other countries to escape high taxes or other obligations, including those of serving in the military service in times of war.[16] Some may organize themselves in lobbies to elicit rents from governmental activities. Some may do little work in their government jobs, thus migrating into laziness, while still receiving government salaries and holding tenured jobs. Some may claim benefits to which they are not entitled, such as false invalids. Some government employees can engage in acts of corruption. Claiming fake disability has been a common problem in several countries. Disability benefits have been received by individuals who had no, or very minor, handicaps. Also the definition of disability may be adjusted, and has been over the years, thus allowing many undeserving individuals to receive disability pensions. Similar problems arise with individuals who get unemployment benefits while they work in the underground economy or simply choose to remain idle. Theories that ignored these real-life possibilities cannot provide useful guidance *in the real world* on the economic role of the state. When these activities become important, as they have in many countries, the signals that come from economic theories may no longer be relied upon. The usefulness of a normative theory depends on how much the reality is likely to diverge from the theory. It is not sufficient that the theory fits an invented, virtual reality as laid out by some "model." Theories must be adjusted to the reality, not the other way around.

Second, even if a "benevolent dictator" knew the *ordinal* preferences of the electorate, it would have to give weights to each individual's preference and find a way of aggregating all the preferences because, as Arrow put it,

"The social choice... is an aggregation of individual preferences" (1951, p. 103). However, given the ordinal ranking, some preferences may be held strongly, some weakly. There is "the problem of measurability of utility" and the problem of "interpersonal comparisons" (ibid., p. 94; see also Sen, 1999). Interpersonal comparisons are always difficult or even impossible to make in economics (Robbins, 1938). Arrow, in his "Impossibility Theorem," pointed out that the problem of "amalgamation of preferences" is impossible to solve. This conclusion, of course, has implications for relying on the outcomes of elections in making economic policy. However, unanimity decisions are very rare.

Third, preferences expressed through the votes of citizens reflect *the views of those who vote*. Quite apart from the fact that, especially in the United States, many citizens do not vote, and that the voting citizens may have limited information on relevant issues and may choose candidates on grounds that have little to do with economic policies, the decisions based on these preferences may not reflect the interest of the "community" *over the long run*. Unborn citizens and young citizens would not have a vote so that their interests would not be represented. There may be principal-agent problems between the true interests of these nonvoting groups and those who claim to represent them. Some groups, such as senior citizens, may vote in high proportions and support policies, such as high pensions financed by public debt, that shift the burden to the young and the unborn. Additionally, behavioral economics has shown that some individuals tend to be myopic or irrational, and some votes may have been conditioned by the existence of fiscal illusions. This leads to other questions about the meaning of preferences, even if it were agreed that the decisions should be based only on those who voted. The consequences might be excessive public debt, excessive transfer of liabilities to future generations, excessive exploitation of the natural environment, and other problems. Some of the most difficult public economics problems in our time have to do with intergenerational economic issues or with environmental sustainability.[17]

Fourth, there is an important point implicit in the work of Ronald H. Coase, the winner of the 1991 Nobel Prize in Economics. The voluntary exchange theories are not explicit about the assumptions that they make about the legal system. Is the legal system assumed to be unchanging over time, so that some of the basic rules under which individuals operate (such as those regarding property rights and the sanctity of contracts) cannot change? Or can the legal system change the relationships that have existed between individuals and property?[18] What is the role of the legal system on the way to the *optimum optimorum*? Zoning laws often change the use and the value of properties. Changes in tax rates and in environmental regulations often do the same. The "enclosure movement" in England, which allowed those who presumably had some rights over large tracts of land to restrict grazing on that land, was important in ending the economic (or pastoral) environment that had characterized the Middle Ages. It also changed, in a fundamental way, the property rights that had existed. The introduction of the patent system, in the late 14th-century Venice, created the concept of intellectual property that allowed some individuals to appropriate the economic benefits from their intellectual output. The reform of the agricultural sector in China after the death of Mao was important in promoting China's growth. All of these examples involved major changes in property rights and had a great impact on economic activities. Time consistency problems, which have attracted the attention of economists in recent years, are often important in these legal changes. Would a "benevolent dictator" be bound by existing property rules, even when the rules would perpetuate inefficiencies? And by changing those rules, what kind of time consistency problems would be created?

This discussion goes to questions raised by Douglass North (1989, pp. 107–15) in his comment on Stiglitz's *The Economic Role of the State*. North made a distinction between the "standard allocative efficiency criteria of the economist" (criteria that seem to be important for the voluntary exchange theories) and the "adaptive efficiency of economies" (which is "derived from a set of political economic institutions – concerned with the tolerance of a society to the acquisition of knowledge and learning, to a society's encouragement of innovation, risk taking, and creative activities of all sorts"; p. 109).[19] North pointed out that property rights that may be important for *static allocative efficiency* may not be the same as property rights that are good for *adaptive efficiency*. "Maximizing behavior by politicians is seldom coincidental with the efficiency criteria of the economist." Finally, "the central and most difficult role of the state is to establish and enforce a set of rules of the game that broadly encourage the creative economic participation of its citizens" (p. 109). The rules must not only reward success but also veto the survival of "inefficient" activities and organizations.[20] They should prevent the continuation of the situation that had existed before the enclosure movement. This may imply changes in property rights. Inefficient activities and organizations may be the outcome of rules, such as those on wealth distributions, and inherited rents that may be protected by current laws on property rights. They may reflect political pressures on policy makers, such as those to protect existing jobs or inefficient regulations.[21]

Protection of property rights in a democratic, political environment inevitably raises the question of the historical legitimacy of these rights. In the real world, and especially where universal franchise has become the norm, this issue cannot be ignored. As we mentioned earlier, it worried laissez-faire economists when universal franchise was being proposed because they were afraid that property rights would be challenged in the new political environment. Under which rules were the properties acquired? Were they acquired legitimately? Should property rights be protected without any consideration of how the properties were acquired? How far back in time must one go to establish legitimacy? Once income or wealth distribution becomes an objective of policy, these questions cannot be avoided. The protection of *existing* property rights, regardless of their (historical) legitimacy, creates a kind of path dependency for the distribution of income that may not be accepted by a democratic society. In such a situation the children of the rich will often continue to be rich, or at least to face much better opportunities than the children of the poor, regardless of how the wealth was acquired. Of course, this conclusion is valid even when the property was acquired legitimately, but in that case the income distribution may be more popularly acceptable. Perhaps, this is one reason why some conservative economists, such as James Buchanan, oppose progressive income taxes but favor inheritance taxes and educational spending. They see these policies as necessary for creating equality of opportunities (Buchanan and Musgrave, 1999, p. 86).

This also raises the important question of whether the three allegedly basic functions of the state – allocation, distribution, and stabilization – are necessarily separable, so that in theory at least each can be assigned to a different branch of the budget office, presumably with firewalls between them, as in Musgrave's conception. Changing the distribution of wealth (and income) often affects efficiency.[22] A state that wants to promote growth, especially over the long run, under some circumstances may have an interest in changing the distribution of wealth.[23] There may be increasing returns to wealth when it is redistributed away from those who use it inefficiently toward those who will use it more efficiently.

This raises the additional but related question of when governments have the right to intervene in contracts. This question became very relevant in 2009 when some governments attempted to block the granting of huge bonuses by private financial institutions to some of their executives and employees. Joseph Stiglitz was aware of this issue when he wrote that "we now recognize that there is not a neat separation between efficiency and distributive issues" because of the impact that uneven distribution has on incentives. Redistribution involves distortions (because the instruments that it may use, such as high marginal tax rates, or expropriation, are likely to affect incentives), but a highly uneven income distribution may also lead to distortions in a democratic government, for the reasons mentioned previously, and also because it may encourage pressures for inefficient, populist policies, such as protectionism and others (Tanzi, 2007).

Finally, if the cardinal preferences for public goods on the part of individuals could be identified, so that each could be made to pay "tax prices" accordingly, the taxes would be based on a benefit-received criterion.[24] Therefore, these taxes would have to be *ad personam* and *lump-sum* taxes. This would rule out progressive or uniform taxes. Individually differentiated lump-sum taxes do not exist in the real world. It is easy to imagine the difficulties that a tax administration would face in determining and applying these taxes. Furthermore, would the theoretical optimum take into account the potential income effects associated with these taxes?[25]

In conclusion, the voluntary exchange theory of public expenditure seems like an "emperor without clothes," in spite of the distinguished economists associated with it. Samuelson was aware of this but tried to justify the effort in developing this theory all the same. He claimed that, "given sufficient knowledge, the optimal decisions can always be found by scanning over all the attainable states of the world and selecting the one which according to the postulated ethical welfare function is best. The solution exists; the problem is how to find it" (Samuelson, 1954, p. 389). The relevant question is whether a solution not "found" can guide real-life policy.

In 2007 three economists who all had strong backgrounds in mathematics received the Nobel Prize in Economics. They were Leonid Hurwicz, Eric S. Maskin, and Roger B. Myerson. The prize was given for "mechanism design," on how to implement social goods (Maskin, 2007). The main question raised by the work of these Nobel Prize winners is, Once social goals are identified, what are the appropriate institutions or mechanisms needed to attain the goals? The normative theory of public finance that we have discussed (broadly) identified the goals and elaborated on the mechanism to achieve those goals. It did this brilliantly. Unfortunately, the mechanism (the institutions) needed to achieve the goals was not one that the real world could duplicate.

An economist who has dedicated a lot of thought to the possibility of "social choice" and who has criticized the traditional approach to it is Amartya Sen (1999). Sen is a very prolific writer. He agrees that, "given the diversity of preferences, concerns, and predicaments of the different individuals within" a society, it may be impossible "to arrive at cogent aggregative judgments" about "social welfare," "the public interest," or even "aggregate poverty," or for that matter aggregate "well-being." However, he believes that society is able to form *proximate* preferences about particularly important issues, preferences that are not based on political elections and thus do not depend on political systems. This is a kind of rough, second-best approach. These preferences ignore "mental states" that exist and are important "when distribution issues dominate and when people seek to maximize their own shares without concern for others" (pp. 354–55). Apart from other difficulties, the existence of envy invalidates the significance of the Pareto optimum in judging the outcome of policies.

Sen suggests that we should get away from comparing utilities or "mental states" and concentrate on the choice of some accounting measures of well-being, as, for example, done by the literature on "basic needs," or by the "Human Development Index" that the United Nations Development Program (UNDP) has been producing. He recognizes that interpersonal comparisons based on these indexes are different from those based on interpersonal utility, but they may be useful in judging policy in spite of their limitations. He believes that the utilitarian approach to the determination of "the public interest" is not required when the issue is to satisfy "basic needs." These "basic needs" can be seen by the population as entitlements. His conclusion seems to be that policy makers should focus on satisfying some "basic needs" for most of the population. This, however, shifts the problem to how the basic needs are defined, who decides at what level they should be satisfied, and how does the change in a country's per capita income change the definition of basic needs.[26] Thse are essential, important, and not easy to answer questions.

## 8.3. The School of Public Choice

A different approach to the economic role of the state came from the "school of public choice." In 1962 James Buchanan and Gordon Tullock published *The Calculus of Consent*, a now-classic book that established the foundation for that school.[27] This book postulated that "the human *individual* is the primary philosophical entity" (emphasis added). It "rejected any organic interpretation of collective activity" (p. 11). Thus, it rejected a basic assumption of the German *Finanzwissenschaft*: the existence of a state that responded to the wishes of a "community" rather than to those of the individuals living in the community at a specific time. For Buchanan and Tullock there is no "general will," no "community will," and no "public interest" that guides or characterizes the people who live in a country, at a given time.

For these authors, the only interests that exist are "the *separate* interests of the individuals who participate in social choice" (p. 12, emphasis added). This implies that the state represents a collection of separate individuals, each with independent goals and interests, and not a community with some historically or culturally determined, or influenced, common goals.[28]

The "social" interests of the individuals can be promoted by marketlike arrangements, entered freely by the individuals, and by the decentralization of political authority that reduces the political power of the state. The objective should be to reduce or minimize the power of the state on individuals and to increase or maximize the independence of the individual. Rules should be agreed that facilitate the free exchange process among individuals. "To improve politics, it is necessary to improve or reform the rules. . . . There is no suggestion that improvement lies in the selection of superior [public] agents, who will use their [public] powers in some 'public interest'" (Buchanan, 1983, p. 11). There are no philosopher-kings in this system. Politicians cannot be saints and cannot escape the pressures that come from their own biases or from their constituencies. Therefore, they will always pursue some vested or special interests that may not coincide with the difficult-to-define "public interest," even if the latter existed. There is here some indirect connection with the theories about the leadership of elites, which was found in the Italian literature and especially in the work of Pareto and Mosca. It is useless and naïve to expect them to do otherwise. Thus, the best that can be hoped for is to restrict the political power of politicians to prevent the bad ones from doing much damage. As Buchanan put it, in a famous debate with Musgrave, "He [Musgrave] trusts politicians, we [public choice economists] distrust politicians" (Buchanan and Musgrave, 1999, p. 88).

Because of this, it is more efficient to try to strengthen rules that prevent the pursuit of vested interests by politicians and to facilitate the free exchange process among free individuals than to try to select better policy makers. The policy makers will always be primarily interested in the maximization of *their* and their group's utility and not that of the broader society. For this reason, their actions need to be constrained by precise rules, including especially constitutional rules. The rules must go beyond "electoral constraints" that make it possible for citizens to "throw the rascals [i.e., misbehaving politicians] out" (Buchanan and Musgrave, 1999, p. 110). Constitutions must exist to *limit* the economic powers of the state and the exercise of political authority by duly elected politicians within established procedures. There must be "limits on collective action" so as to constrain "the range of possible collective outcomes." Constitutions must specify also what the rights of individuals, *qua* individuals, are. Buchanan has been an admirer of the Swiss Constitution because of the strong limitations that it imposes on the Swiss government, including constraints on tax legislation.

Perhaps, in connection with Buchanan's trust in the power of constitutions, it may be worthwhile to cite a contrasting view from Jacob Burckhardt's classic work on the Italian Renaissance. After mentioning that Dante compared his city, Florence, "which was always mending its constitution, with the sick man who is continually changing his posture to escape the pain," Burckhardt (1944, p. 54) commented, "Constitutional artists were never wanting who by an ingenious distribution and division of political power, by indirect elections of the most complicated kind, by the establishment of nominal offices, sought to found a lasting order of things, and to satisfy or deceive the rich and poor alike."

This view seems to be more prevalent in Europe and also in other regions of the world, such as Latin America, where constitutions are frequently changed. For the citizens of these regions the search for the perfect constitution may seem as futile as the quest for a social welfare function. However, as Buchanan put it, "Americans have a sense that constitutions are needed to constrain politicians.... [Europeans] don't have that tradition." Buchanan has been a true believer in the importance and power of constitutions (see Buchanan, 1999, p. 88; for a recent discussion of the economic effects of constitutions, see Persson and Tabellini, 2003).

The school of public choice was established in 1963 by Buchanan and Tullock. It developed into a major field of study that includes among its adherents economists, political scientists, historians, and scholars from some other disciplines. It has its own journals and congresses, and in 1986 James M. Buchanan Jr. was awarded the Nobel Prize in Economics for his contributions to the creation of this field. The work of scholars belonging to the school of public choice has covered different areas. One strand has identified examples in which, regardless of the declared intentions by governments, the public policies that were enacted ended up benefiting (or creating rents for) particular groups rather than promoting the public interest. Much of the modern literature on "rent seeking" relates to this strand. Even when, ex ante, public actions appear to be well intentioned, ex post they often end up benefiting groups different from the declared or intended ones.[29] In one such example, Peltzman (1993, p. 45) reported that "the [US] record of 1965–80 is truly astonishing. Real expenditure per student nearly doubled, and student/teacher ratio declined by about one-fourth ... yet student achievement deteriorated badly by every measure we have." The expenditure must have benefited some groups, most likely teachers or school administrators, rather than the students it was intended to benefit. Thus, this was one of the failures of Johnson's War on Poverty that did not end poverty. Similar conclusions were reached for various programs in Latin American countries (Tanzi, 1974), for health spending in Chile (Aninat et al., 1999), and for other programs in the region. The public choice literature argues that this misdirection of benefits is not random but intentional and normal and cautions against government activism. Some conservative research institutions, such as the Cato Institute and the Heritage Foundation in Washington, the Institute of Social Affairs in London, and the Frazer Institute in Vancouver, have kept track of government programs that presumably have done more damage than good (see, e.g., O'Toole, 2007).

A second strand has tried to identify arrangements, entered voluntarily by individuals, that are capable of producing a "social" output for the components of the groups without any involvement of the government. The school of public choice argues that governments should facilitate these arrangements. This strand has tried to demonstrate that the government is often less necessary than assumed so that much social action could be promoted through free exchange processes among individuals. There are various examples in the literature of "club goods" that, to some extent, deliver "public goods" for the members of the club up to the point where congestion or crowding sets in (Buchanan, 1968). Community swimming pools, private beaches, gulf clubs, toll roads, recreational areas, industrial parks, boarding schools and private universities, shopping centers, or even hotels may be considered examples of these privately produced and limited arrangements that provide "public goods." In all of these private arrangements, an individual who joins or uses them has the option of opting out. However, poor people often do not have the means to get in, even if they would have the freedom to do so.

A recent paper pointed out that in today's United States, about 20 percent of the population (about 60 million people) now lives in *private* community associations (homeowners associations, condominiums, cooperatives, private townships, etc.) that produce, internally to the group, various "public goods" (e.g., security, swimming pools, garbage collection, street lightning, various shared services), which, for the members, are effectively public goods that they can consume freely but are financed collectively and privately. There is no public money used for these public goods. The members of the group, once they become members at their request, cannot be excluded from the consumption of these goods and, up to the point of congestion or crowding, each new member can be added to their use at no extra cost (Nelson, 2008).

These private arrangements reduce transaction costs among members and reduce the need for governmental intervention, just as the existence of various transaction costs in private-sector activities justifies the existence of the firms, as pointed out by Coase (1937).[30] These arrangements allow individuals with similar interests and similar preferences for particular public goods to aggregate themselves freely in legally recognized but private associations.[31] These aggregations are not communities in a traditional sense. They lack most of the characteristics of traditional communities.

Economists that belong to the school of public choice believe that truly national and truly *pure* public goods are very few. Their financing would require a very small share of national income, surely much less than the total public spending now required in most countries.[32] Buchanan has guessed that a government that provided broadly defined but genuine public goods would not need to spend more than 10–12 percent of GDP (Buchanan and Musgrave, 1999, p. 84). It will be recalled that this was the average level of government spending around 1870. Therefore, total public spending could be much smaller than it is now in many countries if governments limited their role mostly to the production of pure public goods. Income redistribution would not play much of a role in determining public spending in this society. The reason is that it would impose limitations on individual liberty through high taxes or other policies. However, expenditures that would contribute to the creation of more equal opportunities for citizens, such as public education, could play a role.

Coase assumed that, in a competitive market, the firm exists mainly because the transaction costs for a (nonfirm) producer of goods and services can become too high, when the use of each purchase of labor, capital, raw material, or other inputs requires a separate transaction and a separate contract. Such (nonfirm) producers do exist in some activities, such as housing construction, in which general contractors hire specific workers and buy needed materials as and when they need them. But this approach has obvious limitations, so the activities of these producers remain small. For larger activities and for more complex projects, it becomes convenient to create firms so as to establish within the internal space of the firms a "command economy" that can reduce transaction costs. Thus, the firm hires workers and buys materials to have them available to it for immediate use. The use of these resources within the firm does not require specific contracts, and the resources can be commanded by management, thus reducing transaction costs. When the firm is not too large and the needed information is easily available, the available resources can be allocated efficiently, within the firm, by command. The allocation problems highlighted by Hayek, Mises, Röpke, and others from the Austrian school for a command economy do not arise in this context because the input used already have prices established outside the firm (see especially Hayek, 1988). However, as firms become very large, the problems identified by Hayek for the command economy begin to surface within the firms in a market economy.

The Coasian argument for the existence of firms in a competitive market might be applicable to the existence of a government. As the number of agents (firms, individuals, associations, etc.) in a country increases, several needs, or problems, arise, such as the need for providing pure public goods; the need for semipublic goods; the need or options for "club goods"; the need to deal with significant positive or negative externalities; conflicts about the limits of individuals' or firms' property rights; growing difficulties on the part of individuals to identify the real value of some products or services (because of complexity, risks, abuses, etc.); the existence of very poor people, some not capable of taking care of themselves. In theory, Coasian solutions, related to externalities, may be feasible for *some* of these problems (Coase, 1960). These solutions would call for private bargaining among the parties. However, as the numbers of agents increase, transaction costs would also increase, making spontaneous, private solutions more difficult to achieve or more costly.[33] Thus, the *demand* for public-sector intervention would rise. This, of course, leaves open the question of how good a job the government would be able to do in meeting that demand and what level of government, in a federal structure, would be capable of doing the best job.[34]

Perhaps a hint of this interpretation is suggested by Stigler (1986, p. 7) when he wrote that

the hypothesis is that the propensity to use the state is like the propensity to use coal: we use coal when it is the most efficient resource with which to heat our houses and power our factories. Similarly we use the state to build our roads or tax our consumers when the state is the most efficient way to reach those goals. . . . When the conditions of society dictate little use of the state, the economy will be characterized as laissez-faire. When the conditions of society dictate much use of the state [as, for example, during a war], the economy will be called collectivistic.

It could be added that in a country in which the private market works well, where income distribution produced by the market is relatively even, and where social norms have generated private activities that help the few people in need, the role of the state could be much reduced.

A third strand of the school of public choice is connected with rules that would constrain or limit the action of the government and thus ensure more individual freedom. A preference for fiscal federalism, or fiscal "decentralization," is also strongly expressed in much of the public choice literature. Fiscal federalism is supposed to create competition among local governments and to reduce the power of the central government (Oates, 1999). In theory, in a highly mobile society, it allows individuals to move to the jurisdictions that more closely match their preferences for the combination of taxes and public services (see Tiebout, 1956, for the classic paper on this issue).[35] It is an open question how mobile most societies are when transaction costs and other considerations such as different languages, religions, and residency requirements are taken into account.[36] Mobility within the United States has declined in recent years. Fiscal federalism is also assumed to reduce the level of public spending, although it is easy to find examples (Belgium, Brazil?) to the contrary (Treisman, 2007). As Brennan and Buchanan (1980, p. 185) put it, "Total intrusion into the economy should be smaller, ceteris paribus, the greater the extent to which taxes and expenditures are decentralized." They ignore the added layers of regulations and other considerations that fiscal federalism may create.

In the past three decades, there has been a growing interest in fiscal federalism and an explosion of writing on this topic, as surveyed by Treisman (2007). More recent writing has pointed to problems that often arise in practice with fiscal decentralization, more than on the options created by fiscal federalism. This has led Oates (2006) to write about the "dark side of fiscal decentralization." It has also pointed to the increasing importance of *global* public goods (see Sandmo, 2003; and Tanzi, 2008).

The school of public choice has been important in calling attention to the fact that there is *market failure* as well as *government failure* and that the latter could be greater than the former. This means that policies should be judged on results rather than on a priori intentions, as argued by Stigler. However, it must face three issues. The first is that regardless of potential public failure, in democratic governments the electorate may, and, often will, demand public action. No existing rules may be able to restrain these demands. It does not help to argue that, if some constraining rules were present, the behavior of governments would be different. Such rules often do not exist and are not going to be introduced. Second, one has to be aware that some countries may be more capable and their electorate more willing of providing public services than other countries. Third, when the income distribution becomes uneven, pressure for governmental intervention to rectify it will grow, regardless of the government's ability to deal with it satisfactorily and regardless of existing rules.

Another school of thought on the role of the government in the economy that deserves at least a brief mention is the Chicago school. Like the school of public choice discussed previously, the Chicago school has been strongly critical of governmental intervention in the economy. As such, it bears a strong affinity with the school of public choice. However, in spite of some similarity of conclusions, its development and its major contributors have been distinct from those of the school of public choice. The Chicago school has been more focused in showing that private markets work, rather than showing that public activity is normally misguided, although it shares this conclusion with the school of public choice. With some important exceptions, the impact of the Chicago school has been largely on regulations rather than on other policy tools. Perhaps it may be worthwhile to mention that, because of the Chicago school's strong belief in the virtue of deregulation, and the role that that belief seems to have played in removing regulations on financial and other markets, it has been associated with what came to be called market fundamentalism and blamed by some for the financial crisis of 2008–9.

## References

Aninat, Eduard, Andreas Bauer, and Kevin Conan. 1999. "Equity-Oriented Policy-Making: Country Experience," in *Economic Policy and Equity*, edited by V. Tanzi, Ke-Young Chu, and Sanjeev Gupta (Washington, D.C.: IMF).

Arrow, Kenneth. 1951. *Social Choice and Individual Values*, 2nd ed. (New York: John Wiley, and Sons; rev. ed., New Haven: Yale University Press, 1963).

Bergson, Abraham. 1938. "A Reformulation of Certain Aspects of Welfare Economics." *Quarterly Journal of Economics* 52: 310–34.

Brennan, Geoffrey, and James M. Buchanan. 1980. *The Power to Tax: Analytical Foundations of a Fiscal Constitution* (Cambridge: Cambridge University Press).

Buchan, James. 2006. *The Authentic Adam Smith: His Life and Ideas* (New York: W. W. Norton).

Buchanan, James M. 1968. *The Demand and Supply of Public Goods* (Chicago: Rand McNally).

　1983. "The Public Choice Perspective." *Economia delle Scelte Pubbliche*, no. 1: 7–15.

　2003. "Endnote," in *The Theory of Public Finance in Italy from the Origins to the 1940s*, edited by D. Fausto and V. De Bonis (Pisa: Instituti Editoriali e Poligrafini Internazionali).

Buchanan, James M., and Richard Musgrave. 1999. *Public Finance and Public Choice: Two Contrasting Visions of the State* (Cambridge, Mass.: MIT Press).

Buchanan, James M., and Gordon Tullock. 1962. *The Calculus of Consent* (Ann Arbor: University of Michigan).

Burckhardt, Jacob. 1944. *The Civilization of the Renaissance in Italy* (London: Phaidon Press; New York: Oxford University Press).

Clark, Colin. 1945. "Public Finance and the Value of Money." *Economic Journal* (December).

___. 1964. *Taxmanship: Principles and Proposal for the Reform of Taxation*, Hobarth Paper 26 (London: Institute of Economic Affairs) Ch. 4.

Coase, R. H. 1937. "The Nature of the Firm." *Economica* 4 (November): 386–405.

___. 1960. "The Problem of Social Cost." *Journal of Law and Economics* 3 (October): 1–44.

Cohen, Adam. 2009. *Nothing to Fear: FDR's Inner Circle and the Hundred Days That Created Modern America* (New York: Penguin Press).

Cornes, Richard, and Todd Sandler. 1986. *The Theory of Externalities, Public Goods, and Club Goods* (Cambridge: Cambridge University Press).

Dupuit, Jules. 1952. "On the Measurement of the Utility of Public Works." *International Economic Paper* 2 (1952): 83–110. Translated from *Annales des Ponts et Chaussees*, 2nd ser., **8** [1844].

Eckstein, Otto. 1958. *Water Resources Development* (Cambridge, Mass: Harvard University Press).

___. 1961. "A Survey of the Theory of Public Expenditure Criteria," in *Public Finances, Needs, Sources and Utilization*, edited by J. M. Buchanan (Princeton, N.J.: National Bureau of Economic Research).

Eusepi, Giuseppe. 2002. "La Logica del Prezzo Fiscale." Paper presented at the conference on the "Attualitá del Pensiero di Antonio De Viti de Marco" (Lecce, November 8–9).

Fogel, Robert William. 2000. *The Fourth Great Awakening and the Future of Egalitarianism* (Chicago: University of Chicago Press).

Greenspan, Alan. 2007. *The Age of Turbulence* (New York: Penguin Press).

Groopman, Jerome. 2010. "Health Care: Who Knows Best?" *New York Review of Books*, February 11, pp. 12–15.

Hayek, F. A. 1988. *The Fatal Conceit: The Errors of Socialism*, edited by W. W. Bartley III (Chicago: University of Chicago Press).

Heller, Walter W. 1966. *New Dimensions of Political Economy* (New York: W. W. Norton).

Kolm, Serge-Christophe. 1985. *Le Contrat Social Liberal* (Paris: Presses Universitaires de France).

Krugman, Paul R. 1991. *Geography and Trade* (Cambridge, Mass.: MIT Press).

Lucas, Robert E. 2009. "Trade and Diffusion of the Industrial Revolution." *American Economic Journal Macroeconomics* 1, no. 1 (January): 1–15.

Maskin, Eric S. 2007. "Mechanism Design: How to Implement Social Goods." Nobel Prize Lecture (December 8).

McKean, Roland N. 1968. *Public Spending* (New York: McGraw-Hill).

Merewitz, Leonard, and Stephen H. Sosnick. 1971. *The Budget's New Clothes* (Chicago: Markham Publishing).

Mokyr, Joel. 2002. *The Gifts of Athena: Historical Origins of the Knowledge Economy* (Princeton: Princeton University Press).

Mueller, Dennis. 1979. *Public Choice* (Cambridge: Cambridge University Press).

Musgrave, Richard. 1998. "The Role of the State in Fiscal Policy," in *Public Finance in a Changing World*, edited by Peter Birch Sørensen (Houndmills: Macmillan), pp. 35–50.

Nelson, Robert H. 2008. "Community Associations: Decentralizing Local Government Privately," in *Fiscal Decentralization and Land Policies*, edited by Gregory K. Ingram and Yu-Hung Hong, Proceedings of the 2007 Land Policies Conference (Cambridge: Mass: Lincoln Institute of Land Policy).

North, Douglas C. 1989. "Comments 2," in *The Economic Role of the State*, by Joseph Stiglitz, (Oxford: Basil Blackwell), pp. 107–15.

Oates, Wallace E. 2006. "On the Theory and Practice of Fiscal Decentralization." Mimeo (March).

1999. "An Essay on Fiscal Federalism." *Journal of Economic Literature* 37: 1120–49.

Olson, Mancur. 1965. *The Logic of Collective Action* (Cambridge, Mass.: Harvard University Press).

O'Toole, Randall. 2007. *The Best-Laid Plans: How Government Planning Harms Your Quality of Life, Your Pocketbook, and Your Future* (Washington, D.C.: Cato Institute).

Peltzman, Sam. 1993. "Political Factors in Public School Debate." *American Enterprise*, July, p. 65.

Persson, Torsten, and Guido Tabellini. 2003. *The Economic Effects of Constitutions* (Cambridge, Mass.: MIT Press).

Peacock, Alan, 1992, *Public Choice Analysis in Historical Perspective*, Raffaele Maltioli Lectures (Cambridge: Cambridge University Press).

Robbins, Lionel. 1938. "Interpersonal Comparisons of Utility: A Comment." *Economic Journal*, December 8, 1992, pp. 635–41.

Samuelson, Paul. 1954. "The Pure Theory of Public Expenditure." *Review of Economics and Statistics* 36 (November): 387–89.

1955. "Diagrammatic Exposition of a Theory of Public Expenditure." *Review of Economics and Statistics* 37 (November): 350–56.

Sandmo, Agnar. 2003. "International Aspects of Public Goods Provision," in *Providing Global Public Goods*, edited by I. Kaul, P. Conceição, K. Le Goulven, and R. U. Mendoza (New York: Oxford Press).

Schäffle, Albert. 1896. *Bau und Leben des Sozialen Körpers*, 2nd ed., Vol. 2 (Tubingen: Laupp).

Sen, Amartya. 2009. "Capitalism beyond the Crisis." *New York Review of Books*, March, pp. 27–30.

1999. "The Possibility of Social Choice." *American Economic Review* 89, no. 3 (June): 349–78.

Solow, Robert M. 1985. "Economic History and Economics." *American Economic Review* 75, no. 2 (May): 328–31.

Stein, Herbert. 1969. *The Fiscal Revolution in America* (Chicago: University of Chicago Press).

1985. *Presidential Economics: The Making of Economic Policy from Roosevelt to Reagan and Beyond*, revised and updated edition (New York: Simon and Schuster).

Stigler, George J. 1986. *The Regularities of Regulation* Hume Occasional Paper, No. 3 (Edinburgh: David Hume Institute).

1988. *Memoirs of an Unregulated Economist* (New York: Basic Books).

Stiglitz, Joseph E. 1989. *The Economic Role of the State* (Oxford: Basil Blackwell).

Tanzi, Vito. 1970. "International Tax Burdens: A Study of Tax Ratios in the OECD Countries," in *Taxation A Radical Approach*, edited by Vito Tanzi, J. B. Bracewell-Milnes, and D. R. Myddelton (London: Institute of Economic Affairs).

2007. "Complexity and Systemic Failure," in *Transition and Beyond*, edited by Saul Estrin, Grzegorz W. Koladko, and Milica Uvalic (London: Palgrave), pp. 229–46.

2008. "The Future of Fiscal Federalism." *European Journal of Political Economy* 24: 705–12.

Tanzi, Vito, and Tej Prakesh. 2003. "The Cost of Government and the Misuse of Public Assets," in *Public Finance in Developing Countries: Essays in Honor of Richard Bird,* edited by Jorge Martinez-Vazquez and James Alm (Cheltenham: Edward Elgar).

Tiebout, C. M. 1956. "A Pure Theory of Local Expenditures." *Journal of Political Economy* 5 (October): 416–24.

Treisman, Daniel. 2007. *The Architecture of Government: Rethinking Political Decentralization* (Cambridge: Cambridge University Press).

Van Overtveldt, Johan. 2007. *The Chicago School* (Chicago: Agate).

Wheen, Francis. 1999. *Karl Marx* (London: Fourth Estate).

NINE

# The Nordic European Economic Theory
# of Fiscal Policy

## 9.1. Introduction

In the 1950s and 1960, there was much writing about "collective action."
In a setting where the preferences of individuals matter and where "the
state is not seen as an organic unit wherein the individual is absorbed in
the 'whole' and there is no benevolent dictator" (Musgrave, 1998, p. 31),
how should the votes of individuals be aggregated to guide policies? The
electors elect their representatives in the government, who, in turn, make
the decisions, presumably on the basis of the promises they made before
the elections. However, the elected representatives might not be able to
interpret correctly the voters' preferences; or, worse, might intentionally
misinterpret them to promote personal gains or the gains of related groups.
An additional complication that was soon recognized was that the voters
might themselves have little interest in investing their time and money to
learn about specific policies because, while such an investment would be
costly for them, their vote, being one among millions, would be unlikely to
change the election results. This problem becomes more significant as the
number of government programs and their complexity increases in line with
an expanded role of the state and the number of voters also increases. Thus,
the electors may choose to remain "rationally ignorant" and cast their vote
mainly on the basis of often-irrelevant impressions or of single, but visible,
issues (see Olson, 1965 and 1982).[1] This makes the concept of the "median
voter" somewhat irrelevant or much less useful than assumed in some of
the academic writing. The writing on "collective action" was interesting and
often brilliant, but it could not have much of an impact on how policies are
actually made. However, it indirectly contributed to the development of the
school of public choice and of other theories that, in turn, may have had
some influence on policy.

193

The Great Depression; the Russian experiment with central planning that, especially in the 1950s and 1960s, was seen by many to have vitality (see, e.g., Rostow, 1953; and Kornai, 1992); and the "Keynesian Revolution," which influenced the thinking of many experts and not just that of economists, had probably a greater and more lasting impact on the future role of the state than the various theories and contributed more to the growth of public spending.

## 9.2. The Economic Theory of Fiscal Policy

Another significant influence came, in the 1950s, from Northern Europe. The Nordic region includes five small countries: Denmark, Finland, Norway, Sweden, and Iceland. Sweden is the largest and the most populated. Under the push of influential economists, sociologists, and other experts, and responding to various political pressures, Northern European countries in the 1950s initiated a process that, within a few years, would transform them into the most advanced "welfare states" in the world (see Chapter 13). This process started in a society in which only two decades earlier "a very uncompromising laissez-faire doctrine [had] dominated the teaching of economics in Sweden" (Myrdal, 1954, p. 111). This transformation was influenced by the powerful intellectual guidance of economists who formulated what came to be called "the economic theory of fiscal policy." In the words of one of its most important contributors, "the aim of economists must . . . be to achieve a model of the economy which provides . . . reasonably accurate information about the effects of fiscal policy" (Hansen, 1955, p. x).[2] The economic theory of fiscal policy borrowed from R. Frisch and J. Tinbergen the view that there are ends that governments want to achieve and there are policies or tools (the means) that can help them achieve those ends. It applied this view to the fiscal area. The theory focused on the ends that governments might wish to pursue and on the tools available to them, as well as on their connection. For this theory, the ends went beyond the Keynesian goal of full employment. The final objective was to improve social or collective welfare. At the time when Hansen wrote his book, the ends were growing significantly in number, although full employment and price stability were still the most important, in a context in which welfare states were being created.

As Haavelmo put it in his 1989 Nobel Lecture, "By welfare state I mean any society where the final objective is the economic well-being of its people, in the short run as well as in the long run" (p. 14). By "starting with some existing society, we could conceive of [the welfare state] as a structure of rules and regulations within which the members of society have to operate. Their response to these rules as individuals obeying them, produce economic results that would characterize the society. As the results materialize, they will stimulate the political process in society towards changing the rules of the game" (p. 15). Thus, over the medium and longer run, the rules are partly endogenous. The rules can be changed as the game develops. This seems to be very different from the views held by James Buchanan – that there are rules, especially those set by constitutions, that cannot be changed except after difficult political processes. Haavelmo stressed that the "question of what is the good society cannot be settled by any mathematical trick" (ibid.). In a society such as the Northern European community, which was at that time characterized by great ethnic and cultural homogeneity and by significant trust in community choices, Haavelmo did not question the political process that selected the goals. He had trust in it.

Major contributors to the theory of fiscal policy, beside Bent Hansen, were Jan Tinbergen, Ragnar Frisch, T. Haavelmo, Leif Johansen, and a few others. Myrdal had had a lot of influence in changing the political debate toward a larger government role. In spirit, if not in geography, Richard Musgrave could be placed among the contributors, even though he was born in Germany, spent his adult life in the United States, and made a more general contribution. There were, of course, also contributors from other regions and especially from North America. Among these were Alvin Hansen, Lawrence Klein, Abba Lerner, Robert Solow, and Paul Samuelson. However, these economists were more directly interested in the stabilization role of fiscal policy than in the promotion of a welfare state.

What are the main elements of the economic theory of fiscal policy? Policy makers are assumed to have no other objectives but the promotion of social welfare through the rules and the policies that they enact. We are thus a long way from the school of public choice or from the Italian *scienza delle finanze*. Social welfare does not depend on any single variable or indicator, such as employment, or the size of GDP, but on several indicators, some of a purely economic nature and some of a more social nature. These indicators are chosen by the policy makers.[3] The way in which policy makers rank these indicators may change with time or with the government in power. In representative democracies, the ranking is assumed to reflect the changing preferences of the citizens as expressed in democratic elections. Those preferences are assumed to be respected by the policy makers. Rules are also expected to change from time to time, as mentioned by Haavelmo.

Examples of *economic* indicators are economic growth, growth of employment, growth of productivity, the rate of inflation, the trade balance, the income distribution, the poverty rate, unemployment among the population of working age or among particular groups, and female participation in the labor force. Examples of *social* indicators are life expectancy, incidence of crime, literacy rates, quality of the physical environment, the incidence of illnesses, and home ownership.

Policy makers responsible for *economic* policy are likely to focus on *economic* indicators and to promote policies aimed at improving them. However, they take account of the preferences of other policy makers. Policy makers have some perception of the weight that each of these indicators, $y_i$, has on the social welfare function, $W$, as the latter is interpreted by the policy makers – for example, how an improvement in the income distribution is weighted against a faster rate of growth, the classic efficiency-equity trade-off (Okun, 1975).

The social welfare function can be written as

$$W = f(y_1, y_2, \ldots, y) \tag{1}$$

With the help of available econometric models, policy makers can predict how the indicators, $y_i$, can be influenced by changes in particular policy instruments, $x_j$. These instruments are the "handles" available to the policy makers to modify the elements that they believe influence the social welfare function and to steer the latter toward an optimum. As Haavelmo put it, "The task of econometrics, from the point of view of human welfare, is to try to extract from past data useful information for whatever economic society it should be found desirable to reach for" (1989, p. 15). Each indicator is a function of the policy instruments. The equations that links indicators to policy instruments can be written as

$$y = f(x_1, x_2, x_3, \ldots, x_j) \tag{2}$$

A particular instrument $x_i$ may be especially efficient in influencing a specific indicator $y_i$. Efficiency in this context refers to the change in an instrument, $\Delta x$, necessary to change an indicator by a given significant amount, $\Delta y$. If a small, realistic change in an instrument can produce a significant change in an indicator, then that instrument is considered an efficient one with respect to that indicator.[4] When efficient instruments are available to promote the desirable social objectives, economic policy becomes easier, both politically and technically.

Examples of fiscal policy instruments are various taxes; particular features of taxes, such as deductions and rates; various categories of expenditures; particular features of the expenditures; and so on. Fiscal deficits can be instruments to pursue stabilization policies, in a Keynesian framework, to promote the goals of full employment. Stabilization and full employment policies were the main preoccupations on the part of American economists around 1960. Nonfiscal, economic instruments, such as the exchange rate, interest rates, and especially regulations, can also be used.

When certain technical conditions are satisfied, the implicit system of equations formed by the relationships mentioned previously can be solved for the values of the instruments that would maximize the social welfare function, $W$.[5] It should be noted that there is no real-life quantification of the social welfare. In reality, $W$ is a virtual concept, essentially nonquantifiable. Thus, it rests on the top policy makers to judge and evaluate the impact that the changes in the indicators have on the welfare function in the real world. Because of this, trust in the policy makers is essential. The mathematical solution may, of course, require large, or even unrealistic, changes in the policy instruments. If inflexible fiscal rules or other constraints are in existence, they may prevent a solution. If the instruments are efficient, the solution of the equation is more likely to require changes in the value of the instruments that are both technically *and* politically feasible. A technical solution does not imply that it will also be a politically feasible solution or that it will be seen as being optimal by the politically important groups.[6]

Stripped to the bare bones, this is the theory of fiscal policy. It came to dominate the thinking in the Nordic European countries and provided the essential theoretical framework or guidance for much fiscal work in those countries and elsewhere. In the Nordic countries, it helped with the introduction of the welfare states, especially in the 1960–75 period. Jan Tinbergen and Ragnar Frisch shared the first Nobel Prize in Economics in 1969 partly for their contribution to the development of this theory and for the needed econometric work that accompanied it. Myrdal and Haavelmo also received the Nobel Prize, in 1974 and 1989, respectively. The theory assumed a particularly benevolent view of the role of governments and attempted to develop the instruments needed to promote a government role deemed desirable. It also assumed that what constituted social welfare could be agreed to, if not measured, in some approximate way. Given the fairly homogeneous societies that prevailed in Northern European countries, their feeling that they were a community, the degree of social cohesion, and the trust in those who represented the government, it was not an unrealistic theory for *these* societies.[7] Still some problems remained.

## 9.3. Assumptions of the Theory of Fiscal Policy

Most theories make assumptions. Sometimes the assumptions are explicit; often they are not. Sometimes they are realistic; often they are not. What are the important assumptions implicit in the theory of fiscal policy? And how realistic are they? Let us briefly discuss the main ones.

*First Assumption:* The first assumption is the existence of a nerve center, that is, of an office or a place where that rather abstract concept that we call the "government" decides which objectives to promote and which policy instruments to use to promote the economic objectives that it considers important to the maximization of social welfare. This could be the office of a president, a prime minister, or a powerful finance minister. This is what Myrdal had defined as "the fiction of a single collective subject" when in fact "there is a multitude of subjects with conflicting political valuations" (Myrdal, 1954, p. 156). The existence of a nerve center implies to a large extent a unitary form of government, because fiscal decentralization can bring complications unless the actions at the subnational level are closely controlled by the center, or unless the subnational governments or agencies largely share the objectives of the national government and coordinate their actions with it. There cannot be any principal-agent problems developing at this level. This is more likely to happen in a homogeneous society. A nerve center also implies a unified and comprehensive budget that leaves only the administration of the spending to decentralized activities; and a prime minister, president, or finance minister with the political power, the administrative instruments, and the technical skills *to set the desired objectives and to change the policy instruments* in the needed direction and by the required magnitude, when needed to achieve the objectives.[8]

This first assumption implies the existence of an all-inclusive budgetary process. No *budgetary* decision is made outside the budget by institutions, such as pension systems, subnational governments, public enterprises, or central banks that are outside the budget; all decisions, whether in or out of the formal budget, must be directly or indirectly controlled by the nerve center. There cannot be any fragmentation of decision making, either because of different levels of government, each with independent power, or because of policy differences among ministries or between agencies.[9] This also implies that the budget for subnational governments, or for extrabudgetary institutions, cannot be a soft one. Furthermore, it implies that policy mistakes made in past years, as for example in the provision of overly generous entitlements and pension rights, can be corrected at any time.

When differences in objectives, or in the use of instruments, exist among policy makers, they must be settled, or ironed out, *within* the nerve center. This assumption deals with political power and administrative controls and with how fragmented the political power is and how it can be used. Obviously, the political power is partly the result of the support that the government receives from the electorate and partly the result of institutional arrangements determined by a country's constitution.[10] In the real world, that power is also partly the result of the real control that the government is able to exercise over the bureaucracy (see Niskanen, 1971; Tullock, 1965; and Jackson, 1982).

*Second Assumption*: Those who represent the government have the public interest of the citizens in mind when they make the policy decisions. They are not influenced by their personal interests or by the special interests of particular groups or geographical areas. There are no powerful and *effective* lobbies operating outside the electoral process, and there is no scope for corruption, rent seeking, or "state capture." Policy makers avoid "populist" policies that go against the public interest, even when these policies have short run appeal that could help those in power win the next election. The electoral cycle plays no role in budgetary decisions. A lot of literature, including the one by the school of public choice, has shown how unrealistic this assumption can be in *some* countries. At the same time, it must be recognized that there are differences between governments and that some satisfy the assumption far better than others.

*Third Assumption*: When it makes its budgetary decisions, the government has available to it the best economic analyses and the best econometric models that money can buy at that time. These analyses and models must be based on reliable data, on unbiased forecasts, and on accepted and hopefully sound economic principles that establish links between changes in policy instruments and changes in policy objectives. From these analyses, the policy makers must be able to predict with a reasonable degree of accuracy that a given change in a policy instrument will cause a given change in a particular objective.[11] These analyses rule out policy decisions based on "gut feelings," impressions, ideology, wrong data, biased forecasts, electoral promises, or simply antagonism toward previous governments.

The Lundberg committee that helped develop "the economic theory of fiscal policy" aimed to achieve this outcome. However, after the initial enthusiasm vis-à-vis Keynesian econometric models in the 1960s, subsequent work by Lucas and other economists raised strong, theoretical questions about the ability of these models to provide reliable predictions. Models related to stabilization policy based on Keynesian assumptions were later criticized for two important reasons. The first was the view that those who made the decisions on policy (the policy makers) were immune from political influences so that their actions would not be influenced by political, or election, cycles. They would run well-calibrated fiscal deficits during slowdown and compensating surpluses during booms, so that the fiscal accounts would remain in equilibrium over the longer run and, as a consequence, there would not be any accumulation of public debt. The second reason was the view that citizens were passive reactors to the policies. They were not able to anticipate those policies or the consequences of those policies and to react rationally to them at times before or during the time the policies were enacted; or worry that the fiscal deficits might become unsustainable, thus affecting the psychology of the economic agents and their decisions. At this time (2010), there is much discussion on these issues (see also Barro, 1974, for an early view, and Tanzi, 2010, for a recent discussion).

*Fourth Assumption*: Fiscal policy instruments are generally imbedded in legislation. Therefore, these instruments can be changed only by enacting specific new laws or by changing current laws.[12] This raises questions about the power that the executive has over the legislative branch of government. The U.S. experience indicates that the executive has limited power. Different parties may control the executive and the legislature. That power may in turn be influenced by how homogeneous the community is and by its fiscal institutions. At times, what goes into the legislative process comes out totally changed and not necessarily for the better. The bills submitted to parliament and the approved laws are also assumed to be specific and to contain as little "opacity" as possible.[13] The laws must not create asymmetric information, or different interpretations, between the government, on one side, and the citizens, on the other; or even between the policy makers and the public servants who write the laws; or between the policy makers and those who must enforce or administer the laws or the regulations.

A law must be identifiable, as much as possible, with a specific policy instrument. It must be possible to determine which instrument a specific law wants to change and which policy objective it wants to influence. In other words, the $x_s$ in equation (2) must be clearly identifiable in the laws. This is rarely the case. To the extent possible, the laws should also avoid dealing with, or be directed toward, multiple objectives. As stressed by Tinbergen, it is generally inefficient, although it is quite common in economic policy, to try to influence more than one objective with one instrument.[14]

*Fifth Assumption*: The executive branch must have as much control over the policy instruments (i.e., over the proposed laws) as is feasible in a democratic society. This assumption has several corollaries, some implicit in the preceding discussion.

First, the legislative branch must, of course, have the prerogative to approve or turn down the proposals submitted to them by the executive. They should also have the prerogative to improve or clarify the proposals, or amend them in relevant ways. However, they should not have the prerogative to change them in fundamental ways, unless the executive agrees to the changes; or to delay unduly action on proposals submitted by the executive. It is the executive branch of government that, within clear constitutional limits, must control the instruments of economic policy, not the parliament.[15]

Second, and related to the first assumption, the various ministries or departments must operate in a harmonious and coordinated way and must not push for conflicting legislation. What we have called the nerve center must be able to deal with and solve any internal conflicts.

Third, most discretionary spending or taxing decisions must be exercised during the budget period. The authorization to spend money authorized in a budget must not stretch out over several budget periods, except for spending connected with large capital projects that, by necessity, may take several years to complete. Obviously, this does not apply to programs that create entitlements that extend over the years, such as pensions, and that reduce the government degrees of freedom. Large unspent resources, or unpaid liabilities, should not characterize the end of the budget period. When they do, the impact of fiscal policy on the economy and the budgetary outcome become more difficult to determine. Of course, there is no essential reason why the budgetary period should be necessarily one year.

Fourth, decisions made upstream, by the executive, and approved by parliament must not be distorted downstream by the existence of principal-agent problems at various levels. Principal-agent problems can occur at the level of ministries, institutions, departments, or even local offices. When principal-agent problems become significant, the signals sent from the top can be distorted in various ways, in their application downstream. By the time they are felt by the citizens, they may have changed substantially in impact (Tanzi, 2000). When these problems become common, the actual impact made by the changes in the instruments can be much different from the expected one. These principal-agent problems become more common when the legislation is more opaque and when heterogeneity may place people from different groups in different positions or levels.

## 9.4. The Positive Theory of Fiscal Policy

What was described in section 9.2 is the framework that many economists, and not just those from Northern Europe, have in mind (even though they might not always be aware of it) when they write academic or policy papers about the role of fiscal policy. That framework originated in the writings of (mostly) Northern European economists in the 1950s.[16] It was a framework based on the assumption that fiscal policies aim at promoting the welfare of the citizens, as interpreted by the policy makers who make the policy decisions. In a more homogeneous society, as was that of the Nordic countries in the 1950s, it could be assumed that the actions of the policy makers reflected more closely the interest of the majority of citizens than would be the case in some other countries. The framework was developed in the hope that econometric models, which were becoming fashionable at that time, would guide government decisions. Unfortunately, it did not reflect the reality that existed in many other countries.

There have been three main challenges over the years to this theory. One comes from the school of public choice already outlined earlier. It challenged especially the view of policy makers as objective promoters of a well-defined social welfare. The second comes from a so-called positive theory of fiscal policy, and the third from the theorists connected with rational expectation.

The positive theory of fiscal policy has been developed by economists such as Alberto Alesina, Guido Tabellini, Alan Drazen, Torsten Persson, J. von Hagen, and a few others (see, e.g., Poterba and von Hagen, 1999). This theory is less suspicious about the motives of policy makers and bureaucrats and more attentive to the impact of fiscal institutions and institutional arrangements on policy outcomes. The fiscal rules that centralize the budgetary process are considered particularly important. This school seems to conclude that with better institutions and better institutional arrangements good policies can be pursued and can deliver better results. In other words, the positive theory of fiscal policy does not necessarily invalidate the theory of fiscal policy, but it argues that the latter will be more successful if given institutions are in place.

The work by Torsten Persson and Guido Tabellini, in particular, has attempted to determine how different political institutions influence the size and the composition of government spending. It is focused on the economic role of the state as pursued through public spending. These authors analyze the role of majoritarian and proportional electoral systems. They also contrast presidential and parliamentary regimes (Persson and Tabellini, 1999, 2003, and 2004). The work by Alesina and others has been more focused on the impact of institutional arrangements on fiscal deficits (Alesina and Perotti, 1995). This literature recognizes that there are different processes that affect the final outcome. There is the planning stage at the executive level, the stage of legislative approval, and the stage of implementation of the legislation. As argued in Tanzi (2000), principal-agent problems can develop at each of these stages.

# References

Alesina, Alberto, and Roberto Perotti. 1995. "The Political Economy of Budget Deficits." *IMF Staff Papers* 42, no. 1 (March): 1–37.

Alesina, Alberto and Ricardo Hausmann, Rudolf Hommes and Ernestr Stein, 1999, Budget Institutions and Fiscal Performance in Latin America," Journal of Development Economics, August, 59: 233–53.

Barro, Robert. 1974. "Are Government Bonds Net Wealth?" *Journal of Political Economy* 82: 1095–1117.

Eichengreen, B., R. Hausmann, and J. von Hagen. 1999. "Reforming Budgetary Institutions in Latin America: The Case for a National Fiscal Council." *Open Economics Review* 10: 4125–4442.

Graff, J. deV. 1957. *Theoretical Welfare Economics* (Cambridge: Cambridge University Press).

Haavelmo, Trygve. 1989. "Econometrics and the Welfare State," Nobel Lecture (December 7). *American Economic Review* 87 (December 1997): 13–15.

Hallerberg, Mark, Rolf Strauch, and Jürgen von Hagen. 2009. *Fiscal Governance: Evidence from Europe* (Cambridge: Cambridge University Press).

Hansen, Bent. 1958. *The Economic Theory of Fiscal Policy* (London: George Allen & Unwin). Original Swedish edition published in 1955.

IDB. 2005. *The Politics of Policies: Economic and Social Progress in Latin America, 2006 Report* (Washington, D.C.: IDB/DRCLAS-Harvard University).

   2009. *Who Decides the Budget? A Political Economy Analysis of the Budget Process in Latin America*, edited by M. Hallerberg, C. Scartascini, and E. Stein (Washington D.C.: IDB/DRCLAS-Harvard University).

Jackson, Peter M. 1982. *The Political Economy of Bureaucracy* (Deddington, Oxford: Philip Allan).

Johansen, Leif. 1965. *Public Economic* (Amsterdam: North-Holland).

Keynes, John Maynard. 1971–89. The Collected Writings, edited by D. Moggridge, vol. 14, *The General Theory and After: Defense and Development* (London: Macmillan).

Kornai, Janos. 1992. *The Socialist System: The Political Economy of Communism* (Princeton: Princeton University Press).

Musgrave, Richard. 1998. "The Role of the State in Fiscal Policy," in *Public Finance in a Changing World*, edited by Peter Birch Sorensen (Houndmills: Macmillan), pp. 35–50.

Myrdal, Gunnar. 1954. *The Political Element in the Development of Economic Theory* (New York: Simon and Schuster).

Niskanen, William A. 1971. *Bureaucracy and Representative Government* (Chicago: Aldine).

Okun, A. M. 1975. *Equality and Efficiency: The Big Trade-Off* (Washington, D.C.: Brookings Institution).

Olson, Mancur. 1965. The Logic of Collective Action (Cambridge, Mass.: Harvard University Press).

Persson, Torsten, and Guido Tabellini. 1999. "The Size and Scope of Governments: Comparative Politics will Rational Politicians, 1998 Alfred Marshall Lecture." *European Economic Review*, vol. 43, 699–735.

2003. *The Economic Effects of Constitutions*, Munich Lectures in Economics (Cambridge, Mass.: MIT Press).

2004. "Constitutional Rules and Fiscal Policy Outcome." *American Economic Review* 94, no. 1 (March): 25–45.

Poterba James, M., and Jürgen von Hagen, eds. 1999. *Fiscal Institutions and Fiscal Performance* (Chicago: Chicago University Press).

Rostow, W. W. 1953. *The Dynamics of Soviet Society* (New York: W. W. Norton).

Tanzi, Vito. 2000. "Rationalizing the Government Budget," in *Economic Policy Reform: The Second Stage*, edited by Anne Kruger (Chicago: University of Chicago Press), pp. 435–53.

2010. "The Return to Fiscal Rectitude after The Recent Escapade." Paper presented at the Annual Research Conference at the European Commission. Brussels, November 17.

Tinbergen, Jan. 1956. *Economic Policy: Principles and Design* (Amsterdam).

Tullock, Gordon. 1965. *The Politics of Bureaucracy* (Washington, D.C.: Public Affairs Press).

von Hagen, J. 1992. "Budgeting Procedures and Fiscal Performance in the European Community." *European Economy Papers* (Brussels) 96.

# TEN

# Policy Tools and Government Roles

## 10.1. Introduction

Generally, a large government role in the economy tends to be associated with a high ratio of public spending into gross domestic product. This, for example, is what characterizes welfare states. The level of public spending in the economy has been the focus of the historical discussion in the second part of this book. However, the state can play its role using policy instruments–the $x_j$ in equation (2) in Chapter 9–other than public spending, as, for example, it did especially during the period of mercantilism in Europe and during recent decades in countries from Asia and Latin America. In these countries, government spending was relatively low, but the governments were very active in the economy, using other policy tools. As far back as 1790, Edmund Burke had recognized that governments have several instruments available besides public spending to promote their goals. In this chapter, we focus on this aspect, recognizing that different countries rely on different instruments; and that in future decades the relative use of different policy tools or instruments is likely to change. We provide a more complete listing of available tools than normally given in public finance books, accompanied by brief comments on each of them.

To appreciate the importance of this discussion, compare Sweden or Denmark with China. Most observers would agree that in these countries the government plays an overwhelming role in the economy. However, in Sweden and Denmark, that role is played mostly through public spending, whereas in China, it is played mostly through various forms of regulations. The difference in the share of public spending into GDP between the Scandinavian countries and China is a huge 30 percent. In Sweden and Denmark private ownership is respected, few enterprises have been nationalized, and regulations are few and transparent. In spite of their high share of spending into GDP, these two countries are ranked high in world competitiveness tables.

At the beginning it must be recognized that some instruments are more efficient than others in promoting particular objectives. Thus, as the objectives change, so should the instruments used by governments. However, at given times, there may be reasons for preferring one type of instrument to others so that, in some circumstance, less efficient instruments may be preferred and used. Strangely, this aspect of choice of instruments and policies has attracted little attention on the part of economists and of students of government. Let us consider reasons that may lead to preferring some instruments over others.

A first reason is that (given the time and the place) some instruments are *administratively* easier to use than others. This implies that the quality of the bureaucracy could be an important determinant of the choice. The more capable the bureaucracy is, the greater will be the degrees of freedom that governments have in their use of instruments. A government that strengthens the quality of its bureaucracy will increase its capacity to play a larger economic role, using a greater range of policy tools. This, of course, assumes that the quality of the bureaucracy is exogenous to the use of the instruments; that may not always be the case. There is a wide literature, by experts in public administration or in sociology, that identifies reasons and policies that make one public bureaucracy more professional and more efficient than others. These reasons range from tradition to social status of bureaucrats, to efficient and nonpoliticized selection and promotion processes of public employees, to levels of wages, and so on. Much of this literature goes back to Max Weber's "ideal" or normative type of rational-legal bureaucracy.[1] Bureaucracies can be assumed to be instruments that can be used to promote welfare and other governments' objectives. The utility or the welfare that they must maximize must be that of the citizens and not their own.[2]

In addition to the basic capacity of the public administration to use efficiently some policy instruments, there is also the question of costs. These costs must be distinguished between the direct costs to the government and those to society at large. Some instruments, such as public spending, are more directly costly to use by the government than others, such as regulations. For this reason, the latter may be preferred by governments, as they are in many countries. This raises an important question of basic asymmetry of costs mentioned by Stiglitz (1989, p. 53): "Public bureaucracies seldom place a value on the time of their clients. While the costs of increased personnel to provide better [public] service are apparent, and [are] reflected in the budget, the benefits are not." Therefore, the benefits (in terms of time saved) to citizens tend to be ignored.

There is a natural tendency to rely on instruments (or on aspects of instruments) that *save money to the government but shift costs* (in time and money) *on the citizens.* In some sense governments ignore social costs, focusing on their financial costs. This could be considered a general outcome of public-sector behavior. For example, self-assessment of income tax liabilities saves "administrative costs" to the tax administration but increases "compliance costs," sometimes by a large degree, for the taxpayers (Tanzi, 2010). This change is often praised by tax administrators for lowering administrative costs to a country.[3] In the provision of other services (getting passports, licenses, etc.), saving on administrative services often results in longer waiting lines for citizens.[4] When governments ignore compliance costs, as they often do, they are not restrained in making tax and other systems progressively more complex (Tanzi, 2006). Another example may be that of regulations that generate large reporting costs on the part of the regulated agents. Reporting costs have increased for enterprises over the years, generating increasing complaints. At the same time, the budgets of the regulatory agencies have been reduced, making it more difficult for them to evaluate the information received and to exercise their functions well.[5]

A second important reason for relying more on some rather than on other instruments is that the use of some instruments is politically easier than the use of others. For example, budgetary instruments (taxes and public expenditures) normally require legislative approval, whereas nonbudgetary instruments often do not. Because legislative approval is a lengthy and, occasionally, difficult and costly process (in terms of political capital), budgetary instruments may be less favored than others. Thus, the use of *non*budgetary instruments increases more than would be desirable in an optimal world. The nature of governments, conservative versus liberal, may also influence the choice. This argument suggests that there may be a bias toward overusing monetary policy over fiscal policy, because the former is politically and administratively easier to use. This became evident in the 2008–9 financial crisis.

In spite of these and other considerations, policy tools may, to some extent, be substitutable among themselves, at least in terms of their impact on the goals that governments wish to pursue. At the same time, ideology may lead governments to favor some over others. For example, governments that prefer lower tax and lower expenditure, as shares of GDP, may choose "tax expenditure" over higher public spending. This, for example, happened during the Clinton administration when it could not increase taxes and spending because the Republicans controlled Congress at the time. History may also be a significant factor. In these substitutions, their full costs to society, and not just to the government, should be considered but often are not. Through its actions, the government may be a generator of negative externalities and not just a corrector of them.

Before discussing the individual policy tools, it may be helpful to recall that, in most economies, the allocation of resources and the generation of incomes among various activities and individuals take place through at least five systems. The government needs different tools or instruments to influence these systems.

The first system is *the private market*. This is often the most important and the one that attracts much of the attention of economists. The market to a large extent generates the distribution of income before the intervention of the government. Neoclassical economists and, especially, economists from the Austrian school have attributed an overwhelming importance to the role that prices play in providing essential information to those who allocate resources and in distributing the national income among the participants in the economy. Wilhelm Röpke notes that "the market is the only efficient way to coordinate the actions of the producers with those of the consumers" (see Pongracic, 1997, p. 129).[6] They have paid less attention to the other four systems that exist and continue to play significant roles in some economies.

The second system involves the activities of civic and religious organizations in the so-called *nonprofit sector*. This sector involves also economic transactions within families, and occasionally through close friends, that escape measurement. Large amounts of resources may be allocated through this sector that may significantly change the distribution of income. We argued earlier that this sector was relatively more important in the past, before it was, in part, crowded out by the growing intervention of the government, especially in welfare states, and, to a lesser extent, by the shrinking of the family and the weakening of family ties. This crowding out was greater in some countries than in others. According to one expert, in Sweden this sector "has been extensively incorporated into central authority" (Boli, 1991, p. 116). The title of Boli's paper is indicative: "Sweden: Is There a Viable Third Sector?" By "third sector" he means the nonprofit sector. The same point has been made by other authors for other countries, including the United States. Röpke (1960) has gone so far as to claim that public assistance and moralism are responsible for destroying charity (*charitas*).[7]

The third system is *the market for, and of, favors*. These favors can be totally legitimate when they involve genuine gifts among friends and relatives or illegitimate when they involve exchanges that reflect hidden acts of corruption or hidden, implicit contracts (Tanzi, 1995). The importance of this system in allocating resources and redistributing income varies from country to country, depending on culture, the role of the family (especially the extended family), and the role of corruption. It remains important in many countries. In some countries, bribes hide themselves as gifts given in exchange for hidden and implicit promises. Reports over the years have indicated that bribes hidden as gifts can be very large in some countries.[8] The importance of this market is likely to be smaller in low-corruption countries, such as Sweden or Denmark, and larger in some other countries.

The fourth system is that associated with *criminal activities*, whether they are organized or not. Burglaries and many other kinds of criminal activities almost always redistribute incomes and lead to actions that reallocate resources away from the allocation that would exist in the absence of these activities. The production and distribution of illicit drugs and such activities as prostitution and gambling add to the (officially measured) national incomes of the countries where these activities are legal but not to those of countries where they are illegal. The smuggling of cigarettes, to avoid high taxes on them, also generates large income for some individuals and higher costs for others. For some countries, the proceeds from these activities, and the resources invested in them, have been reported to be enormous, at times almost as large, as proportions of national income, as the total resources that were available to governments a century ago. Thus, their impact in allocating resources and in redistributing incomes, especially in particular countries, cannot be ignored. These activities form their own markets, with rules and a system of prices, as in the illegal drug industry (see Tanzi, 2001, and Naim, 2005, for more details).

Finally, the last system is the one that involves *the operations of the state* in all its functions. In this system taxes (or loans and fees) are exchanged for public services. As we saw earlier, this activity, as measured by the share of public spending and taxes into national income, grew enormously during the past century. However, the state uses other instruments besides taxing and spending to achieve its various objectives. These other instruments also affect the distribution of income and, in some places or periods, can become very important.

All these systems involve exchanges and require rules. However, only the last two – criminal and governmental activities – involve coercion.[9] The first three do not normally or necessarily involve coercion. Broadly speaking, the more important the last two systems become, the less important the first three are likely to become.

In the next three sections, we identify briefly the most important policy tools. This identification is helpful for later chapters in discussing the outcome of the recent push for the expansion in the role of the state in industrial countries. We list the policy tools under three main categories: fiscal, regulatory, and other tools.

## 10.2. Fiscal Tools

Fiscal tools are the ones normally associated with government budgets. In democratic countries the use of these tools always requires legislative approval, which involves complex procedures.

*Government Expenditures*: Governments need money to pay salaries to public employees, to provide public goods, and to provide services and cash transfers that protect individuals from particular risks with economic consequences. Public spending is needed to build and maintain public infrastructure that, for various reasons, the private sector would not provide, or would not provide in the amounts, conditions, or places that the government desires. In earlier chapters we have shown that over the past century there was a large increase in the share of public spending into GDP in industrial countries, indicating that government expenditure was a favored instrument of government policy.

Both the total *level* of public spending and its *composition* can be considered important policy tools. Even when total spending does not change, governments can significantly change their roles by reallocating spending away from some and toward other functions. Governments that wish to promote economic growth in the long run are more likely to allocate more spending to productive investment, research and development, and other productivity-enhancing uses such as education. Governments that are mostly interested in winning the next election will allocate more public resources to current spending and to higher salaries for public employees. In some cases the money spent may work its way into the pockets of favored groups or of the policy makers themselves.

*Taxes*: Taxes finance public spending with some assistance from borrowing and other sources such as fees, sale of public assets, and occasionally dividends from public enterprises. Over the long run, high public spending requires high taxes. Given the choice, governments will favor some groups with their spending and penalize less favored groups with higher taxes. As is the case with spending, both the *level* and the *structure* of taxation, or the characteristics of specific taxes, are important. There was a time when taxes were collected only, or mainly, with the objective of financing public spending. Their use had no other objective. However, over the past several decades, the tax system became a tremendously versatile tool to promote an increasing number of social objectives. It was used to finance public spending; to redistribute income; to reduce some externalities; to promote good health habits; to finance specific activities, such as the building of roads and the payment of pensions, with earmarked taxes; to promote industrial or regional development through regional or sectoral tax incentives; to promote import substitution; to influence demographic changes and employment objectives; to promote saving or, occasionally, particular consumption; to promote home ownership; and so on.

The tax system has proven to be a very versatile policy tool. "Tax expenditures," based on an analytical concept developed in the 1960s, by Stanley Surrey (a Harvard professor who was working in the U.S. Treasury), became progressively more important with the passing of time (Surrey, 1973). Tax expenditures substituted for public spending in countries that preferred to have lower taxes and lower public spending, such as the United States, while still promoting some socially desirable private consumption (Toder, 2000). There is no question that taxes have acquired a role, as policy instruments, that is far from the traditional and exclusive one of financing public spending and particularly public goods. There is also no question that they have become far more complex.

*Public Debt and Public Loans*: In addition to the use of taxes and public spending, governments also rely on public debt to finance some of their activities and on public lending to individuals or enterprises to encourage some activities. In some circumstances, the amount of borrowing becomes an important tool for promoting particular governments' roles. For example, some economists have advocated borrowing to finance public investment, in what has been referred to as a "golden rule" (e.g., Blanchard and Giavazzi, 2008). This is a policy that the United Kingdom followed in recent years, until it abandoned it in the 2008–9 crisis, and that some other countries, including Germany, had followed in the past. There has been controversy among public finance scholars, going back to the 1960s, on whether public investment should be financed by current revenue or by borrowing, and whether a separate "capital budget" makes sense (see also Balassone and Franco, 2000, for a criticism of the golden rule). The argument has been that, because public investment creates assets that favor future generations, the latter should pay for it. This argument assumes that public investment is always productive.

The *maturity* structure of the public debt can also be considered an instrument that governments can occasionally use to achieve specific objectives.

In theory, the shorter the maturity of the debt is, the more the financial instruments used become substitute for money, and thus the greater may be their potential impact on prices. Governments can influence the yield curve by changing the maturity of their public debt. Increasing the maturity of the public debt is often accompanied by higher interest rates and higher servicing costs. The tax treatment of government bonds can also be seen as another government instrument. Some countries do not tax public bonds, thus reducing to them the direct cost of borrowing and increasing, especially for high-income individuals, the net-of-tax rate of return that they get from lending to the government. This is done by American states and by some national governments. Interest paid to foreigners is often tax free or is taxed at low rates. A government that, for example, does not tax public debt and compensates for the lost revenue by increasing value-added taxes has de facto shifted some tax burden from higher to lower income individuals.

*Public loans* or publicly guaranteed loans are also important budgetary tools to promote particular government objectives. They can be given to public or occasionally to private enterprise and to various categories of citizens (students, farmers, those living in poorer parts of countries, those affected by catastrophes, etc.). When given, it is desirable to give the loans through the budget or to report the anticipated costs. However, they can be, and at times have been, given through the central bank or through development banks that have access to central bank credit or to government guarantees. When this happens, they fall in the category of "off-budget operations." There have been various examples of such "off-budget" loans, especially during the 2008–9 crisis. In the past, such operations have often led, with some lag, to inflation.

In 2008–9 the central banks of several industrial countries, including those of the United States and the United Kingdom, engaged in what was called, "quantitative easing" as a way of stimulating private lending and helping countries to recover from the economic crisis. This was done when the monetary instrument of reducing interest rates was no longer effective, because the rates at which loans by the authority had been given was close to zero. The central banks bought some questionable assets from financial enterprises. This policy increased the assets of the central banks and the reserves that private banks had with the central banks. De facto, the central banks injected large liquidity in the economy. Only time will tell whether the outcome of these "off-budgetary operations" will be inflation, as it usually was in Latin American countries in the 1970s and 1980s, or just higher economic growth. In either alternative, the outcome will influence the economic role of the state in future years.

## 10.3. Regulatory Tools

*Regulations and authorizations* are potentially powerful policy tools that can be used, and are used, by governments to promote various objectives. Historically, they have been important government instruments and are likely to become more important, again, in the future. Regulations can substitute for taxes and public expenditures to promote particular objectives. For example, a government either can provide subsidies to help people with handicaps or can introduce a regulation that requires enterprises to include in their work force a given proportion made up of people who have been certified to be handicapped. Implicitly this regulation is broadly equivalent to a tax on enterprises and a subsidy to the handicapped. Or the government can either subsidize the consumption of a given product or service or constrain the price at which the product can be sold, as is often done in developing countries, and as is done with rent controls in many countries. These latter kinds of regulations often lead, over time, to scarcity of the good or of the regulated service but help those who can access these goods through official channels and not through black markets. Most economic regulations are equivalent to taxes and subsidies, even though at times it is difficult to ascertain their final incidence, a characteristic that they share with taxes. As is the case with taxes, inefficiencies can be generated by their use.

Regulations can be used to provide protection against particular risks for some categories of people. When they are so used, they implicitly tax some sector (say, the enterprises or the agricultural sector) to subsidize some groups (say, the handicapped or the urban workers) (Tanzi, 1998b). Therefore, public spending, aimed at protecting individuals against particular economic risks, can be replaced, to some extent, by well-targeted regulations. Through the use of these regulations, the government can try to achieve specific goals.[10]

The use of regulations for social goals was adopted widely by centrally planned economies where state enterprises were directed to absorb all the workers who became available and to provide them with health care, retirement benefits, and even food and housing. The prices at which the output of these enterprises was sold were determined by the central planners. Centrally planned economies created, de facto, a kind of "regulatory welfare state." Of course, economies organized around these principles could not be efficient, as Hayek, von Mises, Röpke, and other economists have shown. However, their main goal was not efficiency but equity and, perhaps, protection against some risks, at some basic or low level. In the pursuit of these objectives, the centrally planned economies broadly achieved that goal. They did protect their citizens against basic economic risks. Evidence of this was a recurrent complaint, heard especially from senior citizens of economies in transition during the transition period, that the move to market economies had made their lives more risky. The reliable though very basic safety nets that had been provided by the socialist system were no longer there to protect them. It may be inappropriate to assume that economic efficiency is the only criterion to judge economies, as Amartya Sen has argued in various writings. It may also be inappropriate to give excessive weight to equity.

Some uses of regulations in market economies were promoted by labor unions. For example, some American enterprises, such as General Motors, had been providing generous pensions and other nonwage benefits such as health insurance to their workers as parts of their union contracts. These benefits could have been provided directly by the government through public spending. This would have required higher taxes. Thus, there was an implicit welfare benefit for those workers, and for their families, who worked for large, private enterprises (Howard, 1997). To some extent, and for many workers, this social protection was similar to that which workers receive directly from the government in welfare states. These costs became a major problems for the enterprise when they could no longer pass them forward in the prices of the products that they sold, because they had to compete with foreign enterprises (such as Japanese car makers) that were efficient and did not have to cover these costs; or when they were not able to adjust downward the cash wages that they paid to their workers. Another problem was that access to the free or subsidized services was tied to the jobs. Nonworkers did not have access to them; and those who lost their jobs, or changed jobs, lost access to these benefits.

Economically relevant regulations are used, in some countries, in the labor market (e.g., minimum wages, maximum working hours, minimum vacation time, restrictions on firing of workers, requirement to hire disabled individuals); the housing market (rent controls and other restrictions on rental contracts); the credit market (requirement to give subsidized loans or government-guaranteed loans to some sectors, such as farmers, students, home buyers, or enterprises operating in poorer areas); the product market (price controls and other regulations for some products); the foreign trade market (multiple exchange rates, quantitative restrictions on some imports); and public enterprises (requirement to provide services at reduced prices for particular categories of citizens).[11] These regulations are used to pursue particular social objectives that, in principle, could be pursued through the use of taxes and/or government cash subsidies. Thus, they are an integral part of the economic role that the state plays.

The use of these regulations in centrally planned economies but also in the United States and especially in developing countries (such as those in Latin America) can create a kind of rudimentary system of social protection that does not require high levels of public spending or heavy tax burdens (Tanzi, 2004). Because of the use of regulations, the centrally planned economies and especially the developing countries had tax burdens lower than those in the welfare states that remained market economies. These regulation-based protective systems, or safety nets, are easy to criticize, because of the economic inefficiencies that they generate. They have been the object of sharp criticism from mainstream economists, in arguments against the centrally planned economies, and especially from economists from international organization, in arguments against developing countries. They can easily be criticized also because the protection that they provide is not universal but is often limited to particular groups, mainly organized urban workers. In developing countries, the urban middle classes received far more protection than the rural poor; and workers in the official economy received far more than those in the informal economy. Groups that were able to organize and apply pressure on governments, to introduce regulations that helped them, did much better. This has often been also the case with public employees, who often are entitled to various benefits, beside their wages, not available in the private sector. This rudimentary system of protection is important to individuals who are often the most vocal and the best organized.

In market economies, regulations related to the use of land (zoning regulations) are particularly important for the affected people because they can dramatically change the market value of a property and the net worth of its owners. It is no surprise that these regulations often lead to corruption. Of course, these regulations weaken the concept of property rights. They are particularly important at the municipal level.

Governments use various forms of *authorizations* to protect citizens against particular risks. For example, governments establish training and licensing requirements to fly planes, to drive buses, to be a taxi driver, to practice medicine or law, to sell drugs, to operate particular machines, and to cut hair. The training and licensing part may be delegated to particular institutions recognized by the state, such as schools, hospitals, and universities. The declared intention of the authorizations is to protect citizens against incompetence and malpractice. However, the authorizations may and often do become tools for particular categories of individuals to restrict entry into their activities, thus weakening competition and raising their incomes. This, for example, is the case with the American Medical Association, which has the power to limit the number of doctors; or of associations of taxi drivers, and other groups, which restrict their numbers. These are examples of "regulatory capture."

A curious or extreme example of authorizations comes from 16th-century France, where beggars needed a license that authorized them to beg in a particular city or in a specific part of a city (Solomon, 1972). Those who get the licenses have an interest into restricting the number of licenses issued. In today's world, in some countries authorizations are needed to open enterprises, to make some investments, and to operate in foreign countries. Often the requirement to get authorizations slows down economic activity and creates grounds for corruption. "Speed money" may have to be paid to get in front of the line and to reduce the time to get the needed authorization to start a new activity. At the same time, some activities that should be regulated are not or are not regulated effectively, especially when those who should be regulated have strong, political power.

Therefore, countries end up with too many *unnecessary* regulations and too few *necessary* regulations. There is clearly a large misallocation of regulations in most countries. This became evident during the 2008–9 financial crisis. Some participants in the financial market that had strong political power had been able to prevent the introduction of needed regulations in their activities. Many experts now believe that this contributed to the financial crisis and some countries have been introducing legislation to correct some of the more egregious, existing, regulatory failures. However, the operators in the financial market have again been very active in trying to dilute the effectiveness of the new rules. George Stigler is probably the economist who over his long life paid most attention to regulations. His work earned him the Nobel Prize in Economics in 1982. Stigler (1975) believed that the regulators are often captured by the regulated and that regulations rarely or never make a market more efficient.

Besides the more traditional tools mentioned thus far, there are less traditional and more eclectic tools, some of which have became less important in more recent times. On the other hand, some tools that were not important in the past may become important in the future.

## 10.4. Other Tools

*Power of Conscription*: In the past conscription was a major instrument available to governments to force people to build roads and canals, to fight wars, and to pursue other governmental objectives. It often resulted in heavy burdens on the populations subjected to it, because they had to allocate a large share of their time to unpaid, or badly paid, heavy and often dangerous work. In more recent years, especially in democratic countries, this power had been limited to the military draft, and many countries have abandoned even this use, relying on voluntary armies.[12] However, its historical importance should be kept in mind, as well as the possibility that some day governments may find it attractive to return to its use.[13] When the tax burdens in today's countries are compared with those of the distant past, there is a tendency to ignore the implicit burdens associated with forced conscription.

*Ownership*: In all countries, governments own valuable assets and properties. They own natural resources, forests, mountains, some land, buildings, streets, works of art, public libraries, monuments, and so on. They also own some enterprises that may fall in the category of "natural monopolies" or even in categories that should normally be in the private sector. Depending on the ideology of the time and of the country, some "public" enterprises may be completely owned and run by the government, they can be privately operated but regulated by the government, or they can be run largely as commercial enterprises with some public ownership and/or controls. In some cases the government owns a "golden share," a share large enough to allow it to control some important aspects of the enterprises' operations, such as the payment of dividends and the appointment of board members.[14] It can be argued that as governments moved in the past from patrimonial revenues to taxes, they acquired more freedom to spend more because the supply of funds to them became more elastic.

After World War II, reflecting the ideology of the time, and the influence of socialist ideas, there was a wave of *nationalization* of large enterprises in Europe and in other areas. Ideologies associated with socialism called for the control of the "commanding heights" of the economy, while allowing some scope for property rights for citizens. In the 1980s and 1990s there was a wave of *privatization* of previously state-owned or public enterprises starting in the United Kingdom and spreading to other countries. In this period "public-private partnerships" (PPP) were promoted especially in large infrastructure projects. These were privately built and privately run infrastructures, built under agreements with governments, with the understanding that after a number of years, their ownership and their management would return to the government. This allowed governments to reduce their public spending while still pursuing their infrastructure objectives. In some ways, this was a return to what had happened in the 19th century, especially in England (de Molinari, 1849). However, in modern times governments assumed various risks, especially when future developments diverged from those assumed in the agreements (see various papers in Polackova and Schick, 2002).

Government-owned assets can be a small or a large share of a country's total wealth, and the economic return to these assets can be large or small, depending on how efficiently they are used. The value of these assets has been estimated to amount to around 40 percent of GDP in the United Kingdom and more than 120 percent of GDP in Italy (Reviglio and Russo, 2005; and unpublished data). Historical and probably ideological reasons are behind these large differences. In Italy, the value of government-owned assets broadly equals the value of the public debt, leading to occasional proposals to sell the assets in order to pay off the public debt.

Some kinds of public assets (mineral resources) can provide governments with significant incomes that can help finance public expenditure. During periods when commodity prices are high (during so-called commodity booms), governments that own and export natural resources can get a lot of revenue. This happened in recent years to Norway, Russia, Chile, Mexico, Peru, Saudi Arabia, and other countries. This additional revenue can be spent immediately; or it can be kept in special stabilization funds, the return to which can provide the government with a permanent, annual income and allow it to pursue more easily a countercyclical fiscal policy, when needed. This has been the policy followed by some countries, including Norway and Chile. In any case, these resources allow governments to finance, over the long run, levels of public spending above what would be possible with taxes.[15]

The ownership of public enterprises gives governments an important tool to perform various functions, including that of creating government jobs. In some cases, these enterprises establish a monopoly in a lucrative activity. For example, the Italian energy company ENI sells its output at a price high enough to generate large profits that are partly transferred to the government in dividends. However, some public enterprises, such as airlines, railroads, post offices, and others often lose money, requiring government subsidies. For this reason, there are pressures on governments to privatize these loss-making enterprises. There are also examples of internal subsidies within the system of public enterprises, by using the profits of profitable enterprises to cover the losses of unprofitable enterprises. This may allow governments to pursue some of their social objectives.

Governments own some assets that are neither natural resources nor public enterprises. They own works of art (some deposited in the basement of museums and never shown to the public), public libraries, abandoned railroad tracks, buildings that are used as jails or as schools, buildings that in the past had been convents, monasteries, or army caserms, often placed in the middle of cities. Evidence available from some countries indicates that, for various reasons, some having to do with fragmented legal controls, some with poor management, some with the existence of positional rents for some groups that use these assets (associated with historical developments that make any policy change difficult), these assets are often not used efficiently, so that they do not generate much of an income. This is an important example of government inefficiency. It is an inefficiency that has received little attention on the part of economists (Tanzi and Prakash, 2003). An efficient government, that pursued the objective of the maximization of the public interest, would move these assets into functions that could provide the highest possible (social) rate of return. However, in doing so, the government might lose a powerful instrument through which it often dispenses benefits and favors to privileged groups.[16]

*Contingent Liabilities:* This instrument has come to play an important role in modern economies and, especially, in the 2008–9 financial crisis. Contingent liabilities are guarantees (implicitly or explicitly) given by governments to private or quasi-private investors or activities or to particular programs. The importance of this instrument has been growing in recent decades, when the push toward privatization became intense and when it became progressively more difficult to raise tax revenue. Activities that previously had been publicly financed (such as the building of public infrastructures) were taken over by private enterprises often with some government guarantees. Activities that in the past had been totally private (such as those associated with bank deposits) also acquired government guarantees. Other institutions that promoted activities favored by governments, such as private home ownership or students' loans, acquired implicit guarantees. When this instrument is used, the government, or some publicly funded institution, assumes the financial risk in the event the activity fails; or, when it does not meet earnings' expectations spelled out in contracts.[17]

Contingent liabilities may be associated with private activities or also with the activities of subnational governments or quasi-public institutions. Some of the guarantees provided by the government may be implicit rather than explicit. They are not based on formal agreements but on the expectation that the government will intervene, or can be pressured to intervene, if certain events occur. Expectations may be influenced by the past behavior of the government that may have created what economists call "moral hazards," that is, the expectation that the government will come to rescue investors who have taken risks if certain events materialize. Moral hazards encourage economic agents to take more risks. Contingent liabilities become important in connection with activities subjected to catastrophic events. By assuming these potential risks, the government, intentionally or unintentionally, encourages private concerns to expand their activities or to continue operating in riskier circumstances or places.

Common examples of contingent liabilities are those related to investments in major infrastructure projects by private operators through public-private partnerships. In these cases, the governments may guarantee a minimum rate of return on an investment financed and operated by private investors. Another example is the assumption of the liability for acts of terrorism. This protection was provided in some countries for commercial airlines after September 11, 2001. This allowed the airlines to continue flying after the private insurers had suspended their insurance coverage. Another example is the expectation of governments' financial assistance to individuals who build houses in areas subject to earthquakes, floods, hurricanes, or other natural disasters.[18] Without that expectation, fewer houses would be built in those areas. More recently, contingent liabilities related to the financial sector became very important.

As mentioned, these guarantees are at times explicit and at times implicit. The explicit ones are given in advance and are transparent. In this case, the governments may be able to replace some current spending by assuming potential and uncertain future costs for spending financed by others. The implicit ones may remain uncertain until the problems arise. Thus, it is less clear how much of an impact they may have on current spending. In either case, the expected assumption of these risks by the government is likely to promote some activities and to encourage some individuals to invest more and to take more risks. So it has a stimulative effect on the economy, just like expansionary fiscal policy. In some cases, the pressure for the government to intervene during crises may come from the belief that an institution has become "too big to fail" and that its failure would create systemic risks. This may have been the case in the interventions in large financial institutions by the British and U.S. governments in 2008–9. These interventions by governments are likely to create strong expectations about the role of the state in the future.[19] They may also indicate that the government failed in its regulatory function in the past.

The potential but uncertain costs to the government of these implicit or explicit guarantees are not included in the countries' budgets. Therefore, these guarantees do not change the "look" of fiscal policy, although they may change significantly the "substance" of it and the real impact of the true fiscal policy on the economy. In some cases, they effectively put governments at potential risk of large future expenses (Polackova and Schick, 2002). The 2008–9 financial crisis has left many governments with much worsened *actual* fiscal situations and with *changed expectations* about future public-sector interventions.[20]

Accountants have been encouraging governments to give details in budget documents of the *explicit* commitments that they undertake. When this information is provided, which is not always the case, it is contained in footnotes or in memoranda added to the budgets. These footnotes or memoranda rarely attract attention. Furthermore, as mentioned earlier, many contingent liabilities are not visible ex ante, because they are not explicit.[21] The more complex the financial system becomes, the larger its institutions, and the greater the chance of failure, the greater the reason to keep the transparent or visible fiscal policy in good shape, so that it can more easily intervene in times of crisis and assume the extra costs of financial failures. This conclusion has implications for the Keynesian stabilization policies that are pursued in normal times.

Contingent liabilities represent one way in which governments can promote some of their goals – such as the building of infrastructure, keeping commercial airplanes in the air, promoting house buying, or keeping citizens' deposits in the banks – without the (immediate) commitment of public money. The guarantees given to holders of bank accounts are good examples of contingent liabilities, although in some cases fees may be paid by the banks to institutions that are supposed to insure the deposits. These institutions can deal with the failure of an occasional bank but not with systemic failures. Past banking crises have often required very large amounts of public money. These crises have been frequent in recent years and have had major impacts on the countries' fiscal situations by sharply increasing their public debts (Reinhart and Rogoff, 2009).

These contingent liabilities must be distinguished from the future liabilities for governments associated with defined-benefit pensions or with guaranteed public health care systems when the costs of these programs are expected to grow over time and are expected to exceed the contributions to these programs, as in the United States and in many European countries. These future liabilities are also not reported in the current fiscal deficits and thus also lead to statistics that do not correctly measure the real fiscal situation of a country. However, liabilities that arise from demographic changes and from the rising costs of (defined-benefit) pension payments and public health protection are not the result of *unlikely and unanticipated catastrophic events* but are known and anticipated costs. These costs can be estimated within some probability range. A comprehensive system of

accrual budgeting would show them in the current budgets. Their estima-
tion should be subjected to careful sensitivity analysis, to take into account
potential, alternative developments in future years of relevant variables that
might increase or decrease the size of the expected liability.[22]

As already mentioned, some of the contingent liabilities are implicit and
not explicit, making accrual accounting difficult. For example, many had
believed that the liabilities assumed by Fannie Mae and Freddie Mac, the
large U.S. financial institutions that buy the mortgages of many home buyers, had the backing of the U.S. government. This allowed these institutions
to get cheaper credit from the market and to promote home ownership that
was an expressed government goals. Because of the existence of these institutions more houses were built and more people were able to buy houses.
The enormous expansion of these institutions put the U.S. government at
risk of huge liabilities when the institutions failed, forcing the U.S. government to take them over and to become responsible for trillions of dollars
of additional *gross* liabilities (Posner, 2009; Shiller, 2008; and Sinn, 2010).[23]
Expectations have been created over the years that governments will intervene when catastrophic events occur in exposed geographical areas – as, for
example, along the Caribbean coast and the Atlantic coast of the United
States. Expectations have also been created that, when an institution is "too
big to fail," the government will in fact not let it fail. These will inevitably
affect the role of the state in the future.

*Nudging, or Cajolement.* This is another potentially useful instrument
that governments use, or can use, to influence the behavior of citizens and
to make them choose desirable courses of action. The use of this instrument
can potentially reduce future risks and the need for the government to
intervene ex post to deal with the consequences of the risks. Some form
of nudging or cajolement is used by mothers and grandmothers within
families to promote good behavior on the part of children. Recent research
in behavioral economics has suggested ways of influencing often-irrational
individual behavior in positive directions – for example, by inducing people
to save more or smoke less.[24] It represents a "paternalistic approach" on the
part of the government because, in some sense, the government changes the
free actions of individuals. Through this instrument, governments may try
to influence, but not force, the decisions of citizens about health, happiness,
wealth accumulation, and other issues. This instrument is not new, in spite
of recent claims and the results of experiments conducted by behavioral
economists, although its link with presumably irrational behavior may be.
It was used, in various forms, in times of war, when appeals to patriotism
urged citizens to buy government bonds, to volunteer for the army, or to

comply with their tax obligations.[25] In many cases, better behavior can be promoted by the government simply through a better dissemination of useful and important information.

A recent book by Thaler and Sunstein (2008) has provided a useful discussion of potential uses of this instrument (see also Della Vigna, 2009).[26] Recent accounts have described this as "libertarian paternalism" because, through the use of nudging and the spreading of useful information, individuals are encouraged, but are not forced, to take particular lines of action. This "libertarian paternalism" could in some cases be employed in place of other policy tools, thus changing the economic role of the state. However, its uses are likely to be limited. It may become substitutable to other policy tools only in particular circumstances.

Finally, before closing this chapter, it should be repeated that, a government, through the use of regulations and some of the other tools mentioned, can pursue all the major objectives that it normally pursues, such as the allocation of resources, the redistribution of income, and the stabilization of the economy. For example, a government can promote an expansionary policy by relaxing some existing regulations or by assuming greater contingent liabilities. Therefore, discussions of stabilization policy and of allocation and redistribution policies should not be limited to taxing and spending in public finance textbooks. They should recognize that these objectives can also be pursued, and are pursued, with the other policy instruments mentioned.

## References

Andreoni, J. 1988. "Privately Provided Public Goods." *Journal of Public Economics* 35: 57–73.

Auerback, A. J., J. Gokhale, and L. Kotlikoff. 1991. "Generation Accounts: A Meaningful Alternative to Deficit Accounting," in *Tax Policy and the Economy*, vol. 5, edited by D. Bradford (Cambridge: Mass. MIT Press), pp. 55–111.

Balassone, Fabrizio, and Daniele Franco. 2000. "Public Investment, the Stability Pact, and the 'Golden Rule.'" *Fiscal Studies* 21: 207–29.

Blanchard, Oliver, and Francesco Giavazzi. 2008. "Improving the Stability and Growth Pact through Proper Accounting of Public Investment," in *Fiscal Policy Stabilization and Growth: Prudence or Abstinence?*, edited by Guilllermo Perry, Luis Serven and Rodrigo Suescún (Washington, D.C.: World Bank).

Blank, Rebecca. 2000. "When Can Policy Makers Rely on Private Markets?" *Economic Journal* 110, no. 462 (March): 34–49.

Boli, John. 1991. "Sweden: Is There a Viable Third Sector?," in *Between States and Markets*, edited by Robert Wuthnow (Princeton: Princeton University Press), pp. 94–124.

Burke, Edmund. [1790]. 1987, *Reflections on the Revolution in France* edited by J.G.A. Pocock (Indianapolis/Cambridge: Hackelf Publishing Company).

Costa, Raffaele. 2002. *L'Italia dei Privilegi* (Milan: Mondadori).

Della Vigna, Stefano. 2009. "Psychology and Economics: Evidence from the Field." *Journal of Economic Literature*, 47, no. 2 (June): 315–72.

de Molinari, Gustave. 1849. *Les Soirées de la Rue Saint-Lazare.* Translated as *Le Serate di Rue Saint-Lazare* (Macerata: Liberi Libri, 2009).

Evans, Chris. 2003. "Studying the Studies: An Overview of Recent Research into Taxation Operating Costs." *eJournal of Tax Research* 4: 1–38.

Formez (Presidenza del Consiglio dei Ministri, Italy). 2007. *Innovazione Amministrativa e Crescita*, vols. 1–10 (Naples: Ricerca Giannini-Formez).

Gokhale, Jogadeesh, and Kent Smelters. 2003. *Fiscal and Generational Imbalances: New Budget Measures for New Budget Priorities* (Washington, D.C.: AEI Press).

Howard, Christopher. 1997. *The Hidden Welfare State: Tax Expenditures and Social Policy in the United States* (Princeton: Princeton University Press).

Kendall, Jeremy, and Martin Knapp. 1996. *The Voluntary Sector in the UK* (Manchester: Manchester University Press).

Kornai, Janos, Eric Maskin, and Gerard Roland. 2003. "Understanding the Soft Budget Constraint." *Journal of Economic Literature* 41, no. 4 (December): 1095–1136.

Ministero dell'Economia. 2005. *Conto Patrimoniale delle Amministrazioni Pubbliche, Stime 2001–04*, edited by A. Carpinella and E. Reviglio (Rome).

Naim, Moses. 2005. *Illicit* (New York: Doubleday).

Polackova, Ana, and Allen Schick. 2002. *Government at Risk* (Washington, D.C.: World Bank).

Pongracic, Ivan. 1997. "How Different Were Röpke and Mises?" *Review of Austrian Economics* 10, no. 1: 125–32.

Posner, R. A. 1971. "Taxation by Regulation." *Bell Journal of Economics and Management Science* vol. 22, 22–50. (Spring).

2009. *A Failure of Capitalism* (Cambridge, Mass.: Harvard University Press).

Reinhart, Carmen M., and Kenneth Rogoff. 2009. *This Time Is Different: Eight Centuries of Financial Folly* (Princeton: Princeton University Press).

Reviglio, E., and L. Russo, eds. 2005. *Patrimonio dello Stato, Il patrimonio pubblico per classi di disponibilita'* (Rome).

Röpke Wilhelm. 1960. "Il Vangelo Non é Socialista." *La Tribuna*, no. 40 (October 2). Republished in a volume with the same title (Catanzaro: Rubettino, Editore, 2006).

Schiller, Robert J. 2008. *The Subprime Solution: How Today's Financial Crisis Happened and What to Do About It* (Princeton: Princeton University Press).

Sinn, Hans-Werner. 2010. *Casino Capitalism: How the Financial Crisis Came About and What Needs to Be Done Now* (Oxford: Oxford University Press).

Solomon, Howard. 1972. *Public Welfare, Science and Propaganda in Seventeenth Century France* (Princeton: Princeton University Press).

Stigler, George J. 1975. *The Citizen and the State: Essays on Regulation* (Chicago: University of Chicago Press).

Stiglitz, Joseph E. 1989. *The Economic Role of the State* (Oxford: Basil Blackwell).

Surrey, Stanley S. 1973. *Pathway to Tax Reform: the Concept of Tax Expenditure* (Cambridge, Mass.: Harvard University Press).

Tanzi, Vito. 1986. "Fiscal Policy Responses to Exogenous Shocks in Developing Countries." *American Economic Review* 76, no. 2 (May): 88–91.

1995. "Corruption, Arm's Length, and Markets," in *The Economics of Organized Crime,* edited by G. Fiorentini and S. Perltzman (Cambridge: Cambridge University Press). Also published in a revised version, as chapter 6 of Tanzi, *Policies, Institutions and the Dark Side of Economics* (Cheltenham: Edward Elgar, 2000).

1998a. "Corruption around the World: Causes, Consequences, Scope and Cure." *IMF Staff Papers* 45, no. 4 (December): 559–94.

1998b. "Government Role and the Efficiency of Policy Instruments," in *Public Finance in a Changing World,* edited by Peter Birch Sorensen (London: Macmillan), pp. 51–72.

2001. "Transnational Crime and National Jurisdiction," in *National Sovereignty under Challenge,* edited by Ispi (Milan: Egea), pp. 53–72.

2004. "Globalization and the Need for Fiscal Reform in Developing Countries." *Journal of Policy Modeling* 26: 525–42.

2006. *Death of an Illusion? Decline and Fall of High Tax Economies* (London: Politeia).

2007. "Complexity and Systemic Failure," in *Transition and Beyond,* edited by Saul Estrin et al. (London: Palgrave), pp. 229–46.

2008. *Regulating for the New Economic Order: The Good, The Bad, and the Damaging* (London: Politeia).

2010. "Complexity in Taxation: Origin and Consequences." Mimeo.

Tanzi, Vito, and Tej Prakash. 2003. "The Cost of Government and the Misuse of Public Assets," in *Public Finance in Developing and Transitional Countries: Essays in Honor of Richard Bird,* edited by Jorge Martinez-Vazquez and James Alm (Cheltenham: Edward Elgar).

Thaler, Richard H., and Cass R. Sunstein. 2008. *Nudge: Improving Decisions about Health, Wealth and Happiness* (New Haven: Yale University Press).

Toder, Eric J. 2000. "Tax Cuts or Spending – Does it Make a Difference?" *National Tax Journal* 53, no. 3, part 1: 361–71.

Weber, Max. 1947. *The Theory of Social and Economic Organization* (Glencoe, Ill.: Free Press).

1978. *Economy and Society,* vols. 1 and 2 (Berkeley: University of California Press).

Wuthnow, Robert, ed. 1991. *Between States and Markets* (Princeton: Princeton University Press).

# PART FOUR

# THE OUTCOME OF STATE INTERVENTION

A government that takes from Peter to give to Paul can always count on the support of the latter.

George Bernard Shaw

There are no facts, only interpretations.

Friedrich Nietzsche

# ELEVEN

# Evaluating the Impact of Public Spending on Socioeconomic Indicators

## 11.1. The Benefits from Higher Public Spending

Between 1913 and 2000, the share of public spending in gross domestic product for the groups of industrial countries for which data are available rose by about a factor of four. This growth was promoted by the interaction of particular events (wars, Great Depression) with changing views that assumed that government action and more public spending would promote higher social welfare and beneficial structural changes. In much of this period, the strongest pressures on governments were those pushing for higher public spending. They were promoted partly by the growing democratization of countries that had given a vote to a large share of the population.

These pressures for more public spending led to an expansion of the government role in education, with the result that, in many countries, free or at least very cheap schools, at most educational levels, became the norm, and students were required by law to spend increasing numbers of years in school; in health; in the provision of public pensions, reaching eventually a situation where many or most aged individuals (and, increasingly, some not so aged) were receiving, or expected to receive, government-provided pensions; in assistance for the care of the old and the young; in public assistance to the unemployed and the needy in general; in assistance to families with children; in assistance to families unable to find accessible housing; in assistance to loss-making enterprises; and in other less visible programs. A significant part of this growth in spending came in the form of cash transfers. These did not require many public employees to administer. Thus, employment in the public sector increased by less than public spending. These policies are assumed to have contributed to the public welfare in many ways by increasing the literacy rate and human capital in general; reducing infant mortality; lengthening life expectancy; and reducing the trauma and despair that comes with becoming unemployed, incapacitated, or indigent. These are significant achievements. Therefore, it is easy to understand the support that these policies received from many and, increasingly, especially from those who benefited directly from the government programs, whose number was increasing all the time.

A key question to ask, however, is whether there is a continuous, positive relationship between higher public spending and higher social welfare, or whether there may be diminishing returns, in terms of welfare gains, to such spending. This is a complex question for which no theory and no clear methodology exist that can help provide a robust and noncontroversial answer. The approach suggested in this chapter is a modest and, undoubtedly, a controversial one. It consists in linking public spending to a set of important socioeconomic indicators that can be assumed to be related in some ways with social welfare. It is assumed that when the government intervenes, it wants to generate desirable changes to these indicators. To some extent, this approach bears some broad relationship with the Northern European theory of fiscal policy described earlier that aimed at connecting policy instruments to social objectives. The policy objectives are assumed to be the positive or desirable changes in the socioeconomic indicators. The approach goes beyond the traditional one of considering only the impact of public spending on economic growth or on income distribution.

Assume that social welfare, $W$, can be defined and that it depends on the values of various socioeconomic indicators, such as $X_1, X_2, \ldots, X_n$. For example, $X_1$ could be life expectancy, $X_2$ the literacy rate, or school enrollment, $X_3$ the inflation rate, and so on. We can thus write the equation:

$$W = f(X_1, X_2, \ldots, X_n).$$

Improvement in social welfare will depend on changes *in the desired direction* in the values of these indicators. There may be as many of these indicators as the government considers important. Thus,

$$\Delta W = \sum_{i=1}^{n} \frac{\partial f}{\partial X_i} \Delta X_i$$

Assume also that, through public spending (and at times through the use of other policies tools), governments attempt to influence social welfare by promoting desirable changes to these indicators. The greater the positive impact of public spending programs is on these indicators, the greater the improvements in social welfare is assumed to be. Changes in socioeconomic indicators may be taken as proxies for changes in social welfare. (See Tanzi and Schuknecht, 1997, for the first description of this methodology.)

There are obvious shortcomings to this approach. First, more public spending may imply less private spending, at least for some individuals, because the individuals have less disposable income but have access to free, or subsidized, government-provided goods. The availability of the public option allows them to spend less money directly. Higher taxes paid to finance public spending generate for citizens, or for some of them, an opportunity for public spending to replace private spending. This aspect is ignored by the approach followed here, which registers only the positive impact of public spending on the indicators and ignores the cost or the indirect benefit. Second, it is difficult to consider all the social objectives (and, thus, all the socioeconomic indicators) that a government might want to influence with its spending. With the passing of time, there has been a large increase in the number of these objectives. There is no official listing of these objectives. These objectives change over time and differ between different governments. There may also be some objectives that cannot be measured. These are ignored in this exercise. Third, it is difficult to assign weights to these socioeconomic indicators. Therefore, all are given equal weights in our empirical exercise. Also note that this is a cross-country approach, at a given time. It is different from one that would consider the impact of higher spending on the socioeconomic indicators of a country over time. The approach followed here is a rough first step, one that attempts to assess whether more public spending (beyond a given level) has been associated with positive improvements in the indicators assumed to influence social welfare. This may be the most favorable test for assessing the benefits derived from public spending, because it considers the benefits of spending while ignoring the costs in terms of higher taxes.

Three applications of this methodology are presented in this chapter. The first relates to the group of 18 advanced countries shown in Table 1.1. It attempts to link the level of public spending in these countries with achievements in terms of the various socioeconomic indicators. The second expands the number of countries to include also developing countries; however, it uses the United Nations Development Program's Human Development Index (HDI) as a proxy for socioeconomic achievements. The HDI index is itself a composite of different indexes. For the second application, different per capita incomes are likely to play a more significant role than in the first application. Finally, we present results from a more sophisticated

Table 11.1. *Size of government and performance indicators in industrial countries, 1990 (percentage of GDP, or as indicated)*

| Indicator | Size of government[a] | | |
|---|---|---|---|
| | Big | Medium | Small |
| Total public expenditure | 55.1 | 44.9 | 34.6 |
| Public consumption | 18.9 | 17.4 | 15.5 |
| Subsidies and transfers | 30.6 | 21.5 | 14.0 |
| Economic indicators | | | |
| Real GDP growth[b] | 2.0 | 2.6 | 2.5 |
| Standard deviation of GDP growth | 1.6 | 2.1 | 1.9 |
| Gross fixed capital formation | 20.5 | 21.3 | 20.7 |
| Inflation rate[b] | 3.9 | 3.7 | 3.7 |
| Unemployment rate | 8.5 | 11.9 | 6.6 |
| Public debt | 79.0 | 59.9 | 53.3 |
| Social indicators | | | |
| Life expectancy (years) | 77 | 77 | 77 |
| Infant mortality/1,000 births | 6.7 | 7.1 | 6.4 |
| Secondary school enrollment | 92.8 | 99.1 | 89.0 |
| Income share of poorest 40 percent | 24.1 | 21.6 | 20.8 |

[a] Big governments (meaning public expenditure is more than 50 percent of GDP) included, in 1990, Belgium, Italy, the Netherlands, Norway, and Sweden. Medium-sized governments (public expenditure 40–50 percent of GDP) included Austria, Canada, France, Germany, Ireland, New Zealand, and Spain. Small governments (public expenditure less than 40 percent of GDP) included Australia, Japan, Switzerland, the United Kingdom, and the United States.
[b] 1986–94 period.
*Source:* Various official sources. The table is borrowed from Tanzi and Schuknecht, 1997 and 2000.

version of the same basic methodology for the group of advanced countries.[1]

In the first application, we consider as many socioeconomic indicators as it was possible to find data for a large number of advanced countries. Ten such indicators are reported in Table 11.1. They are real GDP growth, the standard deviation of GDP growth, capital formation, the inflation rate, the unemployment rate, the level of public debt, life expectancy, infant mortality, secondary school enrollment, and the income share of the poorest 40 percent of the population. All of these have been considered important by policy makers and in government policies. The relationship between these indicators and general welfare is more direct for some than for others; but in all cases an argument can be made that positive or negative changes in them affect the general welfare in predictable ways.

Table 11.1 has divided the countries into three groups on the basis of the level of public expenditure in 1990: those with public expenditure greater than 50 percent of GDP, those with public expenditure between 40 and 50 percent of GDP, and those with public expenditure less than 40 percent of GDP. The first group is called the "big government" group; the second, the "midsized" or medium government group; and the third, the "small government" group. The indicators, for 1990, have been averaged for each of these groups and are reported in Table 11.1. The table shows also the shares of GDP, for total public expenditure, public consumption, and subsidies and transfers for each group. The objective of the exercise is to see whether the bigger governments, with their higher levels for public spending, have generated (or are associated with) better social and economic indicators. It should be noted that, between big and small governments, there was in 1990 an average difference in total public expenditure of more than 20 percent of GDP.

The table shows that the results are not favorable for the big governments. There is no evidence from the table (or from additional information on indicators not shown in the table) that the big governments generated better indicators. On the contrary, except for the income share of the poorest 40 percent of the population, which is larger for "big governments," most of the other indicators are better for small or medium governments. This could be taken to indicate that, *ceteris paribus*, higher public spending, beyond a given level, does not necessarily lead to better indicators and, in our assumption, to higher welfare.

Let us consider next the second application of this methodology. It uses the Human Development Index, calculated by the UNDP, as a measure of the outcome from public spending.[2] In this application, the reference year is 2005, but the countries are the same as earlier. Once again, the objective is to see whether higher public spending promotes higher levels of HDI. The conclusion reached earlier is strongly supported by the estimations using the HDI and the shares of public spending into GDP for 2005.

The HDIs can be mapped against the share of public spending in GDP for the same year (2005). If more public spending promotes higher levels of "human development," the countries that have higher spending levels should have better levels of human development. Table 11.2 provides, for 19 advanced countries, the shares of public spending in GDP and the ranking of these countries in the HDI for 2005. Figure 11.1 gives a visual representation of the relationship. The interesting result is the lack of a positive relation between public spending levels and HDI rankings. High-spending countries, on average, do not generate better HDI ranks. The four countries with the highest HDI ranks – Norway, Australia, Canada, and Ireland – had in 2005 average spending levels of 37.6 percent of GDP while the four

Table 11.2. *Public spending and indices of human development in industrial countries in 2005*

| | Public spending | | |
|---|---|---|---|
| | % of GDP | Rank | HDI rank |
| Sweden | 56.6 | 1 | 5 |
| France | 54.0 | 2 | 9 |
| Denmark | 52.8 | 3 | 13 |
| Finland | 50.4 | 4 | 10 |
| Austria | 49.9 | 5 | 14 |
| Belgium | 48.8 | 6 | 16 |
| Italy | 48.3 | 7 | 18 |
| Germany | 46.9 | 8 | 19 |
| Netherlands | 45.5 | 9 | 8 |
| United Kingdom | 44.7 | 10 | 15 |
| Norway | 42.3 | 11 | 1 |
| Canada | 39.3 | 12 | 3 |
| New Zealand | 38.3 | 13 | 17 |
| Japan | 38.2 | 14 | 7 |
| Spain | 38.2 | 15 | 12 |
| United States | 36.6 | 16 | 11 |
| Switzerland | 35.8 | 17 | 6 |
| Australia | 34.6 | 18 | 2 |
| Ireland | 34.4 | 19 | 4 |

*Sources:* Public spending data from OECD, 2007; *OECD Economic Outlook*, no. 81 (June 2007); indexes of human development (HDI) from UNDP, 2007.

countries with the highest spending levels – Sweden, France, Denmark, and Finland – had an average HDI rank of more than 9. Their average public spending was 53.5 percent of GDP. The 10 countries that spend between 44.7 and 56.6 percent of GDP have an average rank of 12.7, while those that spend between 34.4 and 42.3 percent of GDP have an average rank of 7. Thus, at least for this group of highly developed countries, with per capita incomes and development levels that are not too different, there is at best no positive relation between public spending and welfare, as measured by the HDI. At worst, there is a negative correlation equal to 0.33 between (higher) spending levels and (poorer) HDI scores as indicated by the line in Figure 11.1. Please recall that a lower number for the HDI index means a higher welfare position. After some level of public spending is reached, which for advanced countries seems to be below 40 percent, more public spending does not seem to improve welfare – at least not as measured by the HDI.

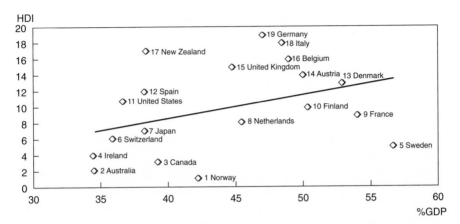

Figure 11.1. Public spending and the Human Development Index. *Sources:* Public spending data from OECD, 2007; *OECD Economic Outlook,* no. 81 (June 2007); indexes of human development (HDI) from UNDP, 2007.

These results are consistent with those reached in the earlier application of the methodology outlined here.

It may be worthwhile to mention that several of the best performers among the advanced countries, which had had very high levels of public spending in the early 1990s, sharply reduced public spending in the following years without apparently suffering any serious consequences with respect to their HDI index (Table 11.3).

The data in Tables 11.1 and 11.2 seem to support the conclusion that public spending of, say, around 35 percent of GDP should be sufficient for the government of a country to satisfy all the genuine objectives that

Table 11.3. *Spending levels in selected countries (percentage of GDP)*

|  | | Public spending | | |
| --- | --- | --- | --- | --- |
|  | HDI Rank | 1992 | 2007 | Difference |
| Norway | 1 | 55.7 | 41.0 | −14.7 |
| Australia | 2 | 38.6 | 34.0 | −4.6 |
| Canada | 3 | 53.3 | 39.1 | −14.6 |
| Ireland | 4 | 45.1 | 34.4 | −10.7 |
| Sweden | 5 | 71.1 | 54.1 | −16.7 |

*Sources:* Public spending data from OECD, 2007; *OECD Economic Outlook,* no. 81 (June 2007); indexes of human development (HDI) from UNDP, 2007.

realistically can be expected to be achieved by the spending action of the public sector in a market economy.[3] If public spending is efficient and well focused, and if the government focuses its attention on making the market work as efficiently as possible so that many citizens can satisfy most of their needs for some services through the market, an even lower spending percentage should be possible, perhaps one as low as less than 30 percent. Unfortunately, in many countries public spending is neither efficient nor well focused, and governments spend much of their energies *in replacing the market* because of its presumed "failures" *rather than in making the market work better*. The result is that higher public spending provides no guarantee that the social welfare and the well-being of the masses, rather than those of smaller selected sectors, are improved by public spending.

When we leave the advanced countries and move to Latin American countries, as representatives of the developing or emerging world, we are faced with the realization or the paradox that in Latin America, and in the developing world in general, there seems to be an apparent greater need for public-sector intervention because of widespread poverty, very uneven income distribution, and the need to improve an institutional and physical infrastructure that in many countries remains inadequate. At the same time, we face the sad reality that the countries' public sectors and the countries bureaucracies and institutions are likely to be less developed and less efficient than those of the countries in Table 11.1. Furthermore, the countries' capacity to raise tax revenue and spend money efficiently is more limited.

This dilemma is reflected in the responses to survey questions by the citizens of the Latin American countries. A recent OECD report (OECD, 2007, p. 37) notes that "most Latin Americans say that the quality of basic public services in their country is not good. According to *Latinobarometro* surveys of public opinion, 92% of Latin Americans express the view that their government should spend more on basic education, and 75% that it should spend more on social security." The OECD also reports that a very small proportion of the population (15 percent in 2003 and 21 percent in 2005) trusts that taxes are well spent and that fiscal policy in Latin America has improved the distribution of income.[4] Thus, we are faced with the classic situation of a customer in a restaurant who complains about both small portions and bad food. Most Latin Americans want the government to spend more on health, education, and social security, but most believe that the spending will do little to improve things. This may be a clear evidence of the fiscal illusion discussed in an earlier chapter. Because more spending

Table 11.4. *Rankings in the Human Development Index for various Latin American countries, 2005*

| | |
|---|---|
| Argentina | 38 |
| Bahamas | 49 |
| Barbados | 31 |
| Belize | 80 |
| Bolivia | 117 |
| Brazil | 70 |
| Chile | 40 |
| Colombia | 75 |
| Costa Rica | 48 |
| Cuba | 51 |
| Dominica | 71 |
| Dominican Republic | 79 |
| Ecuador | 89 |
| Grenada | 82 |
| Mexico | 52 |
| Panama | 62 |
| Paraguay | 95 |
| Peru | 87 |
| St. Lucia | 72 |
| Suriname | 85 |
| Trinidad and Tobago | 59 |
| Uruguay | 46 |
| Venezuela | 74 |

*Source:* UNDP, 2007.

requires more taxes or more public debt, it seems questionable whether more tax money should be spent unproductively.

In the Human Development Index, the ranking of the Latin American countries seems to bear little relation to their level of public spending. Table 11.4 gives the relative positions in the index of various Latin American countries. For these countries, a complicating factor is the large divergence in per capita incomes and economic development that inevitably influences the ranking, because richer countries on average tend to have higher HDI scores regardless of the action of their governments. Still, the position of Brazil is striking because of its low HDI rank, the very high spending level, and the fact that it has a relatively high per capita income.

The higher taxes needed to finance high public spending reduce the disposable income of the taxpayers that pay them, thus restricting their economic freedom and their ability to buy what they need directly from the market. Especially when the services provided by the government are of poor quality, this can be a major problem. Also, over the long run, high tax levels are likely to have at least some negative impact on the efficiency of an economy and on economic growth, especially when the taxes are collected inefficiently and the money collected is spent unproductively.

An obvious question for higher-spending countries is whether the level of public spending (and, consequently, of taxation) should be reduced if this could be done without reducing welfare and without hurting the poorer population. That is to say, if public welfare is not reduced, on any objective criterion, by lower public spending, then public spending and tax revenue could be cut. This would allow most individuals to have discretion over a larger share of their pretax incomes, giving them more access to privately provided goods. The citizens would then decide how to spend this money, not the government. Of course, this argument is not relevant in countries where tax levels and public spending are too low to even provide the minimum resources needed for essential public goods and essential institutions. While public spending can be too high, it can also, obviously, be too low. This possibility should not be ignored (Tanzi and Zee, 1997).

As mentioned earlier, the theoretical reasons advanced by economists to justify the spending role of the state in the economy, including especially the need to help the truly poor, could be satisfied with smaller shares of public spending in GDP than is now found in many countries, if governments could be more efficient and more focused in the use of their tax revenue. Some studies, especially from developing countries, indicate that public spending "benefits" mostly the middle and higher classes. The poor get a relatively small share of it. At the same time, much of the tax "burden" is also likely to fall on the same classes that get the spending. Putting it differently, the government taxes these classes with one hand and subsidizes them with the other, playing the classic role of an intermediary. However, this intermediation, or "tax churning," on the part of the government inevitably creates disincentives and inefficiencies on the side of both taxation and spending.

Before going on with our discussion, let us consider some statistics related to social spending in several Latin American countries. The spending is allocated among the five quintiles (see also OECD, 2007, p. 40). Table 11.5 refers to education, Table 11.6 to public health, and Table 11.7 to social security. The tables tell us what we should already know, but they do it in a striking fashion. The main lesson from Table 11.5 is that, while spending for primary education benefits almost everyone – and it seems even to

Table 11.5. *Distribution of social spending by income quintiles for education in selected Latin American countries, circa 2000*

|  | First | Second | Third | Fourth | Fifth |
|---|---|---|---|---|---|
| Argentina (1998) | 21 | 20 | 21 | 20 | 18 |
| Bolivia (2002) | 17 | 17 | 21 | 22 | 23 |
| Primary | 25 | 25 | 23 | 18 | 10 |
| Secondary | 15 | 18 | 24 | 24 | 19 |
| Tertiary | 3 | 5 | 17 | 30 | 45 |
| Brazil (1997) | 17 | 18 | 18 | 19 | 27 |
| Primary | 26 | 27 | 23 | 17 | 8 |
| Secondary | 7 | 12 | 28 | 33 | 19 |
| Tertiary | 0 | 1 | 3 | 22 | 76 |
| Chile (2003) | 35 | 27 | 19 | 13 | 6 |
| Colombia (2003) | 24 | 23 | 20 | 19 | 14 |
| Primary | 37 | 28 | 19 | 12 | 4 |
| Secondary | 24 | 27 | 23 | 19 | 8 |
| Tertiary | 3 | 8 | 17 | 31 | 42 |
| Costa Rica (2000) | 21 | 20 | 19 | 21 | 19 |
| Primary | 32 | 25 | 19 | 15 | 10 |
| Secondary | 18 | 21 | 22 | 22 | 17 |
| Tertiary | 3 | 8 | 14 | 30 | 45 |
| Dominican Republic | 25 | 26 | 24 | 16 | 9 |
| Ecuador (1999) | 15 | 20 | 20 | 22 | 23 |
| Primary | 35 | 26 | 20 | 13 | 6 |
| Secondary | 15 | 24 | 25 | 22 | 14 |
| Tertiary | 3 | 13 | 16 | 28 | 40 |
| El Salvador (2002) |  |  |  |  |  |
| Primary | 27 | 25 | 23 | 17 | 8 |
| Secondary | 11 | 20 | 26 | 25 | 18 |
| Guatemala (2000) | 17 | 21 | 21 | 21 | 21 |
| Primary | 21 | 25 | 23 | 21 | 10 |
| Secondary | 3 | 12 | 23 | 31 | 32 |
| Tertiary | 0 | 0 | 6 | 11 | 82 |
| Jamaica (1997) |  |  |  |  |  |
| Primary | 31 | 27 | 21 | 15 | 6 |
| Secondary | 10 | 15 | 25 | 30 | 20 |
| Mexico (2002) | 19 | 20 | 19 | 23 | 19 |
| Primary | 30 | 26 | 20 | 16 | 8 |
| Secondary | 14 | 20 | 21 | 26 | 19 |
| Tertiary | 1 | 7 | 15 | 33 | 44 |
| Nicaragua (1998) | 11 | 14 | 20 | 21 | 35 |
| Paraguay (1998) | 21 | 20 | 20 | 20 | 19 |
| Primary | 30 | 26 | 21 | 15 | 8 |
| Secondary | 14 | 18 | 25 | 24 | 19 |
| Tertiary | 2 | 5 | 8 | 29 | 56 |
| Peru (2000) | 16 | 18 | 19 | 21 | 26 |
| Uruguay (1998) | 28 | 23 | 19 | 16 | 15 |

*Source:* Adapted from information collected at the Inter-American Development Bank from various official sources. See also CEPAL (ECLAC), 2006.

Table 11.6.  *Distribution of social spending by income quintiles for health in selected Latin American countries, circa 2000*

|  | First | Second | Third | Fourth | Fifth |
|---|---|---|---|---|---|
| Argentina (1998) | 30 | 23 | 20 | 17 | 10 |
| Bolivia (2002) | 11 | 15 | 14 | 25 | 35 |
| Brazil (1997) | 16 | 20 | 22 | 23 | 19 |
| Chile (2003) | 30 | 23 | 20 | 17 | 9 |
| Colombia (2003) | 18 | 19 | 19 | 22 | 22 |
| Costa Rica (2000) | 29 | 25 | 20 | 15 | 11 |
| Ecuador (1999) | 19 | 23 | 23 | 24 | 11 |
| El Salvador (2002) | 26 | 23 | 21 | 18 | 12 |
| Guatemala (2000) | 17 | 18 | 23 | 25 | 17 |
| Honduras (1998) | 22 | 24 | 24 | 17 | 14 |
| Mexico (2002) | 15 | 18 | 21 | 23 | 22 |
| Nicaragua (1998) | 18 | 23 | 22 | 19 | 18 |

*Source:* Adapted from information collected at the Inter-American Development Bank from various official sources. See also CEPAL (ECLAC), 2006.

benefit the poorest 20 percent of the population more than the richest percentiles, who may send their children to private schools – for secondary and especially tertiary education, the spending share moves up in favor of the richer quintiles. It is the richer quintiles that benefit the most from this spending. This seems to characterize all countries for which there are data and is most pronounced for tertiary education. In Guatemala, a full 82 percent of the spending for the tertiary education goes to the top quintile. In

Table 11.7.  *Distribution of social spending by income quintiles for social security in selected Latin American countries, circa 2000*

|  | First | Second | Third | Fourth | Fifth |
|---|---|---|---|---|---|
| Argentina (1998) | 10 | 14 | 20 | 27 | 30 |
| Bolivia (2002) | 10 | 13 | 14 | 24 | 39 |
| Brazil (1997) | 7 | 8 | 15 | 19 | 51 |
| Colombia (2003) | 0 | 2 | 5 | 13 | 80 |
| Costa Rica (2000) | 12 | 12 | 12 | 18 | 45 |
| Ecuador (1999) | 4 | 7 | 21 | 22 | 46 |
| Guatemala (2000) | 1 | 3 | 5 | 15 | 76 |
| Mexico (2002) | 3 | 11 | 17 | 28 | 42 |
| Uruguay (1998) | 3 | 7 | 15 | 24 | 52 |

*Source:* Adapted from information collected at the Inter-American Development Bank from various official sources. See also CEPAL (ECLAC), 2006.

Brazil, the percentage is 76 percent. In Paraguay, it is 56 percent. It is difficult to justify a spending role of the state that subsidizes the top 20 percent of the population unless it can be argued that the government is much more efficient than the private sector in using these resources. It is also difficult to make a case that the government is more efficient than the private sector in providing higher education. Considerations of externalities cannot be used to justify these policies.

Spending for health seems to be more evenly distributed, creating a stronger case for public spending also because of the greater difficulty for the private sector to provide an efficient market for health that would be affordable on the part of the poor. Of course, this highlights the need for efficiency in this spending (Davoodi, Tiongson, and Asawanuchit, 2003).

It should be recalled from our discussion in Chapter 1 that the data in Tables 11.5 and 11.6 allocate *spending* and not true *benefits* among quintiles. There has been a habit among economists of identifying spending with benefits, under the assumption that the two are the same. However, the two are very different concepts and may diverge significantly. The spending is often received not by the citizens who use the services but by those who deliver them, such as schoolteachers, school administrators, doctors, and nurses. What the citizens get are the services provided by the latter. The benefits are assumed to be received by those who use the services, such as schoolchildren, patients, and so on. In many cases, the providers of services come from higher income quintiles than the beneficiaries of the services who are in the lower percentiles of the income distribution. In some cases, the spending, or much of it, may not become a "benefit" for the recipient, especially when inefficiency, incompetence, or corruption are present, but the spending is always an income for those who deliver the services. Therefore, the usual allocation of spending to the recipients of the services provided by the spending exaggerates the distribution of the benefits to the poorer groups. In some situations, those who deliver the services may appropriate most of the benefits in the form of high salaries or in other ways (see Tanzi, 1974). For example, in some countries, such as Brazil, schoolteachers often do not show up for their classes. This, of course, does not occur with cash benefits, such as pensions that are always received by the intended beneficiaries, who are generally from the upper percentiles.

Table 11.7 gives a clear impression of the extent to which social security benefits are appropriated by higher income classes. For the countries included in the table, the bottom 40 percent of the population received anywhere between a maximum of 24 percent (Argentina) and a minimum of 2 percent (Colombia) of the total. On the other hand, the top 20 percent of the population received between 80 percent (Colombia) and 30 percent (Argentina) of the total.

Those covered by public pensions are a relative minority and are not the poorest citizens who have reached the pensionable age. It is thus difficult to justify a *public* role for pensions on the basis of social needs because the poor, who are often in the informal sector and do not have regular jobs, frequently do not benefit from these programs. It might be much more efficient to provide minimum, basic pensions (that are a small share of per capita income) to anyone who reaches a pensionable age (adjusted for life expectancy) and to finance this spending with *general* taxes. This simple proposal would make pensions much more pro poor. Citizens who wished a higher protection during old age could buy at their expenses private pensions. (See Tanzi, 2006, for a proposal along this line.)

The conclusion is that the "social public spending" in Latin America, which, including social security, has averaged about 15 percent of GDP in recent years and has been growing in the past two decades (see CEPAL [ECLAC], 2005; and Lora, 2007), together with tax systems that are broadly proportional or even regressive (because of the low taxes on personal incomes and on both real and financial wealth), do little to improve the income distribution, which continues to be characterized by Gini coefficients that are the highest in the world. The OECD (2007, p. 31) and the IMF (2007, p. 30) have called attention to the marginal impact that fiscal policy has had in Latin America in reducing Gini coefficients, normally by no more than 1 or 2 percentage points in the whole region and around 4.5 percentage points on average in Central America, mainly because of the good performance by Panama. At the same time, an argument can be made that the attention paid to (inefficient) social spending has distracted governments from their basic role in providing institutional and real infrastructures that are needed by a modern society, and from focusing major attention on the truly deserving poor. The poor are likely to suffer more from crime, lack of personal security, lack of infrastructure that would make them more mobile, and an inefficient justice system than from low social spending.

In spite of *some* progress reported for several Latin American countries in various state reforms (see Lora, 2007), including political reform and reform of the judiciary, the public administration, the tax systems, the fiscal decentralization arrangements, the regulatory framework, and pensions, there is still considerable confusion about what economic role the state should play in Latin America and in other developing countries. Because tax revenues do not seem to have increased significantly in many countries in the past two decades (except in a few countries including Argentina and Brazil), but social spending has increased, there remains the concern that public resources have been diverted from financing fundamental public goods – security, infrastructure, justice, basic education – toward social programs that, for the most part, have not been focused on the truly poor – say, on the bottom quintile of the income distribution. The fact that social policy has been more and more institutionalized in Latin America may accentuate this concern (Székely, 2008).

Recently, more efforts have been made by some Latin American governments to make public transfers better focused. These transfers have been combined with particular incentives for those who receive them, thus making the transfers conditional. Examples of such programs are the Chile solidario; the Bolsa Familia in Argentina, Brazil, Panama, and Peru; Progresa in Mexico; and the Hambre Cero in Nicaragua. These are important programs, but as long as the tax incidence does not change and as long as much social spending continues to significantly benefit the higher quintiles, the impact of these programs on Gini coefficients will be moderate over the longer run.

Finally, we turn to a little more sophisticated application of the methodology outlined at the beginning of this chapter for advanced countries. The objective is to provide proxies for measuring public-sector *performance* as well as for public-sector *efficiency*. We estimate an index of public-sector performance (PSP) and an index of public-sector efficiency (PSE) for 23 OECD countries.[5] Public-sector performance is defined as previously: it is the performance of the public sector of countries in terms of generating several relevant socioeconomic indicators. The public-sector efficiency adjusts the PSP to take into account the cost of that performance in terms of public expenditure. The reason for this adjustment is that if one government spends much more than another government to achieve the same performance, and must thus raise more taxes, it must be considered less efficient. Naturally the same assumptions and qualifications mentioned earlier still apply.

Seven indicators will be used in this exercise to measure public-sector performance. The first four will be called "opportunity indicators." The other three will be called "Musgravian indicators," after Richard Musgrave. The four opportunity indicators are administrative performance; education performance, health performance, and public infrastructure outcomes. These indicators are assumed to promote the opportunities available to the individuals operating in a market economy. The three Musgravian indicators are the income distribution, economic stability, and an economic performance

Table 11.8. *Public-sector performance (PSP) indicators, 2000*

| Country | Public-sector performance index[a] | Rank | Opportunity indicators | | | | Musgravian indicators | | |
|---|---|---|---|---|---|---|---|---|---|
| | | | Administration | Education | Health | Infrastructure | Distribution | Stability | Economic performance |
| Austria | 1.04 | 9 | 1.17 | 1.02 | 0.94 | 1.00 | 0.87 | 1.31 | 1.00 |
| Australia | 1.12 | 4 | 1.21 | 1.00 | 0.98 | 1.10 | 1.22 | 1.28 | 1.01 |
| Belgium | 0.95 | 16 | 0.73 | 1.00 | 0.94 | 0.91 | 1.17 | 1.10 | 0.83 |
| Canada | 1.02 | 12 | 1.11 | 1.05 | 0.95 | 1.16 | 0.92 | 1.00 | 0.92 |
| Denmark | 1.06 | 7 | 1.16 | 1.00 | 1.03 | 1.03 | 1.19 | 1.10 | 0.91 |
| Finland | 1.01 | 14 | 1.26 | 1.07 | 1.04 | n/a | 1.18 | 0.75 | 0.73 |
| France | 0.93 | 17 | 0.72 | 1.03 | 1.03 | 1.01 | 0.90 | 1.12 | 0.70 |
| Germany | 0.96 | 15 | 1.02 | 0.98 | 1.01 | 1.01 | 0.98 | 0.91 | 0.81 |
| Greece | 0.78 | 23 | 0.60 | 0.94 | 0.93 | 0.81 | 0.97 | 0.55 | 0.69 |
| Iceland | 1.03 | 11 | 1.02 | 0.98 | 1.25 | n/a | n/a | 0.59 | 1.29 |
| Ireland | 1.05 | 8 | 1.06 | 0.94 | 0.88 | 1.00 | 0.89 | 1.22 | 1.40 |
| Italy | 0.83 | 21 | 0.52 | 0.96 | 0.93 | 0.84 | 1.10 | 0.76 | 0.69 |
| Japan | 1.14 | 2 | 0.87 | 1.09 | 1.12 | 1.09 | 1.20 | 1.40 | 1.18 |
| Luxembourg | 1.21 | 1 | 1.05 | 0.81 | 0.95 | n/a | n/a | 1.22 | 2.04 |

244

| | | | | | | | | |
|---|---|---|---|---|---|---|---|---|
| Netherlands | 1.11 | 5 | 1.16 | 1.04 | 0.97 | 1.09 | 1.00 | 1.42 | 1.06 |
| New Zealand | 0.93 | 17 | 1.18 | 1.03 | 0.89 | n/a | 0.62 | 0.99 | 0.84 |
| Norway | 1.13 | 3 | 0.97 | 1.04 | 1.09 | 0.94 | 1.17 | 1.45 | 1.26 |
| Portugal | 0.80 | 22 | 0.54 | 0.94 | 0.90 | 0.75 | 0.92 | 0.64 | 0.92 |
| Spain | 0.89 | 20 | 0.77 | 1.00 | 1.10 | 0.86 | 1.02 | 0.82 | 0.67 |
| Sweden | 1.04 | 9 | 1.16 | 1.07 | 1.19 | 1.10 | 1.17 | 0.69 | 0.91 |
| Switzerland | 1.07 | 6 | 1.32 | 0.97 | 1.14 | 1.23 | 0.95 | 0.79 | 1.09 |
| United Kingdom | 0.91 | 19 | 1.00 | 1.05 | 0.91 | 0.99 | 0.79 | 0.78 | 0.84 |
| United States | 1.02 | 12 | 1.15 | 1.00 | 0.82 | 1.08 | 0.76 | 1.14 | 1.20 |
| OECD average | 1.00 | | 1.00 | 1.00 | 1.00 | 1.00 | 1.00 | 1.00 | 1.00 |
| Small governments[b] | 1.07 | | 1.11 | 1.01 | 0.98 | 1.08 | 0.94 | 1.17 | 1.17 |
| Medium governments[b] | 0.97 | | 0.93 | 0.98 | 1.00 | 0.93 | 0.92 | 0.89 | 1.03 |
| Big governments[b] | 1.01 | | 0.99 | 1.02 | 1.01 | 1.01 | 1.12 | 1.03 | 0.85 |

[a] Each subindicator contributes 1/7 to the Public-Sector Performance Index.
[b] Countries with small governments have public spending that is less than 40 percent of GDP in 2000; countries with big governments have public spending that is more than 50 percent of GDP in 2000; medium-size governments have public spending that is between 40 and 50 percent of GDP.

Source: Afonso, Schuknecht, and Tanzi, 2005.

indicator.[6] In the construction of the PSP index, each of the seven indicators is given an equal weight.

To allow easy comparison, the 23-country average for all indicators has been set at 1.00, and the value for each country is calculated in relation to the average. The results for the PSP indicators and the public-sector performance indexes are shown in Table 11.8. They refer to the year 2000. The table shows that 14 of the 23 countries received PSP scores between 0.90 and 1.10. A few countries received the highest total PSP scores. These were Luxembourg (1.21), Japan (1.14), Norway (1.13), Australia (1.12), and the Netherlands (1.11). In these countries, the seven indicators that measure performance were particularly good. A few countries received low scores. These were Greece (0.78), Portugal (0.80), Italy (0.83), Spain (0.89), and the United Kingdom (0.91). In these countries, the seven indicators were somewhat lower than in the rest. Broadly speaking, "small" governments (those with public spending less than 40 percent of GDP) have higher scores than "big" governments (those with public spending more than 50 percent of GDP), thus indicating that spending more does not necessarily produce better results in terms of socioeconomic indicators.

A product could be very good, but if it would cost too much to produce, it would not be a good bargain for consumers. The same rule applies to the citizens vis-à-vis the output of governments. It must be recalled that high spending requires high taxes. Before we can judge the efficiency of the outputs of a government, in terms of socioeconomic indicators, we must consider the costs of producing what it produces. Total government expenditure as a percentage of GDP (G/GDP) is used to calculate the cost of government activities. Once again the average for the 23 countries, for total government expenditure, is set at 1.00, and each country's value is calculated in relation to that average. The PSE index is estimated as the ratio of PSP scores, shown in Table 11.8, to the total public expenditure (G/GDP) that has produced the public-sector outcome or performance. The results are shown in Table 11.9 for each of the seven performance indicators and for the overall PSE index scores, also for 2000. We focus here only on the overall PSE index.

A few countries have scores much above the average, indicating a high efficiency of the public sector in delivering desirable socioeconomic indicators. Very high scores are shown by Japan (1.40), Luxembourg (1.38), Australia (1.29), Ireland (1.27), United States (1.26), and Switzerland (1.20). Low scores are shown by Iceland (0.80), France (0.81), Sweden (0.83), Finland (0.84), Italy (0.85), and Portugal (0.86). Once again, on average countries with small governments perform better than those with large governments.

Table 11.9. *Public-sector efficiency (PSE) indicators 2000*

| Country | Public-Sector Performance Index[a] | Rank | Opportunity indicators | | | | Musgravian indicators | | |
| | | | Administration | Education | Health | Infrastructure | Distribution | Stability | Economic performance |
|---|---|---|---|---|---|---|---|---|---|
| Austria | 1.29 | 3 | 1.25 | 1.09 | 1.04 | 1.17 | 1.53 | 1.66 | 1.27 |
| Australia | 1.06 | 8 | 1.21 | 0.97 | 1.04 | 1.25 | 0.94 | 1.11 | 0.87 |
| Belgium | 1.01 | 12 | 0.68 | 1.19 | 0.87 | 1.67 | 0.91 | 0.98 | 0.73 |
| Canada | 1.03 | 10 | 1.04 | 0.85 | 0.87 | 1.35 | 1.16 | 1.02 | 0.94 |
| Denmark | 0.96 | 14 | 0.89 | 0.70 | 0.91 | 1.72 | 0.93 | 0.88 | 0.73 |
| Finland | 0.84 | 20 | 1.09 | 0.82 | 1.05 | n/a | 0.85 | 0.62 | 0.60 |
| France | 0.81 | 22 | 0.60 | 0.97 | 0.87 | 0.94 | 0.68 | 0.97 | 0.61 |
| Germany | 0.96 | 14 | 1.03 | 1.14 | 0.80 | 1.29 | 0.80 | 0.88 | 0.78 |
| Greece | 0.97 | 13 | 0.81 | 1.91 | 1.21 | 0.71 | 0.95 | 0.54 | 0.68 |
| Iceland | 0.80 | 23 | 0.91 | 0.97 | n/a | n/a | n/a | 0.65 | 1.44 |
| Ireland | 1.27 | 4 | 1.31 | 1.01 | 1.04 | 1.16 | 1.14 | 1.51 | 1.73 |
| Italy | 0.85 | 19 | 0.54 | 1.18 | 0.98 | 1.00 | 0.93 | 0.68 | 0.61 |

| | | | | | | | | | |
|---|---|---|---|---|---|---|---|---|---|
| Japan | 1.40 | 1 | 1.16 | 1.67 | 1.31 | 0.56 | 1.82 | 1.80 | 1.52 |
| Luxembourg | 1.38 | 2 | 1.18 | 1.26 | 1.03 | n/a | n/a | 1.28 | 2.15 |
| Netherlands | 1.05 | 9 | 0.98 | 1.10 | 0.95 | 1.24 | 0.81 | 1.32 | 0.98 |
| New Zealand | 0.95 | 16 | 1.26 | 0.82 | 0.90 | n/a | 0.69 | 1.10 | 0.94 |
| Norway | 1.02 | 11 | 0.90 | 0.73 | 0.99 | 0.83 | 1.15 | 1.36 | 1.19 |
| Portugal | 0.86 | 18 | 0.57 | 0.98 | 1.17 | 0.57 | 1.09 | 0.68 | 0.98 |
| Spain | 0.95 | 16 | 0.86 | 1.19 | 1.24 | 0.70 | 1.10 | 0.88 | 0.72 |
| Sweden | 0.83 | 21 | 0.83 | 0.76 | 1.03 | 1.15 | 0.87 | 0.50 | 0.67 |
| Switzerland | 1.20 | 6 | 1.72 | 0.94 | 1.00 | 1.16 | 1.28 | 0.96 | 1.32 |
| United Kingdom | 1.10 | 7 | 1.02 | 1.10 | 0.98 | 1.85 | 0.87 | 0.89 | 0.96 |
| United States | 1.26 | 5 | 1.48 | 1.06 | 0.84 | 1.24 | 1.02 | 1.53 | 1.62 |
| OECD average | 1.00 | | 1.00 | 1.00 | 1.00 | 1.00 | 1.00 | 1.00 | 1.00 |
| Small governments[b] | 1.28 | | 1.38 | 1.15 | 1.05 | 1.06 | 1.36 | 1.49 | 1.49 |
| Medium governments[b] | 1.00 | | 0.96 | 1.10 | 1.02 | 1.04 | 0.97 | 0.93 | 1.08 |
| Big governments[b] | 0.92 | | 0.85 | 0.96 | 0.96 | 1.28 | 0.87 | 0.88 | 0.73 |

*Note:* These indicators are the expenditure weighted "counterparts" of the indicators of Table 11.1.

[a] Each subindicator contributes 1/7 to the Public-Sector Efficiency Index.

[b] Countries with small governments maintain public spending that is less than 40 percent of GDP in 2000; big government countries have public spending that is more than 50 percent of GDP in 2000; countries with medium-sized governments have public spending that is between 40 and 50 percent of GDP.

*Source:* Afonso, Schuknecht, and Tanzi, 2005; and calculations by author.

The results reported here must, of course, be seen as only indicative. They suffer from various assumptions. However, it is not likely that they could be totally wrong. More careful analysis would likely not change the results significantly. The main point is that good public objectives may at times come at too high a fiscal cost. A broadly similar methodology has been applied by the authors of the study cited earlier to new European Union member states and to emerging markets (Afonso, Schknecht, and Tanzi, 2010). The basic conclusion of this new study is that "many new members states and other emerging markets can still considerably increase the efficiency of public spending by improving the outcomes and by restraining the resource use" (ibid., p. 2161).

A recent study has also looked at the relationship between fiscal size and economic growth, taking into account the efficiency of the public sector, using the method outlined here, for a sample of 64 countries. The study finds that the efficiency of the public sector is an important variable in explaining economic growth (Angelopoulos, Philippopoulos, and Tsionas, 2008).

## References

Afonso, Antonio, Ludger Schuknecht, and Vito Tanzi. 2005. "Public Sector Efficiency: An International Comparison." *Public Choice* 123: 321–47.

——— 2010. "Public Sector Efficiency: Evidence for New EU Member States and Emerging Markets." *Applied Economics* 42: 2147–64.

Afonso, Antonio, Ludger Schuknecht, Vito Tanzi, and Niels Veldhuis. 2007. "Public Sector Efficiency: An International Comparison." *Frazer Alert* (March). The Frazer Institute.

Angelopoulos, Konstantinos, Apostolis Philippopoulos, and Efthymios Tsionas. 2008. "Does Public Sector Efficiency Matter? Revisiting the Relation between Fiscal Size and Economic Growth in a World Sample." *Public Choice* 137, nos. 1–2 (October): 245–78.

CEPAL (ECLAC). 2006. *Panorama Social de America Latina* 2005 (Santiago: Cepol).

Davoodi, Hamid R., Erwin R. Tiongson, and Sawitree S. Asawanuchit. 2003. "How Useful Are Benefit Incidence Analyses of Public Education and Health Spending?" *IMF Working Paper*, WP/03/227.

IMF. 2007. *Regional Economic Outlook, Western Hemisphere*, November (Washington, D.C.: IMF).

Lora, Eduardo. 2007. "Trends and Outcomes of Tax Reform," in *The State of State Reform in Latin America* (Washington, D.C.: IDB and Stanford).

OECD. 2007. *Latin American Economic Outlook, 2008* (Paris: OECD Development Center).

Székely, Miguel. 2008. "Midiendo el Nivel de Institucionalidad de la Politica Social en America Latina." Mimeo (June).

Tanzi, Vito. 2006. "A New Role for the State: Limits of Public Social Security." *D + C, Development and Cooperation* 33, no. 11 (November). 417.21.

2008. "The Role of the State and Public Finance in the Next Generation." *OECD Journal for Budgeting* 8, no. 2 (June): 2–27.

Tanzi, Vito, and Ludger Schuknecht. 1997. "Reconsidering the Fiscal Role of Government: The International Perspective." *American Economic Review* 87 (May): 164–68.

2000. *Public Spending in the 20th Century* (Cambridge: Cambridge University Press).

Tanzi, Vito, and Howell Zee. 1997. "Fiscal Policy and Long-Run Growth." *IMF Staff Papers* 44, no. 2 (June). 179–209.

United Nations Development Programme (UNDP). 2007. *Human Development Report 2007/2008* (Houndmills: Palgrave Macmillan).

TWELVE

# Social Protection in the Modern World

## Some Quantitative Aspects

### 12.1. Introduction

Government-sponsored social protection (or social insurance) is generally considered a European "invention." Its origin has at times been traced to the Workmen Compensation for Norwegian Miners, enacted as far back as 1842, to the Venetian Fund for invalid sailors of 1786, or, more often, to the legislation introduced by Bismarck in Germany in the 1880s. The Social Security Act, introduced by President Franklin Roosevelt in the United States in the middle of the Great Depression, represented a considerable extension and aimed to cover all American *workers* (but not all citizens) who met some requirements, such as age and years of contribution.

In France, the birth of "securité sociale" is attributed to an "ordinance" (a regulation) issued on 4 October 1945, at about the same time when the Beveridge proposals were being considered in Britain. The French public system had been preceded by several private programs of family welfare and social insurance that had been introduced in France after 1914. These had started, generally, with initiatives by employers and by private mutual aid societies. They were later taken over by the government and incorporated in government programs (Dutton, 2002).

In Britain, the introduction of government social protection programs came after World War II, with legislation introduced by the newly elected Labor Party, which implemented the 1942 Beveridge Report proposals. However, the road to social reform had started in a limited scale and coverage much earlier, in the period between 1906 and 1914. In Italy, the first limited step toward social protection came in 1898 with Law no. 80, which created the Cassa Nazionale di Previdenza per l'Invaliditá e la Vecchiaia degli Operai (National Fund for the Disability and the Old Age of Workers). The insurance against work accidents and disability was compulsive; that for old-age pensions was optional for workers. However, for those who chose to join, the state could make a contribution to the cost. Because of this, 1898 can be considered the birth date of the Italian social security system. Very few workers chose to join it. In 1911 there was an intense debate to create a National Insurance Institute that would provide life insurance to the citizens (see Ministero di Agricultura, Industria e Commercio, 1911). In 1919 a new law made it obligatory for workers to join the National Fund. A full reordering of matters related to social protection came in 1952. Later laws brought changes and significant extensions in benefits and in coverage. In 1980 the National Health System was introduced for all Italians and not just for workers. In Sweden the first public pension reform was introduced in 1913. Following the European examples, important social legislation programs were also introduced in Uruguay, Argentina, Costa Rica, and some other Latin American countries around World War II.

With the passing of the years, social legislation was introduced in more countries and included larger shares of the populations. The new programs covered progressively more risks, besides old age and accidents. Additionally, government programs tended to elbow out existing private programs. Voluntarism was replaced by state action. Now all European countries and most countries from the Americas and other parts of the world provide – especially for *workers* in the official part of the economy who pay some obligatory taxes called "contributions" – old-age and survivors pensions, as well as some compensation for work-related injuries and for permanent disability. In many countries, protection against illnesses has been added to the risks against which social protection provides some assistance.

The systems of social protection that now exist in industrial countries and that developed over many decades, especially in the 20th century, developed along different paths in different groups of countries. Some of them established deeper, broader, and more redistributive programs than others. The instruments used to provide social protection have diverged significantly across groups of countries. They can be grouped under three different, broad headings:

1. *Publicly financed programs,* which may consist of cash transfers to individuals and families; or of the provision of real services. In the latter case, public employment tends to rise more than when cash transfers are used. These public programs may in turn be financed by general taxes, as they are in some countries, or by specific "contributions," generally based on wages as they are in others. In the latter case, access to the benefits is restricted to the individuals and the families of those

who have paid the contributions, who are generally workers in the official economy.

2. *"Tax expenditures"* provided to reduce the cost of families' expenditures for education, health, housing and others for individuals who pay income taxes. In this case, tax revenue and public spending are both generally reduced, and the value to the beneficiary of the tax expenditure depends on the taxes saved as a consequence of the tax expenditure.

3. *Various regulations* imposed on individual workers and on enterprises to encourage, or force, them to buy, or provide, some protection. The latter may include the provision of loans and loan guarantees to some categories. In this third instrument the state is only a regulator so that protection can be bought that does not show in the fiscal accounts.

In addition, forms of social protection based on charity remain important in some countries in spite of their sharp reduction in the 20th century. These forms may be stimulated or subsidized by the government through allowances provided through the tax system. This classification may seem unusual because of the emphasis on public spending that characterizes most discussions of social protection. Shares of gross public spending for social protection into GDP are often seen as indicators of the government role in providing social protection. However, they rarely tell the full story.

The relative use on the part of different countries of the various instruments mentioned thus far depends on cultural preferences of the citizens and the policy makers and on the control that different governments have over the policy instruments. Because they generally have better-developed institutions, industrial countries have more choice in the use of the instruments than less advanced countries. The latter are often not able to raise the levels of taxation necessary to finance large public spending. Therefore, regulations often become an easier choice for them.

Following the OECD classification, the social programs now covered by public and by mandatory, private programs of protection are broadly the following:

1. *Old-age protection,* which can come in the form of cash benefits (pension, early retirement pension, and other cash benefits) and benefits in kind (that includes residential care and other benefits). However, the retirement age continues to diverge significantly among countries, by as much as 12 years even when life expectancies are broadly similar.

2. *Survivor protection,* which can also be in cash (pension, other cash benefits) or in kind (funeral expenses, other benefits). The definition

of "survivor" varies from country to country, being more restrictive in some than in others.

3. *Incapacity-related benefits* (in cash or in kind). The definition of invalidity was significantly relaxed over the years, leading to many abuses, and tends to differ across countries.

4. *Health benefits*, in kind or through cash payments made directly to private providers. They may or may not require the payment of some fees by the beneficiaries.

5. *Family benefits*, in cash (family allowances, maternity and parental leave) and in kind (day-care services; or home-help services and others). Tax system also differ widely in the tax treatment of the family.

6. *Various labor market programs*, such as training and assistance in finding jobs.

7. *Unemployment compensation.* This may cover temporary or longer period of unemployment; may or may not require proof of job search; and may be a significant or a small share of the wages that it replaces.

8. *Housing benefits.* These may come in the form of public housing, subsidies to the rent, rent control, deduction of mortgage payment from the income tax, or reductions in the interest paid on mortgages.

9. *Various other social policy areas.*

In the following discussion, we shall try to describe the relative use of the main policy instruments on the part of different groups of countries. By necessity the descriptions cannot be detailed. The programs of social assistance tend to be very complex so that far more information and space would be necessary to provide detailed descriptions. The more generous and wider is the use of these areas of social protection, the more mature is the status of a country as a welfare state.

## 12.2. Industrial Countries

Most but not all OECD countries would be able to use the three instruments mentioned in the preceding section, if they chose to do it. To some extent most of them have tried to do so. However, closer observation reveals that the countries' relative preferences have been widely different. Some countries have used one of these instruments far more intensively than the others. Unfortunately, the information available is limited. Therefore, the following paragraphs are partly based on hard facts and, to a lesser extent, on impressions. The next chapter deals more specifically with the mature welfare states of the Nordic European countries.

Table 12.1. *Gross public social expenditure for country groups in 1997, 2001, and 2005 (percentages of GDP at factor prices)*

| Country | 1997 | 2001 | 2005 |
|---|---|---|---|
| Denmark | 30.7 | 34.2 | 31.9 |
| Finland | 28.7 | 28.0 | 29.8 |
| Norway | 26.1 | 27.0 | 24.1 |
| Sweden | 31.8 | 35.1 | 34.6 |
| Nordic countries | 29.3 | 31.1 | 30.1 |
| Austria | 25.4 | 29.6 | 30.6 |
| Belgium | 27.2 | 28.0 | 29.9 |
| France | n.a | 33.0 | 33.8 |
| Germany | 26.4 | 30.6 | 29.9 |
| Italy | 26.4 | 28.3 | 28.8 |
| Netherlands | 24.2 | 24.3 | 23.6 |
| Spain | n.a | 21.7 | 23.8 |
| Other European countries | n.a | 27.9 | 28.6 |
| Australia | 17.4 | 20.4 | 19.2 |
| Canada | 17.9 | 20.4 | 18.6 |
| Ireland | 17.6 | 15.3 | 19.0 |
| New Zealand | 20.7 | 21.1 | 21.2 |
| U.K. | 21.2 | 25.4 | 24.3 |
| United States | 14.7 | 15.7 | 17.1 |
| Anglo-Saxon countries | 18.3 | 19.9 | 19.9 |
| Japan | 14.0 | 18.5 | 20.1 |
| Korea | 4.3 | 7.1 | 7.8 |
| Mexico | n.a | 5.7 | 8.3 |
| Other countries | n.a | 10.4 | 12.1 |

*Sources:* Arranged from Adema, 2001, table 2; Adema and Ladaique, 2005, table 6; and Adema and Ladaique, 2009, table 5.5.

According to data provided by the OECD, the Nordic countries (and France) have relied more than other countries on public spending (Table 12.1). In 1997 the Nordic countries spent an average of almost 29.3 percent of GDP for public social expenditure. Sweden was the biggest spender. Both Denmark and Sweden spent about 31 percent of GDP. Between 1997 and 2001, these countries (except Finland) increased gross public social expenditure. However, between 2001 and 2005, three of them reduced that spending. The other continental European countries had lower but still significant spending. Some of these countries, and especially France, could have been classified with the big spenders of the Nordic group.

The really big difference is noted between all the continental European countries and the group of six Anglo-Saxon countries. Between these two groups, and between some of the countries in the groups, the differences are very large. For example, between Sweden and the United States the difference in social spending approached a remarkable 18 percent of GDP. Between 1997 and 2005, there were large positive changes in gross public social expenditure as percent of GDP in Japan, Korea, Austria, United Kingdom, Mexico, and a few other countries. Only Norway and, to a lesser extent, the Netherlands reported reductions over that period. The Nordic and some other European countries, such as France, Austria, Belgium, and Germany, have relied more than other countries on public spending for their social protection. These "welfare states" have provided protection against various risks with economic consequences through universal government-financed programs that, being often universal, require high spending. These programs have aimed at protecting all citizens (and increasingly even residents who were not citizens) from the "cradle to the grave." Naturally, to finance these expensive programs, the countries had to impose some of the highest tax burdens in the world (see Table 1.3).

While informative, Table 12.1 creates a somewhat exaggerated picture of the differences in social protection across countries. The reason is that it is focused only on *gross* public spending and ignores some other important aspects. To get a more accurate picture, two important adjustments must be made to that table. The first is to recognize that, while some countries tax as income some of the social benefits that people receive from the government, especially in cash, other countries do not. The second adjustment is to recognize that the private sector plays a significant role in providing social protection in some countries but not in others. The first adjustment provides estimates for *net publicly mandated social expenditures.* The second provides estimates for *net total* (i.e., public and private) social expenditures. Fortunately, some OECD studies have made the various complex adjustments needed so that the desired statistical concepts can be derived. It should be added that social assistance provided by charitable institutions is not shown by the statistics so that they still do not tell the full story.

Table 12.2 provides estimates for the *net publicly mandated social expenditure* for the same countries and for the same groups of countries as in Table 12.1. It adjusts the data for the taxes that the recipients pay on the benefits that they receive. Comparing Table 12.2 with Table 12.1, it is easy to see that the differences in public social expenditure shown in Table 12.1 are significantly reduced, once taxes are taken into account. Especially in the Nordic countries, but also in some of the other continental European

Table 12.2. *Net publicly mandated social expenditure by country groups in 1997, 2001, and 2005 (percentages of GDP at factor prices)*

| Country | 1997 | 2001 | 2005 |
|---|---|---|---|
| Denmark | 26.9 | 25.7 | 24.2 |
| Finland | 24.8 | 21.8 | 23.5 |
| Norway | 25.1 | 23.1 | 20.7 |
| Sweden | 28.7 | 28.3 | 27.5 |
| Nordic countries | 26.4 | 24.7 | 24.0 |
| Austria | 23.9 | 24.1 | 25.5 |
| Belgium | 27.5 | 25.7 | 26.2 |
| France | n.a. | 29.2 | 30.7 |
| Germany | 27.9 | 29.2 | 28.8 |
| Italy | 25.2 | 25.4 | 26.1 |
| Netherlands | 20.8 | 20.9 | 19.7 |
| Spain | n.a. | 18.6 | 21.2 |
| Other European countries | n.a. | 24.7 | 25.5 |
| Australia | 18.8 | 20.2 | 19.5 |
| Canada | 18.7 | 19.6 | 18.7 |
| Ireland | 17.1 | 13.6 | 17.2 |
| New Zealand | 17.0 | 17.7 | 18.4 |
| U.K. | 21.9 | 23.6 | 23.7 |
| United States | 16.8 | 17.2 | 18.8 |
| Anglo-Saxon countries | 18.4 | 18.7 | 19.4 |
| Japan | 15.3 | 19.4 | 20.3 |
| Korea | 6.7 | 9.7 | 8.6 |
| Mexico | n.a. | 6.9 | 9.2 |
| Other countries | n.a. | 12.0 | 12.7 |

*Sources:* Arranged from Adema, 2001, table 7; Adema and Ladaique, 2005, table 6; Adema and Ladaique, 2009, table 5.5.

countries, the individuals experience large reductions in the benefits that they receive because of the taxes they pay on those benefits. For example, in 2005 the average difference between the group of Nordic countries and that of Anglo-Saxon countries is reduced from 10.2 percent of GDP, in Table 12.1, to 4.6 percent of GDP, in Table 12.2. Once this adjustment is made, the differences between the Nordic countries and the other continental European countries largely disappear.

When *private* social expenditures are also taken into account, some remarkable changes are noticed. Table 12.3 shows that net total social expenditure in countries such as the United States and the United Kingdom increases sharply and reaches Nordic, Scandinavian levels. Because these

Table 12.3. *Net total social expenditure by country groups in 1997, 2001, and 2005 (percentages of GDP at factor prices)*

| Country | 1997 | 2001 | 2005 |
|---|---|---|---|
| Denmark | 27.5 | 26.4 | 25.7 |
| Finland | 25.6 | 22.6 | 24.4 |
| Norway | 25.1 | 23.6 | 21.2 |
| Sweden | 30.6 | 30.6 | 29.3 |
| Nordic countries | 27.2 | 25.8 | 25.2 |
| Austria | 24.6 | 24.8 | 26.5 |
| Belgium | 28.5 | 26.3 | 30.3 |
| France | n.a. | 31.2 | 33.6 |
| Germany | 28.8 | 30.8 | 30.2 |
| Italy | 25.3 | 25.3 | 26.6 |
| Netherlands | 24.0 | 25.0 | 25.8 |
| Spain | n.a. | 18.9 | 21.4 |
| Other European countries | n.a. | 26.0 | 27.8 |
| Australia | 21.9 | 24.0 | 21.7 |
| Canada | 21.8 | 23.3 | 23.3 |
| Ireland | 18.4 | 13.9 | 18.3 |
| New Zealand | 17.5 | 18.2 | 18.8 |
| U.K. | 24.6 | 27.1 | 29.5 |
| United States | 23.4 | 24.5 | 27.2 |
| Anglo-Saxon countries | 21.3 | 21.8 | 23.1 |
| Japan | 15.7 | 22.2 | 22.8 |
| Korea | 8.6 | 11.7 | 10.7 |
| Mexico | n.a. | 6.9 | 9.4 |
| Other countries | n.a. | 13.6 | 14.3 |

*Sources:* Arranged from Adema, 2001, table 7; Adema and Ladaique, 2005, table 6; and Adema and Ladaique, 2009, table 5.5.

results are achieved with lower tax levels, and because high taxes are generally assumed to have disincentive effects, these results merit attention. Furthermore, they are presumably consistent with higher individual economic freedom. The more importance we attach to individual economic freedom, and to the disincentive effects of high taxes, the more important these results become. However, they become less significant if the objective of social policy is strictly poverty reduction and reduction in income inequality.

Table 12.3 requires some comments. First, the Nordic countries have much more homogeneous populations so that they may more easily tolerate high taxes that assist other members of their community in need of assistance. They may see the redistribution within the community as they

Table 12.4. *Net total social expenditure by country groups in 2005*

| Country | % of GDP at factor cost | % of GDP at market prices | % of NN1 at factor cost |
|---|---|---|---|
| Denmark | 25.7 | 21.8 | 31.1 |
| Finland | 24.4 | 21.4 | 29.1 |
| Norway | 21.2 | 19.1 | 24.5 |
| Sweden | 29.3 | 24.9 | 34.3 |
| Nordic countries | 25.2 | 21.8 | 29.8 |
| Austria | 26.5 | 23.5 | 32.0 |
| Belgium | 30.3 | 26.8 | 36.4 |
| France | 33.6 | 29.0 | 39.0 |
| Germany | 30.2 | 27.0 | 35.8 |
| Italy | 26.6 | 23.1 | 32.5 |
| Netherlands | 25.8 | 22.8 | 30.7 |
| Spain | 21.4 | 19.1 | 26.3 |
| Other European countries | 27.8 | 24.5 | 33.1 |
| Australia | 21.7 | 19.3 | 27.6 |
| Canada | 23.3 | 20.7 | 27.8 |
| Ireland | 18.3 | 16.1 | 25.7 |
| New Zealand | 18.8 | 16.4 | 24.7 |
| U.K. | 29.5 | 25.9 | 32.8 |
| United States | 27.2 | 25.3 | 31.1 |
| Anglo-Saxon countries | 18.6 | 20.6 | 28.3 |
| Japan | 22.8 | 21.0 | 28.7 |
| Korea | 10.7 | 9.4 | 12.7 |
| Mexico | 9.4 | 8.4 | 10.8 |
| Other countries | 14.3 | 12.9 | 17.4 |

*Sources:* Adapted from table 5.5; table A.3.1.a; and table A.3.1.b of Adema and Ladaique, 2009.

would see redistribution within a family. This would be less so in the United States, the United Kingdom, and some other countries, because of more heterogeneous populations. As the number of immigrants has risen in the Nordic countries, homogeneity has become a less significant characteristic. Second, the public assistance that is provided *publicly* is generally more evenly distributed than the one financed by private, but obligatory, programs. However, social assistance financed through charitable activities is not shown in the table. This is probably more important in the United States and, possibly, in the United Kingdom than in the Nordic countries (Kendall and Knapp, 1996).

Table 12.4 makes further adjustments. This time the adjustment is to the denominator. This adjustment is shown only for the 2005 data. The first column of Table 12.4 is equivalent to the third (last) column of Table 12.3.

It shows net total social expenditure as a percentage of GDP *at factor prices*. The second column shows percentages of GDP *at market prices*. Because this measure of GDP is inflated by the existence of indirect taxes, GDP at *factor prices* may be the preferred denominator. However, domestic product includes income received by foreigners and also the depreciation of capital stock. It might be argued that the best measure is the one that relates *net total social expenditure to net disposable national income at factor prices*. These are the figures shown in the last column of Table 12.4. This calculation shows that social expenditure in the United Kingdom and the United States is in the same order of magnitude as that in the Nordic countries. According to this calculation, the big social spenders are now, in decreasing order, France, Belgium, Germany, and Sweden. Thus, the Nordic countries do not appear as exceptional as they did in Table 12.1.

Table 12.5 provides, for 2005, some additional information for the same groups of countries on selected characteristics of programs of social protection. More specifically, it shows the use of *income testing* by different countries and *private social spending*, divided between "mandatory private" and "voluntary private." As to the use of income testing, the Anglo-Saxon countries stand out. Australia, Canada, and New Zealand especially make a large use of income testing. Surprisingly, the United States does not make much use of income testing. Other countries that make a considerable use of income testing are the United Kingdom, Finland, Ireland, and France. This implies that social benefits are less seen as entitlements, or rights against society, in these countries than in the Nordic countries, except for Finland.

As to *mandatory* private spending, Italy, Norway, Germany, and Australia make more use than others. Some of this is mandatory for the private enterprises. In these countries, workers (or enterprises on the worker's behalf) are required to set aside some current income for future needs. In the *voluntary* private spending category, the major users are, by far, the United States, the Netherlands, the United Kingdom, Canada, and Belgium. For these countries, voluntary private spending ranges from 9.8 percent of GDP for the United States to 4.5 percent of GDP for Belgium. While this spending provides social protection against some risks to the individuals who have chosen to take advantage of the programs, it is not likely to spread the spending equitably or evenly among income groups. Thus, while it does provide protection to the beneficiaries, it does not help much in making the income distribution more even or in reducing poverty. As a consequence, Gini coefficients are changed less by this voluntary private spending (see Förster and Mira d'Ercole, 2005, for estimates of Gini coefficients in the OECD countries).

Table 12.5. *Selected characteristics of programs for social protection, 2005*
*(percentages of GDP)*

| Country | Spending on income-tested programs | Private spending | |
|---|---|---|---|
| | | Mandatory private | Voluntary private |
| Denmark | 1.0 | 0.2 | 2.4 |
| Finland | 2.6 | 0.0 | 1.1 |
| Norway | 1.1 | 1.3 | 0.8 |
| Sweden | 0.6 | 0.4 | 2.4 |
| Nordic countries | 1.3 | 0.5 | 1.7 |
| Austria | 1.1 | 0.9 | 1.0 |
| Belgium | 0.9 | 0.0 | 4.5 |
| France | 1.9 | 0.4 | 2.6 |
| Germany | 1.5 | 1.1 | 1.9 |
| Italy | 0.7 | 1.5 | 0.6 |
| Netherlands | 1.1 | 0.7 | 7.6 |
| Spain | 1.6 | 0.0 | 0.5 |
| Other European countries | 1.3 | 0.7 | 2.3 |
| Australia | 6.3 | 1.1 | 2.6 |
| Canada | 3.3 | 0.0 | 5.5 |
| Ireland | 2.6 | 0.0 | 1.3 |
| New Zealand | 3.4 | 0.0 | 0.4 |
| United Kingdom | 2.7 | 0.8 | 6.3 |
| United States | 1.2 | 0.3 | 9.8 |
| Anglo-Saxon countries | 3.3 | 0.4 | 4.3 |
| Japan | 0.5 | 0.5 | 3.3 |
| Korea | 0.7 | 0.6 | 1.8 |
| Mexico | 0.5 | 0.0 | 0.2 |
| Other countries | 0.6 | 0.4 | 1.8 |

*Sources:* Adapted from OECD Social Expenditure database (www.OECD.Org (els/social/ expenditure) and Adema and Ladaique, 2009.

Table 12.6 provides some information, for the year 2003, on the impact of taxes and social programs on Gini coefficients in Sweden and in the United States. The table shows that, before the actions of the governments are taken into account, the Ginis are relatively high for both countries but especially for the United States. The governments' redistributive actions reduce the Swedish coefficient by 0.22 points, or by 47 percent, while it reduces the U.S. coefficient by 0.109, or by 16.7 percent. Clearly in terms of reducing inequality Sweden is much more successful than the United States.

Other information that may be of interest is that in the mid-1990s the poorest 30 percent of the population received shares of total market income

Table 12.6. *Impact of taxes and social programs on Gini coefficients: United States and Sweden, 2003*

|  | United States | Sweden |
|---|---|---|
| Original market income | 0.503 | 0.468 |
| After social insurance | – | 0.309 |
| After social insurance and taxes | – | 0.288 |
| After social insurance, taxes, and nontaxable transfers | 0.394 | 0.247 |

*Sources:* For U.S. Census Bureau, Current Population Survey, Annual Social and Economic Supplements; for Sweden, Palme, 2006, table 4, p. 23.

that were 9.3 percent in Sweden and 8.9 percent in the United States, while the richest 30 percent received 53.9 and 57.1 percent, respectively (Förster and Pearson, 2002, p. 21).

Some countries have attempted more than other countries to target some public transfers specifically toward those at the bottom of the income distribution. These have been predominantly the Anglo-Saxon countries, together with Switzerland and, to a lesser extent, Norway. On the other hand, some countries, and especially Sweden, have targeted the benefits toward the broad middle classes or the whole population. Compensation of public employees as a share of GDP is particularly large in the countries that use in-kind transfers in their social programs. For example, as percentages of GDPs in 2007, compensation of employees was 16.8 in Denmark, 15.8 in Sweden, 13.7 in Finland, and 13.0 in France. They were somewhat lower in other countries. For example, they were 10.1 and 11.4 percent, respectively, in Ireland and the United Kingdom.

*Tax expenditures* can be used in place of direct public spending to promote some activities that are supposed to be beneficial to citizens. Different countries make different use of them. As mentioned in an OECD report (1995, p. 5), tax expenditures may take different forms:

Exemptions of some income from the tax base
Deductions (allowances against gross income)
Credits against the tax liability
Rate relief (reduced rates for some taxpayers or activities)
Tax deferrals (delays in some tax payments)

While tax expenditures are used by many countries, there is a lot of controversy on how to define and especially on how to calculate them. The attempt by the OECD in 1995 to estimate them on a comparable basis led to controversy, and the OECD did not repeat the attempt. However, many countries now publish regularly estimates of tax expenditures. In several countries, there are legal requirements to do so. In some, the "tax expenditure" report is explicitly linked to the budget process, recognizing that tax expenditures are just a different instrument for promoting particular social goals. The 1995 OECD study provided estimates for 14 countries including six of the G7 countries.

The broad conclusion that can be extracted from that report, and from other information from various countries and sources, is that some countries see these tax expenditures as explicit alternatives to public spending; Anglo-Saxon countries make more use of them than other countries (Nordic countries and several continental European countries make much less use of them, preferring to use public spending); the use of "tax expenditures" lowers the shares of taxes into GDP, reducing the spending capacity of governments, while it provides some assistance to (socially important) expenditure by citizens for education, health, pension benefits, and work-related expenses; the countries that rely on them are more likely to need to target social benefits provided through public spending to the poorest social classes that generally get little or no benefits from tax expenditures; the higher the tax rates are, the more valuable the tax expenditures are to those who benefit from them. Of course, the higher the taxpayer's income is, the greater the benefits are.[1]

Adema (2001, p. 23) reported that "information [on tax expenditure] on Finland, Norway, and Sweden has not been included as it concerns very small items: less than 0.05 percent of GDP." Presumably the same is true for Denmark. None of the Nordic countries prepares tax expenditure budgets. Thus, while the Nordic countries significantly lower the social benefits that beneficiaries get from some public spending by taxing those benefits, the Anglo-Saxon countries reduce the cost of acquiring some privately provided benefits by the use of tax expenditures. In conclusion, the role of taxation is important when comparing the programs of social spending across countries, and it should not be ignored, as it often is, in comparing countries.

## 12.3. Developing Countries

We turn now briefly to the developing countries. With relatively few exceptions, of which Brazil, Argentina, Chile, Uruguay, and perhaps South Africa and India are important but not exclusive examples, developing countries have not tried or, more often, have not had the luxury of choosing the policy instruments mentioned in the preceding section. The structure of their economies (with still large agricultural sectors and much informality), together with political and administrative obstacles to taxation, have kept their average tax revenue low, except for a few countries, including those that could rely on commodity exports during periods of high prices. Because of difficulties in raising tax revenue, most of them have been prevented from using public spending as an effective instrument of universal social protection.[2] When they have tried, often using debt finance, they have got into macroeconomic difficulties. On average, the tax burdens of the developing countries has remained under 20 percent of their GDPs, compared with twice that level for OECD countries. Over the years, the positive impact that administrative improvements could have had on tax revenue was partly neutralized, at least for some of these countries, by the losses of foreign trade taxes, due to the lowering of taxes on foreign trade, or by the reluctance to tax incomes from financial assets, because of fears that these assets would fly out of these countries (Tanzi, 2008).

The second instrument, tax expenditure, has also not been available to many of these countries because, as mentioned earlier, this instrument works best when a country has a personal income tax, with high rates and low personal exemptions, that generates high tax revenue. In general, developing countries have not had progressive and especially productive income taxes on total incomes. However, if the concept of tax expenditure also includes exonerations from value-added taxes and traditional tax incentives for enterprises, some estimates of tax expenditures in developing countries are also high. The definitional problems that these estimates present are, of course, major. Because of the difficulty in raising taxes, most developing countries have been left with the alternative of using the regulatory instrument. Many of them have exploited intensively this instrument, especially to the advantage of the urban middle classes and of organized workers.

Regulations have occasionally been used to keep the prices of agricultural products low by taxing their exports, thus penalizing the agricultural sector in favor of the urban middle classes. This approach has been especially used in Argentina over a long period of time. Regulations, through the use of multiple exchange rates and/or quantitative restrictions on the imports of less necessary products, were used in the past to allow the importation of essential products, such as medicines or basic food, at lower prices in domestic currency. In the past couple decades, these regulations became less common. Regulations kept low for many years the prices of some products and services sold by public enterprises, often creating major financing problems for these enterprises and creating the need for the budget to subsidize them. Furthermore, some of these enterprises, such as those selling electricity and water, were required to apply price discrimination in favor of those who consumed small amount of these products or who could prove to have low incomes. Regulations forced some public enterprises (railroads, bus companies, national airlines) to continue providing services to distant or isolated communities at costs that far exceeded the revenue obtained from these services. This policy invites the interesting question of what responsibility a state should have vis-à-vis citizens who live in far and isolated locations that become too expensive to service adequately.[3] Regulations kept interest rates low or forced banks to extend cheap credit to activities considered socially important. Regulations imposed minimum wages or wage increases not always fully justified by market conditions. In recent years, following the example of Chile, some developing countries privatized their pension systems by forcing workers to set aside a defined share of their wages and to invest the money in special accounts that are regulated by the government but are managed and supervised by private agents.

For those benefiting from them (mostly the urban middle classes), these and other forms of regulations created a kind of rudimentary safety net or even a rough welfare state that was not based on public spending (Tanzi, 2004). It was a safety net that (excluding the privatization of pensions) was easily criticized by economists, because it created economic distortions and inefficiencies. However, to those who benefited from these regulations, the safety net seemed important and real. They often reacted strongly when some of these benefits were removed, or were proposed to be removed, as occurred when public enterprises were privatized in the 1990s, price controls were eliminated, interest rates were set free, and multiple exchange rates were replaced by single flexible rates.

The economic liberalization movement of the 1990s was largely a frontal attack against this regulatory welfare state. Jordana and Levi-Faur (2004, p. 1) have argued that the use of regulations in Latin America started in the 1920s and has continued until the present time. However, along the way its objectives changed. As Jordana and Levi-Faur put it, "Reforms should be understood against the background of four related characteristics of the [Latin American] region: the crisis of the old 'developmental' model (in which the state tried to force development through various policies), the widespread diffusion of economic reforms, democratization, and the problem of state consolidation." With the passing of time, there has been some shift from reliance on taxing and spending, and on redistributive regulations, to rule-making regulations. At first, this shift had been toward giving the state more power and promoting its view of state-led development.

Later, the shift was toward giving more power to progressively more independent regulatory authorities. To the extent that those who ran these regulatory authorities were progressively more market-oriented individuals, the activities of these "authorities" reflected this shift. However, at the time the regulators saw their role not in terms of making the market more efficient but in terms of promoting particular policies that were at times not sustainable.

## References

Adema, Willem. 2001. "Net Social Expenditures, 2nd Edition." *OECD Labour Market and Social Policy Occasional Papers*, no. 52 (Paris: OECD Publishing).

Adema, Willem, and M. Ladaique. 2005. "Net Social Expenditure, 2005 Edition: More Comprehensive Measures of Social Support." *OECD Social, Employment and Migration Working Papers*, no. 29 (Paris: OECD Publishing).

2009. "How Expenditure is the Welfare State? Gross and Net Indicators in the OECD Social Expenditure Database (SOCX)." *OECD Social, Employment and Migration Working Papers*, **92** (Paris: OECD Publishing).

Dutton, Paul V. 2002. *Origins of the French Welfare State: The Struggle for Social Reform in France, 1914–1947* (Cambridge: Cambridge University Press).

Förster, M. F., and M. Mira d'Ercole. 2005. "Income Distribution and Poverty in OECD Countries in the Second Half of the 1990s." *OECD Social, Employment and Migration Working Paper*, no. 22 (Paris: OECD Publishing).

Förster, Michael, and Mark Pearson. 2002. "Income Distribution and Poverty in the OECD Area: Trends and Driving Forces." *OECD Economic Studies*, no. 34: 7–39.

Jordana, Jacint, and David Levi-Faur 2004. "Toward a Latin American Regulatory State?" Mimeo (February).

Kendall, Jeremy, and Martin Knapp. 1996. *The Voluntary Sector in the UK* (Manchester: Manchester University Press).

Ministero di Agricultura, Industria e Commercio. 1911. *Discorso Pronunciato da S.E. l'on. Francesco Nitti* (Rome: Tipografia Nazionale di G. Bertero e c.).

OECD, Committee on Fiscal Affairs. 1995. "Tax Expenditures: Recent Experiences" (Paris: distributed September 19).

Palme, Joakim. 2006. "Income Distribution in Sweden." *Japanese Journal of Social Security Policy* 5, no. 1 (June): 16–26.

Pipkin, Charles W. 1927. *The Idea of Social Justice: A Study of Legislation and Administration and the Labour Movement in England and France between 1900 and 1926* (New York: Macmillan).

Tanzi, Vito. 2004. "Globalization and the Need for Fiscal Reform in Developing Countries." *Journal of Policy Modeling* 26:- 525–42.

2008. "Introduction: Tax Systems and Tax Reforms in Latin America," in *Tax Systems and Tax Reforms in Latin America*, edited by Luigi Bernardi, Alberto Barreix, Anna Marenzi, and Paola Profeta (New York: Routledge).

U.S. Census Bureau. 2006. Current Population Survey, Annual Social and Economic Supplement (LISA: Government Printing Office).

THIRTEEN

# The Role of the State and Economic
# Performance in the Nordic Countries

## 13.1. Introduction

Those who have strong preferences for a large economic role of the state often point to the Nordic countries of Europe as examples of mature welfare states that prove that high public spending and high tax levels, combined with wide social protection, can coexist with good economic performance. In recent decades, the Nordic countries have had the highest levels of public spending in the world, the highest tax levels, the lowest Gini coefficients, and the lowest poverty rates. They have the most effective safety nets among countries while managing to retain very favorable rankings in countries' competitiveness leagues, such as those prepared by the World Bank, on "The Ease of Doing Business"; in "economic freedom" indexes, prepared by the Heritage Foundation and the *Wall Street Journal*; and in the "Corruption Perception Index," prepared by Transparency Internationals. According to the April 16, 2010, special edition of *Forbes*, these countries even included 17 of the world billionaires. In the 2010 rankings on the Index of Economic Freedom, Denmark ranked 9th, Finland ranked 17th, and Sweden ranked 21st out of 122 countries.

The Nordic countries seem to defy the notion that large public spending and the high tax levels that it requires are necessarily damaging to the economic performance of countries and to the economic freedom of individuals. The inevitable question that arises is, If this is true for these countries, why should it not be true for other countries? Why should governments not aim at high public spending if that spending can provide high levels of social protection, efficient safety nets, better income distribution, and low poverty, without having to pay a high price in terms of economic efficiency and economic freedom? Is there something special about the

Nordic countries that make them avoid some of the costs of high taxes and high spending that are assumed to characterize other countries?

It would not be possible here to examine, in a comprehensive and fully satisfactory fashion, the many aspects of these questions. Many books and articles published over the years have attempted to provide answers. However, their conclusions often reflect the known biases of the authors of these studies, proving that there is no such thing as "valueless" economics, as maintained by Korpi (1996). In spite of strong claims to the contrary, economics is not a pure science. Those who, for whatever reasons, give more weight to equity and poverty reductions, and thus favor the policies of the welfare states, tend to focus on the positive outcomes of these policies and to minimize the costs (among these authors, see, e.g., the papers in Costabile, 2008; and Atkinson, 1999). Those who give more weight to efficiency and the economic freedom of individuals, and less to equity, tend to focus more on the costs (see, e.g., Lindbeck, 1997 and 2000; Thakur et al., 2003; Rosen, 1996; and also the various articles in the special issue on welfare states in *Oxford Review of Economic Policy*, 2006).

In this chapter, we discuss the experience of the Nordic countries, focusing particularly on Sweden, the largest of these countries and the one for which there is more information available. Except for details and for some specific policies, the experiences of these countries are fairly similar, so the special attention given to Sweden should not provide a significantly distorted picture. The chapter presents information that may help readers better understand developments and form some informed and objective impressions. Our conclusion is that the relatively good economic performance of these countries in recent years (until the economic crisis of 2008–9 and after their crises of the early 1990s) may have been influenced by significant reforms, aimed at improving economic incentives. These reforms were introduced especially in the decade of the 1990s. This conclusion may imply that the good, recent performance may not tell much about the impact of high spending and high taxes on the economies of these countries and on how these countries' economies will perform *over the long run*. In any case, it may be a mistake to assume that, especially over the short and medium run, economic growth is affected significantly by only one factor (high taxes) when there are many other factors that may be influencing it in a given period. It should be added that Norway stands in a special category because it is a major oil exporter, so that the price and the production of oil have a major impact on its economic performance. The revenue from oil has been well managed and has allowed Norway to promote generous social policies without the need to impose high taxes, just as Saudi Arabia, Kuwait, Qatar, and some other oil- or gas-rich countries have done. Norway has accumulated huge foreign assets and, by using annually only an "income" out of them, has been able to cover its yearly social expenses without depleting the assets or raising taxes.

## 13.2. The Period until the 1950s

Until the end of the 19th century, the Nordic countries, with the exception of Denmark, which had a higher per capita income, were very poor. At that time many of their citizens were forced to migrate, especially to the United States. During the decade of 1880s, more than 1 percent of the population of Sweden and Norway emigrated annually (Einhorn and Logue, 1989, p. 9). Between 1850 and 1910, more than a million Swedes (a large proportion of the total population) emigrated to the United States, mainly to Minnesota and other midwestern states.

Somewhere around 1870 Sweden started to industrialize and to develop rapidly. During that period, strong grass-roots organizations came into existence, including trade unions, temperance groups, and independent religious groups (see "Sweden" in Wikipedia). In 1899 the Swedish Trade Union Confederation (Landsorganisationen I Sverige) was founded. It developed strong links with the Social Democratic Party, the party that would dominate political developments in Sweden for much of the 20th century and would play a large role in the creation of the Swedish welfare state. The creation of a welfare state was an alternative to socialism, an ideology that in Sweden had created a strong political movement at the beginning of the 20th century and especially at the time of the Bolshevik Revolution in Russia in 1917. The fact that Sweden avoided both World Wars I and II and that it was able to peacefully develop its considerable natural resources within a strongly democratic setting (with a stable constitutional monarchy) helped it to grow rapidly and to become one of the richest countries in the world by the middle of the 20th century.

Much has been written about "the Nordic alternative," the "Nordic welfare states," and the societal characteristics that made the introduction of the reforms needed to create a welfare state possible and relatively smooth. These characteristics may have reduced the perceived burden of high taxes, making these taxes easier to bear and less damaging to personal incentives. They may also raise questions of whether the policy changes toward a welfare state were necessary, except in their goal of preventing the introduction of full-fledged socialism. The early societies that existed in the Nordic region were made up of "loosely knit clans and villages, sometimes united under a local chieftain. . . . [Within the clans and villages,] decisions were taken at popular assemblies called Ting, where all enfranchised men had the right to speak and vote" (Rexed, 2000, p. 4). Some of these decisions involved assisting families in need. At that time, women had still little formal power, but their power would grow enormously with the formal welfare state, and they would become the strongest supporters of the policies of such a state.

The Nordic region had never experienced the feudal system that had been common in other parts of Europe during the Middle Ages. This helped the people in the region develop a clear sense of a community made up of relatively free, even though poor, individuals willing to assist one another. The clans and villages had some of the characteristics of extended families within which mutual support was considered natural. After the Reformation in the 16th century, the Catholic Church, with its extended charitable network, had been replaced by Protestantism, which lacked the hierarchical structure that characterizes the Catholic Church. The role that the Catholic Church had played in social activities was eliminated and replaced by other means. Within the community – or, better, the communities made up of the various villages – a "strong work ethic, solidarity and a bias for [spontaneous] collective action dominated" (Rexed, 2000, p. 5). The decentralized character of this collective action has continued to define various government programs of social assistance. These programs are generally financed nationally but administered locally. Mutual support has been and has remained an important social objective; however, it has been "nationalized." The income distribution and the alleviation of poverty have been spontaneous and long-run concerns in this society and not goals imposed by distant bureaucrats or policy makers. In some way the welfare state nationalized the existing social network while maintaining some of its basic characteristics.

It has been frequently argued that natural aspects of Nordic society – such as the strongly felt social norms and the trust in collective actions that had prevailed in the small agrarian communities – had created a culture that smoothed the way for and facilitated the introduction of the Nordic version of welfare state. Especially important among these social norms were *egalitarianism* and *conformism* with the values and the objectives developed by the community. When decisions were made in the past, at the popular assemblies (the Ting), they were accepted by the individuals and became the community's decisions. They were not challenged by dissenting individuals. This is an example of communal trust and a "communal state" described in Chapter 7. In this "communal state," the individual is an integral part of the community, and the community develops, jointly and democratically, norms that are not challenged by the individuals and that influence the current and future policies. Once developed, the community norms prevail over the personal incentives and even over the freedom of individuals. People do not see a conflict between their own objectives and those of the community. These collective norms came to be assimilated by the trade unions and by the political parties that came into power in the 20th century and that guided the country's policy.

The fact that the population of the Nordic countries was then ethnically homogeneous, before these countries started attracting large number of immigrants from the rest of the world, must have facilitated the development of the welfare states. Many scholars have referred to these characteristics. For example, Jeffrey Sachs (2008, p. 5) wrote that "social-welfare systems [have proved] to be most effective and popular in ethnically homogeneous societies, such as Scandinavia, where people believed that their tax payments were 'helping' their own." He added that "in the end, the social-welfare model relies on a form of trust... people are more willing to withstand high rates of taxation if they know that their taxes are paying for programs that help people like them" (p. 265). The relation between trust and social cohesion has been discussed in several places (e.g., Fukuyama, 1995; O'Hara, 2004; and Putnam, 2000).

In a formal or statistical sense, which puts the emphasis on government programs and on shares of taxes and public spending into GDPs, the welfare state of the Nordic countries was not introduced until *after* World War II. It was only at that time that those shares of GDP started rising fast, from the low levels that had prevailed until World War II. Within a short time they became very high. This inevitably raises the question of whether the formal arrangements created by the government were necessary, and whether it could not have been possible to maintain the past, informal protection that had been provided, without government intervention, through spontaneous, private, but social arrangements. Perhaps, the transaction costs for these informal arrangements were becoming too high in the new industrial environment, thus requiring governmental intervention as argued in an earlier chapter.

Some have argued that the seeds for the welfare state in Sweden were planted much earlier than the period after World War I. In 1847 and 1853 Sweden enacted "poor relief laws" and, as we mentioned earlier, in 1898 the powerful Swedish Trade Union Confederation was founded. In 1913 the Liberal Party government started to broaden the scope of social benefits, reflecting a trend that was developing, at that time, in various parts of Europe. In that year Sweden adopted the first universalistic, social insurance program. The program was far from generous and was funded by taxes imposed by the central government. However, it covered everyone. The Social Democratic Party had assimilated the prevailing social norms widely shared by the members of the trade union. In the following period, it started the creation of what would in time become the most mature welfare state in the world. However, the process would be slow and, as we shall see, in 1950 the level of public spending and taxes into GDP, both in Sweden and in the other Nordic countries, was still very low, and lower than in other advanced countries.

An interesting aspect of the Swedish experience that does not seem to have attracted much attention is that the drive for egalitarianism and conformism came initially not from the use of redistributive taxes and social public spending for universal programs but from operations that, directly, had little to do with the fiscal or budgetary actions of the government. Discussions of the Nordic welfare states, and of Sweden in particular, routinely stress the low Gini coefficients that these countries managed to achieve and link these low Ginis to the budgetary actions of the welfare state. They show that, in the 1980s, these coefficients became as low as 0.20 (or 20 percent) making these countries the most egalitarian, in terms of income distribution after the action of the government, among the market economies of the world. The impression that is given is that these low Ginis were the direct result of the high and progressive taxes and of high and universal spending programs and that without these programs the income distribution would have been much more uneven.

Although the income distribution of these countries, and especially of that of Sweden, for which there is good information, became more even in the 1960s when taxes and public spending increased rapidly and sharply, there had been major changes toward more equality in income distribution in the first half of the 20th century, or well before the state-sponsored welfare programs were introduced.

A study of the evolution of top incomes in Sweden over the 1903–2004 period has shown that Sweden started the 20th century with significant *market* inequality, at least as measured by the share of income going to the top percentile, *before* any *informal* redistribution took place (Roine and Waldenström, 2008). However, as the century progressed, and until around 1980, there was a sharp drop in the share of total income received by the top 1 percent. The drop was particularly pronounced between 1915 and 1950 and continued until the early 1980s, although at a much slower pace, before inequality started rising again. In 1981 the Gini coefficient for *disposable* income reached its lowest value of 0.199, according to *Statistics Sweden*. The Gini remained very low until 1988 and rose significantly afterward. What is interesting about this pattern is that the fall in the share of income going to the top 1 percent between 1915 and 1950 could not have had much to do with the welfare state – associated with the taxing and spending activity of the government – simply because the welfare state had not yet been created. It is also questionable whether the increase in the Gini between 1981 and later years was all the result of the withdrawal of the welfare state, although some reforms were introduced in that period that may have increased inequality.

These results are important because they indicate, or at least suggest, that the distribution of income may be as much associated with *changing social attitudes* toward income distribution as with *objective market developments* of the kind stressed by economists (such as globalization, technological changes, and other objective factors) or specific government policies such as taxing and spending. This seems to be a point made by Paul Krugman in some of his writings in which he has stressed that the increasing unevenness of the income distribution in the United States in recent decades may have been due more to changes in attitudes than to changes in objective, measurable factors. Economists tend to put emphasis on measurable technical or policy factors and to ignore more sociologically based explanations that do not lend themselves to econometric analysis or testing (see also Esping-Andersen, 2007). This may be due to their habit, or frame of mind, of seeing the economy as a machine in which different variables must be related only in specific and precise ways. "There is a single universally valid model of the world" in Solow's words (cited in Chapter 8, note 5). This raises the question of whether the use of mathematical models always helps us to better understand reality. Do they truly capture reality? Is it possible that the elegance of these models helps convince us that they are in fact a representation of reality, when they are not? This may have happened with the efficient market hypothesis that convinced many investors that it was a faithful representation of reality. Human beings may be too varied or too irrational in their reactions to be fully captured by formal models.

The assumption that markets work efficiently and precisely so that the compensation that individuals get for their economic activities is the natural and precise result of market forces has been widely accepted, especially in recent decades. This assumption has tended to justify huge incomes or high compensations for some people. The view has been that if the market has generated those incomes, those who received them must have earned and merited them. That assumption tends to ignore the fact that some individuals are in particular positions that give them a lot of power in determining their own compensation or income. This is especially the case for managers of large private enterprises that in Keynes's words have socialized themselves and in which the shareholders, who are the legal owners of the enterprises, tend to play a limited, if any, role, especially in the short run. There may be various ways in which the value added created by an enterprise can be shared among the workers, the managers, and the shareholders. That sharing could be much influenced by the prevailing social attitudes and, to some extent, by market forces. In recent decades, the social attitudes have favored the managers and especially those of widely held enterprises, who could choose the board members who approve or determine their salaries. The power of "benchmarking" often contributes to the outcome, because higher compensation for some managers provides a good justification for others to ask for, or to be paid, higher total compensation. This has been a common argument to justify huge bonuses in the financial market and large salaries for the managers of enterprises, even for managers who had not performed particularly brilliantly. The argument has been that if we do not pay million-dollar bonuses or high salaries, and others do, we shall lose the best talent. A global market for some of these individuals has contributed to this trend. The losers have been the workers and, to some extent, the shareholders (Johnson and Kwak, 2010).

It can be theorized that the compensation of the top earners rise when society at large comes to accept the view that these individuals deserve high compensation and falls when society comes to doubt the net value of these individuals. In the past couple of decades, particular individuals came to be seen by society as contributing significantly to "economic value" with their work. This perception made it easier for some individuals to demand and get much greater compensation than they would have gotten in the past. In some ways, these individuals replaced the nobles of the past in their natural right to a greater share of the cake. They, too, were assumed to deserve high incomes because their position in society suggested that outcome.

During this period, the difference between the incomes of the top earners and the average incomes of normal workers increased sharply (Johnson and Kwak, 2010, p. 115). While the latter stagnated in many countries, those of the top earners went through the roof. Multimillion-dollar compensations, including golden parachutes, and huge bonuses came to seem normal. This was seen to be the price that societies had to pay to the lucky few, presumably to get more efficient economies and faster growth rates. Because of the assumption that markets operated efficiently, and that the judgment of the market must always be correct, the compensation that these individuals received was seen as reflecting the economic value that they were creating. The key assumption was that all compensations are objectively, market determined and competitively established so that it would not be efficient to interfere with them.[1] It is doubtful that, *ceteris paribus*, these salaries would have prevailed under different social attitudes.

Let us return to Sweden. The period between 1915 and 1950 saw some interesting political and social developments in that country. In this period, Sweden became widely unionized and much more urbanized and industrialized than it had been in earlier years. In 1938, in a small town called Saltsjöbaden, an important formal agreement was reached between unions and confederations of employers. This agreement, which came to be called the Saltsjöbaden spirit, established ways in which workers and enterprises could cooperate. By implication, the agreement broadly determined how the country's total income, produced in the industrial sector, should be distributed. The egalitarian spirit that had characterized the Swedish society was reaffirmed by this agreement, and government policy was called upon to validate the main objectives of the agreement that had been reached, in free negotiations, between workers and employers. It became normal in Swedish enterprises to have representatives of workers sit in the management boards of the enterprises. This helped contain the salary differences between managers and workers.

The two sides agreed that wages as well as managers' compensation would be leveled significantly so that income inequality within the labor market would be reduced, making lower-paid workers better off and higher-paid workers, as well as managers and supervisors, worse off. This change by itself would make the *market* distribution of income more even. Between the mid-1930s and 1950, there was the sharpest fall in the share of total incomes received by the top percentile. Note that this was *before* the welfare state was introduced. Furthermore, this change meant that the cost of the average worker became more expensive for enterprises that hired (now better-paid) low-skill workers and less expensive for those enterprises that hired (now lesser-paid) skilled workers. This encouraged enterprises to prefer high-skilled workers and to promote technologically more advanced activities. Given the objective of full employment, this change required and was accompanied by a lot of attention paid to retraining low-skilled workers, especially on the part of large enterprises. Low-skilled workers were retrained and helped to transfer to other enterprises.

Another important part of the cooperation achieved in Saltsjöbaden was that enterprises were encouraged, through the tax system, to retain and invest profits, rather than pay them out to shareholders in dividends. This also contributed to a better income distribution (especially excluding unrealized capital gains) and provided more resources to invest for the more productive enterprises. Much attention was directed toward the retraining of workers and increasing the educational level so that technologically more advanced enterprises would be able to find and to hire better-trained individuals. By the way, the school system was also highly egalitarian and did not reflect differences promoted by social classes.

This kind of "developmental role of the state" was not achieved through commands, by politicians or government bureaucrats, but by spontaneous cooperation between workers' and employers' representatives. It was facilitated and made possible by the existing trust that existed in the Swedish society and by the societal preference for more equality. It would not have been possible in less homogeneous and less trusting societies.[2]

Aided by the fact that it stayed out of the Second World War, Sweden developed at a fast pace after World War II. By the early 1970s it had become the third-richest country in the world, behind Switzerland and the United States (Thakur et al., 2005, p. 23). Also, "in many industrial areas Swedish companies took a position at the technological frontier" (Schön, 2008, p. 2). As Schön put it, "The most notable feature of long-term Swedish growth is the acceleration in growth rates during the period 1910–1950" (p. 9). The fast growth continued until around 1970, although in this postwar period some European countries were growing at a faster pace. In conclusion, during the period when the *formal* welfare state was being introduced, after 1950, the growth rate of Sweden had started to lag that of some other European countries (Krantz and Schön, 2007). This may imply that it was not the trend toward egalitarianism that may have played a role in slowing the economy (a trend that had been going on at least since World War I) but possibly the transfer of that role to the state. It required sharply increasing taxes that accompanied the introduction of the *formal* welfare state.

### 13.3. The Period between the 1950s and the 1980s

Until the early 1950s, the Nordic European countries had taxes and public spending ratios to GDP broadly similar to or lower than those of other industrial countries. For example, the ratio of total taxes to GDP in 1940 in Sweden was only 15.1 percent (Table 13.1). Therefore, the incomes of the citizens of these countries were not much reduced by taxes, and they still depended very little on public spending. Assistance to families in need did not come from entitlement but from spontaneous social actions, and it was greatly influenced by social norms that did not condone laziness and that

Table 13.1. *Sweden: Taxes as percentages of GDP, 1900–2007*

|       | Direct taxes | Indirect taxes | Social security contributions | Total |
|-------|--------------|----------------|-------------------------------|-------|
| 1900  | 2.7          | 4.9            | 0.0                           | 7.7   |
| 1912  | 4.8          | 3.7            | 0.0                           | 8.5   |
| 1924  | 6.7          | 4.0            | 0.3                           | 10.9  |
| 1930  | 5.5          | 4.3            | 0.2                           | 10.1  |
| 1940  | 9.4          | 5.4            | 0.3                           | 15.1  |
| 1950  | 12.3         | 7.4            | 1.3                           | 21.0  |
| 1960  | 14.7         | 10.0           | 3.6                           | 28.3  |
| 1970  | 20.2         | 12.4           | 7.6                           | 40.2  |
| 1980  | 21.9         | 13.7           | 14.4                          | 50.0  |
| 1990  | 23.4         | 17.2           | 15.1                          | 55.7  |
| 2000  | 22.3         | 15.1           | 15.1                          | 52.6  |
| 2007[a] | 19.2       | 16.9           | 14.4                          | 50.5  |

[a] The data for 2007 are from the Statistical Annex of European Commission, *Public Finance in EMU 2009.*

Sources: Rodriguez, RRV, *Statens Finanser*, RSV. The table is drawn from Sweden, National Tax Authorities Statistics, 2008, table 14.5.

encouraged egalitarianism.[3] In 1960 the shares of public spending into GDP in the Nordic countries were still relatively low: 24.1 percent in Denmark, 26.0 percent in Finland, and 31.0 percent in Sweden. Even though they had been rising rapidly in the previous decade, they were still lower than in France, Germany, and the United Kingdom. Even the United States, at 26.2 percent of GDP, had a broadly similar expenditure level in 1960.

Table 13.1 provides data on the growth of total taxes and some breakdown by major tax categories in Sweden for the whole of the 20th century until 2007. The table shows that total taxes were *very* low until 1930. They were still low, by international standards, in 1950. After 1950, the tax collection increased sharply until the tax level (and the level of public spending) reached a world record, around 1990, before starting to fall. Table 13.1 shows also that social security contributions almost did not exist as late as 1950 and were still low in 1960. This again confirms that the formal, government-based, welfare state (of the "tax and spend" type) was created only in the second half of the century, after 1950. Similar developments took place in the other Nordic countries (see Table 13.2 for the 1925–2006 period). Therefore, the movement toward welfare states in these countries is a relatively recent phenomenon. Between 1950 and 1980, these countries introduced the most universal and generous social welfare systems that the

Table 13.2. *Total taxes as percentages of GDP: Selected countries, 1925–2000*

| Years | Sweden | Denmark | Norway | Finland | U.K. | Germany |
|---|---|---|---|---|---|---|
| 1925 | 16.0 | 19.6 | 20.9 | 21.6 | 22.6 | 17.8 |
| 1933 | 18.9 | 20.1 | 25.1 | 20.1 | 25.2 | 23.0 |
| 1950 | 21.0 | 19.8 | n.a. | 27.8 | 33.1 | 30.1 |
| 1960 | 28.7 | 25.3 | 32.0 | 27.5 | 27.3 | 33.9 |
| 1970 | 39.8 | 40.4 | 34.9 | 32.5 | 37.0 | 32.9 |
| 1980 | 47.5 | 43.9 | 42.7 | 36.2 | 35.2 | 33.1 |
| 1990 | 53.6 | 47.1 | 41.8 | 44.7 | 35.9 | 32.6 |
| 2000 | 54.2 | 48.8 | 40.3 | 46.9 | 37.4 | 37.9 |
| 2006[a] | 49.1 | 49.1 | 43.9 | 43.5 | 37.1 | 35.6 |

[a] The data for 2006 are from OECD, *Revenue Statistics, 1965–2007* (OECD, 2008).

*Sources:* Enriguez Rodriguez, *Den Svenska Skattehistorien* (1925–77); and OECD, *Revenue Statistics* (2001). The table is drawn from Sweden, *National Tax Authorities Statistical Annual Report* (2003, in Swedish), table 14.4.

world had even seen. Public spending and taxes were pushed up at a record pace, and both reached the highest levels among countries.

Between 1950 and 1995, public spending as a share of GDP rose to world record levels of 67.1 percent in Sweden, 61.4 percent in Finland, and 59.2 percent in Denmark. As shares of GDP, the 1950 levels of public spending rose until 1995 by 36.1 percentage points in Sweden, 35.4 percentage points in Finland, and 35.1 percentage points in Denmark. The explicit declared goal of these increases in public spending was to provide social protection "from the cradle to the grave" to all citizens through *formal* government-financed programs and through legal *entitlements*.

While at the beginning of the 20th century Sweden and the other Nordic countries had been relatively poor, so that many individuals had migrated to America, by the time they introduced the welfare states they had become rich. There must have been a view that, with their wealth, these countries could buy the best formal protection that the welfare states could provide *as a right of the citizens.* As Lindbeck notes, "It is well known that Sweden's economy grew faster than nearly all other countries during the 1870–1970 period." In the 1950–70 period, the rate of growth of Sweden "was about the same as the average for rich OECD countries" (Lindbeck, 2000, p. 13). It fell significantly afterward. In 1970 its GDP per person placed it at the 3rd place among OECD countries. In 1980 it was 7th. In 1991 it was 14th, and in 1998 it was 18th. By comparison, Denmark and Finland, which had not pushed taxes and spending as far as Sweden, did not experience similar major positional changes over the period (Thakur et al., 2003, p. 23).

Table 13.3. *Growth rates of selected OECD countries, 1960–2008*

| Countries | GDP per employed person at constant domestic prices | | | | GDP growth per capita | |
|---|---|---|---|---|---|---|
| | 1960–70 | 1970–80 | 1980–90 | 1990–2000 | 1997–2007 | 1973–97 |
| Denmark | 3.5 | 1.8 | 1.5 | 1.9 | 1.7 | 1.8 |
| Finland | 4.7 | 2.5 | 2.5 | 2.9 | 3.1 | 1.9 |
| Iceland | 2.8 | 3.6 | 1.1 | 1.6 | 3.8 | – |
| Norway | 3.5 | 3.2 | 1.8 | 2.3 | 1.8 | 3.1 |
| Sweden | 4.0 | 1.0 | 1.4 | 2.4 | 2.9 | 1.2 |
| Average | 3.7 | 2.4 | 1.7 | 2.2 | 2.7 | – |
| Germany | 4.2 | 2.6 | 1.7 | 1.4 | 1.5 | 1.7 |
| Luxembourg | 2.9 | 1.4 | 2.7 | 4.5 | 4.5 | – |
| Austria | 5.2 | 3.0 | 2.1 | 2.0 | 2.0 | 2.1 |
| Italy | 6.2 | 2.9 | 2.1 | 1.7 | 1.0 | 2.1 |
| Belgium | 4.2 | 3.2 | 1.7 | 1.7 | 2.2 | 1.8 |
| Greece | 8.5 | 4.0 | 0.6 | 1.6 | 4.0 | – |
| Spain | 6.6 | 4.1 | 2.3 | 1.4 | 2.5 | 1.9 |
| France | – | 2.6 | 1.9 | 1.4 | 1.7 | 1.5 |
| Netherlands | – | 2.6 | 1.3 | 0.8 | 2.0 | 1.7 |
| Switzerland | 3.2 | 1.1 | 0.2 | 0.7 | 2.0 | 0.6 |
| Average | 5.1 | 2.8 | 1.5 | 1.7 | 2.3 | |
| Ireland | 4.2 | 3.8 | 3.7 | 3.5 | 5.7 | – |
| Australia | 2.7 | 1.9 | 0.9 | 1.9 | 2.2 | – |
| United Kingdom | 2.6 | 1.8 | 1.9 | 1.8 | 2.4 | 1.7 |
| Canada | 1.8 | 1.1 | 1.0 | 1.4 | 2.3 | – |
| United States | 1.2 | 0.6 | 1.5 | 1.8 | 1.8 | 1.6 |
| New Zealand | 1.2 | 0.6 | 1.5 | 0.7 | 2.0 | – |
| Average | 2.3 | 1.6 | 1.8 | 1.9 | 2.7 | – |

*Sources:* For the three columns that cover the 1960–90 period the data are from Lindbeck, 2000, p. 23; the data for the 1990–2000 period and for the 1997–2007 period are from OECD, *Economic Outlook.* The data for 1973–97 (last column) are from Maddison, 1999.

Table 13.3 provides some information on the growth performance of these countries and other developed countries over five decades. Please note that the data for the last two columns are not comparable with those of the first four columns. A significant weakening of growth performance can be noticed between the 1960–70 period, when the welfare states were being created, and the following two decades, when the transformation toward welfare states was complete. However, broadly similar deterioration is observed in several other countries over the same period. Therefore, one should not see an immediate or necessary cause and effect between the introduction of the welfare state and the slowdown in the growth rates, even though Sweden experienced one of the sharpest reductions.[4]

At this point, it may be worthwhile to describe briefly some of the unique characteristics of the formal, government-sponsored, welfare state that was introduced in Sweden and, with some variations, in the other Nordic countries between 1950 and the mid-1970s. The description is mainly focused on Sweden, the largest and most influential of these countries. The Swedish model of welfare state is different from that of other continental European countries that rely less on universalistic programs and more on institutional arrangements that cover specific categories of individuals; or, in the case of Mediterranean countries, on family-based institutional arrangements. It is also different from the social protection that exists in the Anglo-Saxon countries, which relies more on "tax expenditures," targeted programs, and private arrangements that provide protection to those who have them but not to others.

It ought to be reiterated that the Nordic countries had been egalitarian *before* the welfare state was introduced and had had a population that was ethnically and culturally homogeneous, until immigration started changing it. In these countries, those who represented the government had more legitimacy, were trusted, and perhaps had been expected to step in with new programs when the region became industrialized and richer and when locally based protection started to face difficulties because of structural changes in economic relations and because of increasing urbanization. It must have seemed normal, at that point, to institutionalize the existing, informal social protection.

Several specific features make the Nordic model of welfare state different from those set up outside of Scandinavia. A Scandinavian author has identified several significant characteristics of the Nordic model. They are reported here in a shorter and somewhat edited version.[5] The characteristics are the following:

1. There is greater and more active involvement by the state that guarantees, *to all qualified residents, basic* pensions and free or highly subsidized health and other social services. Private action has been largely driven out and absorbed by governmental action. (See Boli, 1991, for details.)

2. Compared with the situation in other countries, a larger proportion of the labor force is employed in the provision of *in-kind*, social, health, and educational services. Social and educational services are largely provided by government employees who work for local governments

and especially for municipal governments. Thus, there is a close relationship between the citizens who receive the services and the government employees who provide them. Both are from the same local community and share the same community spirit.

3. National systems coordinate the organization of social services, such as *basic* pensions, sick-leave benefits, child allowances, and health services. As mentioned, most of these services in kind are provided by *local* and not by national organizations.

4. There is a high degree of trust in the governments of these countries. This is very different from the situation that exists in countries such as the United States and Italy where governments are less trusted by large shares of the population.

5. There is reliance on universal, or category-specific, social insurance systems that ignore differences in incomes on the part of the recipients. Nobody is excluded because of his or her higher income, or because of other factors such as gender or family status. The benefits are directed to individuals on their own right and not as members of families. Residency is the only condition to be satisfied, in order to be entitled to the *basic* benefits. Present or past participation in the labor force is not required for basic services.

6. There is no class or occupational biases to the *basic* benefits.

7. The *basic* benefits are financed through general taxation and not through specific "contributions." Thus, everyone contributes to financing them, through the taxes paid. However, some *nonbasic* benefits are based on the incomes that individuals have earned in particular periods during which they have paid specific contributions, thus accumulating rights that may differ between individuals. These latter benefits have become more important in recent years.

8. There is a much greater use than in other countries of benefits provided *in kind* rather than in *cash payment* (for child care, old-age care, in house assistance for the very old and the very ill). During the retrenchment in benefits in the 1990s, the in-kind benefits were protected against reductions over the cash benefits. For example, in 2007 the public spending on long-term care in Sweden was 3.5 percent of GDP, the highest share among the EU-27, against the average of only 1.2 percent of GDP (see Przywara, Diez Guardia, and Sail, 2010, p. 6).

9. Full employment is seen as a very important social objective, both as an end in itself and as a means to finance the welfare state. Various government policies are directed toward this goal and there are strong social pressures on individuals to stay employed.

Until relatively recent years, there had been strong popular support in the Nordic countries for this model of social assistance. This support may have weakened a little in recent years for several reasons, including the increasing access to benefits by immigrants and the related fact that the populations were becoming less ethnically homogeneous. In Sweden, immigrants now account for about 12 percent of the population. Also reports of abuses and arguments by some influential economists that the welfare state was damaging the economic performance have increased the number of those demanding reforms and have weakened support for some of the policies. This may have also led to the election of more conservative governments in some of these countries.

Before leaving this list, and at the cost of some repetition, it may be useful to highlight some key aspects that make the Nordic model different from that prevailing in other high-spending, European welfare states. First, most *basic* benefits are *universal* and are under the direction of *central* government agencies. The main exception is the unemployment benefits system, which is largely managed by labor unions. Second, the benefits are directed to individuals and not to families. They do not depend on family status or on rights acquired by other family members. Thus, the family has largely disappeared as a legal entity, as far as basic services are concerned, while it often remains central in the welfare systems of other countries. Since 1971, even the payment of income taxes is attached to individuals. There is no aggregation of family income that, in a progressive income tax system, can be a disincentive to the employment of spouses or other dependents; or the splitting of the income with children, as in France, which can reduce the progressivity of income taxes. At the same time, there are particular (nonbasic) benefits (especially some pension rights) that are linked to the past "contributions" of the beneficiaries that give them an incentive to continue working and earning more income. Third, the welfare system requires a high labor force participation to finance it and to provide the in-kind social services made available to the population. The labor force participation by women increased significantly during the past decades, because of the opportunities created for them by jobs and programs connected with the welfare state. In the Nordic countries, the employment rate for both men and women, but especially for women, is very high. It is among the highest in the world (Alesina and Giavazzi, 2006, p. 62).

In terms of employment, the Swedish and other Nordic countries' welfare systems have not been gender neutral. They have definitely benefited women who were hired by the local governments to provide the in-kind, social services paid for by the national governments. According to Rosen (1996,

p. 729), "Two basic facts dominate the [employment] data. First, the local public sector has accounted for all employment growth in Sweden since the early 1960s. Second, almost all of it has been by women." In more recent years, this was no longer true. The Swedish welfare state has provided many government jobs to women, jobs that have liberated them from tasks – taking care of their own children and of their own old relatives – that they had performed in the past within their families and that are still performed within the family in other countries (e.g., in Italy and Japan). The difference is that now the women are paid for performing these tasks, whereas before, and in other countries still now, they were, and still are, not paid. This has liberated women from family obligations, giving them financial and social independence. At the same time, this change must have weakened the role of the family as a social institution. For example, available data show that only 4–5 percent of individuals live with their family, and only a very small fraction of individuals care for elderly relatives, compared with much higher percentages for Mediterranean countries.

Apart from the impact that this expansion of state activity has had on the family, it raises the important economic question of whether national accounts statistics are not distorted by this outsourcing of domestic activities. This point can be made by quoting from one of my earlier papers:

In some of these countries, such as Sweden, as much as 30% of the labor force works for the government compared with about half that number in Italy. Many of these public employees . . . are used in activities that deal with child care centers, old age homes, in-house assistance for the elderly and the chronically ill, public housing, and so on. Many of these public employees are women. Thus, the welfare state has created working opportunities within the public sector, for women. It has also liberated them from the need to deal with old or handicapped relatives. It has sharply raised the labor force participation of women . . . The Swedish and Danish participation in 2003 at 71.5 and 70.5% compared with 42.7% participation in Italy. (Tanzi, 2005, p. 28)

In judging the welfare impact of this change, one should measure that impact from the point of view of those who provide the care (the women) and those who receive the care. The results or the valuations are likely to differ (Tanzi, 2008, p. 181).

These government-supported activities have replaced some household production. . . . they may have distorted the comparability of international statistics on per capita incomes. . . . In countries such as Sweden and Denmark these activities are counted in the national income statistics. . . . in Italy similar activities take place within the household and are not counted in the statistics. (Tanzi, 2005, p. 31)

This may mean that the GDP of Sweden and its per capita income are overestimated compared to those of Italy and that the rate of growth of Sweden was inflated by the increasing hiring of women during the years of expansion for the welfare state, especially in the 1950s, 1960s, and 1970s. It also raises inevitable questions about the impact of the welfare state on the family as a social institution. The more weight one assigns to the importance of the family, the less attractive the Swedish welfare state appears. In this unintentional impact on the family, the Nordic welfare states have approached the intentions of the Bolshevik reformers that had little use for the institution of the family. Women were probably the greatest winners, at least in terms of individual freedom, making them the strongest supporters of government spending and welfare policies.

### 13.4. From 1990 to the Present

Although it has been often reported that the Nordic welfare state is popular with the majority of the citizens of these countries, there were always shares of the population that were less enthused with it. These included some prominent economists, such as Assar Lindbeck. They worried about the *long-run* impact on incentives of high taxes and spending programs. Even within egalitarian and homogeneous populations, these disincentive effects could become important with the passing of time. It is realistic to hypothesize that the disincentive effects are likely to grow over time, especially if some social norms begin to weaken. The years used by some economists to assess the impact of the welfare states on growth rates were too few to fully reflect what Lindbeck (1995) called the "hazardous long-run dynamic." Furthermore, as mentioned earlier, economic growth is likely to be influenced by more than one factor, and there were various factors that were changing over the years.

The strong social norms that existed in these countries imply that it may take longer for the negative impact of the disincentive effects of the welfare state to be fully felt in these countries than in countries where such norms do not exist or are less strong. However, as time passes the high tax burdens could induce some of the most talented individuals, and some enterprises, to decide that they would gain by locating in more fiscally friendly environments. A more globalized world makes this more likely and easier, and there have been threats from some enterprises that they might move to lower-tax countries. In addition, the generous, universal social programs could encourage a growing number of individuals to reduce their effort and their active participation in the economy. They could do this by faking illnesses, invalidity, and other disabling characteristics or by delaying their entrance in the labor force. Absenteeism from work, justified by fake illnesses, and delayed entrees in the work force have, in fact, been reported to have become an increasing problem. Finally, more immigrants might be encouraged to move in and become residents by the generosity of the programs (Mehrez, 2002; and Henreckson and Person, 2002). Immigrants now account for a significant share of the Swedish population and probably for a larger share of the population at the working age. Immigrants have increased the fiscal costs of the welfare state and, in both Denmark and Sweden, have stimulated some conservative reaction against welfare programs. More conservative governments have also been voted in. It is difficult to predict how the hazardous, long-run dynamic that was forecast by Assar Lindbeck will evolve and how the welfare states of the Nordic countries will look, say, two three decades from now. This dynamic must be empirically important and must grow with time in order to have an impact not only on the static efficiency of these countries (on the level of their GDPs) but also on their dynamic efficiency (on their rate of growth). For the latter, it may depend on what they do in other policy areas. It is likely that the welfare systems will become less generous than they are now and far less generous than they were a couple decades ago.

In the 1980s, after the welfare states had become fully mature, and after the golden period of economic growth was over, the need for some adjustment to the policies that had been introduced after 1950 became evident. The economies of Scandinavian countries slowed down considerably in the 1970s and the 1980s (Table 13.3). Denmark was the first of these countries to face an economic crisis, in the late 1970s and early 1980s. Finland and Sweden followed in the early 1990s. Sweden experienced a sharp recession in the 1990–93 period, when its rate of growth turned negative for three consecutive years.[6] In Finland, the breakup of the Soviet Union, which had been a major trading partner, contributed to the deep crisis.

These slowdowns or recessions indicated that some policy changes were necessary. Major reforms were introduced, and they contributed significantly to the revival of the economies of these countries over the following years. While some of the generosity of the welfare state was scaled down, its main characteristics remained. It can be argued that the positive effects of the new reforms on the economy counterbalanced the disincentive effects that the welfare policies might still be having over the following years. It is difficult to tell whether, over the long run, the positive impact of the more recent reforms or the negative impact of the earlier reforms will prevail. In any case, after the reforms of the 1980s and, especially, the 1990s were introduced, the growth rates of several of these countries recovered (Table 13.3). The recovery in the growth rates was accompanied by some increase in income inequality. These countries have had significant increases in Gini coefficients between the mid-1980s and mid-2000s.

The main reforms introduced concerned the tax system, large reductions in public spending, and reforms in pension systems. In addition, several specific efficiency-enhancing policies were enacted. These reforms were important enough to make a difference, for years to come, in the performances of these economies.

The *tax reforms* aimed largely at reducing the disincentive effects that the existing tax systems were having, or were believed to be having, on economic activities. Thus, a major objective of the tax reforms was the reduction in marginal tax rates, without losing too much in total tax revenue. As two Swedish economists put it, "The major tax reform [in Sweden] in 1991 essentially implied a broadening in the tax base, a considerable decrease in marginal tax rates, especially for high levels of income, and an increase in the value-added tax." The objective was to induce higher-income workers to increase their work effort while preserving tax revenue. Similar reforms were introduced in other Nordic countries. All of them now have the highest rates for the value-added taxes, taxes that in other countries are considered damaging taxes to lower-income people, and relatively normal tax rates on workers and especially on high-income individuals. To compensate for some of the negative effects of these changes on the income distribution, transfer payments to household with children were increased by that reform (Aronsson and Palme, 1998, p. 39).

A large literature has attempted to determine empirically the impact of high tax burdens and, especially, of high marginal tax rates on labor and capital incomes on the economic performance of countries in general and Nordic countries and Sweden in particular (e.g., Gustafsson and Klevmarken, 1993). Much of the theoretical literature on taxation has argued that high marginal tax rates and high tax burdens must have negative effects on economic incentives and on economic growth. For example, Ed Prescott, who won the Nobel Prize for Economics in 2004, analyzed the effects of high labor tax wedges on hours worked (Prescott, 2002). He attributed differences in living standards between the United States and large EU countries to differences in these wedges. Martti Hetemäki (2003) has also shown that high tax rates on labor reduce the number of hours worked (Figure 13.1; also see Alesina, Glaeser, and Sacerdote, 2005; T. Andersen, 2010; and Strand, 1999). No economist has argued that high tax rates have positive impacts on work or other incentives.

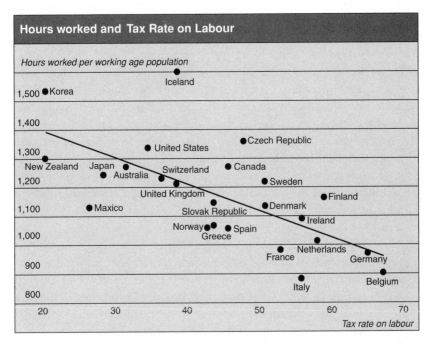

Figure 13.1. Hours worked and tax rate on labor. *Source*: Hetemäki, 2003, p. 211.

The literature that links taxes to growth, however, suffers from two fundamental shortcomings: it ignores how revenue is used; and it attributes economic performance to only or mainly to one factor, taxes, while, over a period of time, there are many other potentially important changes in economic policies going on. These policies may reinforce or neutralize the effect of taxes on economic performance. However, an important study by an IMF team on Sweden concluded that while "links between growth and government intervention . . . are complex, and still imperfectly understood . . . there is good reason to suppose that the high levels of taxation . . . have depressed growth" (Thakur et al., 2003, p. 45).

A major tax innovation that aimed at reducing the disincentive effects of high marginal tax rates in Nordic countries was the introduction of dual income taxes (DIT). These taxes separate the incomes received by enterprises and individuals from the returns to their capital investments and the incomes received by dependent workers and by self-employed operators from their economic activities. The former income (the income from capital sources) is taxed by the DIT at final, proportional and lower rates, whereas the income from labor activities (for dependent or independent workers) is taxed at progressive rates (Sørensen, 1994).

In the past, all the income of individuals had been aggregated and taxed at highly progressive rates. This meant that the income from capital sources (interest, dividends, capital gains, rents) often became the marginal or top income, the one taxed at the highest marginal rates, for individuals who also had labor income. This high taxation of capital income encouraged individuals to take the money out of the countries, to invest it abroad, often in tax haven locations. It led to capital flight and encouraged tax evasion. This incentive was strengthened when inflation distorted the capital incomes through the effect (e.g., the "Fisher effect") that inflation has on incomes from interest and from other capital sources. The combination of the effect from inflation with the high marginal tax rates created situations in which the real, effective tax rates on the capital incomes of individuals could easily exceed 100 percent (Tanzi, 1980 and 1988).

The dual income tax reduced the rate on capital incomes to make it broadly equivalent to the corporate income tax rate that in Nordic countries has been a modest 28 percent in Sweden and Norway and an even lower 25 and 26 percent in Denmark and Finland. The change to the DIT improved incentives significantly, while it probably contributed to increases in Gini coefficients. At the same time, the top statutory tax rates were also lowered, reducing tax wedges and, once again, potentially increasing income inequality.

An OECD questionnaire, on redistribution by government, indicates that the redistributive impact of direct taxes in the Nordic countries is among the weakest of the countries surveyed: at the time of the survey, in 2000, the richest 30 percent paid a smaller proportion and the poorest 30 percent paid a higher proportion of total taxes than other country groups (Table 13.4).[7] The contrast in the redistributive effect of taxes between the Nordic countries and the Anglo-Saxon countries is particularly sharp. In the Nordic countries, the poorest 30 percent pays taxes equivalent to 11.3 percent of the total, whereas in the Anglo-Saxon countries it pays only 5.1 percent. On the other hand, the richest 30 percent pays 53.1 percent of total taxes in the Nordic countries and 63.8 percent in the Anglo-Saxon countries. This different is partly explained by the fact that the Nordic countries have more even *market income* distributions and, in greater part, by the fact that tax policies in Anglo-Saxon countries attempt to concentrate the tax payment more on the richer groups.[8] Broadly similar results were also reported by the data in Table 1.5.

Table 13.4 shows also the distribution of general government transfers among different income deciles.[9] Once again there are significant differences among the three groups of countries shown in the table. In the Anglo-Saxon

Table 13.4. *Distribution of taxes and government transfers on different income deciles for selected countries*

| Countries | Taxes | | General government transfers | |
|---|---|---|---|---|
| | Poorest 30% | Richest 30% | Poorest 30% | Richest 30% |
| Denmark | 14.1 | 48.7 | 43.4 | 17.7 |
| Finland | 9.8 | 56.8 | 43.2 | 16.4 |
| Norway | 10.2 | 53.8 | 45.1 | 18.3 |
| Sweden | 11.0 | 53.3 | 33.7 | 25.8 |
| Average | 11.3 | 53.1 | 41.4 | 19.5 |
| Belgium | 3.9 | 63.5 | 36.0 | 22.5 |
| France | 8.7 | 67.9 | 35.6 | 25.1 |
| Germany | 10.0 | 53.6 | 31.7 | 30.7 |
| Italy | 6.7 | 62.3 | 20.5 | 34.5 |
| Netherlands | 11.7 | 52.2 | 45.8 | 18.1 |
| Average | 8.2 | 59.9 | 33.9 | 26.2 |
| Australia | 3.7 | 65.1 | 62.3 | 6.5 |
| Canada | 6.2 | 60.4 | 41.5 | 20.8 |
| Ireland | 3.3 | 66.4 | 47.1 | 14.8 |
| United Kingdom | 6.0 | 61.0 | 54.5 | 11.7 |
| United States | 6.3 | 65.3 | 41.4 | 23.0 |
| Average | 5.1 | 63.8 | 49.4 | 15.4 |

*Sources:* OECD questionnaire on distribution of household incomes (2000). Arranged from table 7, p. 31, of Förster and Pearson, 2002.

countries, those in the poorest 30 percent were the major beneficiaries of these transfers. They received almost 50 percent of the total. In the European (non-Nordic) countries, the poorest 30 percent of the individuals received marginally more than 30 percent of government transfers (33.9 percent), whereas the richest 30 percent received a little less than 30 percent (26.2 percent). In the Nordic countries, the poorest 30 percent received 41.4 percent of transfers, whereas the richest 30 percent received 19.5 percent. The contrast between Italy and Australia is particularly striking. In Italy the poorest 30 percent receives only 20.5 percent of government transfers, whereas in Australia it receives 62.3 percent.

Additional information gathered by the OECD questionnaire indicates that between the mid-1980s and the mid-1990s there were large shifts in government transfers and indirect taxes among the different income deciles (Table 13.5). Table 13.5 seems to indicate that, during the troubled decade between the mid-1980s and the mid-1990s, the governments of the Nordic countries attempted to protect the poorest 30 percent of the population by transferring some benefits from the top 70 percent of the population,

Table 13.5. *Changes in redistribution between mid-1980s and mid-1990s*
*(percentage points)*

| | Government transfers | | | Taxes | | |
|---|---|---|---|---|---|---|
| Country | Poorest 30% | Middle 40% | Richest 30% | Poorest 30% | Middle 40% | Richest 30% |
| Denmark | 5.1 | −1.4 | −3.7 | 0.2 | −2.2 | 2.0 |
| Finland | 2.2 | 1.5 | −3.8 | −1.1 | −1.0 | 2.1 |
| Norway | 3.2 | −1.3 | −2.0 | −2.9 | −1.8 | 4.6 |
| Sweden | 1.3 | 0.6 | −1.9 | −1.3 | −0.7 | 2.0 |

*Sources:* OECD questionnaire on distribution of household incomes (2000). Arranged from table 7, p. 31, of Förster and Pearson, 2002.

and especially from the top 30 percent, toward the poorest 30 percent. At the same time, there were higher taxes on the richest 30 percent and tax reduction on the lower 70 percent. Thus, the introduction of the DITs must not have been immediately and relatively damaging to the poorer groups, at least up to the mid-1990s.

We shift now to the *changes* that took place *in government expenditure* after 1995, when the countries emerged from the crises and were moving toward a period of improved growth and normal conditions. It has not been appreciated how much these countries reduced their public spending in this period. Table 13.6 shows the behavior of total government expenditure and some categories of spending between 1995 and 2007 for which there are data collected on a strictly comparable basis by the European Commission. Unfortunately, data for Norway are not available. It should be noted that

Table 13.6. *Government expenditure in selected countries, 1995–2007*
*(percentages of GDP)*

| | Denmark | | Finland | | Sweden | |
|---|---|---|---|---|---|---|
| | 1995 | 2007 | 1995 | 2007 | 1995 | 2007 |
| Social benefits in kind | 17.0 | 17.6 | 14.3 | 14.8 | 18.7 | 19.2 |
| Social transfers not in kind | 19.5 | 15.8 | 21.9 | 16.2 | 20.4 | 16.9 |
| Interest payments | 5.9 | 1.5 | 4.0 | 1.3 | 6.7 | 1.8 |
| Other expenditures | 16.8 | 15.1 | 21.2 | 17.5 | 21.3 | 17.7 |
| Total expenditure | 59.2 | 50.0 | 61.4 | 49.8 | 67.1 | 55.6 |

*Note:* The table is based on ESA 95 definitions.
*Sources:* Arranged by author from the Statistical Annex to *Public Finance in EMU, 2008* (European Commission).

the data start in 1995, when some of the adjustment had already been made. The table shows that over the 1995–2007 period total public expenditure, as a share of GDP, was cut by 9.2 percent in Denmark, 11.6 percent in Finland, and 11.6 percent in Sweden. These are, indeed, very large cuts. In spite of these reductions, or because of them, the economies of these countries performed very well in this period.

Table 13.6 indicates that there was no reduction in spending for "social benefits *in kind*" and, thus, presumably no firing of government employees engaged in these activities. However, there were significant reductions in "social transfers *not in kind*," which are largely cash transfers. In this category the cuts, as percentages of GDP, were 3.7 in Denmark, 5.7 in Finland, and 3.5 in Sweden. The table shows also large savings in interest payments connected with the fall in public debts and the fiscal surpluses that developed over the period. There were savings in other expenditures not connected with welfare, and these savings helped finance the expenditure on in-kind social benefits.

These are interesting results, especially when it is recalled that the cut in public spending and the reduction in public debts and in fiscal deficits did not damage economic performance but rather seem to have strengthened it; and that, although there was some increase in inequality, as measured by Gini coefficients, the position of these countries in the UNDP Human Development Index did not change. In 2006 information from *Eurostat NewCronos* database gave the following Gini coefficients for these countries: 0.24 for Denmark, 0.26 for Finland, and 0.24 for Sweden.[10] These countries continued to have indexes of poverty that were among the lowest in the EU-25.

We now turn to *the pension reforms* that introduced one of the most innovative reforms in the 1990s. In the 1980s the Swedish pension system had started to be seen as financially unsustainable in its then present form because of the sharp deceleration of the growth rate of the economy and the increasing life expectancy of the Swedish population. Following guidelines established by the Swedish Parliament in 1994, and after several years of intense political debate, a new pension system was introduced in June 1998. The new system would apply fully and immediately to those born after 1953, but it would be phased in gradually for those born between 1938 and 1956. The new system is somewhat complex. The following are its main characteristics.

The reformed Swedish pension system is largely financed through contributions paid by workers and employers and not through general taxes. The basis for the "pensionable income" includes wages and salaries and all cash benefits (sickness benefits, unemployment benefits, study grants, parental benefits, and so on) that individuals receive from the state or the employers. There is an upper limit to the pensionable income. The total contribution to the pension fund is 18.5 percent of the pensionable income, of which 16 percent goes to an "income pension" and 2.5 percent goes to a "premium pension." The 18.5 percent paid creates pension entitlements on the part of residents. The 16 percent and the 2.5 percent are placed into two separate (fictitious) pension accounts. The value of these accounts grows in line with the annual amounts contributed, the years of contributions, and the "interest" earned by the accounts. The "interest" received by the "income pension" (by the 16 percent) is determined by the annual growth rate of wages and salaries in Sweden. It is thus a virtual interest rate. For the 2.5 percent that goes to the "premium pension," the future pensioners can choose the securities in which to invest the money set aside. The return to this account is determined by the actual rate of returns on these securities. The pensioner is free to change, at any time and without cost, the choice of investments in the premium account.

There is also a state-financed "guarantee pension" for all individuals with low or no "income pensions." This "guarantee pension" can be drawn only at age 65 or later. There is no set pensionable age at which individuals must retire in Sweden, but individuals can start to draw "income" or "premium" pensions at the age of 61 if they choose. The longer they wait, the larger becomes the annual income pension, because the postponement makes the account grow and the (remaining) life expectancy of the pensioner (the years that remain at the time of retirement) fall. The pension received at retirement is set in line with the *average* life expectancy at that age. The Swedish pension system (income and premium pension) is largely designed to be a pay-as-you-go (PAYG) system. There is an automatic "balancing mechanisms" that adjusts the liabilities of the pension system in line with the growth in average income (for more details, see Thakur, et al. 2003, p. 95; and Settergren, 2001). The "guarantee pension" is financed by the central government budget. It takes into account pensions (below the limit) that the individuals may be receiving and complements them.

In Sweden there are now two types of social insurance benefits: those based on rights acquired at work, and those acquired through official residence. A "guarantee pension" is acquired only by residing in Sweden. However, one need not live in Sweden to receive an "income pension" or a "premium pension."

The pension rights of each person are established by the social insurance office every year. These rights make up the pension balance of each individual form. As mentioned earlier, the reform of the pension system was forced by the slowing down of economic growth in Sweden in the 1970s and 1980s, which had made the existing system clearly unsustainable. There were also some perceived inequities that needed to be corrected. In 2010 the employer's contribution was 10.21 percent of wages, while employees paid 7 percent. In time, the two sides of the contributions will become equal. Because of the way contributions and payments are structured (the "balancing mechanism"), the system is expected to remain broadly in balance in future years.

For the pension systems of the other Nordic countries, we limit ourselves here to short descriptions of their main features. Norway introduced a comprehensive national insurance reform called Folketrygden in 1966. It replaced several different insurance systems (old age, disability, sickness, unemployment, assistance to families with children) with one system. Initial steps toward a pension coverage for the whole population in Norway go back to the 1880s, at the time of Bismarck's reforms in Germany. In 1894 a parliamentary worker commission was set up. It prepared reports in 1899 and 1902, but no legislation followed (Ervik, 2001). These and other steps did not lead to any reform until 1935, when an old-age pension system, financed by a 1 percent tax on the income of individuals and companies, was enacted. The pension was universal, but it was very low and "means tested," so that not every old person received it. The income testing was abolished in 1957 when the pension system became universal.

In 1967 an additional, income-related pension was introduced. The required earning period to get a full pension was set at 40 years. Thus, the first full pensions would be paid only in 2007. A special income supplement for low pensions was added in 1969. With several modifications, that basic system continued after 1967. As in Sweden, the slowdown in economic growth in the 1980s and demographic changes raised questions of future sustainability and the need for reform. In the period between 1985 and 2000, there was a debate on the need for pension reform. In 1995 a committee was set up to assess the finances of the pension system. The system is expected to undergo further reform in future years.

The Norwegian pension system is broadly similar to but not identical with the Swedish one. The pensionable age is set at 67. The system consists of a "basic pension," to which all official residents are entitled, and a "supplementary pension" that is earnings related. Those with no or small supplementary pensions are entitled to a special supplement to the basic pensions that is income tested. A full public pension is received after 40 years of contributions, which are made between the ages of 16 and 66. There are means-tested supplements for spouse and children. There are also disability pensions for those who have earned the right to a pension but whose capacity to work has fallen by at least 50 percent. Surviving spouses have a right to a pension if they meet some conditions.

The full "basic" pension for a single person that is 15.6 percent of *average* earnings, plus any special supplement forms the "minimum" pension. Starting in 2003, the minimum pension has been indexed to average earnings. Increases in the special supplement were introduced in 2008 and in 2010. The minimum pension is about 31 percent of average earnings. Starting in 2006, employers have been required to make a minimum contribution of 2 percent of the earnings of their employees, up to a given level, to a defined-contribution pension plan. The benefits can be taken out only after the age of 67 and over a minimum period of 10 years. There are, additionally, voluntary private occupational pension schemes.

About two-thirds of employees work in businesses that participate in early retirement programs. The scheme, introduced in 1989, allows retirement from age 62. Individuals can also retire after the age of 67. In this case, they can work and receive a pension at the same time. The extra work does not entitle them to higher pension rights. Until 1973, the pension age had been 70. As in Sweden, the income from pension is taxed but at lower rates than normal labor income.

In Finland, the first general pension system was introduced in 1938. It was an earnings-based system with individual accounts. In 1956 the system was changed to an income-related pension. After 1956, the central labor organizations have played a major role in the reforms of the system. From 1961 to 1993, private employers provided all the funding for earnings-related pensions. However, the recession of the early 1990s made this system unsustainable. In 1992–93 it was agreed that employees should also contribute. Their initial contribution was 3 percent of wages, against 15 percent paid by the employers. However, the understanding was that in the future the two sides would contribute equal shares. Other changes were introduced at that time to reduce the cost of pensions, including the raising of the retirement age and extending the period of employment used to calculate the pensionable income.

In 2005 another significant pension reform introduced the following changes:

1. Employees could choose to retire any time between the ages of 63 and 68. The early retirement pension was abolished.

2. The pension accrual was raised from 2.5 to 4.5 percent between the ages of 63 and 68, and from 1.5 to 1.9 percent between the ages of 53 and 62.
3. Benefits would be calculated on the basis of the whole working life earnings, and not on the basis of selected best years.
4. The age limit for part-time pensions was raised.
5. A life expectancy coefficient was introduced. An automatic cut in pensions will accompany increases in life expectancy.

The reform's objectives were to encourage individuals to extend their working life; to take into account changing demographics, including increasing life expectancy and the shrinking labor force, to make pension systems sustainable; and to relate the pensions more closely to actual contributions. The 2005 reform applies only to pensions that accrue after 2005.

Finland has two statutory pension systems, a national pension, financed through general revenue, and an earnings-related pension, financed through contributions. The first provides all residents with a very small income. The second is related to earnings and to years of work, and can provide much higher pensions. To qualify for the national pension, one must have lived in Finland for at least three years, after the age of 16, and must be covered under the Finnish social security system. Also one must not receive other pensions or benefits above a given level. No contribution is necessary to qualify for this national pension. Old-age pensions can be obtained at age 65 (or for a lower pension at 62). Waiting beyond 65 increases the amount received in line with the fall in the average life expectancy at that age. There are also disability and (long-term) unemployment pensions. The unemployment pension can be received only by individual born before 1950, so not too many qualify.

The earnings-related pensions depend on the years of contribution and on the size of the earnings. Since 2010, the pension benefits has been reduced to reflect the increase in life expectancy from that date on. There is no floor and no ceiling to pensionable earnings. Differences in costs of living among municipalities are taken into account in determining pension payments. These differences can be substantial. In 2008 the average annual contributions *by employers* to social insurance schemes were 16.80 percent of wages and salaries for the employees pension, 2.06 percent for unemployment insurance, 1.51 percent for the national pension insurance, 1.97 percent for the national health insurance, and 1.05 percent for employment accident insurance. For *the insured*, the social insurance contribution rates for 2008 were contributions to employment pensions: 4.10 to 5.20; to unemployment insurance, 0.34 percent; to medical care coverage, 1.24 to 1.41; and to daily allowance coverage, 0.67 to 0.81. Between 1993 and 2008, the share of all pension expenditure into GDP fell from 13.8 percent to 11.0 percent (see Kela, 2009).

The pension system of Denmark is broadly similar to that of other Nordic countries (OECD, 2005). There is a public *basic* scheme that is equivalent to about 17 percent of average earnings in the country and is income tested for low-income pensioners and is indexed annually in line with average earnings. The income testing is against all sources of income additional to the basic pension amount. The normal pension age is 65 and requires 40 years of residence.

In addition to the public basic scheme, there are two other schemes based on individuals' contribution records, the ATP and the SP, the special pension saving scheme. The ATP (labor-market supplementary pension) was introduced in 1964. The contributions for the ATP are split between the employer, who pays two-thirds, and the employee, who pays one-third. The contribution amount depends on the hours worked per month and not on the wages earned. The voluntary occupational schemes are fully funded, defined-contribution schemes with almost universal coverage. The contributions, agreed between social partners, vary between 9 and 17 percent of earnings and are withdrawn at retirement time as annuities. The interest rate paid on the accounts is 1.5 percent. Pension payments are subject to income taxes.

## 13.5. General Conclusions

In judging the economic performance of the Nordic countries in recent years, several factors must be kept in mind. First is the significant adjustment in *macroeconomic policies* that these countries made especially in the second half of the 1990s and the large cuts in public spending and in tax rates. These may have set in motion a virtuous cycle that would be expected to bring economic benefits for some time to come. Finland, which cut public spending and taxes on labor income the most, also grew at the fastest rate in the following years. Second, these countries undertook several other important *structural reforms*, aimed at making their economies more efficient. For example, they invested more than other countries in "training," not only for younger workers but also for older workers who had been displaced from their jobs. They increased their spending in research and development (R&D). This helped make some of their enterprises highly innovative and global leaders in particular area. They simplified the procedures and reduced the cost of starting a new business. This was particularly important in Denmark, where it takes now only a few days and zero cost to start a new business. This compares with hundreds of days and high costs in many other countries. They were quick in introducing information technology in the schools. The ratio of students to computers has been reported to be 2.8 in Denmark, 5.0 in Finland, and 3.4 in Sweden, much lower than in other countries.

The quality of their education systems, especially at the tertiary level, is considered particularly good, particularly in Finland, followed by Denmark and, to a lesser extent, Sweden. Denmark does quite well in the area of labor regulation, an area in which the other two countries, and especially Sweden, do less well. None of the three countries performs well in terms of unemployment legislation, which is seen by economists as being too generous. The "net replacement rates" for unemployed workers, at the average production wage level, remain high (around 80 percent) for periods that are considered too long, thus potentially encouraging workers to stay unemployed for longer periods. However, social pressures on the unemployed and a "good work ethic" reduce this problem. Good "social norms" continue to help these countries. Firms (and government offices) encounter fewer obstacles in firing and hiring workers than in most other continental European countries. The average days lost per year because of strikes have been reported to be very low for Sweden and relatively low for Denmark and Finland. However, standard working time per year is low, especially in Denmark. Annual weeks worked were low, and absences from work for various reasons were high (Alesina and Giavazzi, 2006, p. 48).

In the field of regulations in general, Finland scores well, followed by Denmark and Sweden. By and large, the three countries do well in this area, showing that a high level of public spending and taxes is not inconsistent with efficient regulatory quality (Kaufman, Kray, and Mastruzzi, 2009). Good scores are also obtained by these countries in the area of corruption, governance, red tape, and quality of the judiciary. Remarkably, Finland, Denmark, and Sweden have among the best scores in the Global Competitiveness Index, prepared by the World Economic Forum. This is a consequence of their good and transparent regulatory system and the fact that these countries, and especially Sweden and Finland, are seen as innovation drivers.

Going back to the question of the level and the quality of public spending, as mentioned earlier, recent studies have concluded that the public sectors of these countries, and especially those of Finland and Sweden, do well in terms of "performance." They deliver good results in terms of those socioeconomic indicators that governments presumably wish to improve. The present discussion broadly confirms this picture. But when the ratio of public spending, which is very high, is also taken into consideration and is considered as a cost of producing those indicators, these countries do less well in terms of "efficiency." In other words, the good results in the socioeconomic indicators are obtained at too high a cost in terms of taxes paid and perhaps of personal liberty lost (Afonso, Schuknecht and Tanzi, 2005). Recent surveys by the OECD have shown that workers in Nordic countries share (with their Japanese counterparts) the lowest opportunities for advancement in their work. Furthermore, Swedes report that they find work "most stressful" and would prefer to spend less time at their working places. As mentioned earlier, they work the lowest number of hours and weeks per year and are absent from their jobs more often.

In conclusion, focusing only on the level of taxes and public spending would lead one to conclude that in terms of economic performance, and over the long run, these countries ought to perform less well than countries with lower taxes and lower disincentives connected with them. This is the aspect that has been stressed by some economists. However, there are so many other policies pursued by these countries in which they have done very well that inevitably the question must be asked as to which factors have the strongest impact. For the time being, the economies of these countries have been benefiting from the cuts in marginal tax rates, in public spending, in public debts, in fiscal deficits, in the future cost of pensions, and from other important structural reforms. How long the inertial speed created by these relatively recent reforms will be maintained is uncertain. However, the conclusion must inevitably mention that particular characteristics of these countries (community spirit, more homogeneous populations, little corruption, and so on) seem to indicate that they are more likely to be more immune than other countries to the consequences of high public spending and high taxes. This may mean that if other countries attempted to have the same welfare states as the Nordic countries, they would pay a higher price in terms of economic growth. Their systems have changed more than most observers realize since the early 1980s. The welfare systems that were introduced in the countries of Northern Europe are probably not exportable because they depend on social characteristics that do not exist elsewhere. Only time will tell whether the "hazardous welfare dynamics," mentioned by Lindbeck, will grow in strength to the point of damaging these economies and making these systems unsustainable.

# References

Afonso, Antonio, Ludger Schuknecht, and Vito Tanzi. 2005. "Public Sector Efficiency: an International Comparison." *Public Choice* 123: 321–47.

Alesina, Alberto, and Francesco Giavazzi. 2006. *The Future of Europe: Reform or Decline* (Cambridge, Mass.: MIT Press).

Alesina, A., E. Glaeser, and B. Sacerdote. 2005. "Work and Leisure in the US and Europe: Why so Different?" *NBER Macroeconomics Annual,* edited by Mark Gertler and Kenneth Rogoff (Cambridge Mass.: MIT Press).

Andersen, Carsten, and Peter Skjodt. 2007. "Pension Institutions and Annuities in Denmark." World Bank, Policy Research Working Paper No. 4437 (December).

Andersen, Torben M. 2010. "Why Do Scandinavians Work?" CESifo Working Paper No. 3068 (May).

Anderson, Martin, and Christen Gunnarsson. 2005. "Egalitarianism in the Process of Modern Economic Growth: The Case of Sweden," background paper to *World Development Report 2006: Equity and Development* (Washington, D.C.: World Bank).

Aronsson, Thomas, and Marten Palme. 1998. "A Decade of Tax and Benefit Reforms in Sweden: Effects on Labour Supply, Welfare and Inequality." *Economica,* n.s., 65, no. 257 (February): 39–67.

Atkinson, Anthony B. 1995. "The Welfare State and Economic Performance." *National Tax Journal* 48: 171–98.

1999. *The Economic Consequences of Rolling Back the Welfare State* (Cambridge, Mass.: MIT Press).

Atkinson, Anthony, B., and G. V. Mogensen, eds. 1993. *Welfare and Work Incentives: A North European Perspective* (Oxford: Clarendon Press).

Boli, John. 1991. "Sweden: Is There a Viable Third Sector?," in *Between States and Markets,* edited by Robert Wuthnow (Princeton: Princeton University Press), pp. 94–124.

Barr, Nicholas. 1992. "Economic Theory and the Welfare State: A Survey and Interpretation." *Journal of Economic Literature* 30, no. 2: 741–803.

2004. *Economics of the Welfare State* (New York: Oxford University Press).

Costabile, Lilia, edited by, 2008. *Institutions for Social Well-Being: Alternatives for Europe* (Houndmill, Basingstoke and New York: Palgrave Macmillan).

Disney, Richard. 2000. "The Impact of Tax and Welfare Policies on Employment and Unemployment in OECD Countries." IMF Working Paper WP/00/164.

Einhorn, Eric, and John Logue. 1989. *Modern Welfare States: Politics and Policies in Social Democratic Scandinavia* (New York: Praeger).

Erixon, L. 2008. "The Rehn-Meidner Model in Sweden: Its Rise, Challenges and Survival." Research Papers in Economics, Department of Economics, Stockholm University.

Ervik, Rune, and Stein Kuhnle. 1996. "The Nordic Welfare Model and the European Union," in *Comparative Welfare Systems: The Nordic Model in a Period of Change,* edited by Bengt Greve (Basingstoke: Macmillan, 1996).

Ervik, Rune, 2001. "Pension Reform in Norway." Norwegian Centre for Research in Organization and Management (February 28).

Esping-Anderson, Gosta. 1985. *Politics against Markets: the Social Democratic Road to Power* (Princeton: Princeton University Press).

1990. *The Three Worlds of Welfare Capitalism* (Cambridge: Polity Press).

2007. "Sociological Explanations of Changing Income Distributions." *American Behavioral Scientist* 50, no. 5: 639–57.

European Commission. 2009. Public Finance in EMU, 2008, Brussells.

Forbes. 2010. "Billionaires, The World's Richest People," Special Edition, April 26.

Freeman, Richard B., Robert Topel, and Birgitta Swedenborg, eds. 1997. *The Welfare State in Transition: Reforming the Swedish Model* (Chicago: University of Chicago Press).

Förster, Michael, and Mark Pearson. 2002. "Income Distribution and Poverty in the OECD Area: Trends and Driving Forces," *OECD Economic Studies*, no. 34.

Fukuyama, Francis. 1995. *Trust: The Social Virtues and the Creation of Prosperity* (New York: Simon and Schuster).

Golinowska, Stanistawa, Peter Hengstenberg, and Maciez Zukowski, eds. 2009. *Diversity and Commonality in European Social Policies: The Forging of a European Social Model* (Warsaw: Friedrich-Ebert-Stiffung and Wydawnictwo Naukowe Scholar).

Gustafsson, Bjorn. 1995. "Foundations of the Swedish Model." *Nordic Journal of Political Economy* 22: 5–26.

2008. "The Swedish Model in the Era of Integration and Globalization," in *Institutions for Social Well-Being*, edited by Lilia Costabile (Houndmills: Palgrave Macmillan), pp. 176–97.

Gustafsson, Bjorn, and N. Anders Klevmarken. 1993. "Taxes and Transfers in Sweden: Incentive Effects on Labour Supply," in *Welfare and Work Incentives: A North European Perspective*, edited by Anthony Atkinson and G. Mogensen (Oxford: Clarendon Press), pp. 50–134.

Henreckson, Magnus. 1996. "Sweden's Relative Economic Performance: Lagging Behind or Staying on Top?" *Economic Journal* 106: 1747–59.

Henreckson, Magnus, and Mats Person. 2002. "The Effects of Sick Leave on Changes in the Sickness Insurance System." SSE/EFI *Working Paper Series in Economics and Finance*, no. 444 (Stockholm).

Henriksson, Jens. 2003. "The Use of Fiscal Rules in Sweden," in *Fostering Economic Growth in Europe*, Oesterreichische Nationalbank, 31st Economics Conference (Vienna).

Hetemäki, Martti. 2003. "Experience with Public Sector Reform in Finland," in *Fostering Economic Growth in Europe*, Oesterreichische Nationalbank, 31st Economics Conference (Vienna).

Johnson, Simon, and James Kwak. 2010. *13 Bankers: The Wall Street Takeover and the Next Financial Meltdown* (New York: Pantheon Books).

Kaufmann, D., A. Kraay, and M. Mastruzzi. 2009. "Governance Matters VIII: Aggregate and Individual Governance Indicators, 1996–2008." Policy Research Working Paper No. 4978.

Kela (Finland). 2009. *Statistical Yearbook of the Social Insurance Institution, 2008*.

2010. "Finland Pensions" (Home Page).

Korpi, Walter, and Joakim Palme. 1996. "Eurosclerosis and the Sclerosis of Objectivity: On the Role of Values Among Economic Experts." *Economic Journal* 106: 1727–46.

1998. "The Paradox of Redistribution and Strategies of Equality: Welfare State Institutions, Inequality, and Poverty in Western Countries." *American Sociological Review* 63, no. 5 (October): 661–87.

Krantz, Olle, and Lennart Schön. 2007. *Swedish Historical National Accounts, 1800–2000* (Lund: Almqvist and Wiksell International).

Kuhnle, Stein. 1998. "The Nordic Approach to General Welfare." *Nordic News Network,* www.nnn.se (March).

Lindbeck, Assar. 1995. "Hazardous Welfare-State Dynamics." *American Economic Review, Papers and Proceedings* 85 (May 1995): 9–15.

——— 1997. "The Swedish Experiment." *Journal of Economic Literature* 25 (September): 1273–1319.

——— 2000. "Swedish Economic Growth in an International Perspective." *Swedish Economic Policy Review* 7, no. 1 (Spring): 7–37.

Lindbeck, Assar, S. Nyberg, and J. W. Weibull. 1999. "Social Norms and Economic Incentives in the Welfare State." *Quarterly Journal of Economics* 114: 1–37.

Maddison, Angus. 1999. "Perspective on Global Economic Progress and Human Development." *Academy of the Social Sciences,* 1.

Mahler, V. A., and D. K. Jesuit. 2006. "Fiscal Redistribution in the Developed Countries: New Insights from the Luxembourg Income Study." *Socio-Economic Review* 4: 483–511.

Mehrez, Gil. 2002. "Sick Leave in Sweden." *Sweden: Selected Issues,* IMF Country Report 02/160 (Washington, D.C.).

OECD. 2008. "Explaining Differences in Hours Worked across OECD Countries." *Economic Policy Reforms* 1: 66–81.

——— 2005. *Pensions at a Glance: Public Policies across OECD Countries* (Paris: OECD).

O'Hara, Kieron. 2004. *Trust: From Socrates to Spin* (Duxford, Cambridge: Icon Books).

*Oxford Review of Economic Policy.* 2006. Vol. 22, no. 3.

Palme, Joakim. 2005. "Features of the Swedish Pension Reform."

——— 2006. "Income Distribution in Sweden." *Japanese Journal of Social Security Policy* 5, no. 1 (June).

Pierson, P. 1994. *Dismantling the Welfare State? Reagan-Thatcher, and the Politics of Retrenchment* (Cambridge: Cambridge University Press).

Prescott, E. C. 2002. "Prosperity and Depression." *American Economic Review* 92, no. 2: 1–15.

——— 2004. "Why Do Americans Work So Much More Than Europeans?" *Economic Theory* 32: 59–85.

Przywara, Bartosz, Nuria Diez Guardia, and Etienne Sail. 2010. "Future Long-Term Care Needs and Public Expenditure in EU Member States," in CESifo Dice Report. *Journal for Institutional Comparisons* 8, no. 2 (Summer).

Putnam, Robert D. 2000. *Bowling Alone* (New York: Simon and Schuster).

Rexed, Knut. 2000. "Public Section Reform: Lessons from the Nordic Countries, the Swedish Experience," Swedish Agency for Administrative Development, Mimeo (May 19).

Rodriguez, Enrique. 1980. *Offentlig inkomstexpansion* (The Expansion of Public Revenue) (Lund: Gleerup).

Roine, Jesper, and Daniel Waldenström. 2008. "The Evolution of Top Incomes in an Egalitarian Society: Sweden, 1903–2004." *Journal of Public Economics* 92, nos. 1–2: 366–87.

Rosen, Sherwin. 1996. "Public Employment and the Welfare State in Sweden." *Journal of Economic Literature* 34, no. 2 (June): 729–40.

Sachs, Jeffrey D. 2008. *Common Wealth: Economics for a Crowded Planet* (New York: Penguin Books).

Schön, Lennart. 2008. "Sweden-Economic Growth and Structural Change, 1800–2000." EH. *Net Encyclopedia*, edited by Robert Whaples, February 10. Available at: http://eh.net/encyclopedia/article/schon.sweden.

Settergren, Ole. 2001. "The Automatic Balance Mechanism of the Swedish Pension System," Stockholm: National Insurance Board of Sweden (unpublished manuscript).

Sinn, Hans-Werner. 1995. "A Theory of the Welfare State." *Scandinavian Journal of Economics* 97: 495–526.

Sørensen, Peter Birch. 1994. "From the Global Income Tax to the Dual Income Tax: Recent Tax Reforms in the Nordic Countries." *International Tax and Public Finance* 1, no. 1 (February): 57–79.

Strand, Henning. 1999. "Some Issues Related to the Equity-Efficiency Trade-Off in the Swedish Tax and Transfer System." *OECD Economics Department Working Papers*, no. 225.

Sweden, Ministry of Health and Social Affairs/National Social insurance Board. 2003. *The Swedish National Pension System* (September).

Sweden, National Tax Authorities. 2008. *Statistical Annual Report, 2008*. In Swedish.

Tanzi, Vito. 1980. "Inflationary Expectations, Ecomomic Activity, Taxes, and Interest Rates," *The American Ecomomic Review*, Vol. 70, No. 1 (March) 12–21.

———. 1988. "The Tax Treatment of Income Taxes and Expenses in Industrial Countries: A Discussion of Recent Changes," in *Taxation*, Proceedings of the 80th annual conference of the National Tax Association – Tax Institute of America (Columbus, Ohio), 128–136.

———. 2005. "Social Protection in a Globalizing World." *Rivista di Politica Economica*, Anno XCVM, Serie III, Fascicolo III–IV, Marzo–Aprile, pp. 25–45.

———. 2008. Review of *Institutions for Social Well-Being: Alternatives for Europe*, edited by L. Costabile (Houndmills: Palgrave Macmillan, 2008). In *Rivista di Politica Economica*, Anno XCVIII, Serie III, Fascicolo V–VI, Maggio-Giugno, pp. 173–87.

Thakur, Subhash, Michael Keen, Balázs Horváth, and Valerie Cerra. 2003. *Sweden's Welfare State: Can the Bumble Bee Keep Flying?* (Washington, D.C.: IMF).

PART FIVE

# ON THE ECONOMIC ROLE
# OF THE STATE IN THE FUTURE

Laissez-faire is all well and good until something goes wrong.
    John Gutfreund, former chief executive of Solomon Brothers

How majestic is the equality of the Law, which permits both rich and poor alike, to sleep under the bridges at night.
    Anatole France (cited by Paul Samuelson, 1968)

# FOURTEEN

# The Economic Role of the State in the Future

## Concluding Reflections

### 14.1. Introduction

What should be, or is likely to be, the economic role of the state in the 21st century? Various factors and different forces are likely to influence that role in the years to come. In the previous chapters that described historical developments from the 19th century on, we reported how countries had managed, some not too badly, with widely different economic roles and different levels of public spending and taxes. Until the 1930s, these levels were very low by modern standards, even though they had been increasing for several decades. For example, in 1930 public spending and taxes were as low as 15 percent of GDP in Sweden and the United States. By comparison, the fiscal deficits in the United States and Great Britain in 2009 and 2010 have been not far from that level. These low tax and spending levels and the government role that they supported must have seemed normal at that time, even though, as reported earlier, some economists, including Keynes, had started calling for more intervention by governments, and the laissez-faire attitude that had prevailed in much of the 19th century was no longer popular. Governments had started to be viewed as potential promoters of social reforms by changed social forces that were acquiring much more political power.

During the second half of the 19th century and much of the 20th century, there was a persistent upward trend, in most advanced countries, in the share of public spending (and tax revenue) in GDP. The increase was justified by expectations that more spending would help satisfy unmet social needs and would increase public welfare. As George Stigler put it half a century ago, ex ante, each expansion in public spending seemed to be justified, and a good case could be made for that additional spending. Generally, the *potential benefits* from the spending attracted much more public attention

305

than the *potential costs* of the taxes (or the additional public debt) needed to finance it. The reason was the classic one, common in economics, and recognized as far back as by Machiavelli 500 years ago in his classic study, *The Prince*: those who receive the benefits are often easily identified, whereas those who bear the costs are more difficult to identify. Thus, the latter have greater difficulties in organizing opposition to spending or to the taxes or the borrowing needed to pay for it.

With the passing of the years, the additional public spending was increasingly connected with programs that, once passed, made that spending difficult to reverse. This created strong political constituencies and expectations that transformed the benefits from the spending into "entitlements," or legal claims against society. As a consequence of this spending, public budgets became larger, less flexible, and less discretionary, tying the hands of future governments. In today's world, the truly discretionary part of the yearly budgets of most countries is often very small, making it difficult to cut public spending without fundamental reforms.

Once the population of a country (or, more often, groups within it) comes to see the government as a potential cow that can be milked, there is no longer a limit to the demands for more public spending. There are literally infinite "needs" of the population, and infinite groups capable of organizing politically, to press for more government spending or for other governmental actions that would benefit them. Especially when the costs are diffused, as they are with public borrowing and with *general* taxes, while the benefits are concentrated on specific groups, as they often are when new programs are introduced, the pressures on governments to spend more will always be present, especially when attitudes toward a larger government role have become more favorable.[1] In these circumstances, there is no longer a specific, identifiable limit to the spending role of the state. The requests for higher spending can continue ad infinitum, as long as there is a political response to them. More democratic governments can justify themselves by their attempts to bring more equality through more generous public spending programs. Because of these pressures, effective constitutional limits, as they exist in Switzerland, can play a role in limiting the increase in the public spending. But even in Switzerland, public spending has increased significantly over the years.

Because of these considerations, it can be asserted that in the real world, and in a political sense, there is no such a thing as an "optimal" level of public spending, or an "optimal" role of the state, as it would seem to be implied by the economic literature on public goods and on market failures that makes the government role seem apolitical. That literature refers to objectively identifiable "market failures" and to specific "public goods" that could be corrected or provided through the action of the state. Therefore, the aggregation of the various governmental interventions to deal with these well-identified failures implies an optimal economic role of the state and one that is apolitical. In the real world, however, the economic role of the state is determined largely by politics and is constrained mainly by financing difficulties and possibly by political and institutional arrangements (constitutions, fiscal rules, etc.) that make it easier or more difficult for policy makers to resist the requests that are continually coming from different groups of citizens. Thus, one can agree with Paul Samuelson: "There are no rules concerning the proper role of government that can be established by a priori reasoning" (1968, p. 37).

In a democratic setting, with a market economy, politics has a direct impact on *all* government functions – resource allocation, redistribution of income, and stabilization of the economy. It may even have an impact on that less well-defined function, the promotion of economic growth or employment. In our earlier survey of developments in the 20th century, we saw that, in the second half of the century, the allocation of resources, used to generate genuine public goods, took a back seat to those used in the redistribution of income (the distribution function) and to the related protection against particular risks (the insurance function), together with the occasional stabilization of the economy.[2] This occurred even though the generation of genuine public goods is far more fundamental to a society than the redistribution of income or stabilization. Societies had existed for thousands of years without the two latter functions being satisfied. However, they could not exist without *some* significant allocation of resources to fundamental public goods (e.g., defense, justice, personal protection) and to essential institutions. Therefore, *the allocation of resources* should, and probably *will, receive more attention in the coming decades*, compared with what it had received in the past half century. But the allocation of resources may take different forms than in the past.

To give some sense of realism to the preceding conclusion it may be pointed out that in the United States federal government purchases (as measured by the National Income and Product Accounts) fell by more than 5 percent of GDP between 1970 and the year 2000, when they reached only about 6 percent of GDP. This level, which has increased only a little since the year 2000 and includes military spending, is very low, perhaps as low as it prevailed a century ago. At the same time, the federal taxes collected barely cover the government transfers that have continued to increase significantly. It is easy to see how low public spending and taxes could be if the U.S.

government focused only on the allocation function, a function that is mainly connected with government purchases (data reported by Marron and Toder, 2011).

## 14.2. Factors Likely to Change the Role of the State in the Future

In Chapter 10, it was argued that there has been an excessive concentration (in the public finance literature) on spending and taxing as tools of fiscal policy and that *all* the fundamental economic functions of the state can be promoted using a wider range of policy instruments. When countries face difficulties in raising revenue to accommodate higher public spending, different instruments, and especially those associated with regulatory tools and with the assumption by government of contingent liabilities, become more important. This is likely to occur in future years because of increasing difficulties to raise the level of taxation in many countries.[3] Thus, the future economic role of the state should not be assessed exclusively in terms of the level and structure of taxes and public spending. That role can change significantly, even without major changes in tax and spending. More attention should be paid to the other policy instruments, although this will make the monitoring of policies more difficult than in the past. These other instruments became much more important during the financial-economic crisis of 2008–9 than they had been in the past. Their importance is likely to increase further in future years.

So far the discussion of the economic role of the state has been country specific. It has been focused on the role that the government of a country has played or plays within the confines of the country's borders. The implicit assumption has been that the economic role of a (national) government stops at the borders of its country. What happens beyond these borders is not its concern. However, we live in an increasingly globalized and interconnected world, and in one where spillovers across countries are becoming more important and visible all the time. These spillovers now increasingly come from the cross-country financial activities of the financial sector. Developments beyond the immediate control of national governments are becoming increasingly significant for each country. Issues of *allocation of resources, redistribution of income*, and *stabilization of economic activity* are thus no longer country specific. They *have an increasingly important global component in today's world.*

This global component has become progressively more important, with the passing of years, because of globalization, new technologies, a global financial market, the consequences of economic and population growth, emigration, and other developments. In some sense, the countries are becoming spacially smaller, and cross-country externalities and connectivity have become larger.[4]

The government role in allocating resources, to deal with public "goods" (or often public "bads") and with significant externalities, has generally been played by *national* governments and has been related to the needs that have existed within a country's borders. However, in today's world, there is a growing necessity to deal with *global* public goods (or "bads") and other allocation problems. The necessity to deal with these global issues is likely to continue to grow in future years. Global problems related to the environment and the global financial market, climate change and global warming, global epidemics, pollution of the air and of the oceans, the excessive exploitation of marine life, global terrorism (some potentially involving atomic devises or biologic agents), global crime, and global conflicts are all examples of global public goods (or "bads") and of significant cross-country externalities that cannot be dealt with by the independent action of national governments. *There is no invisible hand to do the coordinating at the global level.* One should add to these truly *global* public goods the *regional* public goods that are receiving increasing attention on the part of the authorities of different regions (Estevadeordal, Frantz, and Nguyen, 2004; ADB/ADBI, 2009; and Tanzi, 2005).

The international dimension is not limited to the allocation of resources. It extends to stabilization and income redistribution. Stabilization was traditionally considered in relation to the policies of specific countries. This, at least, was the way countercyclical policy was interpreted and explained by students of Keynes in the past. It was the responsibility of the government of a country hit by an economic slowdown to introduce policies (fiscal and monetary) that would compensate for the deficient aggregate national demand. When we thought of the government being the "balancing factor" for aggregate demand, we thought of the *national* government playing the role, as Musgrave (1959) had argued in his influential book. However, the opening of economies, the globalization of the financial market, and other global factors have reduced the countercyclical power of *national* policy and the ability of countries to act independently from other countries. They have also increased the exposure of countries to developments in other countries. Greater economic openness has reduced the size of the fiscal multipliers, as several recent studies have indicated.

To be effective, or more effective, stabilization policy now requires some degree of international cooperation and coordination in the response, coordination that was not required in the past. However, there is no global government and no clear mechanism in place that can ensure that joint actions will be forthcoming, and forthcoming at the needed level. The growing role of regular international meetings, by heads of state or by economic ministers, such as those of the G20, and of some international institutions, such as the IMF, the European Union, the OECD, and the UN, have to a limited extent substituted for the role that a global government would play. *This global role is likely to grow in importance with the passing of time.* National governments must find ways to contribute, and adjust, to this growing global role.[5] No government should consider itself exceptional and thus above this coordinating role.

It might be thought that at least the function of income redistribution would remain strictly national. As we saw earlier, this function became important and contributed significantly to the growth of public spending during the 20th century in many countries. However, the greater interconnection of countries' economies and the negative cross-border externalities, generated by both poor and rich countries, are bound to influence the global distribution of income in direct and indirect ways. In some cases, poor countries generate what could be considered significant, negative externalities by exporting illegal immigrants, illegal drugs, and in some cases individuals who are more likely to engage in criminal activities for a variety of reasons. This has become, or has been seen to be, a growing problem, especially in Europe but also in Asia and in some American states. Immigration has become a hot topic in several countries.[6] It might become of more interest for rich countries to increase their economic assistance to poor countries, to help them develop and create domestic jobs to reduce migratory flows. Rich countries generate other kinds of cross-border or global negative externalities. For example, they contribute more to environmental problems and to global warming. It would be in the interest of many poorer countries that are much affected by them to have these externalities reduced.

Income is distributed unevenly not only within countries but also among countries. The Gini coefficient, estimated for the whole world, is very high. The rich countries have a much larger share of the world total income than they would have in a world in which per capita income were the same among countries. As we saw earlier, many governments are very active in redistributing income *within* the borders of their countries. Redistribution at the global level, across countries, receives much less attention. There is no global government, or institution, capable of promoting large cross-countries income transfers. Cross-countries pressures on rich national governments are less effective than within-countries pressures, mainly because foreigners do not vote in national elections. The pressures applied by existing international organizations, including the United Nations and the World Bank (which to some extent could be considered as proxies or ministries for the nonexisting world government), are of limited effectiveness (Tanzi, 2008). It is likely, though far from certain, that in future years there will be increasing pressures on rich countries to transfer more of their income to the poorer countries and pressures on all countries to deal more effectively with global and regional public goods.[7]

These examples point to the need for some coordinated international response unless one believes that there is an invisible hand operating internationally that already coordinates national responses to guide them toward an optimum. The examples highlight the contrast that exists between countries, which have a national government, and the world, which does not. As *global* needs become more intense, pressures on national governments to respond to them are bound to increase. Some of the responses will require spending that may be channeled through international organizations or that can be allocated directly and globally by specific national governments to the poorer countries. Some response may also come through international agreements that may or may not be accompanied by specific (binding?) regulation. We are likely to see more and more activity in this area in future years.[8] It will likely change, to some extent, the traditional economic role of the (national) state (Tanzi, 2008 and 2009a).

## 14.3. The Role of the State and the Financial Market

A concrete evidence of the need for coordination was presented by the global financial crisis of 2008–9. That crisis pointed to the need for some coordination of stabilization responses and of regulation of the global, financial market. Financial stability is a clear example of an important *global* public good. Without financial stability, many things can go wrong. The financial market became truly global in the preceding two decades because of the liberalization of capital movements on the part of many countries and because of the widespread use of the Internet and of powerful computers. As a consequence, national governments became less able to control the financial market activities in their territory that were often much influenced by decisions of financial operators in other countries. Many important decisions on the supply and demand for progressively more complex financial instruments were made abroad, at times in offshore centers or from tax havens. While the financial market became truly global, the (limited) regulations that existed remained national and were directed toward specific *national* objectives, such as encouraging home ownership in the United States and in other countries. Often, the regulations were widely different among countries, making regulatory arbitrage by financial institutions easy (see especially Sinn, 2010; Johnson and Kwak, 2010; and Rajan, 2010). The argument, often forcefully made, that the financial market was self-regulating and thus it did not need formal monitoring proved to be a costly illusion.

A combination of increasing complexity, opacity, and greed on the part of some operators, some misguided national policies, and complacency or incompetence on the part of national authorities created a time bomb that was destined to go off at some point (Tanzi, 2007b, especially p. 234 for an anticipation of this explosion). That combination also created situations whereby financial market operators were able to skirt national laws without fear of legal consequences.[9] The bomb did go off and in a spectacular way in 2008, forcing many governments to intervene on a massive and unprecedented scale, through operations of central banks and through public budgets. Soon the financial crisis morphed into an economic crisis and, with a lag, into a fiscal or sovereign debt crisis. The fiscal accounts of many countries, and probably their potential output, suffered sharp, long-term deteriorations, with unavoidable consequences for the future.

Some countries are now facing immediate, or delayed, dangers of default. Additionally, moral hazards were created for the future, because of the use of previously little-used policy tools – such as "contingent liabilities" and "quantitative easing" associated with extremely low interest rates – and the likely expectation by market operators that if governments had intervened this time to save financial institutions they would do it again. This expectation was enforced by the fact that some financial institutions that had been considered "too big to fail" had become even bigger because of the disappearance of some competitors (Scherer, 2010). The intervention to deal with the crisis may have contributed to raising the probability of future crises, and such crises would come when governments and central banks would find more difficult to intervene because of their weakened situations (Johnson and Kwak, 2010; and Tanzi, 2010b).

"Market fundamentalism," the belief that markets, and especially the financial market, are always self-correcting, a belief strongly held by many before the crisis in both academia and the financial market, proved to be wrong. Several recent books have elaborated on this conclusion.[10] Some of the leading advocates of market fundamentalism, such as Alan Greenspan, were forced to admit, even though reluctantly, that they were wrong in their belief (Dash, 2010).[11] The options available to governments, and especially to the American government, to deal with the consequences of the crisis for the financial market were few.

A first option was a "do-nothing option." It would have assumed that the crisis was a random, a one-in-a-century event requiring no major policy change, except for the need to deal with some of the mess left behind in the fiscal accounts and in the accounts of central banks. The need for immediate rescue operations of banks and other financial institutions, without any regulatory reform, was seen as necessary by some, including those running the big banks, but not by all. This option is the one that many financial market operators would have liked, and what their lobbyists pushed policy makers to do. This option would (as to a large extent it did) have socialized the losses, while leaving most of the gains to the operators. However, it would have protected the financial system. The argument was that any increased control on financial operations would damage economic growth or would reduce a country's competitiveness in financial operations.

In late 2009 and in 2010, large banks returned to the huge profits of past years and went back to paying large bonuses to their managers and employees, as if nothing had happened. The huge losses caused to the economy had been largely socialized. The return into profitability for the banks had much to do with the very low borrowing rates by the banks, due to central banks policies. This implied that large implicit subsidies were being provided by the central banks to the borrowing institutions. These low rates favored the banks more than the enterprises and especially the small enterprises that had to pay much higher rates to get loans from the banks, when they could get the loans. In spite of the return to profitability by the banks, lending to enterprises remained relatively low. This, in a way, defeated the purpose of keeping the rates low. The banks could earn profits simply by borrowing from the central banks and lending to governments.

This "do-nothing option" over the long-run *might* even generate a higher rate of (conventionally measured) economic growth because it would continue to encourage technological developments (and increasing complexity) in the financial market and generate large profits for those who operate in it. These profits would continue to be counted as genuine incomes on which economic growth statistics are measured. The " do-nothing option" would also make periodic financial crises more likely, through the creation of asset bubbles that would hurt large sectors of the economy and through the increasing complexity of financial market operations. As long as the occasional losses continued to be socialized, and the large gains continued to be privatized, large incomes would continue to be received by the financial market operators. This would perpetuate, or aggravate, the uneven income distribution that existed in recent years.[12] In time, this would inevitably give rise to popular resentment and lead to populist reactions against the market economy, which would disrupt its operations (as argued in Tanzi, 2007a).

A first objection to this " do-nothing option" is that the GDP growth rate cannot be the only or final yardstick of economic policy, just as the Gini coefficient cannot be. In this " do-nothing option," there is no mechanism that – in a fashion consistent with traditional welfare economics (which relies on the Pareto optimum criterion) but with an actual compensation mechanism – would allocate some of the income earned by the top managers and the operators in the financial market, *during periods of high growth*, toward the many workers who would lose their jobs and their assets *during crises and recessions*. At the end of 2010, there were still millions of workers in the United States and elsewhere who had not regained the jobs that they lost, and millions of families that had lost their homes because they were not able to keep paying their mortgages or because they gave back their houses to the banks when the value of the houses they had bought, with loans from banks, fell below the value of their mortgages. Unemployment benefits had run out for U.S. workers, while many bankers had gone back to getting large bonuses.[13] The value of a dollar earned by the lucky few in the financial markets cannot be assumed to be equivalent, in generating welfare, to the value of a dollar lost by average workers unless there is real compensation. Therefore, the criterion of the theoretical Pareto optimum, without compensation, cannot be accepted as a valid one for this situation.

As a short digression on this first option, a growing number of recent papers has connected the 2008–9 financial crisis, especially in the United States, to the deteriorating income distribution before the crisis. The deterioration was partly due to the increasing share of profits absorbed by the financial sector that led to sharply higher incomes for those who operated in that sector. It has been argued that the deteriorating income distribution had promoted policies on the part of politicians, such as "bribing" borrowers to increase their borrowing with cheap loans partly promoted or guaranteed by government programs such as mortgages, student loans, and others. The U.S. Federal Reserve Bank had been encouraged to maintain exceptionally low interest rates for much too long to contribute to this borrowing. (See a review article on this issue by Kumhof and Rancière, 2010.)

A second objection to this " do-nothing option" is that, to the extent that banks and other enterprises remain "too big to fail," or have become even more so, governments would be forced to intervene in future crises. A case can also be made that significant parts of the large incomes earned by managers and by financial market operators not only did not contribute real value to the economy but were effectively "rents" rather than genuine incomes (Tanzi, 2007b; and Philippon, 2010). There is no convincing evidence that proves that the incomes appropriated by the financial market in recent years contributed equivalent *genuine value* to the economy (see also note 12). The incomes generated were often associated with bets that were pure gambling or "casino" activities. They had little or, at times, nothing to do with the real economy. In these activities, they largely redistributed incomes from losers to winners, and the losers were often pension funds, municipalities, universities, or normal individuals who had little understanding of what they or those who managed their funds were investing in. The incomes of some of the winners were also derived from the production of goods and services that should not have been produced in the first place. For example, millions of unneeded houses were built in several countries during the housing boom that preceded the crisis. That boom was, to a large extent, a "bubble" created by an artificial and partly "manufactured" demand. Asymmetric information, complexity, misguided Fed and other federal policies, and shady practices all played significant roles in manufacturing the large demand for new homes. That boom preceded the crisis and, while it created large incomes for some, it did not generate genuine lasting economic value for society. The subsequent deflation in the value of the houses built, and the abandonment of many of them that were subsequently vandalized or even destroyed, proved that the genuine value created was far less than the incomes earned. This implies that the growth rate in the years before the crisis was distorted because it reflected the inflated value of the houses built and the incomes earned by the financial market operators from the housing boom.[14] Thus, the fall in the growth rate in 2008–9 ought to be adjusted to reflect the inflated growth rates before 2008.

A second, more difficult but preferable option on the part of governments would be that of following faithfully, efficiently, and ruthlessly what could be considered the truly fundamental economic role that the state should play in a market economy. As we saw earlier, it is a role implied, but not spelled out, by Adam Smith in *The Wealth of Nations*. It is *to make the market operate as efficiently as a market can be made to operate*. This would require governmental intervention that is well thought out and efficient.[15] In this intervention, the government would aim at eliminating market failures that *are not natural and that can be eliminated*. Such an intervention would not be limited to the financial market. Of course, the government should refrain from itself introducing distortions in the market, as it did in the housing market in the United States by essentially subsidizing borrowing for the acquisition of houses. This attempt at eliminating nonnatural market failures might have some negative consequences in the short run for the economy, but it would pay high dividends in the longer run.

It must be recognized that many market failures are *not* natural but man-made. Often, the government itself has allowed them to exist or has even created them. These include nonnatural monopolies, "too big to fail" institutions, positional rents for various categories, and abuses connected with limited or false disclosure. It is easy to despair whether governments could ever play the right role. Economists such as George Stigler and others of the Chicago school, and public choice scholars and market fundamentalists, and not just them, would be highly skeptical that governments could ever do this. However, it must be recognized that governments have concentrated too much on *replacing* the market with public-sector activities when the market presumably failed and in shuffling income, presumably to make economic outcomes fairer and the income distribution more even, and not enough in trying harder to *prevent* market failure. Many markets fail in part because the government has allowed them to create the conditions that lead to failure. *Governments should concentrate their activity on prevention, much more than on ex post repair or correction.* This should be a fundamental principle guiding the economic role of the state.

An important tool for this ambitious, normative option might be a clear political and legal framework that defined a market economy and indicated clearly the market failures that ought to be corrected. In a way, this idea borrows from Buchanan's view that the government should establish clear rules to guide the behavior of citizens. That framework would include the development of regulatory and other instruments and institutions that would be used to eliminate or reduce some of the market failures, and these institutions should be given the means and the authority to carry out their function without political interference. The difficulties that would be met in this approach are, of course, monumental. It is easy to make arguments, as they were made by George Stigler and other exponents of the Chicago school half a century ago and by laissez-faire economists of the 19th century, that regulations have often been used for the wrong purposes. Additionally, the regulators have often been captured by the regulated or have been rendered impotent by misguided guidelines, lack of resources, incompetent staff, or signals that they have received from their political masters who did not believe in the necessity of regulations or who had fallen victims of special interests and lobbies.[16] This is the reason why a clear, binding, legal guideline may be necessary. Such a guideline should almost play the role of a good economic constitution, with an efficient enforcement mechanism.

If one truly believes in the virtue of a market economy, one not corrupted by some of those who operate in it, or distorted by bad economic policies, he or she should not resist but should favor the elimination of monopolies, monopolistic practices, and other abuses that corrupt it, regardless of what the original justification for these practices may have been. This may require corrections that may reduce the short-run growth of the economy. This outcome should not prevent the government from intervening in the market for market failure when intervention is genuinely needed. However, the intervention should be with instruments that are the least distorting to the market. It would be an intervention aimed at truly correcting for *fundamental* market failures or for changing very uneven income distributions and not at using the failures as excuses for replacing the market or for socializing private losses.

It should be recognized that if the government is incapable of exercising the role outlined here, as some or even many economists may believe, the future of the market economies becomes highly questionable, because the increasing complexity of modern markets is making and will continue to make abuses much easier. It would be unwise to rely mainly on self-enforcing mechanisms. They will not work. It is important to acknowledge this sad conclusion and to act on the consequences that arise from it[17] (Tanzi 2007a). Like an expensive machine, the market economy needs attention and occasional repairs to continue operating efficiently.

Evidence from several industries – energy, mining, railroads, airlines, financial market, food, pharmaceutical – both in the United States and elsewhere indicates that, without effective monitoring, some market operators tend to cut corners, in terms of safety, and try to maximize profits not through fair competition and honest dealings with their customers but through unfair and occasionally dangerous practices. A combination of opaqueness, greed, limited liability for operators, and lack of clear and effective regulations, applied intelligently and fairly, have often created situations that have allowed operators in various industries to skirt or break the law occasionally with disastrous consequences, as in the BP Gulf explosion or in mining disasters. This has raised the question asked earlier: whether the market economy can remain truly efficient and fair over the long run without more effective controls and constraints. To keep its main market characteristics, the market will need the continued political support necessary in a democracy. A rule-based system, one not complemented by good principles, may ironically have made the skirting of the law easier. Rules are established to deal with *past* situations. They may become inadequate to deal with new unanticipated situations, especially when the latter are created by innovations that may have been developed or stimulated exactly to get around the increasingly anachronistic existing rules.[18] *Rules tend to follow developments,* and often they do so with long lags. For this reason, *rules need to be complemented by broader principles, and there must be some institutions, such as the U.S. Supreme Court, that determine whether the right principles are being followed.*[19]

In the financial market, institutions, if they are truly seen as "too big to fail," should be forced to shrink to a size at which they could be allowed to fail. If their incentive systems make them take excessive risks, the incentive structure must be corrected. Financial enterprises operating in that market should be required to disclose *all* the information necessary to allow citizens to invest with full knowledge of the risks they would be taking. Furthermore, the information should be provided in the most transparent and user-friendly way possible. Some risk should remain with those who initiate the financial instruments, and the instruments should not be quickly downloaded (with their full risks and lack of transparency) on other less-informed or ignorant investors, as happened during the subprime crisis with securitized subprime mortgages. The institutions that make the loans or assume other risks should have enough genuine and immediately usable capital to cover eventual losses. Thus, excessive leverage must be prevented.

Furthermore, in a global market, the regulations must be as global and as well defined as possible to avoid regulatory arbitrage among different countries and different regulators. There must be a global regulator, or the countries' regulatory agencies should harmonize their regulations and coordinate their actions closely under some global umbrella, while exchanging needed information. Also the possibility available to financial institutions of shopping for the easiest regulator within a country, as has often been the case within the United States, must be eliminated. Both micro- and macroeconomic regulations are required to deal with the problems of both specific institutions and the whole system. Macro-prudential regulation is now attracting more attention than in the past, recognizing that whole systems, and not just single entities, can fail.

These suggestions can be criticized with the often-heard argument that they will make the financial market less efficient by slowing down technological development and advances in financial engineering.[20] Once again, presumed efficiency – a concept not always easy to define, except in theory, and even more difficult to measure, especially in the financial market– cannot be the only criterion for judging the performance of this sensitive industry, especially when it can have and often has had large undesirable effects on income distribution and on short-term economic activity

(Reinhart and Rogoff, 2009).[21] The crisis that the financial market caused in 2008–9 is a sufficient reason to argue that the financial market needs significant and not just cosmetic reforms. Unfortunately, memories may be short, and the pockets of those who operate in the financial market are deep. There is thus the risk that soon the crisis period will again come to be seen as normal or as "the new normal."

In 2010 there has been a lot of activity regarding regulatory reforms of the financial system, in both the United States and Europe. The United States has enacted a complex financial reform bill that was thousands of pages long. However, in spite of its length, many decisions are awaiting the regulations that will give the law real substance. The reform in the United States has not been fully coordinated with reforms in Europe. The lobbies have become very active in trying to influence the regulations that will be needed to give operational content to the bill passed. The final outcome will have a major impact on future economic developments and also on the economic role of the state in this sector. Whether the reforms will be able to prevent future financial crises, only time will tell. That final outcome will be influenced by the strong current interest in reforms on the part of various governments and by the resistance to major changes on the part of those who operate the financial system and who rely on powerful lobbies, representing their interests, and have the money to finance the activities of the lobbies.

## 14.4. Taxes and Public Spending in the Future

Let us return to fiscal policy in its narrower definition, involving the use of taxes and public spending, and consider its future role. Estimates made in 2010 by the IMF, the European Union, the OECD, and other sources indicate that many countries came out of the 2008–9 crisis with fiscal accounts in far worse shape than the already precarious ones they had faced before the crisis. The average public debts of the G20 countries on the basis of current policies is forecast to approach 120 percent of GDP within a decade. The fiscal deficits are expected to remain high for years to come. For several countries, the efforts needed to bring the fiscal situation to long-term sustainability would have to be truly extraordinary. (See IMF, 2010; and Tanzi, 2010a and 2010b.)

There has been continuing talk about the need for "exit strategies" to bring fiscal deficits and public debts to levels at which they could be managed without excessive difficulties. These strategies will require improving the structural primary balances (the balances that exclude interest

payments) of many countries by *very* large amounts. The required adjustments over the next decade for some of the countries – Japan, United
Kingdom, Spain, United States, Ireland, Greece, Portugal, and others –
are huge. These adjustments would come at the same time when fiscally
unfriendly demographic developments begin to have their full impact as
the baby boomers retire. The 2008–9 crisis lowered the potential growth rate
of many countries, while the interest rates, which have been kept artificially
low by central banks' actions and by the spare capacity created by the crisis,
should be expected to go up considerably at some point in the future unless
the countries remain in a state of crisis. The crisis has increased unemployment, and its structural aspects may have reduced the size of the work force
for years to come because some elderly workers may not return to work if
their skills are no longer required. A 50-year-old worker who lost his job in
the housing industry will have a hard time being reabsorbed in the work
force. Some will probably drop out of it permanently.[22]

Large reductions in public debts and in fiscal deficits can come from each,
or a combination, of four possible developments: significant falls in interest
rates for government debt, high economic growth, unanticipated inflation,
and reforms in taxes and in public spending associated with a major change
in the role of the state in the economy that lead to large reductions in public
spending and/or to significant increases in tax levels.

Interest rates are now so low in many countries that they can only go up;
and they could go up significantly, increasing the difficulties for financing
the public debts, as Greece, Ireland, Portugal, and some other countries
have been experiencing. The fact that the average maturities of the public
debts were generally reduced in many countries in recent years to reduce
interest expenses makes an increase in interest rates a worrisome aspect.[23]
Servicing large public debts at higher interest rates could significantly and
quickly increase public spending, thus worsening the fiscal situation. As an
example of what could happen, between 1978 and 1985 the share of net
interest payments into GDP for the United States more than doubled, from
1.5 to 3.1 percent, mainly because of the increase in interest rates.

For various reasons, some mentioned earlier, fast economic growth is
not likely to characterize most of these economies at least over the medium
run. Significant structural adjustments remain to be made, for example,
to the U.S. balance of payment, which continues to be in large dise-
quilibrium. The high public debt will divert some creditors away from
making long-term private-sector investments, because of concerns about
the fiscal situation, uncertainty, or higher future taxes. Animal spirits are
likely to be dimmed. Also, because of the high risk that will continue to

prevail, loans to small enterprises will be limited and will carry high interest costs.

Inflation cannot be ruled out, because of the huge amount of liquidity that has been injected in the past couple years in the banking system by the actions of the central bank. In fact, in some countries, such as Great Britain, the inflation rate has recently gone up more than expected. There are suggestions by some commentators that public borrowing might be financed directly by the central banks, and there has been a huge expansion in the balance sheet of the Fed, the European Central Bank, the Bank of England, and other central banks, which has helped finance the large fiscal deficits. It may be difficult to wipe out all that liquidity before it starts to put significant pressure on prices. As the economies begin to recover, the pressures on prices may start in some sectors, including commodities, and spread to others. If inflation were anticipated, it would inevitably and quickly affect the willingness of savers to invest, especially in longer-term government bonds, unless the rates on these instruments were adjusted to reflect the savers' inflationary expectations. Longer-term interest rates have in fact been going up, especially when related to the continued talk about deflation.

This leaves, as a possible and more realistic long-term adjustment strategy, the redefinition of the economic role of the state in the economy, in terms of taxing and spending. Taxes could be increased quickly, and public spending could be reduced over the medium run. Some major European countries have declared their intentions to follow this option. At the same time, there continue to be pressures on most governments to increase their spending and on some, such as the U.S. government, to maintain the high fiscal deficit until a full recovery of the economy is clearly under way (Tanzi 2010a).

In earlier chapters it was shown that, during much of the 20th century, tax levels had been pushed continuously upward to finance progressively higher public expenditures. By the end of the century, the taxes had reached very high levels in most countries. In the new century, however, in several countries, the tax levels had stopped rising or had started to come down (Tables 1.3 and 4.5). The reductions in tax levels were promoted by growing concerns about disincentives and tax avoidance actions, created or simulated by high marginal tax rates and by technological developments (combined with increasing international tax competition) that were making it more costly and more difficult for some countries to increase tax rates or to maintain high tax levels. Some of these factors were defined as "fiscal termites" because of the damage that they were causing to the foundations of tax systems (Tanzi, 2001).

The need to promote higher economic growth, in the more difficult circumstances that are likely to prevail in the next few years, will make most, though not all, countries hesitate to use *significant* tax rate increases as the way to bring the fiscal accounts under control.[24] However, some tax increases may become necessary and may be possible, at least for some countries, and should not be excluded. Some of the increases may be in more acceptable taxes, such as environmental taxes and, perhaps, taxes on financial market activities aimed at bringing the tax burden in line with that in other sectors. Stories about hedge fund managers and other billionaires in the financial market who have been paying significantly lower tax rates on their incomes than the drivers who take them around are not a good publicity for a market economy or for the governments that have allowed these inequities to develop. They are likely to stimulate populist reactions over the long run. But these increases are likely to have a modest impact on revenue. Sharp reductions in tax expenditures would help. In some countries and especially in the United States and Japan, more significant measures, such as the introduction of a value-added tax in the United States and a significant increase in the existing VAT in Japan, may become necessary. This leaves the option of attempting significant reduction in public spending as the potential, main adjustment tool *for the medium run*. This book has argued that this option, though politically difficult, may not be as painful as many believe it to be in terms of welfare reduction. However, it will require well-thought-out and major structural reforms and not just cosmetic ones.

A combination of a better-regulated and better-working private market, which would make it easier for most, though not all, citizens to buy directly from the market services that protect them against particular risks (some of the services that they now get from the government), combined with well-thought-out "libertarian" regulations that directed and required them to do so, and with a good dose of "libertarian paternalism," could be a combination that could go a long way toward reducing public spending over a number of years and especially over the long run without abandoning the fundamental role of the state in terms of its various objectives.

The government would be putting more of its effort and activity toward *reducing risks rather than correcting, ex post, for bad outcomes that could have been prevented*. This approach can be applied in several areas, including the health sector, the educational sector, and the financial market. In this scenario, the government would inevitably have to direct more specific attention toward the truly "deserving poor," those who, because of serious and genuine handicaps and other difficulties, cannot be expected to be able to take care of themselves. However, the "deserving poor" would have to be and to remain a small share of the population. The broad middle class would be encouraged to rely more on the market for protection against risks and for some social services. Because of potentially lower taxes made possible by the spending reductions, over the long run they would have more (after tax), disposable income to be able to buy the desired and needed protection directly from the market. This is not an easy way out from the current fiscal mess, but it may be the only realistic one for many countries over the long run. It would require reinventing and reengineering the role of the state rather than continuing on a road with increasing difficulties. It may also require introducing fiscal rules that would reduce the recourse in the future to facile fiscal policy.

Before bringing this chapter, and this book, to a close, there are other important issues that merit some mention because of the role that they might or are likely to play in the future. A full treatment of them will be left for another occasion. The two most important issues among these are preparation for disasters and the increasing problem of complexity in fiscal policy and in government operations in general.

## 14.5. The Government Role in Major Disasters

Recent events (Katrina, major earthquakes, the Indonesian tsunami, oil explosion in the Gulf of Mexico, biblical floods in Pakistan, huge fires in Russia) have reminded us that we live in a world in which Mother Nature, with significant assistance from human activity or stupidity, from time to time makes this a dangerous world. Because of population growth and the increasing need to settle in disaster-prone areas, natural and other disasters have become more frequent in recent years and their impacts on human beings more significant (Cavallo et al., 2010; Kron, 2010; Hallegatte and Przyluski, 2010). When major disasters strike, all the talk about free market and laissez-faire is quickly forgotten. It is the government that is expected to play the leading role in dealing with their consequences and in alleviating the pain and the suffering of those affected by them. Governments should spend much more time and energy and should allocate more resources than they normally do to be ready to intervene effectively in these emergencies. However, they almost always seem to be taken by surprise and are caught unprepared. There may not be more fundamental responsibilities for governments than to help those in need during major catastrophes.

However, this is clearly an area where "moral hazard" can become a significant problem, at least in particular countries and places. The expectation of governmental financial and physical intervention in disasters (hurricanes, earthquakes, floods, cyclones, major fires, tidal waves) may encourage some individuals to build vacation houses, establish some economic activities, and even choose to live in the areas where these events are not rare. This is a significant problem in the United States, especially in areas occasionally visited by hurricanes, along the East Coast and the Gulf of Mexico. At the same time, it must be recognized that there are communities that, historically, were established in dangerous areas, long before there was any expectation of governmental intervention. The people who live in these areas have not done it by choice, because of expected governmental assistance in case of catastrophes. They may also be too poor to have much choice.

Some countries (or areas within countries) are more exposed to particular calamities (e.g., earthquakes, floods, fires, cyclones) than others. Furthermore, catastrophes can hit areas that had not been considered exposed before. Therefore, governments should be ready to intervene immediately, to the best of their ability, when *major* catastrophes strike.[25] Governments should adopt policies that would reduce the incentives that people have to live in exposed areas for the people who have choices. These policies should also require all people to be better prepared for expected disasters. New houses should not be built in areas subjected to occasional floods, and effective and well-enforced building regulations should exist in areas where earthquakes are not rare, as they exist, for example, in California. This regulatory guidance should be considered an important economic role of the state. It is a role that is played much more effectively in some countries (Chile) than in others (Haiti). Differences in per capita income may not account entirely for the differences.

The government role ought to be focused on prevention and on preparation for potential, damaging events but also on ex post assistance, although this should also be part of the preparation. Regulations are the major policy instrument to perform the prevention role. Laissez-faire is not a realistic alternative. The same approach (i.e., prevention) is applicable to other situations that may not appear to have the characteristics of disasters.

Some disasters are so huge as to overwhelm the available local resources. Therefore, global collaboration becomes essential. A world government, if it existed, would be expected to play a natural role in dealing with major disasters. The UN plays an important role but one that depends on ad hoc contributions from national governments. These contributions are often inadequate or come too late to be fully helpful. A special UN or World Bank fund could be created that could accumulate annual, national contributions. These would be similar to insurance fees. The fund's resources earmarked and kept in relatively liquid form would be readily available to help deal with *major* disasters. At the national level, the countries' military could be given the formal responsibility of preparing and dealing with *national* disasters when they occur. Most of the time, armies are not fighting wars. Why not have them prepare and be ready to deal with other kinds of national emergencies, which are likely to become more frequent than wars? It would make the resources invested in military expenditure more productive and useful.

### 14.6. The Growing Role of Government in Preventing and Dealing with Significant Externalities

The role that governments should play in prevention against various dangers other than major disasters is likely to move to the front line of the battle between libertarians, who want little governmental intervention, and liberals, who expect governments to protect citizens against an increasing number of risks and to assume more responsibilities. This battle has (directly) less to do with redistribution and much to do with risk prevention. It, nevertheless, does have implications for the incidence of governmental intervention on individuals in different income deciles and in different citizen categories. It is a battle that has been drawn over smoking; the requirement to buy health insurance, a requirement that exists in various countries; or the provision of free public health services, as exists in several other countries; the creation of an effective consumer protection agency not only to protect consumers but also to teach them how to protect themselves; regulation of some of the activities of the financial market; and so on. This battle, which in the United States often acquires constitutional implications, already took place in 1935, with the requirement for American workers to be part of the federal social security system. It is taking place again now with the law to reform the health system.

In the United States, the debate has to do with the power of the federal government to impose obligations on citizens, when the citizens' rights and obligations are not specifically spelled out by the U.S. Constitution, or when unanimity or an overwhelming majority has not demanded a given course of action. The regulatory tool is likely to become the most important among the tools used by governments to perform their role in risk prevention. It is important that it be used with moderation and not abused.

As modern societies develop, and as the proportion of people forced to live in close proximity, in huge megalopolises, goes up, new needs arise, and new products and ways of producing old products become common.[26] These developments bring with them not only opportunities for citizens to achieve higher standards of living but also dangers. New negative externalities are created by the contacts and the asymmetries in information on the quality and the safety of products and services exchanged between producers, or providers, and users. As the share of services and of nontraditional products (such as new drugs, car repairs, vacation packages) increases in the consumption basket of individuals, the role that prices play in providing, ex ante, full information to the buyers, as described by Hayek and other Austrian school economists, is reduced. The role of asymmetries in information, ex ante, increases. This may promote the need for more action by governments to protect individuals.

Also, while individuals continue to have rights as individuals, the rights of *collective entities*, as distinguished from those of individuals, rise in importance. These two rights must somehow be made to coexist in a democratic, market economy. In a desert, one may have the right to dispose of his garbage as he wishes, or to drive at any speed. In a crowded city, these individual rights are no longer realistic. This is true in many other activities. The choice and the right to live in a crowded community come with the obligation to give up some individual freedoms. When people lived in relative isolation, at least vis-à-vis nonfamily members, some of the collective needs, created by urbanization and by richer economies, were not perceived. Take, for example, the habit of smoking. Before the creation of public health services (which shifted to the collectivity some or all of the individual financial costs of being ill) and when most individuals lived in isolation (so that they did not smoke around strangers), smoking was not a problem requiring the attention of society or government. The individual's right to smoke, whenever and wherever he wanted, and to get ill because of it, was not challenged. But once crowding and a public health system are added, the rights of collective entities to impose healthy behavior rise in importance, vis-à-vis those of individual smokers. This is a second-best argument. At that point, rules created by the community become necessary and justified as long as they are fair and efficient.

A similar but more complex example is provided by the production and use of products (coal, petroleum) that beside being useful to the individuals contribute to generalized, or global, pollution and to other environmental problems. Many scientists now believe that this kind of pollution is causing "global warming," a development that, if they are right, may become the mother of all negative externalities (McKibben, 2010). The current debate on global warming is reminiscent, to some extent, of the earlier debate on smoking (Stern 2010). In earlier years many had affirmed the right of citizens to smoke whenever and wherever they wanted, and the right of cigarette manufacturers to sell tobacco and to advertise their tobacco products. For a long time they denied that smoking had any negative health effects on those who smoked and on those in the close proximity of smokers who passively shared the smoke. With the passing of the years, science settled this matter. Similar questions are now being raised about global warming. Does it really exist? If the answer is positive, are its effects significant? Do governments have the right to intervene vis-à-vis consumers of particular products (petroleum, coal) and producers of those products to reduce the amount of carbon dioxide in the air? The impact of potential governmental restrictions on the rights of individual to use these products is clear. The rights of "collective entities" are equally clear, under the assumption that the science behind the global warming concern is correct.[27] Should this "potential disaster" be ignored, letting individuals continue to live as they have for the past 200 years, trusting that the free market will somehow solve the problem or that the problem simply does not exist?

Unlike smoking, global warming has a global, spatial dimension that makes it far more difficult to cope with it, or with its effects, through *national* government policies. In this phenomenon, free-rider problems are very important, and the free riders may be whole nations. This is an area in which the absence of a world government, or at least of a global institution with the power to require and enforce changes, makes the solution more difficult. In this sense, it is a different problem from the one created by smoking, for which the cross-countries' spillovers are limited to cigarette smuggling. An economist who has paid particular attention to the potential implications of global warming, in addition to Nick Stern et al. (2007), is Martin Weitzman (2007 and 2009). His analysis of global warming, which uses sophisticated statistical methods that take into account the large uncertainties in the data, has led him to the conclusion that the probability of worldwide, catastrophic increases in temperature is "worrisomely large." He has estimated at 5 percent the probability that in the next 200 years the temperature of the Earth would increase by 10 degrees Celsius (18 degrees Fahrenheit), and at 1 percent that it would increase by 20 degrees Celsius. In either case the world as we know it would cease to exist.

If Weitzman is right, it would be wise to pay the price necessary to significantly reduce that probability and, of course, it would be easier if there were a global government, or a global institution, capable of doing something about the problem and of fully representing the interests of generations not yet born. It would be highly irresponsible for governments to hide behind the possibility that predictions such as these may be completely wrong, given the growing weight of evidence. Wishful thinking can be a poor choice when the consequences of it could be that catastrophic. However, future generations do not vote and markets that would reflect the demand by them for a livable earth do not exist. Governments that for the most part give far more importance to the interests of those living and especially of the individuals who vote are not likely to give full weight to the possibility of immense disasters in a distant future that come with low probability.

Even without a global government, or a global institution, the proper economic role of the state for each national government would require not ignoring this potentially terminal, global catastrophe. It remains to be seen whether the various governments will be able to rise above the parochialism and the vested interests that often determine their actions. This is an area where laissez-faire is clearly not an option. Or, if it is, it is one that could potentially leads to the end of the world.

Various new activities that use new technologies (use of the Internet, cloning of animals, use of genetic therapy, genetically modified crops, nanology, oil extraction in deep water, use of atomic energy) and the production of new and old products, at times produced with poorly understood new techniques, are creating a greatly expanded range of choices and opportunities for the populations. At the same time, some of these new activities and products are creating potential dangers, some of which are minor and are clearly overwhelmed by the advantages that the products provide. This is the case with new drugs that sometimes have minor side effects. Some new products or technologies used are, however, potentially disastrous, as the BP oil disasters in the Gulf of Mexico demonstrated. National regulators are charged with preventing some of the potential problems, under the assumption that the operators cannot always be trusted to be prudent and transparent and to keep the welfare of the populations in mind. Regulators are blamed when problems arise that they have not been able to prevent. And they are blamed, often by the regulated industries, for being too strict and for allegedly overstepping their regulatory power and slowing down economic activity. A common complaint is that regulations raise the costs of production and the prices that consumers have to pay.

There is clearly a conflict between the freedom of individuals and that of enterprises. More freedom for enterprises is often accompanied by greater potential dangers for citizens. Many products are frequently recalled because of significant defects (cribs that kill children, foods that poison people, cars that have major and potentially dangerous problems). Regulators initiate some of these recalls. Others are, spontaneously, initiated by the producers themselves concerned about their reputation and their potential liabilities. Whatever the origin, the recalls have become so frequent that "recall fatigue" has been reported to have set in: the recalls tend to be ignored by the consumers of the recalled products. At other times, and as an increasingly frequent evidence of asymmetry in information, those who have bought the defective or dangerous products are not informed of these defects, because of difficulties or an inability of the producers to contact them (Layton, 2010). The producers of defective products have a natural incentive to minimize, or hide, the defects or the side effects, for obvious economic reasons. This has been a frequent problem in connection with new drugs. Thus, "asymmetry of interests" between producers and consumers and "asymmetry of information" combine to make reliance on the spontaneous action of producers in correcting the problems a dubious regular option. Additionally, at times there is little agreed-upon science at the time when a decision is or must be made on particular issues. Enterprises can easily find paid experts who will support their side. The government may not have much (independent) information, and the information provided by the producers may be biased.[28] Asymmetry in information may also exist between the true but unknown scientific facts and the facts that are provided by the enterprises that sell the products. In conclusion, the market is moving away from the world of Hayek in which the prices provided all the needed information to both buyers and sellers. Now a large part of consumer spending is for products for which the prices that are requested ex ante do not convey as much information to consumers as Hayek assumed. In some cases, consumers are charged for services over which their capacity to control the work done is limited, as for car repairs or medical tests.

Perhaps Wagner's Law of a progressively expanding role of the government, as economies grow and develop, has been misinterpreted by assuming that it referred specifically to the ratio of public spending into GDP. It seems more realistic to assume that the expanding government role may refer to the regulatory role. It can be hypothesized that governments must play progressively larger roles than in the past couple centuries in their attempt to protect citizens against potential dangers and damages from significant negative externalities or from abuses coming from both the production and the consumption side. This regulatory role of the state should be focused on prevention rather than on benefiting specific groups, as was generally the case during the mercantilist period. How efficiently the regulators will be able to perform this role, given all that can go wrong with it, remains an open question. Whatever the result, it is reasonable to expect that market economies will have more regulations and possibly less public spending over the long run. The invisible hand is less likely to play a less prominent role in the future.

## 14.7. The Growing Problem of Complexity

The last issue to be briefly discussed in this chapter is the growing complexity in the conduct of economic and especially fiscal policy, which characterizes modern economies. It is a problem that is becoming progressively more serious, with the passing of time, but has not yet received the full attention that it deserves. If past trends continue in the future, the problem of complexity could become a truly intractable one for policy makers. (See especially Tanzi, 2007b, 2007c, and 2010b, for some examples of this complexity.) In this context, we limit ourselves to only a few observations on different aspects or angles of this problem. It is a problem not limited to fiscal policy, but it seems to be particularly serious in the fiscal area.

As we saw in earlier chapters, over the years, as the economies developed, governments took more and more responsibilities and assumed more and more functions. Those functions have become larger in numbers and more specific, or more tailor-made, for some groups or categories of citizens or enterprises. They have also become more and more complex. Just think of tax systems. The laws that are approved by the legislative branches these days are often thousands of pages long and require thousands of additional pages of enacting explanations and regulations. Public budgets have also become documents that almost nobody understands. Furthermore, the number of laws that are still active keeps growing because laws are rarely abolished. They are just modified. In some countries, such as Italy, it has been estimated that there are some 150,000 laws in existence. The process is a cumulative one so that complexity increases with time.

The statistics that are supposed to determine the fiscal situation of countries (fiscal deficits and public debts), or to assess the performance of various programs, are more and more open to misinterpretation, misreporting, and manipulations. The assignment of responsibilities for specific activities (authorizations, monitoring, particular actions) and to specific institutions, within the public administration, have become confused and have often led to conflicting signals and to serious omissions. For examples from outside fiscal areas, just think of Katrina, the Gulf of Mexico disaster, the regulations of financial activities, and the monitoring of national security in the United States. In some countries, authorizations obtained from one institution within the public administration are later challenged, or even revoked, by another institution. This may happen after private investors have spent large amounts of money in the previously authorized activity or investment.[29]

While this problem has been growing, another problem has become more acute. Public spending has gone up in most countries; however, some essential inputs in the operations of governments, inputs essential to the process of policy making, have remained unchanged over time. Perhaps the most extreme example is that of the role of heads of government or of states (prime ministers or presidents), especially in countries where, as in the United States, the same person performs the tasks of head of government and head of state. It is not feasible to have more than one president, for a country such as the United States, or more than one prime minister, for parliamentary democracies. This essential input has not changed over time, while the activities and the individuals that formally report or should report to the president or to the prime ministers have increased enormously. The United States had one president in 1800, and it still has one president. However, the individual who occupies this top position is expected to supervise all the activities of the government, to read the laws that must be approved, and to understand them, while making an incredible number of other decisions and performing a large number of ceremonial or campaign functions. It is obvious that there is a major and growing problem here. Today's world is far more complex than it was in 1800. It is a problem that has become progressively more serious with the increasing number of responsibilities assumed by the governments. And it is getting worse all the time.

Legislators and ministers are not spared this problem, even though there are many of them. There is increasing evidence that some of the complex bills that are sent to the legislative bodies for approval into laws – as, for example, the bill that reformed the health system and the bill that reformed the financial system in the United States – are voted on without being read by most of those who must vote on them. The reason is their length, often in the thousands of pages, their complexity, and the lack of time to do the reading. It is also obvious that the president who signs these bills into laws does not have the time to read and fully understand them.

Both the legislators and the president rely on assistants, thus opening the door for "principal-agent problems" and making the work of lobbyists, who can more easily access and influence the assistants, much easier.[30] How complex some public systems can become can be seen from the U.S. federal tax system, which now requires more than 70,000 pages of laws and regulations. How many people know or can know what is contained in those 70,000 pages? Strange and previously unnoticed special tax preferences, often worth billions of dollars to some industry or even to a specific company, find their way into these laws, and occasionally surface, surprising everyone except those who had inserted them or had lobbied for them (Tanzi, 2010c). We often read about "obscure provisions contained in laws" that had been so obscure that they had not been noticed by anyone when the laws were approved or when regulations based on the laws were written.

This increasing complexity and its consequences may be the ultimate price to pay for the expansion of the role of the state in the economy and the greatest future danger for a market economy and a democracy (Tanzi, 2007b). That complexity will make reality progressively different from the perception of it. It may be an extreme form of Puviani's fiscal illusion, but it will be a fiscal illusion difficult to understand and monitor. When the activities of institutions (firms, organizations) exceed the supervisor's capacity to monitor and manage them, either the activities must be reduced or the supervisors (the principals) will lose control over them. In this case, the final supervisors or the principals are the citizens.

In 1968 George Stigler saw a part of this danger when he wrote, "As [an] organization grows, the able subordinate must get able subordinates, who in turn must get able subordinates, who in turn must get able subordinates, who in turn – well, by the time the organization is the size of the [U.S.] federal government, the demands for ability begin to outstrip the supply of even mediocre genes" (1968, p. 10). However, Stigler connected the danger to the supply of able individuals. While this is an important aspect, it may be far less important than the principal-agent problems that develop in those situations (Tanzi, 2000). It is an illusion to assume that the president of a country such as the United States, however able he may be, is truly in charge of the policies and the actions of the government.

Complexity is likely to become the most significant issue in governmental operations in the future. If not checked, it will increasingly lead to "state capture" by those who have more resources, or to a popular backlash in the form of populism that will challenge the market economy. To deal adequately with this problem would require deep and possibly unrealistic changes in the way states operate. This is an area where it is not difficult to be pessimistic.

### References

ADB/ADBI. 2009. *Infrastructure for a Seamless Asia* (Manila and Tokyo: Asian Development Bank and Asian Development Bank Institute).

Boeri, Tito, Gordon Hanson, and Barry McCormick, eds. 2002. *Immigration Policy and the Welfare State* (Oxford: Oxford University Press).

Cavallo, Eduardo, Sebastian Galiani, Ilan Noy, and Juan Pantano. 2010. *Catastrophic Natural Disasters and Economic Growth* (Washington, D.C.: IDB).

Dash, Eric. 2010. "So Many Ways to Almost Say 'I am sorry.'" *New York Times*, April 18.

Darvas, Zsolt, and Jakob von Weizsäcker. 2010. "Financial Transaction Tax: Small Is Beautiful." *Bruegel Policy Contribution*, no. 2 (February).

Estevadeordal, Antoni, Brian Frantz, and Tam Robert Nguyen, eds. 2004. *Regional Public Goods: From Theory to Practice* (Washington, D.C: Inter-American Development Bank and Asian Development Bank).

Hallegatte, Stephane, and Valentin Przyluski. 2010. "The Economics of Natural Disasters: Concepts and Methods." Policy Research Working Paper No. 5507 (December 1, World Bank)

IMF. 2009. "The State of Public Finances Cross-Country *Fiscal Monitor.*" SPN/09/25 (November).

2010. "Strategies for Fiscal Consolidation in the Post-Crisis World" (IMF Policy Paper, February 4).

Johnson, Simon, and James Kwak. 2010. *13 Bankers: The Wall Street Takeover and the Next Financial Meltdown* (New York: Pantheon Books).

Kaul, Inge, and Pedro Conceição. 2006. *The New Public Finance: Responding to Global Challenges* (Oxford: Oxford University Press).

Kaul, Inge, Pedro Conceição, Katell Le Goulven, and Ronald U. Mendoza. 2003. *Providing Global Public Goods: Managing Globalization* (Oxford: Oxford University Press).

Kron, Wolfgang. 2010. "Natural Catastrophes: Do We Have to Live with Them?" *CESifo Forum* 11, no. 2 (Summer):1–13.

Kumhof, Michael, and Romain Rancière. 2010. "Leveraging Inequality." *Finance and Development* 47, no. 4 (December): 28–31.

Layton, Lyndsey. 2010. "As Product Recalls Pile Up, Consumers Risk Getting Lost." *Washington Post*, July 1, p. 1.

Lowenstein, Roger. 2010. *The End of Wall Street* (New York: Penguin Books).

Marron, Donald, and Eric Toder. 2011. "Measuring Leviathan: How Big is the Federal Government?" (Washington, D. C.: Urban Institute and Brookings Institution, Tax Policy Center, January 14), Powerpoint presentation.

McKibben, Bill. 2010. *Earth: Making a Life on a Tough New Planet* (New York: Times Books).

Monti, Mario, ed. 1989. *Fiscal Policy, Economic Adjustment and Financial Markets* (Washington, D.C., and Milan: International Monetary Fund and Centro di Economia Monetaria e Finanziaria).

Musgravi, Richard, 1959, *The Theory of Public Finance* (New York: McGraw Hill).

Philippon, Thomas. 2010. "Are Bankers Over Paid?" Available at: http://sternfinance. blogspot.com/2008/11.

Plender, John. 2010. "To Avoid the Backlash, Executives Need to Act on Pay." *Financial Times*, April 3–4.

Posner, Richard A. 2004. *Catastrophe: Risk and Response* (Oxford: Oxford University Press).

2009. *A Failure of Capitalism* (Cambridge, Mass.: Harvard University Press).

Rajan, Raghuram. 2010. *Fault Lines: How Hidden Fractures Still Threaten the World Economy* (Princeton, N.J.: Princeton University Press).

Reinhart, Carmen M., and Kenneth Rogoff. 2009. *This Time Is Different: Eight Centuries of Financial Folly* (Princeton: Princeton University Press).

Samuelson, Paul. 1968. "The Economic Role of Private Activity," in *A Dialogue on the Proper Economic Role of the State*, by George Stigler and Paul A. Samuelson. Selected Papers no. 7 (Graduate School of Business, University of Chicago).

Scherer, F. M. 2010. "A Perplexed Economist Confronts 'Too Big to Fail.'" RWP10-007, Faculty Research Working Paper Series, Harvard Kennedy School.

Sinn, Hans-Werner. 2010. *Casino Capitalism: How the Financial Crisis Came About and What Needs to Be Done Now* (Oxford: Oxford University Press).

Stern, Nicholas. 2010. "Climate: What You Need to Know." New York Review of Books, June 24, pp. 35–37.

Stern, Nicholas, et al. 2007. *The Economics of Climate Change* (Cambridge: Cambridge University Press)

Stigler, George. 1968. "The Government of the Economy," in *A Dialogue on The Proper Economic Role of the State*, by George J. Stigler and Paul A. Samuelson. Selected Papers no. 7 (Graduate School of Business, University of Chicago).

Tanzi, Vito. 1989. "International Coordination of Fiscal Policies: Current and Future Issues," in *Fiscal Policy, Economic Adjustment and Financial Markets* (Washington, D.C.: International Monetary Fund), pp. 7–37.

1992. "Structural Factors and Tax Revenue in Developing Countries: A Decade of Evidence," in *Open Economies: Structural Adjustment and Agriculture*, edited by I. Goldin and L. A. Winters (Cambridge: Cambridge University Press).

2000. "Rationalizing the Government Budget," in *Economic Policy Reform*, edited by Anne Krueger (Chicago: University of Chicago Press).

2001. "Globalization, Technological Developments, and the Work of Fiscal Termites." *Brooklyn Journal of International Law* 26, no. 4: 1261–84.

2005. "Building Regional Infrastructure in Latin America." Inter-American Development Bank, Intal-ITD Working Paper No. SITI-10.

2007a. "Tax System Reform Can Address Unrest over High Pay." *Financial Times*, March 2.

2007b. "Complexity and Systemic Failure," in *Transition and Beyond*, edited by Saul Estrin, Grzegorz W. Kolodko, and Milica Uvalic (London: Palgrave), pp. 229–46.

2007c. "Fiscal Policy and Fiscal Rules in the European Union," in *Europe after Enlargement*, edited by Anders Aslund and Marek Dabrowski (Cambridge: Cambridge University Press), pp. 50–64.

2008. "The Future of Fiscal Federalism." *European Journal of Political Economy* 24 (June): 705–12.

2009. "The Future of Fiscal Federalism and the Need for Global Government: A Reply to Roland Vaubel." *European Journal of Political Economy* 25, pp. 137–139.

2010a. "The Return to Fiscal Rectitude after the Recent Departure." Mimeo. Paper presented at the annual research Conference at the European Commission in Brussels (November 23).

2010b. "Comments on Recent Fiscal Development and the Exit Strategy." *CESinfo Forum* 6, no. 3: 57–64.

2010c. "Complexity in Taxation: Origins and Consequences." Unpublished manuscript.

Time. 2010. "The Best Laws Money Can Buy," July 12.

Walvin, James. 1988. *Victorian Values* (Athens: University of Georgia Press).

Weitzman, Martin L. 2007. *Review of The Stern Review on the Economics of Climate Change. Journal of Economic Literature* 45 (September): 703–24.

2009. "On Modeling and Interpreting the Economics of Catastrophic Climate Change." *Review of Economics and Statistics* 91, no. 1 (February): 1–19.

# Notes

## Chapter One: General Introduction and Main Issues

1. However, even in a perfectly working market, in a democratic setting, the electorate may ask the state to perform some redistributive or other functions, just as management is expected to coordinate private enterprises in a competitive market. See Coase, 1937. Coase's argument for why firms exist, even when the market works well, also has some implications for the government. It might be too costly to coordinate privately some social activities, even if that were possible.

2. Whether the state would be capable of performing this regulatory function well is an issue that we leave to a later chapter. An extensive literature, mainly connected with the "Chicago school," questioned the effectiveness or even the need for regulation on the part of the government. Much of that literature has focused on the regulation of industrial monopolies and, until more recent years, much less on the regulation of financial and other markets. For the sake of the historical record, it may be worthwhile to mention that conclusions similar to those of the Chicago school (with respect to the need for regulations) had been endorsed by some proponents of "laissez-faire" as far back as 1849. See, especially, de Molinari, 1849 [2009], for arguments against regulations of monopolies similar to those advanced much later by economists associated with the Chicago school. De Molinari, an influential Belgian economist in his time, lived in Paris for much of his long life.

3. Countercyclical policy has two dimensions: continuous fine-tuning and discretionary intervention during recessions. Fine-tuning was popular mainly in the 1960s and 1970s. Intervention during recessions remained more popular all along. Fine-tuning reflected an exceptional degree of confidence on the part of policy makers in their ability to determine the need for government intervention and to influence economic activity in the desirable direction. See especially the 1962 *Economic Report of the President* for a clear statement of "fine-tuning." For a recent general criticism of stabilization policy, see Tanzi, 2007.

4. In general, the average voter is not well informed and tends to remain "rationally ignorant," according to Anthony Down's expression (Down, 1957). This has become more of a problem in recent years when the number of issues on which

voters are expected to be informed has grown exponentially. On the other hand, specific groups of individuals (lobbyists) acquire a lot of information and power and push for specific policies. The lobbyists acquire far more information about the results of policies or the content of laws than those who make the decisions. Thus, the asymmetry in information becomes important.

5. For a fascinating account of the growth of the welfare state, see Ritter, 1996. For statistical evidence on the growth of public spending in industrial countries over a century, see Tanzi and Schuknecht, 2000.

6. In the United States and a few other countries, independent "think tanks" provided information that allowed for a less biased assessment of the official programs. However, truly independent "think tanks" have become rare in today's world.

7. In this connection, it may be worthwhile to mention, even though it should be obvious, that the fact that the government may assume this role does not increase the resources available to a country to deal with these risks. Over the longer run, governmental intervention may even reduce the resources available to the country.

8. The concept of the tax price goes back a long way. It was clearly stated in the writing of Italian public finance economists, such as Antonio De Viti De Marco, more than a century ago when taxes and public spending were low. See also chapter 7 of Myrdal, 1954, for a discussion of the concept.

9. Horizontal redistribution is more easily accepted *within* families, or within *closely knit* groups, where the claims for assistance can be more easily checked and where there is a stronger spirit of altruism among the groups' members than among strangers.

10. For example, the abusive absences from public jobs amounted to 17.1 days per year in Italy in 2005. In parts of the Italian public sector, the absences were as high as 31 days. Reported in *Corriere della Sera*, 8 September 2008, p. 18. High absenteeism has also been reported in Sweden and other European countries. The fake claims of invalidity have been a major problem in several countries.

11. Over the past decade, compensation of employees in general government jobs was 8 percent of GDP *higher* in Nordic countries than in Germany. The European Commission has estimated that the share of *productive* public spending (R&D, public transport, and education) was generally less than 20 percent of primary spending in 2005. See European Commission, 2008, p. 140. Primary spending is total public spending less interest payments on the public debt. In the United States, the Office of Management and Budget has reported a large fall in public spending for capital accumulation in recent years. See www.OMB.gov.

12. The high taxes introduced a large wedge between the cost of labor to private enterprises and the after-tax wages of employees. They also increased the cost of products and services freely bought from the market.

13. The vertical redistributive effects have received far more attention than the horizontal redistributive effects.

14. This spirit is probably higher in Nordic European countries than, say, in Anglo-Saxon countries. It is likely to be influenced by the trust that citizens have in the people in the government and in the political institutions. A recent

survey has indicated that this trust is highest in the Nordic countries of Europe. See European Foundation, 2008. As a high-level Swedish official put it, "One plausible hypothesis why the Nordic peoples accept a relatively high taxation is that most of their direct taxes goes to public services in their own community." See Rexed, 2000, p. 9.

15. The question of the efficiency in public spending is taken up in later chapters. It must be recognized that the welfare costs associated with given tax rates may differ from country to country, depending on the citizens' attitude vis-à-vis taxes and public programs, and depending on the structure and the efficiency of the tax systems.

16. It should again be mentioned that many of the arguments made by the modern school of "public choice" were made in less sophisticated or less formal ways in the French and Italian public finance literature of more than a century ago.

17. The goal of having "national champions" is another example of the pursuit of goals that often have little to do with the activity of particular enterprises and the delivery of services to citizens.

18. The question of whether individuals are myopic or, more generally, irrational has been addressed in recent books and articles. See Ariely, 2008; Thaler and Sunstein, 2008; and Della Vigna, 2009. They have shown that individuals do tend to make irrational choices. Some of these choices may imply myopia, including undersaving. However, irrationality may also lead to excessive saving, as in the classic case of misers or, perhaps, in the general Keynesian assumption of underconsumption. Furthermore, policy makers, as individuals, are subjected to the same irrationality. There is no filter that guarantees that those who become policy makers and make government decisions are immune from these irrationalities. See also, for specific application of behavioral economics to public finance, McCaffery and Slemrod, 2006.

19. These liabilities have been identified by the large literature on generational accounts. See, for example, Auerback, Gokhale, and Kotlikoff, 1991.

20. See also Rizza and Tommasino, 2008.

21. This has already happened in some countries.

22. The Keynesian revolution, with its emphasis on aggregate demand and its implicit and at times explicit fear of underconsumption, changed saving from being a virtue to being almost a defect of human behavior. In today's society, good credit rating is a more valuable asset than the absence of debts. To have good credit rating, one needs to have not savings but debts that have been serviced adequately. Those who have saved and have not borrowed cannot have a good credit rating. By making saving a defect, rather than a virtue, the Keynesian revolution implicitly gave governments programs that support individuals in need a more favorable role.

23. For example, it has been reported that in the mid-19th century, 95 percent of English children went to private schools and that their parents spent for education a share of total national income broadly equivalent to today's public spending for children of the same ages. See Tooley, 1996, and West, 1970. Furthermore, the schools provided the students with an education and training that matched more closely the market's needs than public schools now do. Thus,

it was more productive education. For an interesting discussion of formal and informal education in the Western world, see Cipolla, 1969.

24. Charitable giving in the United States is about 2 percent of GDP. This figure excludes the time given to charitable activities by volunteers and also informal giving. These could add a significant amount to the formal giving. See Andreoni, 2006.

25. For examples from different areas and for many statistics, see the chapters in Beito et al., 2002.

26. In fact, the situation could be considered worse because the private mutual assistance associations that had existed earlier would no longer be there to help.

27. By the way, Nozick's position is similar to that of various classical French economists of the 19th century such as J. B. Say, F. Bastiat, and G. de Molinari.

28. Perhaps, it should be added that the private network of assistance that had existed in the past, and that had been crowded out by the government programs, may not come back after the government programs have been abolished and the taxes reduced. Also Nozick would probably argue that nobody would prevent me from freely encouraging the poor to move away from where I live, through the payment of some money. *In theory*, Coasean contracts could deal with this externality. See Coase, 1960. In practice, it is not likely that these contracts would take care of the problem.

29. See Coase, 1960.

30. In the United States, some consider a federally imposed requirement to buy health insurance as unconstitutional. The federal government is being challenged in the courts on this issue. Similar objections were made in the 1930s against the requirement for workers to be part of the Social Security System.

31. "Home-schooling" has been growing in popularity in some countries, including the United States and the United Kingdom.

32. Up to the current financial crisis, the assumption had been that the rate of return on these privately invested pension funds would be higher than the rate of return on government pensions. That assumption could now be challenged, especially for short periods, although it remains valid for long periods, given the impact of the crisis on government finances. However, once again, it may be an illusion to assume that there are no risks in government pensions. The question should be, which is the greater risk and which alternative is better for the majority of citizens?

33. These defined contributions programs have been introduced in recent years in the welfare states of the Nordic European countries. See Chapter 13.

34. There are at least 11 countries (plus the state of Massachusetts) that now require mandatory health insurance. See World Bank, 2008. One country (Singapore) requires health accounts. The United States will also require that people buy health insurance.

35. In spite of the crisis of 2008–9, most real markets still operated fairly efficiently.

36. However, the inefficiency in the provision of universal public services must be kept in mind.

37. Also questions of incentives created by poverty traps must be dealt with. These problems become less pronounced when the assistance is not an entitlement.

38. The income declared must be backed up by other information such as the place of residence, car ownership, and educational level.

39. Of course, as argued by Sen in various publications and by other economists before him, development consists of more than just economic growth. Therefore, we should not go to the other extreme of assuming that only growth matters.

40. It is unlikely that, if the recipient of the benefits had received the money in cash rather than the public services, they would have bought willingly the same services.

41. To some extent, this is already happening in Europe where immigrants from Eastern Europe now care for many old people.

42. The 2008–9 crisis indicates that the risks are not limited to particular countries or to the private sector. See the experiences of Iceland, Greece, Ireland, and Portugal. If governments had major difficulties in meeting future obligations in pensions and health before the crisis, they will have even greater ones in the future. In 2010 Ireland and Greece faced serious difficulties in financing their public debt.

43. See also de Molinari, 1849, for arguments similar to those of the Chicago school vis-à-vis the regulation of monopolies.

### Chapter Two: The Role of the State in the Pre–World War II Period

1. Actually the way in which Marx's ideas were used was different from the way he had intended. As a biographer has put it, "Marx... would have been appalled by the crimes committed in his name." See Wheen, 1999, p. 2. For Marx, the state was assumed to be an instrument of the working class. In time it would disappear. It was left to writers from the Austrian school to argue that a command economy inevitably leads to an authoritarian government. It is also an open question the extent to which "laissez-faire" as normally interpreted reflects faithfully Adam Smith's views. J. M. Keynes suffered the same faith. Keynesian economics probably went far beyond where Keynes himself would have liked it to go. In his recent biography of Keynes, Peter Clarke quotes Keynes, who in 1944, after attending a meeting of Keynesian economists in the United States, commented that "[he] was the only non-Keynesian there." See Clarke, 2009.

2. Speaking of the United States, in a comment written in 1983, on H.C. Simons's *A Positive Program for Laissez Faire*, Milton Friedman would say that, in 1934, when Simons's book appeared, "close to a majority of the social scientists and the students in the social sciences at the University of Chicago were either members of the Communist party or very close to it." Cited in Van Overtveldt, 2007, p. 201. The proportions were probably higher in many European universities.

3. It should be recognized that governments have many other responsibilities beside the direct, purely economic ones. In the period before the Great Depression, many social laws that were indirectly important for the economy (rights to unionize, to strike, to vote, to vacation, to safe jobs, etc.) were being pushed and enacted in various countries. These laws did not require much higher public spending but different social relations in the private sector. They did, however,

call for an efficient bureaucracy capable of enforcing the new legislation. See Weber, 1947.

4. A standard remark was that in capitalist countries unemployment was in the streets, out of the enterprises; in centrally planned countries, it was in the enterprises.

5. Especially various French economists of the 19th century carried some of Smith's ideas well beyond where Smith might have liked. Among these economists, one should mention F. Bastiat, J. B. Say, de Molinari, Comte, and Dunoyer. These economists left very little scope to the government. See Weinburg, 1978.

6. Besides Buchan's recent biography of Adam Smith, two other good introductions to Smith are Winch, 1978, and Muller, 1993.

7. See on this the fascinating book *La fine dell'economia* (2006; The End of the Economy), by Sergio Ricossa, especially the chapter titled "Contro il comercio" (Against Commerce).

8. See Ricossa, 2006, p. 51, citing Gerschenkron.

9. Actually it could be argued that the policies recommended by Smith, by increasing trade and specialization, would generate growth.

10. It should be reiterated that this "market fundamentalism" had found strong defense much earlier among some classical economists such as de Molinari (1849). De Molinari strongly defended property rights and did not believe that monopolies existed, or that they could remain monopolies for long without the support of the state. During his long life, de Molinari, a Belgian-born economist living in France, was well known and influential, even though he is not much remembered today.

11. In 1776 capital markets were not developed as they became later so that it was much more difficult for private operators to get financial resources for large public works. Also the state may find it easier to deal with legal obstacles that often exist in the execution of large infrastructure projects.

12. Say, de Molinari, and other laissez-faire economists would question this government role.

13. As a recent biographer has put it, "The world in which Adam Smith was writing was not a modern economy, but had as much to do with the Roman Empire as [with] the age of Alan Greenspan and Gordon Brown." See Buchan, 2006, p. 5.

14. As Cicero had put it, in 43 B.C., "the national budget must be balanced. The public debt must be reduced. The arrogance of the authorities must be moderated and controlled. Payments to foreign governments must be reduced if the nation does not want to go bankrupt. People must again learn to work, instead of living on public assistance." David Hume, a contemporary of Smith, is also worth citing: "It is tempting to a Minister to employ such an expedient, as enables him to make a great figure during his administration, without overburdening the people with taxes, or exciting any immediate clamours against himself. The practice, therefore, of contracting debt will almost infallibly be abused in every government." Therefore, "the consequences . . . must indeed, be one of . . . two events; either the nation must destroy public credit, or public credit will destroy the nation." Hume, 1955.

15. Note that in the Nordic states of Europe the church had been incorporated by the state in the 16th century during the Reformation so that the church, as a

church, could no longer play this role independently from the state. In England, Henry VIII had dissolved monasteries and friaries in the 1530s and taken over their assets, often using the pretext of corruption. See MacCulloch, 2003, p. 46.

16. Perhaps a word of caution is necessary here. At that time, there were no official national income statistics. Therefore, the data available must be seen as approximations rather than precise figures.

17. J. B. Say, the French laissez-faire economist famous for the law that stated that the supply creates its own demand, had defined the growth of public spending at that time as a "universal evil."

18. Jean-Baptiste Colbert was the famous finance minister of Louis XIV, the king of France. He was much connected with mercantilism in France.

19. See also an article by Bruno Frey (1985).

20. Thus, they would have been amused by the literature on social welfare maximization and social welfare functions that assumes a benevolent and all-knowing dictator. They would be skeptical about voluntary exchange theories. See Fausto and De Bonis, 2003.

21. The Netherlands succeeded in reducing public spending significantly after imposing those limits.

22. In the 1880s the English income tax "varies from . . . twopence in the pound to a mere sixpence half-penny." See Trevelyan, 1942, p. 558. During the war the threshold was reduced from 160 to 130 sterling per year and the income tax rate was raised from 5.8 to 30 percent. See Stevenson, 2007, p. 178.

23. The borrowing was justified on grounds that future generations should contribute to the financing of the war. Strong patriotic appeals were directed to citizens to buy government bonds. Those who did ended up financing a lot of the war because of the inflation that followed the war and that wiped out the value of their bonds.

## Chapter Three: Forces That Changed the Role of the State

1. See Hegel, 1956.

2. See *Le Encicliche Sociali: Dalla Rerum Novarum Alla Centesimus Annus*, 6th ed. (Paoline Editoriale Libri, 2003).

3. In later decades, better roads and the introduction of some public transportation and bicycles allowed workers to cover greater distance.

4. As an Italian book has put it, quoting from *Il Grido del Popolo* (The Cry of the People, a weekly magazine) of November 25, 1899, "The slave 'could look at the future without fear. . . . the wage earner instead lives by the day. . . . He is free to starve." See Ricossa, 2006, p. 34 (my translation). By that time, strikes were becoming common and occasionally violent, and the right to strike had become a major social issue. Insecurity had also become an issue as indicated by Bismarck's reference to it in a major speech in 1884. See article on Otto von Bismarck in Wikipedia.

5. Some countries now provide basic, minimum pensions to anyone reaching an official retirement age. Pensions that are relatively low are not linked to contributions made during the working life. See Chapter 13.

6. Because pensions were rare in the late part of the 19th century, the *Rerum Novarum* urged the state to educate the workers to the need to save (p. 60).

7. How much the world has changed can be seen from the following: "An act of 1802 safeguarding the interests of poor-law apprentices in factories limited the daily work of children to twelve hours.... The house of commons agreed in 1818 to fix a limit of eleven hours a day a child of nine or ten could be expected to spend at work.... the house of lords... postponed the bill.... It was reintroduced in 1819, and passed with a limit of twelve hours a day, exclusive of meal times, for children between the ages of nine and sixteen" (Woodward, 1962, pp. 12–13).

8. Life expectancy has been increasing by about 1 year or more every 10 years in industrial countries.

9. It can be argued that modern societies are characterized by too much formal education and too little practical training. Governments support education for people to become poets but not training to become plumbers. When schools were mostly private, this problem did not exist. Several writers of the past expressed a preference for technical and activities-related education over general education. In modern societies, enterprises complain that even during recessions they cannot find some skilled workers.

10. See Wheen, 1999, pp. 4–5.

11. Williamson has shown that globalization led to higher income inequality both in the period before World War I and in the current period. Income inequality has been a strong force for higher governmental intervention in democratic societies.

12. These levels might have been seen as too high by libertarians who advocated a minimal state, such as Bastiat and de Molinari. As we saw earlier, there were frequent complaints in the literature of the 19th century about *excessive* government spending and about *waste* in that spending. Even mainstream economists shared these views.

13. Obviously, even if one accepts Wagner's conclusion, as often interpreted, there must be a limit to the levels that public spending can reach in a market economy before that market ceases to be a market economy. It will be argued later that this level may have been reached, or even exceeded, around the year 2000 by several countries.

14. This was different from the socialist notion that would abolish private property, and thus the market economy, by transferring the means of production to the state.

15. It should be reiterated noted that the trilogy does not include economic development or economic growth, an objective often explicitly promoted by governments.

16. Seligman (1913) had also questioned the use of income taxes.

17. It should be noted that, while the *Rerum Novarum* of Pope Leo XIII had called attention to the need to save more on the part of workers, the implicit recommendation of the Keynesian Revolution might be interpreted as a need to save less. Saving ceased to be an obvious virtue, and, of course, lower saving exposes individuals, *qua* individuals, to higher risks, creating a presumption for greater government intervention in protecting individuals from economic risks.

18. As Ebenstein (2001) put it, "Socialism was considered, particularly by academic intellectuals, to be society's next ethical and empirical step" (p. 116). He cites the 1989 edition of Paul Samuelson's *Economics* textbook that, on p. 837, stated that the "Soviet economy is proof that contrary to what many skeptics had earlier believed, a socialist command economy can function and even thrive." The timing of this statement, just a short time before the collapse of the Soviet Union, was particularly unfortunate for Samuelson. The fact that Russia avoided the Great Depression, while undergoing other major difficulties, may have given more weight to the Soviet experiment.

19. The data are from Herbert Stein (1984, p. 399). It should be mentioned that the large growth in public spending in the United States between 1929 and 1958 was in part due to the large increase in defense spending over the period.

20. Richard Musgrave's identification of the three roles for governmental action was not new. For example, an article by a Greek economist, published in 1950, had referred to these three roles and had described, in considerable detail, what policies each role should promote (Angelopoulos, 1950). However, Musgrave refined and popularized the concept, especially in the Anglo-Saxon world. His book remains the most influential public finance book in the past 50 years.

21. Van Creveld's interpretation may be stretching the truth a bit. While the Atlantic Charter mentions (fifth principle) "the object of securing, for all, improved labor standards, economic advancement and social security" and the hope that "all the men in all the lands may live out their lives in freedom from fear and want" (sixth principle), the United States had not yet entered the war at the time the charter was signed on August 14, 1941.

22. In the United States, the Eisenhower administration would prevent any increase in public spending during its years, 1952–60. There were vocal opponents of the new programs. Even in 1964, during the Kennedy administration, "added expenditure programs faced very great resistance" (Heller, 1967, p. 113). However, the opponents of new expenditure programs became more and more isolated voices. See, for example, Hayek, 1942; and de Jouvenel, 1952.

23. Libertarians would even question this point.

24. In the 1940s, immediately after the end of the war, there was a great fear conditions typical of the Great Depression would return because of excessive saving by the population and because of the reduction in war spending.

25. The low-spending countries of Asia seem to have been affected less by the crisis. However, the reasons may be different ones.

### Chapter Four: Growth of Public Spending and Taxation in the 20th Century

1. Some of the information in this chapter comes from Tanzi and Schuknecht, 2000.

2. The share of public spending into GDP rose in some countries, including the United States, during the Great Depression, partly because of the fall of economic activity. For the United States, see Stein, 1984, p. 399, and U.S. Office of Management and Budget, 2009.

3. In 1946 the share of public debt into GDP in the United States was 121.7 percent. By 1953 it had fallen to 71.4 per cent of GDP. Unlike what happened at the end

of the First World War in some European countries, the Second World War was not followed by high inflation in the United States but by low inflation. However, the debt had been issued at long maturity and at very low interest rates. Thus, the low inflation that prevailed in the years after the war, combined with better economic performance, was sufficient to reduce the debt quickly. By 1960 the share of gross federal debt into GDP had been reduced to 56.0 percent. In the years after the war, the *real* return on the public bonds acquired during the war was taxed at more than 100 percent.

4. In the United States, the growth was moderate also because the fall in defense spending accommodated some increase in civilian public spending and because, as we discuss later, the United States followed a different social model. Between 1960 and 1999, U.S. federal receipts rose from 17.8 percent of GDP (in 1960) to 20.0 percent (in 1999). Federal outlays rose from 17.8 percent of GDP (in 1960) to 18.6 percent (in 1999). For general government (that includes state and local governments), the increases were from 25.2 percent (in 1960) to 30.1 percent of GDP (in 1999) for government receipts, and from 26.2 percent of GDP (in 1960) to 29.3 percent of GDP (in 1999) for outlays. See U.S. Office of Management and Budget, 2009, table 1.2, pp. 24–25, and table 15.3, pp. 326–27.

5. The Kennedy administration had wanted to increase public spending, but the programs and the legislation that would have allowed it were not in place. These programs had to wait for Johnson's War on Poverty. During the Johnson administration, U.S. public spending increased by more than 3 percent of GDP. As Heller (1966) put it, "Added expenditure programs faced very great resistance. The use of tax reduction made it possible to induce a coalition of conservative and liberal forces to endorse and work for an expansionary fiscal policy" (p. 113).

6. Housing was also subsidized by the operations of institutions (Fannie Mae and Freddie Mac) that contributed to lower interest rates for mortgages. These institutions were created in the 1960s.

7. The prevailing view was that income taxes had an "income effect" that stimulated the taxpayers to work more and a "substitution effect" that would favor taking more leisure. The conclusion was that the two effects neutralized each other. Paul Samuelson, in his *Foundations of Economic Analysis* (1947), dismissed the notion of elasticities as playing a significant role in the response of individuals to high marginal tax rates. In later years many came to believe that the substitution effect was much more important for high-income people and especially for the internationally mobile ones, as well as for particular categories of individuals.

8. The Keynesian revolution had also removed the stigma of fiscal deficits and public debts. See Heller, 1966, pp. 36–37. An earlier sin became a virtue.

9. During the preparation that led to the 1986 comprehensive tax reform in the United States, there was some discussion of the value-added tax but nothing came out of it. See Tanzi, 2010, pp. 35–36.

10. See table 15.1, pp. 322–23 of U.S. Office of Management and Budget, 2009.

11. For a quantitative analysis of this process in the Italian case, see Franco, 1993, especially table 51, on p. 187.

12. Some discussion of pension reforms in Nordic countries is provided in Chapter 13.

13. Inflation also distorts tax bases but corrections for these effects are much more complex, and only some Latin American countries with high inflation (Argentina, Brazil, Chile, Mexico) attempted them.

14. Many U.S. states had retail sales taxes. But these were much less productive than the value-added taxes. Also tax competition among the states kept state taxes low. See Tanzi, 1995, chap. 3.

15. During the Clinton years, "tax expenditures" increased significantly. To some extent they substituted for public spending. See Toder, 2000.

16. Total government revenue (not just taxes) exceeded 60 percent of GDP in 1993–94 and in 1998 in Sweden and 56 percent of GDP in 1987–89 and in several years after 1993 in Denmark.

17. Between 2000 and 2008, federal receipts fell from 20.9 to 17.7 percent of GDP. In 2009 they fell to an estimated 15.1 percent of GDP. Outlays increased from 18.4 percent of GDP in 2000 to 21.0 percent in 2008 and to an estimated 28.1 percent in 2009.

18. It might be a coincidence but all three countries that increased cash transfers would face fiscal difficulties in 2010. All the countries that decreased cash transfers would face much fewer difficulties.

## Chapter Five: The Role of the State in Social Protection: Historical Landmarks

1. This is more so in some parts of the world than in others. The large size of the (extended) family has been considered a negative factor in economic development by development economists. It is assumed to reduce the incentives of individual members of the family. The benefit from higher effort on the part of one individual is distributed to other members of the extended family rather than benefiting just the individual and his immediate family. However, the reduction of the size of the family in recent decades must have been a major contributor to the growth of social spending.

2. This is perhaps a major distinction from some government-supported programs. The latter try to anticipate needs and not just to react to the events that create these needs.

3. According to Angus Maddison, in 1820 the level of GDP per capita (in 1990 international dollars) was 1705 in the United Kingdom, 1264 in the United States, and 675 in Japan. In the whole West, it was 1956 in 1870 and 3843 in 1913. See Maddison, 1999, tables 1 and 6. Some economic historians now question Maddison's estimates.

4. Recent research in economic development has concluded that when safe and easily accessible opportunities for investing their savings are available to poorly paid workers, they are more likely to save. Postal saving systems were created in some countries to facilitate the investment of savings, especially in rural areas and in small towns.

5. As mentioned earlier, in the United States charitable contributions account for about 2 percent of GDP, excluding the value of the time that many volunteers

allocate to this activity and the assistance provided through informal channels, which could be significant.

6. Ashley, 1904, pp. 16–17, reports that in England there was an Accident Insurance System, broadly compared with that introduced in Germany, but the Friendly Society Organization, "supplemented by various union and other Trade Societies," was far less comprehensive in coverage for old age and infirmity than that introduced by Bismarck.

7. In 1900 life expectancy in Germany at birth was 47. See Maddison, 1999, table 4. Life expectancy for men at the age of 40 was somewhat higher. For the years 1894–97, it was 26 in Prussia and 25 in England beyond the life expectancy at birth. Data reported in Ashley, 1904, p. 48. Still, few would reach the age of 70.

8. The two major Italian economists of the time, Vilfredo Pareto and Maffeo Pantaleoni, encountered difficulties in their academic careers in this period because of their opposition to interventionist government policies that were becoming common. See Are, 1974, chapter 5.

9. Another change would be that with the passing of time the retirement age would become a progressively lower ratio of average life expectancy. The time in retirement increased in relation to the time spent at work.

10. For a concise and early account of the Roosevelt reform, see Schlesinger, 1959, especially chapter 18, "The Birth of Social Security." See also Stein, 1984, especially chapter 2, "Hoover and Roosevelt: The Depression Origin of Liberal Economics."

11. In 2008 social insurance and retirement receipts were about $900 billion or 35.7 percent of total federal receipts. That percentage had not changed from the mid-1980s. Before the mid-1980s it had been growing over the years. As a share of GDP, it had grown to reach about 6.5 percent in the late 1980s and afterward. See U.S. Government, 2009.

12. See Feldstein, 1974; and, for a criticism of Feldstein's conclusion, see Barro, 1978.

13. Furthermore, additional support for this category came from the increasing use of "tax expenditures," especially in the decade of the 1990s.

14. The marginal tax rates for welfare recipients who got a job and lost the benefits were very large, thus creating a poverty trap.

## Chapter Six: Globalization and Public Spending

1. In Chapter 14 we discuss other ways in which globalization and more specifically growing cross-border externalities are changing the economic role of the state.

2. By Keynesian ideas, it is meant here those of the Keynesian school and not necessarily those of J. M. Keynes himself.

3. Once the attention shifted to the supply side, it was inevitable that some of the policies that had led to the expansion of the role of the state would be subjected to growing scrutiny by economists.

4. The privatization of many previously state-owned or public enterprises reversed a process that had characterized the period after World War II when nationalization of many large enterprises had been popular.

5. Reading Schlesinger's 1959 description of what happened during the Great Depression, one gets the impression of reading accounts of the 2008–9 crisis. As he put it, "Few things were more demoralizing to the middle class in 1933 than the threatened loss of homes through mortgage foreclosure.... The mounting foreclosure rate weakened the position of saving banks and insurance companies.... The real estate market and the construction industry alike seemed headed toward collapse" (p. 297).

### Chapter Seven: Theories of Public-Sector Behavior: Taxonomy of Government Types

1. For a good introduction to the theory of public finance in Italy, see Fausto and De Bonis 2003.
2. The first Italian edition of his major work in public finance – *Il carattere teorico dell' economia finanziaria* – was published in 1888.
3. Among the collective wants that he lists, he ranks, in terms of importance, defense first and protection against poor hygiene and against private monopolies last.
4. See Mill, 2004, p. 788.
5. Ibid.
6. The dislike for direct taxes goes back in time. It has been reported that, in the 13th and 14th centuries, Siena had a direct tax (the *dazio*) that was much hated. The citizens preferred an indirect tax (*contado*). See Bowsky's article in Herliky et al., 1969. The first English-language book ever written on Italy, in 1549, by a Welsh traveler who lived in Italy during the late 1540s, reported with amazement on the large amount of taxes collected by the Venetian state, an amount "rather to be wondered at than believed, considering they raise it not upon lands but upon customs." He adds that "there is not a grain of corn, a spoonful of wine, a corn of salt, egg, bird, beast, fowl, or fish bought or sold that payeth not a certain custom." See Thomas, 1549, p. 69. Perhaps the reluctance of the United States in using indirect taxes has contributed much to keeping its tax burden and its public spending lower than in other countries.
7. Letter written by Pareto to Griziotti. See Griziotti, 1944, p. 137 (my translation).
8. See Dalton, 1967, p. 33.
9. Ibid, p. 34.
10. See Amilcare Puviani, *Teoria dell' Illusione Finanziaria* (Milan: ISEDI, 1973). The first edition of this book was published in 1903. For a long time, Puviani's ideas were not extensively discussed in the literature. For example, they attracted a total of six lines in Dennis C. Mueller's comprehensive survey, *Public Choice* (Cambridge: Cambridge University Press, 1979), p. 90. The interested reader can find some description in James M. Buchanan, *Public Finance in Democratic Process* (Chapel Hill: University of North Carolina Press, 1967). Chapter 10 of that work deals with the "fiscal illusion." An interesting interpretation of Puviani's work is Franco Volpi's introduction to the 1973 edition of the *Teoria dell' Illusione Finanziaria*. For some uses of this concept, see R. E. Wagner, "Revenue Structure, Fiscal Illusion, and Budgetary Choice," *Public Choice* 25 (Spring 1976): 25, 45–61; and Vito Tanzi, "Taxpayers' Preferences and the Future

Structure of State and Local Taxation," in International Institute of Public Finance, *Issues in Urban Public Finance,* New York Congress, 1972 (Saarbrücken, 1973), pp. 459–66. In recent years, Puviani's name has become better known.

11. Perhaps this is an unfair interpretation of that theory because it is a *normative* rather than a *positive* theory; thus, it is supposed to tell us only how governments *should* behave and not how they behave. Also at this point we ignore the question of aggregation, to large groups, of benefits and costs of public-sector programs.

12. Puviani, 1973, p. 5 (my translation).

13. Ibid. p. 7 (my translation).

14. Ibid.

15. Ibid., pp. 7–8.

16. Many, but not all, of the ways outlined in this paragraph are illustrated in Puviani's work with historical examples.

17. Thus, a report by the surgeon general that cigarette smoking causes cancer will be followed by tax increases on cigarettes. There is some evidence that this, in fact, is what happened in the United States. Similarly, reports of excessive incomes for managers of enterprises and for operators in the financial market may lead to tax increases on these groups. Or reports that car use leads to global warming may facilitate tax increases on gasoline. Of course, these tax increases may also be explained by the existence of externalities. But externalities may themselves become excuses for higher taxes.

18. The most complete treatment of this particular aspect of the Italian literature is found in Fasiani, 1951. However, Fasiani's treatment draws considerably from the work of other economists including De Viti de Marco. The discussion that follows is an interpretation of that literature.

19. Pareto believed that, regardless of the form of government, the political power is always exercised by a leading group, an elite. See Pareto, 1923. See also Mosca, 1884, 1933, and 1966.

20. For a discussion along these lines, see Tanzi, 1974.

21. It may also be limited by the ability to extract high taxes from the population.

22. Musgrave, 1959, p. 86.

23. *Whether this summation* is possible is an interesting question but one not relevant to our immediate discussion. See on this Arrow, 1951, and rev. ed. 1963; and Mueller, 1979, pp. 184–206. See also Amartya Sen's Nobel Lecture 1999, which contains a very extensive bibliography on the topic.

24. It was presumably in this spirit that Ronald Reagan, when he was governor of California, attempted to abolish the withholding-at-the-source system for the payment of the state income taxes. In his view, that system decreased the taxpayers' awareness of the true cost of public spending and, by thus creating a fiscal illusion, led to a larger public sector.

25. In the Hegelian version of the state, the state has its own personality or "mind" and finality that might be distinguished from that of the governments, which may change over time. These may not coincide with those of the individuals who make up the state at any one moment. See Weil, 1950.

26. A government may appear paternalistic with respect to some policies, monopolistic with respect to others, and may follow the individualistic model with respect to still others.

27. Of course, it is difficult to identify what are "significant" externalities. However, small externalities are so prevalent that, if one used them to justify governmental intervention, the government would be involved in most activities. It can be argued that the government's attempt to deal with many externalities has been one reason for the expansion of public sector's activities over the years. This is a point often made by Buchanan, who has argued that governments have politicized and exploited externalities to expand their scope.

28. This amalgamation has become more difficult because of the inclusion in personal preferences of distributional concerns and environmental concerns.

29. This, of course, raises the question of whether each vote reflects or should reflect the same weight.

30. See Parravicini, 1970, p. 92 (my translation).

31. It is interesting to note that this conception is similar in spirit to that contained in "Charity in Truth," the third encyclical letter released on July 7, 2009, by Pope Benedict XVI, on the eve of the G-8 meeting in L'Aquila (Italy).

32. See Putman, 2000.

33. There are even treaties that require the return of stolen "national heritage works of art" that have been taken to other countries.

### Chapter Eight: Voluntary Exchange and Public Choice Theories

1. Perhaps North's is too strong a view. In the Republic of Venice, in Florence, and in other city-states during the Renaissance, there was concern about the performance of the economy and of the government and its effect on the public good (*bene commune*). Also, the United States was born with a different kind of government than the one described by Douglass North. The magnificent frescos by Ambrogio Lorenzetti in the Sala dei Nove in the Palazzo Pubblico in Siena, painted between 1338 and 1340, describe his vision of the Buon Governo (the Good Government) and the Mal Governo (the Bad Government) and their effects on society. They are among the best-known works of the Renaissance and are a clear witness that, at least during the Italian Renaissance, there was a vision of what citizens expected from their government. Whether they got it, is another story.

2. Buchan (2006, pp. 1–2) is sharply critical of Alan Greenspan's interpretation of Adam Smith's ideas. See also Greenspan, 2007, pp. 260–66, for his description of Smith's ideas.

3. In 1950 the share of total taxes into GDP in Sweden had been only 21 percent. In 1930 it had been 15 per cent. By 1980 it had reached and surpassed 50 percent of GDP. Broadly similar changes occurred in some other countries. See also Tanzi, 1970.

4. For the United States one could argue that the tipping period might have come with the Roosevelt administration during the Great Depression, which changed the expectations of many Americans toward what the government's responsibilities were. Cohen (2009) has written that FDR's Agricultural Adjustment Act was the "first law that [in the United States] committed the [federal] government to caring for the destitute citizens." There had not been any Poor Laws in the United States. The Eisenhower administration would attempt to restore to

some extent the previous government role. After the Eisenhower administration, there was an alternation of administrations that tried to expand or contain the growth of the role of the state. Especially important was the "War on Poverty" by the Johnson administration in 1965. The net result was a smaller increase, over future years, in public spending than in European countries. There was no increase in the share of *total* public spending into GDP between the late 1960s until 2009. However *social* spending grew, financed by cuts in defense spending. The 2008–9 crisis and the advent of the Obama administration is likely to lead to an increase in the share of total public spending in GDP in future years. For a good description of historical developments in the attitude, in the United States, vis-à-vis the economic role of the state, see Stein, 1969 and 1985.

5. One of my Harvard professors in 1961–62, Professor Edward Chamberlin, of monopolistic competition fame, stated during one of his classes that economics was then becoming a "haven for mediocre mathematicians." This was clearly much too strong an opinion. However, it became more and more frequent for economists to start as mathematicians or physicists or even engineers and then move to economics, bringing with them their mathematical tools and, more importantly, a mental frame that assumed that the economic system is similar to the physical world or even to machines and that, like a machine, it follows specific rules and responds in a specific, precise, and consistent way to changes in particular variables. On this point, it may be worthwhile to cite a top economist and Nobel Prize winner, Robert Solow. He wrote, "My impression is that the best and brightest in the profession proceed as if economics is the physics of society. There is a single universally valid model of the world" (1985, p. 330). There is thus the view, or the illusion, that there are precise relationships among economic variables that are not influenced by historical circumstances, irrationality, or societal characteristics, including the institutions that they have created.

6. It should be recalled that, especially in the Anglo-Saxon world, public spending had been traditionally considered unproductive and thus not worthy of analysis. This view has continued to prevail among more conservative political agents. It was an article of faith during the Reagan administration. During the early part of that administration, the head of the General Service Administration declared that public salaries should be low because public jobs did not need to attract able individuals. However, for an increasing proportion of economists, fiscal tools became important instruments for solving many social problems. The "War on Poverty" by the Johnson administration in the United States had been an expression of this thinking. See Heller, 1966.

7. For a short history of the use of cost-benefit analysis in public works and other techniques, see Merewitz and Sosnick, 1971.

8. This already brings legal considerations. In the United States citizenship is connected with the place where one is born. Thus, the only consideration is the status of the individual. In many other countries, citizenship is acquired through blood relationship among citizens (the *jus sanguinis*). Thus, community, or family links, enter the legal decisions on citizenship.

9. It should be pointed out that in "failed states," and not just in them, the government may compete with other groups, such as terrorist groups or organized crime, in the use of force. See, for example, the current situation in Mexico.

10. For a recent discussion of this concept, see Eusepi, 2002.

11. An argument can be made that, at the time when the theories about tax prices were formulated, much of what the government produced (defense, protection, justice, administration, and large public projects) consisted of "public goods" assumed to benefit everyone. There was little purely and explicitly redistributive expenditure. Thus, the main question was whether the expenditure was productive or not.

12. Peacock, 1992, p. 16, comments that "Pareto considered that his criteria for allocative efficiency applied only to the private economy." He would have been surprised to see the application of that concept to the public sector.

13. The concept of a "social welfare function" had been developed by Bergson, 1938. Such a function would encourage exchanges that maximized the welfare of society. A problem has remained that welfare cannot be measured unless one identifies it with total output, such as GDP or some similar concept. Thus, it has remained a virtual concept.

14. Globalization has made tax evasion easier especially for higher income individuals.

15. Current estimates of underground economic activities are large and growing in many countries.

16. For example, the American citizens who escaped to Canada during the Vietnam War to evade the draft.

17. These difficulties were recognized in discussions of the proper social rate of discount. Marxists assumed a zero rate of discounts. Others (Baumol and Eckstein) assumed that there is a rate of discount for individuals acting individually and for individuals acting in groups. Eckstein concluded that "the choice of interest rates must remain a value judgment." Eckstein, 1961, p. 460.

18. This can happen when some groups have the discretion to make legal decisions or when the meaning of laws can be reinterpreted, say by a Supreme Court.

19. See on this Mokyr, 2002.

20. In a recent article that tried to explain differential growth rates over the long run in a group of countries, Robert Lucas (2009) concluded that the flow of ideas was probably the main factor in explaining those differences. This would be consistent with North's adaptive efficiency. Countries where institutions facilitate the flow of ideas and the use of those ideas are more likely to grow and develop over the long run. What government role generates these institutions?

21. For an example of rules that lead to significant misuse of resources, see Tanzi and Prakash, 2003.

22. It may affect differently short-run and long-run efficiency.

23. This used to be a common assumption made by those who promoted land reform, especially in those Latin American countries characterized by *latifundio*, that is, large estates.

24. Even this raises problems. Is the benefit related to the *availability* of the public service (say, health or education), or to the actual *use* of the service? If it is for

the actual use, the tax prices can be determined only ex post, after the service has actually been used. In this case they would truly become prices, similar to those in the market. This would rule out any redistributive feature.

25. It should be recalled that De Viti de Marco would tax incomes proportionately under the assumption that they were a good, practical measure of the benefits that individuals received from public goods and services. But, as mentioned earlier, in his time most public spending was on public goods because income redistribution was not yet considered a legitimate policy objective.

26. The debate about health reform in the United States in 2009 and early 2010 indicated how difficult these questions can be. At what level of health provision is the basic need for health assumed to be satisfied? See Groopman, 2010, for a physician's view.

27. In 1955–56 James Buchanan spent a sabbatical year in Italy and became acquainted with the Italian scienza delle finanze. As he put it in a recent article, "De Viti de Marco was [his] entry point into the Italian research program" (2003, p. 283).

28. Because of the young age of the United States, and the fact that its population came from different parts of the world (with different ethnic, religious, and historical backgrounds), it is less of a "community" than the population of many other countries. Thus, the Buchanan and Tullock assumption may be more realistic for the United States than for other, older and more homogeneous countries.

29. As George Stigler (1988, p. 8) put it, "Ex ante, every public action is expected to be non-mistaken, ex ante, the state is infallible."

30. The similarity between Coase's argument for private firms and Nelson's argument for these private community associations is striking.

31. One could argue that these arrangements contribute to the breakdown of the community spirit and, perhaps, to a decline in social capital except for those who operate within the private associations. They may lead to a fragmentation of the true community spirit.

32. Members of the Chicago school to which Coase belonged also believe that regulations are rarely needed and that there are rarely natural monopolies that justify governmental intervention. See Van Overtveldt, 2007.

33. Also externalities become more diffused and, at times, less immediately recognized or concentrated to lend themselves to Coasean solutions.

34. This "Coasean" approach to the role of the state may be implicit in the work of Albert Schäffle, as reported in Musgrave, 1998, pp. 43–44. Schäffle took a biological perspective to society, which he saw as a set of interacting organisms that could be coordinated by the state in the realization of communal interests. See Schäffle, 1896.

35. The Tiebout argument assumes away the existence of horizontal inequities in the allocation of taxes and public spending. It also faces the problem that, as more people move to a new jurisdiction, their number may force the jurisdiction to change the composition of their taxes and expenditure.

36. When mobility is restricted, jurisdictions may compete as communities, as they did during the Italian Renaissance, leading to different conclusions. See Burckhardt, 1944.

## Chapter Nine: The Nordic European Economic Theory of Fiscal Policy

1. When they vote, voters vote for candidates and not for specific policies. Electoral promises may not be honored or may be changed after the elections. Often the candidates are not specific about the policies that they would follow if elected. Furthermore, they may change the policies on the grounds that the circumstances have changed, thus justifying the change. In particular cases, single, emotional issues dominate the choices.

2. Bent Hansen was part of a committee, chaired by Erik Lundberg, that had been appointed by the Swedish minister of finance to investigate policies needed to keep stable prices and full employment. Its work was completed in 1955 at a time when the transformation of Sweden and other Nordic countries had just started.

3. There was a lot of discussion at that time on the difference between economic growth and economic development. The latter was considered a broader and more significant concept.

4. It must be recognized that changes in instruments can be constrained by laws, politics, international agreements, or administrative difficulties. Small changes in instruments are more likely to be feasible than large changes.

5. The conditions to be satisfied are specified in Johansen, 1965.

6. Passing from the mathematical to the economic solution, it must be realized that the mathematical solution may imply unrealistic changes in the instruments. Thus, a mathematical solution does not imply a feasible policy. The larger the changes are, the more difficult it will be to use econometrically derived results to predict the outcome. Also large changes might make results based on past data less reliable.

7. In more recent years, because of the impact of immigration, the Northern European countries have become ethnically less homogeneous societies. Thus, some previously accepted policies have become more controversial and the governments have become more conservative.

8. Thus, the question of who decides the budget becomes an important one. In recent years, there has been much literature on this question.

9. Coalition governments are less likely to satisfy this first assumption.

10. This is an area where the work of Persson and Tabellini, 2004; von Hagen, 1992; Alesina et al., 1999; and IDB, 2005 and 2009, is relevant.

11. It must be recognized that the economic principles on which the empirical relationships are based may change with time because of the results of new research. Furthermore, as Myrdal recognized, "there exists widespread doubt about the supposed scientific character of economics" (Myrdal, 1954, p. xiii). Keynes (1971–89, 14:297), of course, shared the same doubts.

12. This is an area where fiscal policy is fundamentally different from monetary policy. The changes in the instruments of monetary policy do not require legislation and can be made by a few individuals, whereas those of fiscal policy always require legislation and the involvement of many actors. This makes the conduct of fiscal policy much more difficult and more political. This has led to proposals to create "fiscal councils" that would have power within certain limits to force or encourage changes in policies. Such councils were established in Sweden,

Hungary, and a few other places. But in 2010 the Hungarian government cut the budget for the council, and the Swedish government reduced its budget. It remains to be seen how these councils will operate over the long run and how much real political power they will have.

13. At times, the bills are thousands of pages long and are not read by those who have to approve them. For example, the bill sent by the Obama administration to stabilize the economy (February 2009) was thousands of pages and, it turned out, contained more than 8,000 earmarks. It was reported that few, if any, of those who had to vote on it read (or had the time to read) the bill. The same happened with the health bills. The law to reform the financial system, approved in July 2010, is 2,300 pages long. It will need thousands of additional pages in regulations that are still to be written.

14. There is also the big question of estimating the long-run cost of new legislation. Major mistakes are often made with respect to this objective.

15. This, for example, is a requirement well satisfied by the legislation of Chile where the constitution limits the initiative of parliament in promoting policies that have fiscal implications (IDB, 2005). It is clearly not satisfied in the United States, where major fiscal changes often originate in Congress with limited input from the executive branch. It is, however, true that the U.S. president has the power to veto legislation that he does not like. On the other hand, changes that are not attractive to the president can be imbedded in legislation that the president wants to be approved.

16. The clearest description of it is, perhaps, in Johansen's book (1965).

### Chapter Ten: Policy Tools and Government Roles

1. See Weber, 1947, and, especially, Weber, 1978, volume 2, chapter 11. See also the monumental study, in ten volumes, prepared by Formez (Presidenza del Consiglio dei Ministri, Ministero per la Pubblica Amministrazione e L'Innovazione), Italy, 2008. A better bureaucracy is also a less corrupt one. See Tanzi, 1998a.

2. For a study that argues that, at least in Italy, the bureaucracies maximize their own utility, see Costa, 2002. The Italian public finance literature has frequently shown skepticism about the role of bureaucracies in promoting the national rather than their interest.

3. As an author has put it, "Sensible tax law design must be informed by an understanding of the impact that design will have on the burden that taxpayers will face and the administrative costs that the revenue authority will be required to carry" Evans, 2003, p. 2.

4. This, in turn, may give rise to corruption when citizens pay bribes to public employees to get in front of the line. There is a lot of literature on corruption that has called attention to this aspect. See Tanzi, 1998a.

5. Perhaps, it should be added that fiscal rules that constrain the quantitative outcomes of fiscal policy might lead to increases in these compliance costs by citizens, because, in order to comply with the rules, governments shift the burden on the citizens. Also relevant here is the fact that outsourcing often reduces the financial costs to the governments but not the costs to the citizens. For example, getting a passport has become expensive in the United States

since this service was privatized. Outsourcing may also increase some forms of corruption.

6. Recent literature connected with the work of Akerlof, Stiglitz, and others has qualified the role of prices, because of asymmetry in information and other factors. See also Tanzi, 2007.

7. There is an extensive literature that deals with this sector. See, for example, Andreoni, 1988; Blank, 2000; and Kendall and Knapp, 1996.

8. Transparency International and some international institutions have attempted to measure the bribes paid.

9. We are assuming here that corruption does not involve coercion. When it does, it becomes explicitly a criminal activity.

10. The regulations may aim at putting the cost of the protection on the individuals themselves or on the employers. When it is on the latter, they may create a "hidden welfare state." This is the case with health and pensions. See Howard, 1997.

11. These are the "internal subsidies" within the system of public enterprises identified by Posner, 1971.

12. The Iraq War was "privatized" to a considerable extent because soldiers as well as a large number of "contractuals" were hired for pay to perform various war-related tasks. However, the costs were borne by the government.

13. During the Iraq War, there were some calls for a return to the draft.

14. These aspects give some policy makers, often the economy ministers, a lot of power.

15. For an early discussion of this issue, see Tanzi, 1986.

16. It should also be realized that the social, implicit costs of some incentives given in the past may change dramatically over time. For example, a tax-free status, given many years ago to a private school or to a religious establishment when the land on which the school is located was cheap, becomes progressively more costly in terms of opportunities when the value of the land increases. See Tanzi and Prakash, 2003.

17. In some countries, public enterprises and subnational governments also benefit from these implicit guarantees, making them face "soft budgets." For an analysis of soft budget constraints, see Kornai, Maskin, and Roland, 2003.

18. This creates an interesting theoretical question. In some cases the houses are built in areas not occupied before, such as the Atlantic or Caribbean coasts of the United States, subject to hurricanes, or on potential flood areas. In other cases, the houses are built in old cities known to be subject to earthquakes. Does the government have the same obligation in both cases in case of catastrophe?

19. This creates another interesting theoretical question. If an enterprise or an institution has become too big to fail, creating the perception or the expectation of governmental assistance, shouldn't the government have intervened *before* to prevent the institution from becoming too big to fail? Thus, the failure to intervene ex ante creates the expectation for intervention ex post.

20. It will also leave some countries with even larger financial institutions than the previous "too big to fail" ones.

21. It can be added that when the government officials who must make the decisions have come from the financial sector, and with increasing frequency from the

"too big to fail" institutions, there is a greater probability and expectation that they will convince the government to intervene.

22. The literature on intergenerational accounts has dealt with this aspect. See, inter alia, Auerback, Gokhale, and Kotlikoff, 1991.

23. The net liabilities are likely to be lower because some of the assets will be sold.

24. As a simple example, placing a television in front of a treadmill machine creates an incentive to spend more time on the treadmill. Going on the treadmill during a favorite program will increase the incentive.

25. When Alexander the Great jumped in front of his soldiers during battles, to encourage them to protect him and save their honor, he was de facto using a form of nudging.

26. See McCaffery and Slemrod, editors, 2006, for some examples of behavioral public finance. Over the years, several Latin American countries have used lotteries to induce buyers of goods and services that are subject to value-added taxes to request receipts for payments. The receipts become the lottery tickets.

## Chapter Eleven: Evaluating the Impact of Public Spending on Socioeconomic Indicators

1. This section draws from works listed in the references that I have done with Antonio Afonso and Ludger Schuknecht, and from Tanzi, 2008.

2. "The . . . HDI is a composite index that measures the average achievements in a country in three basic dimensions of human development: a long and healthy life; access to knowledge; and a decent standard of living. These basic dimensions are measured by life expectancy at birth, adult literacy and combined gross enrolment in primary, secondary and tertiary level education, and gross domestic product (GDP) per capita in purchasing power parity in US dollars." See UNDP, 2007, p. 225. The lower the HDI index is, the higher the HDI level is. Norway, with a ranking of 1, is considered to have the best index.

3. In fact, 35 percent of GDP may be too high if the countries are efficient in the use of their public money.

4. The percentages of those who thought that taxes are well spent ranged from a low of 10 percent in Peru to a high of 37–38 percent in Chile and Venezuela.

5. The following discussion is based on Afonso, Schuknecht, and Tanzi, 2005, and Afonso et al., 2007.

6. For details, the original articles should be consulted.

## Chapter Twelve: Social Protection in the Modern World: Some Quantitative Aspects

1. In some cases the "tax expenditures" lose their value when incomes become high because of vanishing characteristics of the "expenditures" contained in the tax laws.

2. As mentioned earlier, several of these countries are now experimenting with the use of public spending directed to the poorest and most vulnerable groups.

3. This, for example, is a major problem for Italy where there are 8,000 municipalities, some located in not easily accessible places and too small to justify the provision of schools, post offices, and other public services.

## Chapter Thirteen: The Role of the State and Economic Performance in the Nordic Countries

1. According to Internal Revenue Services statistics in the United States, the share of income received by the top 1 percent of U.S. taxpayers rose from 9.6 percent in 1979 to 21.6 percent in 2000, before falling slightly afterward. These data do not include unrealized capital gains. It would be difficult to accept the view that market forces alone, as distinguished from changed political and sociological attitudes, brought about this trend.

2. The economic framework followed by Sweden from the 1950s on was drafted by two economists who were closely associated with the labor unions: Gosta Rehn and Rudolf Meidner. Their program aimed at creating a welfare state while at the same time promoting policies that would lead to full employment and rapid growth. There was little nationalization of enterprises in Sweden. Most enterprises remained in private hands. State-owned enterprises played a much smaller role in Sweden than in many other European countries.

3. On the relation between egalitarianism and economic growth in Sweden, see Andersson and Gunnarsson, 2005.

4. Perhaps it should be added that several of the non-Nordic European countries were also creating their own version of welfare states in this period.

5. This description is based on Stein Kuhnle, 1998. See also Gustafsson, 1995.

6. As Jens Henriksson, state secretary in the Swedish Ministry of Finance, notes, "When the Social Democrats came to power in October 1994, the Swedish public deficit was above 10% of GDP. The interest rate differential vis-à-vis Germany came to 450 basis points and the unemployment rate stood at more than 8%.... Public debt was expected to be 128.2% of GDP.... There was a big crisis." See Henriksson, 2003, p. 205.

7. The direct taxes include income taxes and social security contributions.

8. In the United States, the fact that there is no value-added tax and that families get large deductions from income subject to the income tax means that many poor families pay hardly any taxes.

9. These are cash transfers only. They exclude transfers in kind that are particularly important in Nordic countries.

10. Please note that the Gini coefficient for Sweden given by *Eurostat NewCronos* diverges from the one given by Statistics Sweden reported earlier.

## Chapter Fourteen: The Economic Role of the State in the Future: Concluding Reflections

1. Over many years, the impact of taxes tended to become more diffused because of the introduction of *general* income and sales taxes, while the government programs became less linked to public goods and more to programs aimed at redistributing income. These changes must have contributed to increasing requests for spending.

2. In several countries, infrastructure, both physical and institutional (schools, bridges, roads, justice, and other essential services), has often been starved for funds to accommodate distributional and insurance functions. In some countries, prisoners have had to be released from jails because there were not

enough jails to accommodate them. In other countries, judicial processes last decades because there are not enough judges to deal with them in a more timely fashion. In some places bridges fall because of poor maintenance.

3. Measures associated with "libertarian paternalism," which try to change attitudes of individuals so as to reduce some risks to them and to others (smoking, getting fat, driving too fast, eating too much salt, etc.), or to induce them to take more initiatives to prevent some bad outcomes, are likely to become more important. If not reduced, these risks eventually increase government expenditure.

4. In many cases, cross-country externalities originate from emigration, pollution, and criminal and terroristic activities.

5. How this will be achieved is likely to be an important topic in future summit meetings of G7, G20, or other groups.

6. Of course, immigrants can also be an important positive externality for a country. For example, a significant proportion of American Nobel Prize winners, over the years, were foreign born. Immigrants can be a problem for the welfare states by creating pressures on schools, health systems, and so on. See Boeri, Hanson, and McCormack, 2002. Thus, countries are likely to make greater distinctions in the future in the access to public services, and especially to health and education, between citizens, on one hand, and immigrants, on the other hand.

7. See the various papers on global public goods in Kaul et al., 2003; and the papers, on regional public goods, in Estevadeordal et al., 2004. See also Tanzi 2005. There will also be greater pressures on developing countries to use more effectively the assistance that they receive.

8. Of course, from this it does not follow that a coordinated action will not suffer from (global) government failure. But, without coordination, failure will be certain. We shall leave to future policy experts to decide which failure would be more damaging. For an earlier and skeptical view of the possibility of international coordination of fiscal policy, see Tanzi, 1989. The best coordination of fiscal policy would be one in which all countries keep their fiscal accounts in order.

9. In several cases, clearly ethically questionable practices could take place without legal consequences because the practices had not been anticipated by rules that would have made them illegal.

10. See inter alia, Lowenstein, 2010; Sinn, 2010; Johnson and Kwak, 2010; and Rajan, 2010.

11. However, this did not prevent them from keeping, in several cases, hundreds of millions of U.S. dollars earned, not always ethically, in their financial market activities. See Dash (2010).

12. Top U.S. executives have been reported to have earned, in 2008, 319 times more on average than the average U.S. worker. In 2009, the year of the crisis, the chief executives of the 100 largest U.K. companies earned 81 times the average pay of U.K. full-time workers. See Plender, 2010, p. 7. Bloomberg reported that, in 2008, the top 25 hedge fund managers in the United States earned total incomes equivalent to the GDP of Kenya, with its 30 million inhabitants. It would be easier to accept these levels of compensation if a good case could be made that these were payments for real value contributed by these people to the economy.

Unfortunately, it is difficult to make such a case. See Tanzi, 2007a. It could be added that a "norm" attributed to the first Nobel Prize winner in economics, Jan Tinbergen, stated that the difference between lowest and highest incomes in an enterprize should not exceed 1 to 5.

13. In both the United States and the European Union, new legislation might limit or tax these large bonuses. Financial transaction taxes have been attracting increasing attention since Tobin first suggested their use. See Darvas and von Weizsäcker, 2010.

14. Philippon and Resheff, of NYU Stern School of Business, have argued that in recent years, and not just before the crisis, bankers have been overpaid by about 50 percent. This large rent implied also, in their view, that, because of the rents, highly skilled individuals chose to go into banking, rather than, say, regulatory activities, thus contributing to regulatory failure. They add that deregulation of financial markets played a significant role in this process. See Philippon, 2010, for a summary of their views.

15. It assumes that the intervention of the government can be truly complementary to the work of a market economy.

16. In the United States, in recent years, resources were reduced for regulators, and they were essentially told to close their eyes and trust the market. The regulated industries themselves often filled the forms that indicated whether they were following regulatory guidelines. This contributed to disasters, such as the "Madoff scheme," the Gulf of Mexico disaster, mining tragedies, and other problems. It has been reported that some of the regulators working for the Security and Exchange Commission in the United States, in the period before and during the 2008–9 crisis, spent their time watching porn on the Internet. The *Washington Post*, April 28, 2010, p. 83, reported that none of these people had been fired.

17. Of course, some will make a case that, with all its problems, an unregulated private market will deliver better economic results than a regulated market. Whether this conclusion is correct, not only in terms of economic growth but also in terms of general welfare, only careful empirical analysis can answer.

18. This is likely to have happened in the financial market where some highly objectionable practices connected with newly developed financial instruments developed that were widely seen as wrong but were not forbidden by the existing rules.

19. This issue arises in tax "evasion," which relates to the intentional breaking of tax laws. Tax "avoidance" may achieve the same objective as tax evasion by exploiting complexities or ambiguities in the laws but without strictly breaking the laws. A rule-based system does not penalize tax avoidance but only tax evasion. However, the legal systems of some countries (e.g., India) penalize both if the intention of the taxpayer is clearly seen by a special court to be that of evading the payment of taxes.

20. Perhaps, technological development needs to be slowed down if the needed institutions cannot adjust fast enough to keep up with it, and if those who operate in the market have difficulties in understanding what is going on. Fast technological development cannot always be assumed to be a beneficial development for society.

21. The costs of transactions imposed by the financial market on the real economy have become much too high to justify the incomes that the industry appropriates. The benefits that may come from more risk spreading must be evaluated against the increasing transaction costs. These transaction costs raise legitimate questions about whether the financial market is generating real economic value equivalent to the incomes it receives.

22. A large part of the increase in unemployment is due to structural adjustments (e.g., the sharp fall in demand for new houses).

23. With the difference of the United Kingdom, the average maturity on outstanding government debt is below eight years. In the United States it is around five years.

24. The United States, a low-tax country by international standards, may be forced to join the rest of the world by introducing a value-added tax. Because of very worrisome intergenerational accounts, it may be one of the few countries that may have to rely on significant tax increases to deal with current and future fiscal deficits. Some countries (United Kingdom, Spain, and others) have been forced to increase the rate of the value-added taxes. However, significant tax increases will encounter strong resistance in several countries, including Japan and the United States.

25. For an analysis of the government role vis-à-vis catastrophic events, and for a definition of major disasters, see Posner, 2004 also 2009. For several papers dealing with natural disasters, see *CES ifo Forum* 11, no. 2 (Summer 2010), and Cavallo et al., 2010.

26. For an interesting historical example of the role that urbanization played in England in increasing risks and promoting a larger role of the state, see Walvin, 1988. For a statistical analysis that highlights the impact of urbanization on tax levels, see Tanzi, 1992.

27. In the view of a minority, this is still an unsettled issue.

28. This is common in the pharmaceutical industry in which companies often invest hundred of millions of dollars to develop new drugs. They will, thus, tend to minimize or occasionally hide potentially serious side effects in order to recover their investments. A new, arising issue is, for example, whether cellular phones may increase the incidence of brain cancer, especially in children. As is often the case, the science is unsettled and limited at this point. The city of San Francisco is planning to require the producers of these phones to report how much radiation they generate.

29. Some countries have introduced the concept of the "single window," a single office where all authorization can be obtained, but the problems created by conflicting authorizations persist.

30. A recent article in *Time* 176, no. 2 (2010), has concluded that the best investment for enterprises and industries these days is the hiring of lobbyists, who for relatively small investments can get enormous financial returns for their sponsors from lawmakers. The view that *the government is now for sale* is becoming predominant. It is not surprising that many of the lobbyists were the assistants to the legislators, or often they are those who were policy makers and legislators themselves in previous years.

# Index

Accident Insurance Bill of 1884 (Bismarck), 115
Adema, W., 263
Agricultural Adjustment Act, 349–50n
Aid to Dependent Children (ADC), 118, 120–21, 346n
Alesina, A., 202
Allocation of resources function, 4, 59
Argentina
  education spending in, 239t
  HDI rankings in, 237t
  public transfer focusing in, 242–43
  social protection programs historically, 251–52
  social security spending in, 240t, 241–42
Arrow, K., 176, 177–78
*Ateliers nationaux*, 81
Atkinson, T., 63, 77, 79
Atlantic Charter of 1941, 87, 343n
Australia
  cash transfers as GDP percentage in, 102t
  defense spending as GDP percentage in, 103t
  distribution of taxes, government transfers by income deciles, 289t
  government expenditure growth, 9t, 101t
  gross public social expenditures in, 255t
  HDI rankings *vs.* public spending in, 233–34, 234t, 236
  income testing use in, 260, 261t
  mandatory private spending for social protections in, 260
  net total social expenditure in, 258t, 259t
  paradox of redistribution in, 27t

  publicly mandated social expenditure in, 257t
  public sector performance/efficiency measures, 244t, 246, 247t
  social protection program characteristics, 261t
  social transfers as GDP percentage, 10t, 64t, 235t, 288–90
  taxation, disposable cash income effects, 16t
  tax revenue, 1960–2000, 95t
  tax revenue changes, 1960–2007, 104t
Austria
  cash transfers as GDP percentage, 101–102, 102t
  defense spending as percentage of GDP, 102–103, 103t, 104
  government expenditure growth, 9t, 101t
  gross public social expenditures in, 255t
  growth performance in, 279t
  HDI rankings *vs.* public spending in, 234t
  net total social expenditure in, 258t, 259t
  publicly mandated social expenditure in, 257t
  social protection program characteristics, 261t
  social protection program public spending, 254–63
  social transfers as GDP percentage, 10t, 64t
  taxation, disposable cash income effects, 15, 16t
  tax revenue, 1960–2000, 95t
  tax revenue as share of GDP, 1960s, 97–98
  tax revenue changes, 1960–2007, 104t
Authorizations, 215–16, 330

Bahamas, 237t
Banking, 80–82
Barbados, 237t
Bastiat, F., 6, 340n
Belgium
    cash transfers in, 102t
    defense spending as GDP percentage in,
        103t
    distribution of taxes, government
        transfers by income deciles, 289t
    government expenditure growth, 9t, 101t
    gross public social expenditures in, 255t
    growth performance in, 279t
    HDI rankings *vs.* public spending in,
        234t
    mandatory private spending for social
        protections in, 260
    net total social expenditure in, 258t, 259t
    paradox of redistribution in, 27t
    publicly mandated social expenditure in,
        257t
    public sector performance/efficiency
        measures, 244t, 247t
    social protection program characteristics,
        261t
    social protection program public
        spending, 254–63
    social transfers as GDP percentage, 10t,
        64t, 100–101
    taxation, disposable cash income effects,
        15, 16t
    tax revenue, 1960–2000, 95t
    tax revenue as share of GDP, 1960s, 97–98
    tax revenue changes, 1960–2007, 104t
Belize, 237t
Beveridge Report, 87, 123–24, 124t
Bismarck legislation, 114–16, 346n
Boettke, P., 47
Bolivia
    education spending in, 239t
    HDI rankings in, 237t
    social security spending in, 240t
Brazil
    education spending in, 238–39, 239t, 241
    HDI rankings in, 237t
    HDI rankings *vs.* public spending in, 237
    public transfer focusing in, 242–43
    social security spending in, 240t
Buchan, J., 170, 349n
Buchanan, J., 17–18, 67, 161–62, 171–72,
    182–88, 352n

Buon Governo, 349n
Burckhardt, J., 184
Burton, J., 161–62
Bush, George W., 118

Cajolement, 222–23, 356n
Canada
    cash transfers as GDP percentage,
        101–102, 102t
    defense spending as percentage of GDP,
        102–103, 103t, 104
    distribution of taxes, government
        transfers by income deciles, 289t
    government expenditure growth, 101t
    gross public social expenditures in, 255t
    growth performance in, 279t
    HDI rankings *vs.* public spending in,
        233–34, 234t, 236
    income testing use in, 260, 261t
    mandatory private spending for social
        protections in, 260
    net total social expenditure in, 258t, 259t
    paradox of redistribution in, 27t
    publicly mandated social expenditure in,
        257t
    public sector performance/efficiency
        measures, 244t, 247t
    social protection program characteristics,
        261t
    social transfers as GDP percentage, 10t,
        64t, 235t
    taxation, disposable cash income effects,
        16t
    tax revenue, 1960–2000, 95t
    tax revenue changes, 1960–2007, 104t
Casino capitalism, 135
Chicago School, 57, 133–34, 189, 352n
Chile
    education spending in, 239t
    HDI rankings in, 237t
    health spending in, 185
    public transfer focusing in, 242–43
    social security spending in, 240t
China, 205–206
Cicero, 340n
Citizenship in voluntary exchange theory,
    173, 350n
Clark, C., 170
Clinton, William J., 121
Coase, R. H., 178–80, 186–87, 352n
Colbert, J.-B., 341n

Colombia
 education spending in, 239t
 HDI rankings in, 237t
 social security spending in, 240t, 241–42
Command economy (centrally planned
   system)
 historically, 43, 45–48, 339–40n, 343n
 private firm's use of resources in, 186–87
Communal state philosophy, 74–75
Community associations
 historically, 108
 mutual assistance societies, 109, 132
 in Nordic countries, 270–71, 280–81
 role in education, 53
 role in social protection, 19–21, 42,
   108–109
 Smith on, 53, 59
 in United States, 185–86, 352n
 Wagner on, 74–75, 82–83
Confraternity role in social protection,
   109
Conscription, power of, 216–17, 355n
Constitution's role in constraint of
   politicians/states, 183–84, 354n
Contingent liabilities, 219–20, 355n
Cooperative movement, credit provision
   (banking), 80–82
Cooperative republic theory, 81
Costa Rica
 education spending in, 239t
 HDI rankings in, 237t
 social protection programs historically,
   251–52
 social security spending in, 240t
Cost-benefit analysis historically, 172
Countercyclical policy (stabilization,
   fine-tuning), 5, 335n
Credit provision role in social protection,
   109
Cuba, 237t
Czech Republic, 16t

Dalton, H., 154
*Das Capital* (Marx), 44
Defense spending as percentage of GDP,
   102–103, 103t, 104
Deficit financing, 98, 153–54
De Molinari, G., 335n, 340n
Denmark
 cash transfers as GDP percentage,
   101–102, 102t

changes in redistribution, 290t
choice of policy instruments in, 205–206
defense spending as percentage of GDP,
   102–103, 103t, 104
distribution of taxes, government
   transfers by income deciles, 289t
economic crises in, 279t, 285
government expenditure growth, 101t
government expenditure reforms, 290t,
   290–91
gross public social expenditures in, 255t
HDI rankings *vs.* public spending in,
   233–34, 234t, 236
net total social expenditure in, 258t, 259t
paradox of redistribution in, 27t
pension reforms in, 296
publicly mandated social expenditure in,
   257t
public sector performance/efficiency
   measures, 244t, 247t
public transfer targeting in, 261–62
social protection program characteristics,
   261t
social protection program public
   spending, 254–63
social transfers as GDP percentage, 10t,
   64t, 100–101
taxation, disposable cash income effects,
   16t
taxation level growth in, 20th century,
   104–105
tax burden as percent of GDP, 95t, 100,
   276–78, 345n
tax expenditures for, 263
tax revenue, 1960–2000, 95t
tax revenue as share of GDP, 97–98,
   276–78
tax revenue changes, 1960–2007, 104t
Developmental role of government, 54–56
 *See also* Income redistribution, market
   stabilization
De Viti de Marco, A., 66–67, 93, 152–53,
   347n, 351–52n
Director's Law, 28–30
Disasters, state intervention roles in,
   323–25, 359n
Dominica, 237t
Dominican Republic, 237t, 239t
Down, A., 335–36n
Drazen, A., 202
Dual income taxes (DIT), 287–88

Eckstein, O., 172
Econometric models, 199–200, 353n
Economic theory of fiscal policy
  assumptions of, 197–201, 353n, 354n
  overview, 194–97, 352–53n
Ecuador
  education spending in, 239t
  HDI rankings in, 237t
  social security spending in, 240t
Education
  community associations role in, 53
  Smith on subsidies for, 53, 58
  spending in Jamaica, 239t
  spending in Latin America, 238–39, 239t,
    241
  state intervention roles, 342n
Eisenhower, Dwight D., 343n, 349–50n
Elementary and Secondary Education Act of
  1965, 119
El Salvador, 239t, 240t
Entitlements. *See also* Welfare state
  government intervention in historically,
    112–13, 306
  growth of in Nordic countries, 278
  Sen on, 181–82
  War on Poverty (*See* War on Poverty)
Equality of conditions, 40–41
Equality of outcomes, 41
Executive branch effects on policy
  instruments, 200–201, 354n
Executive compensation
  in Nordic countries, 273–75
  in United States, 274–75, 313–14, 357n,
    358–59n
Extended families role in social protection,
  108, 345n

Family Allowances Act of 1945 (Beveridge),
  123–24
Fasiani, M., 173
Financial market future roles, 311–19
Finland
  cash transfers as GDP percentage,
    101–102, 102t
  changes in redistribution, 290t
  defense spending as percentage of GDP,
    102–103, 103t, 104
  distribution of taxes, government
    transfers by income deciles, 289t
  economic crises in, 279t, 285
  government expenditure growth, 101t

government expenditure reforms, 290t,
  290–91
gross public social expenditures in, 255t
HDI rankings *vs.* public spending in,
  233–34, 234t, 236
income testing use in, 260, 261t
net total social expenditure in, 258t, 259t
paradox of redistribution in, 27t
pension reforms in, 294–96
publicly mandated social expenditure in,
  257t
public sector performance/efficiency
  measures, 244t, 246, 247t
public transfer targeting in, 261–62
social protection program characteristics,
  261t
social protection program public
  spending, 254–63
social transfers as GDP percentage, 10t,
  64t, 100–101
taxation, disposable cash income effects,
  16t
tax expenditures for, 263
tax level reduction in, 102t, 105
tax revenue, 1960–2000, 95t
tax revenue as share of GDP, 97–98,
  276–78
tax revenue changes, 1960–2007, 104t
Fiscal drag, 99, 345n
Fiscal federalism, 187–88, 352n
Fiscal illusion theory
  generally, 152–57, 347n, 348n
  monopolistic governments, 158–59
  voting effects, 178, 351n
Fiscal policy instruments, 200, 353n, 354n
  *See also* Policy instruments
Fiscal termites hypothesis, 140
Fogel, R., 172–73
Foster Act of 1870, 53
*The Fourth Great Awakening and the Future
  of Egalitarianism* (Fogel), 172–73
France
  authorizations in historically, 216
  cash transfers as GDP percentage,
    101–102, 102t
  defense spending as percentage of GDP,
    102–103, 103t, 104
  distribution of taxes, government
    transfers by income deciles, 289t
  government expenditure growth, 9t, 101t
  gross public social expenditures in, 255t

growth performance in, 279t
HDI rankings *vs.* public spending in, 233–34, 234t, 236
income tax introduction in, 68
income testing use in, 260, 261t
net total social expenditure in, 258t, 259t
paradox of redistribution in, 27t
publicly mandated social expenditure in, 257t
public sector performance/efficiency measures, 244t, 246, 247t
public transfer targeting in, 261–62
social protection program characteristics, 261t
social protection program public spending, 254–63
social protection programs historically, 251
social transfers as GDP percentage, 10t, 64t, 100–101
taxation, disposable cash income effects, 15, 16t
tax revenue, 1960–2000, 95t
tax revenue as share of GDP, 1960s, 97–98
tax revenue changes, 1960–2007, 104t
World War I financing in, 68
Friedman, M., 133–34, 339n
Frisch, R., 195, 197

*The General Theory of Employment, Interest and Money* (Keynes), 85
Germany
Accident Insurance Bill of 1884 (Bismarck), 115
Bismarck legislation in, 114–16, 346n
cash transfers as GDP percentage, 101–102, 102t
defense spending as percentage of GDP, 102–103, 103t, 104
distribution of taxes, government transfers by income deciles, 289t
employee compensation in historically, 336n
government expenditure growth, 9t, 101t
gross public social expenditures in, 255t
growth performance in, 279t
HDI rankings *vs.* public spending in, 234t
income tax introduction in, 68
mandatory private spending for social protections in, 260
net total social expenditure in, 258t, 259t

paradox of redistribution in, 27t
publicly mandated social expenditure in, 257t
public sector performance/efficiency measures, 244t, 247t
social protection program characteristics, 261t
social protection program public spending, 254–63
social transfers as GDP percentage, 10t, 64t, 100–101
taxation, disposable cash income effects, 15, 16t
taxation level growth in, 20th century, 104–105
tax revenue, 1960–2000, 95t
tax revenue as share of GDP, 1960s, 97–98
tax revenue changes, 1960–2007, 104t
World War I financing in, 68
Gide, C., 81
Globalization effects on public spending
compensation hypothesis, 140–41
economic historically, 129–32
education, 137
efficiency hypothesis, 140
empirical analysis, 141–43, 143f, 144f
financial crises, safety net provision, 135–36
fiscal termites hypothesis, 140
future factors affecting, 308–11, 358n
historically, 82, 132–37, 342n
Internet in, 134–35
overview, 129
protectionism, 132–33
risk probabilities, 137
state's capacity in, 136–37
tax competition, 94
tax evasion, 351n
trade liberalization/individual income risk relationships, 137–41
Government expenditures as policy tool, 210
Graziani, A., 51–52, 60–61
Greece
cash transfers as GDP percentage, 101–102, 102t
defense spending as GDP percentage in, 103t
financing of public debt in, 339n
government expenditure growth, 101t
growth performance in, 279t

Greece (*cont.*)
  public sector performance/efficiency
    measures, 244t, 246, 247t
  social transfers as GDP percentage, 10t,
    64t, 100–101
  taxation, disposable cash income effects,
    16t
  tax level reduction in, 102t, 105
  tax revenue, 1960–2000, 95t
Greenspan, A., 312–13
Grenada, 237t
Guatemala
  education spending in, 238–39, 239t,
    241
  social security spending in, 240t

Haavelmo, T., 194–95, 197
Hagen, J. von, 202
Hagertrom, K. G., 66–67
Hansen, A., 195
Hansen, B., 194, 353n
Harvey Road mentality, 161–62
Hayek, F. A., 47–48, 54, 133–34, 186–87,
  213–14
Health (or Sickness) Insurance Bill of 1883
  (Bismarck), 114–15
Henriksson, J., 357n
Historical perspectives
  community associations, 108
  countercyclical policy (stabilization,
    fine-tuning), 5, 335n
  equality of conditions, 40–41
  equality of outcomes, 41
  globalization effects (*See* Globalization
    effects on public spending)
  income redistribution, market
    stabilization (*See* Income
    redistribution, market stabilization)
  Industrial Revolution (*See* Industrial
    Revolution effects)
  19th century, 60–64, 64t, 68, 339–40n,
    341n
  on poverty, 39–40
  social hierarchy, 41–42
  20th century, 6–9, 9t, 10t, 13, 335–36n
  World War I, financing of by taxation, 68,
    341n
Honduras, 240t
Human Development Index (HDI), 231–32,
  233–43, 356n
Hume, David, 50–51, 340n

Hungary, 15, 16t
Hurwicz, L., 181

Iceland
  defense spending as GDP percentage in,
    103t
  growth performance in, 279t
  public sector performance/efficiency
    measures, 244t, 246, 247t
  taxation, disposable cash income effects,
    16t
  tax revenue as share of GDP, 1960s, 97–98
Impossibility Theorem, 177–78
Income redistribution, market stabilization
  contract intervention, 180–81
  "do-nothing" option effects on, 314,
    359n
  efficiency effects, 180, 351n
  future factors affecting, 308–11, 358n
  Keynes on, 83–85
  Mill on, 75–76
  personal interest influences on, 306–307,
    357–58n
  political developments in, 85–89, 343n
  property rights protections, 178–80,
    351n
  service state, 162–63, 348–49n
  Smith on, 59, 340n
  Wagner on, 75, 82–83, 342n
  welfare state, 163–64, 349n
Industrial Revolution effects
  cooperative movement, credit provision
    (banking), 80–82
  on income redistribution, market
    stabilization (*See* Income
    redistribution, market stabilization)
  Leone XIII on, 76, 79
  overview, 72–73, 76–77, 79, 82, 89–90
  political developments, 85–89,
    343n
  retirement, pensions, 78–79, 341n,
    342n
  unemployment, labor protections, 77–78,
    341n, 342n
Insurance, 112–13
Internet in globalization historically, 134–35
Ireland
  cash transfers as GDP percentage,
    101–102, 102t
  defense spending as GDP percentage in,
    103t

distribution of taxes, government
transfers by income deciles, 289t
government expenditure growth, 9t,
101t
gross public social expenditures in,
255t
growth performance in, 279t
HDI rankings *vs.* public spending in,
234t, 233–34, 236
income testing use in, 260, 261t
net total social expenditure in, 258t,
259t
publicly mandated social expenditure in,
257t
public sector performance/efficiency
measures, 244t, 246, 247t
social protection program characteristics,
261t
social transfers as GDP percentage, 10t,
64t, 100–101, 235t
taxation, disposable cash income effects,
16t
tax level reduction in, 102t, 105
tax revenue, 1960–2000, 95t
tax revenue changes, 1960–2007,
104t
Italy
abusive leaves in, 336n
cash transfers as GDP percentage,
101–102, 102t
defense spending as GDP percentage in,
103t
distribution of taxes, government
transfers by income deciles, 289t
government expenditure growth, 9t,
101t
gross public social expenditures in,
255t
growth performance in, 279t
HDI rankings *vs.* public spending in,
234t
mandatory private spending for social
protections in, 260
net total social expenditure in, 258t,
259t
pension fund obligations in, 18–19
public finance studies in, 151–52
publicly mandated social expenditure in,
257t
public sector performance/efficiency
measures, 244t, 246, 247t

social protection program characteristics,
261t
social protection programs historically,
251–52
social transfers as GDP percentage, 10t,
64t, 288–90
taxation, disposable cash income effects,
15, 16t
tax revenue, 1960–2000, 95t
tax revenue changes, 1960–2007, 104t
World War I financing in, 68

Jamaica, 239t
James, H., 135, 140
Japan
cash transfers as GDP percentage,
101–102, 102t
defense spending as GDP percentage in,
103t
government expenditure growth, 9t, 101t
gross public social expenditures in, 255t
HDI rankings *vs.* public spending in, 234t
intellectual aristocracy in, 161–62
net total social expenditure in, 258t,
259t
publicly mandated social expenditure in,
257t
public sector performance/efficiency
measures, 244t, 246, 247t
social protection program characteristics,
261t
social protection program public
spending, 254–63
social transfers as GDP percentage, 10t,
64t, 100–101
taxation, disposable cash income effects,
16t
tax revenue, 1960–2000, 95t
tax revenue changes, 1960–2007, 104t
Johansen, L., 195
Johnson, Lyndon B., 99–100, 118–20, 344n,
349–50n

Keynes, J. M.
*The General Theory of Employment,
Interest and Money,* 85
historical impact of, 5, 169
historical perspectives on, 170
philosophy of, 73, 83–85, 124–26
Keynesian Revolution, 133–34, 337n, 342n,
344n

Klein, L., 195
Korea
  defense spending as percentage of GDP,
    102–103, 103t, 104
  gross public social expenditures in, 255t
  net total social expenditure in, 258t,
    259t
  publicly mandated social expenditure in,
    257t
  social protection program characteristics,
    261t
  social protection program public
    spending, 254–63
  taxation, disposable cash income effects,
    16t
Krebs, T., 138–39
Krishna, P., 138–39
Krugman, P., 171–72, 273

Laissez-faire system
  historically, 42–43, 46
  Keynes on, 73, 83–85, 124–26
  Senior on, 73
  Smith on, 49–50, 340n
  Wagner on, 74–75
  Woodward on, 73
Landlord and Tenant (Rent control) Act of
  1949 (Beveridge), 123–24
Latin America
  education spending in, 238–39, 239t, 241
  HDI rankings *vs.* public spending in,
    236–37, 237t, 239t, 240t, 243
  land reform in, 351n
  program benefit failures in, 185
  social protection programs historically,
    251–52
  social security spending in, 240t, 241–42
  tariff rates historically, 131
  trade openness/public spending
    relationships, 141–43
Legislation length effects, 354n
Leone XIII, 76, 79, 342n
Lerner, A., 195
Leroy-Beaulieu, P., 60–61, 62
Libertarian paternalism, 358n
Lindbeck, A., 268, 278, 279t, 284–85, 298
Lindert, P. H., 66
Lorenzetti, A., 349n
Lucas, R., 351n
Luxembourg
  cash transfers as GDP percentage in, 102t

  defense spending as GDP percentage in,
    103t
  government expenditure growth, 101t
  growth performance in, 279t
  public sector performance/efficiency
    measures, 244t, 246, 247t
  social transfers as GDP percentage,
    100–101
  taxation, disposable cash income effects,
    16t
  tax revenue, 1960–2000, 95t
  tax revenue changes, 1960–2007, 104t

Maddison, A., 345n
Mal Governo, 349n
Maloney, W., 138–39
Market efficiency
  hypothesis, 140
  income redistribution, market
    stabilization effects, 180, 351n
  measures of, 244t, 246, 247t
  Smith on, 59
  state intervention roles, 315–17, 359n
  voluntary exchange theory, 180, 351n
Market fundamentalism, 57, 312–13,
  340n
Market stabilization. *See* Income
  redistribution, market stabilization
Marx, Karl
  historical impact of, 44, 169, 339n
  historical perspectives on, 170
  philosophy of, 74
Maskin, E. S., 181
Mercantilism. *See* Laissez-faire system
Mexico
  education spending in, 239t
  gross public social expenditures in, 255t
  HDI rankings in, 237t
  net total social expenditure in, 258t,
    259t
  publicly mandated social expenditure in,
    257t
  public transfer focusing in, 242–43
  social protection program characteristics,
    261t
  social protection program public
    spending, 254–63
  social security spending in, 240t
  taxation, disposable cash income effects,
    16t
Mill, James, 65–66

Mill, John Stuart, 75–76, 153
Mises, L., 47, 213–14
Musgrave, R., 6, 54, 86–87, 159, 162–66, 176, 195, 343n
Mutual assistance society role in social protection, 109, 132
Myerson, R. B., 181
Myrdal, G., 197, 198, 353n

National Health Service Act of 1946 (Beveridge), 123–24
National Insurance (Industrial Injuries) Act of 1946 (Beveridge), 123–24
National Insurance Acts of 1948 and 1949 (Beveridge), 123–24
Nerve Center assumption (decision-making centralization), 198–99
Netherlands
cash transfers as GDP percentage, 101–102, 102t
defense spending as percentage of GDP, 102–103, 103t, 104
distribution of taxes, government transfers by income deciles, 289t
government expenditure growth, 9t, 101t
gross public social expenditures in, 255t
growth performance in, 279t
HDI rankings *vs.* public spending in, 234t
net total social expenditure in, 258t, 259t
paradox of redistribution in, 27t
publicly mandated social expenditure in, 257t
public sector performance/efficiency measures, 244t, 246, 247t
social protection program characteristics, 261t
social transfers as GDP percentage, 10t, 64t, 100–101
taxation, disposable cash income effects, 16t
taxation limitations historically, 67, 341n
tax level reduction in, 102t, 105
tax revenue, 1960–2000, 95t
tax revenue as share of GDP, 1960s, 97–98
tax revenue changes, 1960–2007, 104t
New Deal, 86, 343n
New Zealand
defense spending as GDP percentage in, 103t

government expenditure growth, 9t
gross public social expenditures in, 255t
growth performance in, 279t
HDI rankings *vs.* public spending in, 234t
income testing use in, 260, 261t
net total social expenditure in, 258t, 259t
publicly mandated social expenditure in, 257t
public sector performance/efficiency measures, 244t, 247t
social protection program characteristics, 261t
social transfers as GDP percentage, 10t, 64t
taxation, disposable cash income effects, 16t
tax revenue, 1960–2000, 95t
tax revenue changes, 1960–2007, 104t
Nicaragua
education spending in, 239t
public transfer focusing in, 242–43
social security spending in, 240t
Niskanen, W., 17–18, 198–99
Nitti, F.S., 58, 61
Nordic countries. *See also* Denmark; Finland; Iceland; Norway; Sweden
changes in redistribution, 290t
disincentive effects, 284–85
distribution of taxes, government transfers by income deciles, 289t
economic crises in, 279t, 285
employment of women in, 282–84
executive compensation in, 273–75
government expenditure reforms, 290t, 290–91
growth performance in, 279t, 279–80
historically pre-1950, 269–76
impact of welfare state on family model, 282–84
overview, 267–69, 296–98
pension reforms in, 291–96
sense of community in historically, 270–71
social transfers as GDP percentage, 288–90
tax reforms in, 289t, 290t, 286–90
welfare state model in, 280–82
welfare system reforms in, 279t, 285–86
Normative theories, 3–5, 335n
North, D., 169, 172–73, 179, 349n

Norway
    changes in redistribution, 290t
    defense spending as percentage of GDP,
        102–103, 103t, 104
    distribution of taxes, government
        transfers by income deciles, 289t
    government expenditure growth, 9t
    gross public social expenditures in, 255t
    growth performance in, 279t
    HDI rankings *vs.* public spending in,
        233–34, 234t, 236
    mandatory private spending for social
        protections in, 260
    net total social expenditure in, 258t, 259t
    oil exports in, 268–69
    paradox of redistribution in, 27t
    pension reforms in, 293–94
    publicly mandated social expenditure in,
        257t
    public sector performance/efficiency
        measures, 244t, 246, 247t
    public transfer targeting in, 261–62
    social protection program characteristics,
        261t
    social transfers as GDP percentage, 10t,
        64t, 235t
    taxation, disposable cash income effects,
        16t
    tax expenditures for, 263
    tax revenue, 1960–2000, 95t
    tax revenue as share of GDP, 1960s, 97–98
    tax revenue changes, 1960–2007, 104t
Nozick, R., 22–23, 338n
Nudging/cajolement, 222–23, 356n

Obama, Barack, 116, 122–23, 349–50n,
    354n
Old Age and Infirmity (or Disability) Bill of
    1889 (Bismarck), 115
Olson, M., 17–18, 193
*The Origin of Development Economics*
    (Jomo/Reinert), 54–55
Owen, R., 80–81
Ownership, 217–19, 355n. *See also* Property
    rights protections

Panama, 237t, 242–43
Pantaleoni, M., 346n
Paradox of redistribution, 26–27, 27t, 29f,
    31, 339n
Paraguay, 237t, 238–39, 239t, 241

Pareto, V., 153–54, 346n, 348n
Patient Protection and Affordable Care Act
    of 2010, 116, 122–23
Payroll deductions, 112
Peacock, A., 65, 172, 351n
Pension Act of 1947 (Beveridge), 123–24
Pensions
    financial outlay progression in, 121–23
    Germany, Bismarck legislation, 115, 346n
    historically, 252
    in Latin America, 240t, 241–42
    Old Age and Infirmity (or Disability) Bill
        of 1889, 115
    reforms in Nordic countries, 291–96
Personal, political interests influences on
    policy making, 199, 306–307, 357–58n.
    *See also* Bismarck legislation
Personal Responsibility and Work
    Opportunity Reconciliation Act of
    1996 (Welfare Reform Act), 121, 122
Persson, T., 202
Peru, 237t, 239t, 242–43
Pigou, C., 57
Poland, 16t
Policy instruments
    contingent liabilities, 219–20, 355n
    cost considerations, 206–207, 354n
    criminal activities and, 209
    executive branch effects on, 200–201,
        354n
    favors market and, 208–209
    fiscal tools, 210–13
    future factors affecting, 308–11, 358n
    nonprofit sector and, 208
    nudging/cajolement, 222–23, 356n
    overview, 196–97, 205–206, 223, 353n
    ownership, 217–19, 355n
    political considerations, 207–208
    power of conscription, 216–17, 355n
    private market system and, 208, 355n
    quantitative easing, 212–13
    regulatory tools, 213–16, 355n
    state operations and, 209
Portugal
    cash transfers as GDP percentage,
        101–102, 102t
    defense spending as GDP percentage in,
        103t
    government expenditure growth, 101t
    public sector performance/efficiency
        measures, 244t, 246, 247t

taxation, disposable cash income effects, 16t

taxation level growth in, 20th century, 104–105

tax revenue, 1960–2000, 95t

tax revenue changes, 1960–2007, 104t

Positive theory of fiscal policy, 201–202

Poverty, historical perspectives on, 39–40

Power of conscription, 216–17, 355n

Prebisch, R., 132–33

Property rights protections
  as policy instrument, 217–19, 355n
  voluntary exchange theory, 178–80, 351n

Public debt/loans (credit) as policy tool, 211–13

Public-private partnerships
  contingent liabilities in, 219–20, 355n
  historically, 134
  as policy instrument, 217–19
  School of public choice on, 185, 352n
  in United States, 185–86, 352n

Public spending policies
  bureaucratic corruption in, 18
  cash transfers as GDP percentage, 101–102, 102t
  De Viti de Marco on, 152–53
  disposable cash income effects, 15, 16t
  fiscal deficits in, 98
  future perspective on, 319–23, 360n
  globalization effects on (*See* Globalization effects on public spending)
  as growth of historically, 20th century table, 8, 10t
  historically 19th century, 60–64, 64t, 68, 339–40n, 341n
  historically 20th century, 6–9, 9t, 10t, 13, 335–36n
  inequalities (horizontal redistribution) in, 13–14, 15–17, 336n
  limitations on, 306, 342n, 357n
  loss of freedom of choice due to, 15, 336n
  minimalist state approach to, 21–23, 338n
  paradox of redistribution, 26–27, 27t, 29f, 31, 339n
  scientific phase of, 171–72, 350n
  as share of GDP, 8, 9t
  social transfers, 64–65, 100–101, 101t

universal suffrage in, 65–67

war effects on, 93–94, 343–44n

waste, inefficiency in, 342n

welfare, efficiency costs, 17–18, 336–37n

zero price effect, 11, 336n

Public spending policies benefits
  HDI evaluation, 231–32, 233–34, 234t, 235f, 235t, 237t, 239t, 240t, 243, 356n
  limitations, 231
  methodology, 230–31
  overview, 229–30
  public sector performance/efficiency measures, 244t, 243–46, 247t
  socioeconomic indicator evaluation, 232t, 232–33
  spending *vs.* benefits, 241

Puviani, A., 154–55, 159, 347n

Quantitative easing, 212–13

Raiffeisen, F. W., 81–82

Reagan, Ronald, 133–34, 348n

Redistribution paradox, 26–27, 27t, 29f, 31, 339n

Regulatory capture, 215–16

Regulatory function of state
  in economic theory, 4–5, 335n
  future applications of, 317–19, 359n, 360n
  historical perspectives on, 83–85
  policy instruments, 213–16, 355n

*Rerum Novarum* (Leone XIII), 76, 79, 342n

Rexed, K., 59

Ricardian equivalence, 153–54

Ricossa, S., 39

*The Rise and Decline of the State* (Van Creveld), 87

Rochdale Society of Equitable Pioneers, 80–81

Rodrik, D., 137–38, 141–43

Roman Catholic Church role in social protection, 109, 270

Roosevelt, Franklin D., 349–50n

Roosevelt, Theodore, 86

Röpke, W., 208, 213–14

Sachs, J., 271

Saltsjöbaden spirit, 275–26, 357n

Samuelson, Paul, 176, 181, 343n, 344n

Saving
  education of people to, 342n
  government intervention in historically,
    111–12, 345n
Say, J. B., 51–52, 340n, 341n
Schäffle, A., 352n
School of public choice, 182–88, 352n
Schulze-Delitzsch, H., 81
Schumpeter, J., 55
Scienza delle Finanze, xiii, 58, 66–67,
    151–52, 174, 195
Sen, A., 170, 181–82, 213–14
Senior, N., 73
Serra, A., 55
Shaw, G. B., 8
Slovak Republic, 16t
Smith, Adam
  on allocation of resources, 52–53, 59
  on assistance to very poor, 52–53, 59, 113,
    340–41n
  on division of labor, specialization, 51, 53
  on government's duties, roles in economy,
    51–52, 56–58, 340n
  on higher education subsidies, 53, 58
  historical perspectives on, 49–50, 170,
    340n
  on human nature, 51
  impact of on government perspective, 169
  "laissez-faire" economics and, 46
  on market efficiency, 59
  on mercantilism, 48–49, 51, 58–59
  on merchants in government, 53–54
  personal history, 50–51
  *The Theory of Moral Sentiments*, 43–44
  *The Wealth of Nations*, 43–44, 48–49
Social hierarchy, historical perspectives on,
    41–42
Social protection programs
  abuse, escape from obligations to, 177,
    351n
  application of instruments in, 253
  benevolent dictator concept, 176–77
  charity-based, 253
  confraternity role in, 109
  coverage generally, 253
  developing countries, 263–66
  extended families role in, 108, 345n
  financial outlay progression in, 121–23
  Germany, Bismarck legislation in,
    114–16, 346n
  government options for, 111–14

historically, 19–21, 107–11, 251–52,
    337–38n, 345n
  industrial countries, 255t, 254–55, 257t,
    258t, 259t, 263
  instruments used to provide, 252–53
  Keynes on, 124–26
  mutual assistance society role in, 109, 132
  regulatory tools in, 213–16, 355n
  Roman Catholic Church role in, 109, 270
  tax expenditures for, 262–63
  United States historically, 118t, 116–18,
    123, 251–52
  voluntary exchange theory, 171–82, 350n,
    351n, 352n
  voting effects, 178, 351n
Social Security system
  contributions in tax revenue, 99
  historically, 118t, 116–18, 346n
Social welfare function, 196–97, 353n
Solow, R., 195
Soviet experiment, 343n
Soviet Union, 68
Spain
  cash transfers as GDP percentage in, 102t
  defense spending as GDP percentage in,
    103t
  government expenditure growth, 9t, 101t
  gross public social expenditures in, 255t
  growth performance in, 279t
  HDI rankings *vs.* public spending in, 234t
  net total social expenditure in, 258t, 259t
  publicly mandated social expenditure in,
    257t
  public sector performance/efficiency
    measures, 244t, 246, 247t
  social protection program characteristics,
    261t
  taxation, disposable cash income effects,
    16t
  taxation level growth in, 20th century,
    104–105
  tax revenue, 1960–2000, 95t
  tax revenue changes, 1960–2007, 104t
Speed money, 216
St. Lucia, 237t
State intervention roles
  assumptions justifying growth of, 13–16,
    16t, 19, 336–37n
  Coasian approach to, 187, 352n
  contracts, 180–81
  developmental, 54–56

De Viti de Marco on, 152–53
education, 342n
expansion of, post Industrial Revolution,
  87–88, 170, 349–50n
externalities, 325–29, 358n
factors affecting, 42, 79
future factors affecting, 308–11, 358n
growing complexity problem, 330–32,
  360n
historically 20th century, 6–9, 9t, 10t, 13,
  335–36n
income redistribution, market
  stabilization (*See* Income
  redistribution, market stabilization)
as intermediary, 238
major disasters, 323–25, 359n
market efficiency, 315–17, 359n
minimalist approach to, 21–23, 113,
  338n, 342n, 345n
mixed economies, 44–45
overview, 5–6, 44–45, 88–89, 305–307
paternalistic approach to, 23–26, 338n
Puviani on, 154–55, 347n
regulatory (*See* Regulatory function of
  state)
social protection (*See* Social protection
  programs)
social protection program options,
  111–14
State types
  communal, 164–66, 349n
  flawed, 166, 350n
  individualistic, 159–60, 348n
  monopolistic, 158–59, 348n
  Musgrave on, 162–66
  overview, 157, 348n
  paternalistic (tutorial), 160–62, 348n
  service, 162–63, 348–49n
  welfare, 163–64, 349n
Stigler, G., 187, 332, 352n
Stiglitz, J., 173, 180–81
Supply-side revolution, 134
Suriname, 237t
Sweden
  cash transfers as GDP percentage,
    101–102, 102t
  changes in redistribution, 290t
  choice of policy instruments in, 205–206
  defense spending as percentage of GDP,
    102–103, 103t, 104
  disincentive effects, 284–85

distribution of taxes, government
  transfers by income deciles, 289t
economic crises in, 279t, 285
employment of women in, 282–84
Gini coefficients, pre-1950, 272
Gini coefficients, taxes/social program
  impact on, 261, 262t, 272
government expenditure growth, 9t, 101t
government expenditure reforms, 290t,
  290–91
gross public social expenditures in, 255t
growth performance in, 279t, 279–80
HDI rankings *vs.* public spending in,
  233–34, 234t, 236
historically pre-1950, 269–76
impact of welfare state on family model,
  282–84
income distribution as result of changing
  attitudes in, 272–73
net total social expenditure in, 258t, 259t
paradox of redistribution in, 27t
pension reforms in, 291–93
public debt in, 357n
publicly mandated social expenditure in,
  257t
public sector performance/efficiency
  measures, 244t, 246, 247t
public transfer targeting in, 261–62
Saltsjöbaden spirit, 275–76, 357n
sense of community in historically,
  270–71
social protection program characteristics,
  261t
social protection program public
  spending, 254–63
social protection programs historically,
  251–52, 357n
social transfers as GDP percentage, 10t,
  64t, 100–101, 235t
taxation, disposable cash income effects,
  16t
taxation level growth in, 20th century,
  104–105
tax burden as percent of GDP, 95t, 100,
  276–77, 277t, 278t, 278, 345n
tax expenditures for, 263
tax level reduction in, 102t, 105
tax reforms in, 289t, 290t, 286–90
tax revenue, 1960–2000, 95t
tax revenue changes, 1960–2007,
  104t

Sweden (*cont.*)
  welfare state model in, 280–82
  welfare system reforms in, 279t, 285–86
Switzerland
  defense spending as percentage of GDP,
    102–103, 103t, 104
  government expenditure growth, 9t,
    101t
  growth performance in, 279t
  HDI rankings *vs.* public spending in,
    234t
  paradox of redistribution in, 27t
  public sector performance/efficiency
    measures, 244t, 247t
  public transfer targeting in, 261–62
  social transfers as GDP percentage, 10t,
    64t
  taxation, disposable cash income effects,
    16t
  tax revenue, 1960–2000, 95t
  tax revenue as share of GDP, 1960s, 97–98
  tax revenue changes, 1960–2007, 104t

Tabellini, G., 202
Tanzi, V., 283
Taxation
  benefit-received criterion, 181, 351–52n
  deficit financing *vs.*, 153–54
  demand factors, 63–64
  direct *vs.* indirect, 153, 347n
  disposable cash income effects, 15, 16t
  future perspective on, 319–23, 360n
  general theory of tax structure change,
    131–32
  historically, 20th century, 11–13, 92, 170,
    343n, 349n
  Leroy-Beaulieu on, 62
  level increases, factors affecting, 93–94,
    343–44n
  limitations on historically, 67, 341n
  personal (income) tax as disincentive, 97,
    344n
  personal (income) tax manipulation, 20th
    century, 94–95, 95t, 97, 344n
  as policy tool, 210–11
  pre-World War I, 62–63, 341n
  Puviani on, 154–55, 347n
  revenue as share of GDP, 1960s, 97–98,
    344n
  revenue increases, sources of post-1965,
    95t, 98–99, 104–105, 344n

  substitution effect, 344n
  supply factors, 67–68, 341n
  tax expenditures, 97
  tax revenue changes, 1960–2007, 104t
  universal suffrage in, 65–67, 93
  value-added taxes (VAT), 95t, 98, 344n,
    360n
Tax avoidance, 359n
Tax churning, 238
Thatcher, Margaret, 133–34
"Theory of Fiscal Policy," 86–87
*The Theory of Moral Sentiments* (Smith),
    43–44
Thiers, Louis Adolphe, 110–11
Tinbergen, J., 195, 197
Tocqueville, A. de, 20, 39–41, 65–66
Toqueville, Alexis de, 40–41
Trade liberalization/individual income risk
    relationships, 137–41
Trinidad and Tobago, 237t
Tullock, G., 17–18, 182–88
Turkey, 16t

United Kingdom
  Accident Insurance System, 346n
  Beveridge Report, 87, 123–24, 124t
  cash transfers as GDP percentage in, 102t
  defense spending as GDP percentage in,
    103t
  distribution of taxes, government
    transfers by income deciles, 289t
  government expenditure growth, 9t, 101t
  gross public social expenditures in, 255t
  growth performance in, 279t
  HDI rankings *vs.* public spending in, 234t
  income tax introduction in, 68, 341n
  income testing use in, 260, 261t
  mandatory private spending for social
    protections in, 260
  marginal tax rates in, 96
  net total social expenditure in, 258t, 259t
  paradox of redistribution in, 27t
  publicly mandated social expenditure in,
    257t
  public sector performance/efficiency
    measures, 244t, 246, 247t
  quantitative easing as policy tool, 212–13
  social protection program characteristics,
    261t
  social protection program public
    spending, 254–63

social protection programs historically, 251–52

social transfers as GDP percentage, 10t, 64t

taxation, disposable cash income effects, 16t

tax revenue, 1960–2000, 95t

tax revenue as share of GDP, 1960s, 97–98

tax revenue changes, 1960–2007, 104t

voting rights in, 66

welfare spending in, 1900–1995, 124t

World War I financing in, 68

United States

benefits for destitute in, 349–50n

cash transfers as GDP percentage, 101–102, 102t

charitable giving in, 338n, 345n

command economy in, 339n

defense spending as GDP percentage in, 103t

distribution of taxes, government transfers by income deciles, 289t

executive compensation in, 274–75, 313–14, 357n, 358–59n

family income tax deductions in, 357n

Federal outlays, receipts trends, 20th century, 92–93, 99–100, 344n, 345n, 349–50n

Gini coefficients, taxes/social program impact on, 261, 262t

government expenditure growth, 9t, 101t, 343n, 349–50n

gross public social expenditures in, 255t

growth performance in, 279t

HDI rankings *vs.* public spending in, 234t

housing boom economic effects, 314–15, 359n

income tax introduction in, 68

income testing use in, 260, 261t

mandatory private spending for social protections in, 260

marginal tax rates in, 96

net total social expenditure in, 258t, 259t

paradox of redistribution in, 27t

pension fund obligations in, 18–19

private community associations in, 185–86, 352n

public debt in, 343–44n

publicly mandated social expenditure in, 257t

public sector performance/efficiency measures, 244t, 247t

public transfer targeting in, 261–62

quantitative easing as policy tool, 212–13

retail sales taxes, 345n

social protection program characteristics, 261t

social protection program public spending, 254–63

social protection programs historically, 116–18, 118t, 123, 251–52

social transfers as GDP percentage, 10t, 64t, 100–101

taxation, disposable cash income effects, 16t

taxation level growth in, 20th century, 104–105, 344n

tax burden as percent of GDP, 95t, 100, 345n

tax revenue, 1960–2000, 95t

tax revenue changes, 1960–2007, 104t

Universal suffrage, 65–67

Uruguay

education spending in, 239t

HDI rankings in, 237t, 240t

social protection programs historically, 251–52

Value-added taxes (VAT), 95t, 98, 344n, 360n

Van Creveld, M., 87–88, 343n

Venezuela, 237t

Voluntary exchange theory

abuse, escape from obligations, 177, 351n

benevolent dictator concept, 176–77

contract intervention, 180–81

efficiency effects, 180, 351n

Impossibility Theorem, 177–78

overview, 171–82, 350n, 351n, 352n

property rights protections, 178–80, 351n

taxation benefit-received criterion, 181, 351–52n

voting effects, 178, 193, 351n, 352–53n

Voting effects

universal suffrage, 65–67

voluntary exchange theory, 178, 193, 351n, 352–53n

Wagner, A., 7–8, 74–75, 82–83, 159, 161–62
Wagner's Law, 7–8
Walvin, J., 61
War on Poverty, 99–100, 118–20, 185, 344n, 346n, 349–50n
Washington Consensus, 134
*The Wealth of Nations* (Smith), 43–44, 48–49
Wealth ownership *vs.* income, 65–66
Webb, R. K., 40
Welfare Reform Act of 1996 (Personal Responsibility and Work Opportunity Reconciliation Act), 121, 122
Welfare state. *See also* Economic Theory of Fiscal Policy; Entitlements; Nordic countries

described, 163–64, 349n
empirical analysis, 141–43, 143f, 144f
establishment of historically, 110–11
immigrants in, 358n
income redistribution, market stabilization in, 163–64, 349n
Williamson, J., 342n
Wolfe, A., 39–40
Woodward, L., 39–40, 73
World War I, financing of by taxation, 68, 341n
Wuthnow, R., 20

Zero price effect, 11, 336n